PENGUIN BOOKS

THE TRAVELLER'S TREE

Patrick Leigh Fermor was born in 1915 of English and Irish descent. After a 'stormy' school career and his year-and-a-half journey on foot to Constantinople, he lived and travelled in the Balkans and the Greek Archipelago. During that time he acquired a deep interest in languages and a love of remote places. He enlisted in the Irish Guards in 1939, joined the 'I' Corps in 1941, became liaison officer in Albania, and fought in Greece and Crete to which, during the German occupation, he returned three times (once by parachute). Disguised as a shepherd, he lived for over two years in the mountains organizing the resistance and the capture and evacuation of the German Commander, General Kreipe. He was awarded the DSO in 1940 and the OBE in 1943, and was made Honorary Citizen of Herakleion, Crete. Patrick Leigh Fermor has also written *A Time to Keep Silence*, *The Violins of Saint Jacques*, *Mani*, winner of the Duff Cooper Memorial Prize and a Book Society Choice, and its companion volume, *Roumeli*, *A Time of Gifts*, winner of the 1978 W. H. Smith & Son Annual Literary Award and the 1992 Prix Audiberti de la Ville d'Antibes, described by Jan Morris as 'nothing short of a masterpiece' and its sequel, *Between the Woods and the Water*, winner of the 1987 Silver Pen Award and the Thomas Cook Travel Book Award, and *Three Letters from the Andes*, an account of the author's first expedition. Patrick Leigh Fermor now lives in Greece in a house he designed and built. He is a visiting member of the Athens Academy, has been awarded the Gold Medal of Honour of the Municipality of Athens, and is Hon. D.Litt. at the University of Kent.

The Traveller's Tree is an account of Patrick Leigh Fermor's journey – by steamer, aeroplane and sailing ship – through the long island chain of the West Indies, and of the idiosyncratic and distinct civilizations that have sprung up amongst the Caribbean Islands. It received considerable critical acclaim: Raymond Mortimer in the *Sunday Times* said, 'He is the ideal traveller, inquisitive, humorous, interested in everything, and vivid in depicting all that he has observed; and Harold Nicolson in the *Observer* wrote 'Being a natural romantic . . . possessing as he does a vivacious sympathy for all who are ill-adjusted, lonely or repressed, he was able to probe the hidden recesses of this mixed civilization and to present us with a picture of the Indies more penetrating and original than any that has been presented before.' *The Traveller's Tree* won the Heinemann Foundation Prize for Literature in 1950 and the Kemsley Prize in 1951.

The Traveller's Tree, like all the human beings who now inhabit the Antilles, was originally a stranger to these regions. It is a remarkable tree, native of Madagascar and Reunion, with a straight stem reaching thirty feet in height, and bearing at the top a number of large, long-stalked leaves which spread vertically like a fan. The leaf has a large sheath at the base in which water collects in such quantity as to yield a copious draught – hence the name. The plant is known botanically as the RAVENALA MADAGASCAR-IENSIS – Encyclopaedia Britannica.

A. Costa

PATRICK LEIGH FERMOR

THE TRAVELLER'S TREE

A Journey through the Caribbean Islands

Penguin Books

PENGUIN BOOKS

Published by the Penguin Group
Penguin Books Ltd, 27 Wrights Lane, London W8 5TZ, England
Penguin Books USA Inc., 375 Hudson Street, New York, New York 10014, USA
Penguin Books Australia Ltd, Ringwood, Victoria, Australia
Penguin Books Canada Ltd, 10 Alcorn Avenue, Toronto, Ontario, Canada M4V 3B2
Penguin Books (NZ) Ltd, 182–190 Wairau Road, Auckland 10, New Zealand

Penguin Books Ltd, Registered Offices: Harmondsworth, Middlesex, England

First published by John Murray 1950
Published in Penguin Books 1984
9 10 8

Frontispiece by A. Costa
Sketch-map of the Caribbean Islands by H. W. Hawes
The drawing on p. 230 by Patrick Leigh Fermor

Printed in England by Clays Ltd, St Ives plc
Filmset in Monophoto Photina

FOR
BALASA CANTACUZENE
WITH LOVE

Ἕνα σωρὸ κομμάτια ἀπὸ ὑαλί
κόκκινα, πράσινα ἢ γαλάζια.

CAVAFY

CONTENTS

PREFACE

Geographically, the Caribbean archipelago is easy to split up into component groups. With the exception of an occasional coral island like Barbados, the islands are the emerging summits of a range of drowned volcanoes, a submarine continuation of the same geological upheaval as the Andes, and on the map they swing northwards from the South American continent like the dislocated vertebrae of a spinal column based upon the *os coccyx* of Trinidad; northwards, and then westward through the Windward and Leeward Isles to the terminus of the Lesser Antilles in the scattered Pleiades of the Virgin Islands. Only a few dozen miles have so far separated them, and all except a few minute and scattered islets can be dimensionally reckoned by comparison to English counties. After the Virgin Group, however, a new world begins: the Greater Antilles. Much larger distances lie between the four great islands of Puerto Rico, Hispaniola, Jamaica and Cuba. The intervening sea sinks to vast depths, mountains rise in forbidding cordilleras, and distances measured from the sea's floor to certain Cuban peaks would overtop the Himalayas. The islands are few and enormous, comparable no longer to the shires, but to European states. Populations become reckonable in millions, and independent republics outnumber colonies by three to two. Cuba, floating on the confines of the Mexican Gulf, is the beginning of Latin America.

No such brisk summing-up can be formulated for the inhabitants of these islands: the ghostly Ciboneys, the dead Arawaks and the dying Caribs; the Spaniards, the English, the French, the Dutch, the Danes and the Americans; the Corsicans, the Jews, the Hindus, the Moslems, the Azorians, the Syrians and the Chinese, and the all-obliterating Negro population deriving from scores of kingdoms on the seaboard and hinterland of West Africa. Each island is a distinct and idiosyncratic entity, a civilization, or the reverse, fortuitous in its origins and empirical in its development. There is no rule that holds good beyond the shores of each one unless the prevalence of oddity, the unvarying need to make exceptions to any known rule, can be considered a unifying principle. The presence of religious eccentrics like the Kingston Pocomaniacs and the adepts of Voodoo in Haiti and the survival of stranded ethnological rock-pools like the Poor Whites in the Islands of the Saints or the semi-independent hospodarate of the Maroons of the Jamaican mountains –

all this, and the abundance and variety of superstitions and sorceries and songs, of religious and political allegiances, and the crystallization of deracination and disruption into a new and unwieldy system, almost, of tribal law – all this excludes any possibility of generalization. Nothing is more than four and a half centuries old, and all is improvised. It is with these aspects of the Caribees that this book is concerned, with their life as it impinges on an interested stranger, their buildings and food and religions, their history and the perceptible texture of their existence. Short of writing a thesis in many volumes, only a haphazard, almost a picaresque, approach can suggest the peculiar mood and tempo of the Caribbean and the turbulent past from which they spring; and this was the only trace of method or guiding principle that prompted my two companions and myself on our Odyssey through the islands: a journey almost as unco-ordinated and involved as the island itinerary three thousand years ago to Ithaca from Troy.

There ought, perhaps, to be a warning, in case this book should be mistaken for a guide to the Caribbean. It is, alas, nothing so satisfyingly complete. Of the strange world of the Dutch islands of the Spanish Main, for instance – Curaçao, Aruba and Bonair – we only caught a few hours' glimpse when our ship called for fuel on the journey home from Panama: an astonishing vision of coloured roofs and steep Netherlandish gables, a city of Vermeer or Peter de Hoogh transported beyond the Tropic of Cancer. St Vincent was no more than a mountain of cloud underneath our aeroplane; and of the smaller of the Lesser Antilles, those remote and bird-haunted islets lying far from the currents of ordinary travel we saw only a few. St Croix, the former stronghold of the Knights of Malta, remains in our memory as little but a mysterious and fascinating shadow on the horizon south of our line of flight. Descriptions of islands that were formerly Spanish, with the exception of a few pages about Cuba, I have reluctantly left out; not because their importance failed to interest us, but because they are so enormous. Their history and social structure radically diverge from the rest of the archipelago, and their inclusion would have completely altered the scope of the book. Our ignorance of Spanish (of which we were later to acquire a smattering in Guatemala and Nicaragua) was then almost complete, and I found, when the book was finished, that my chapters on Puerto Rico, San Domingo and Cuba were luxuriating a little too floridly over the barley-sugar columns of baroque cathedrals, the silver spurs with rowels the size of marguerites, the saddles like elephants' howdahs or jousting equipment from the Field of the Cloth of Gold; with never a word spoken, nothing to break the silence of a uniquely visual contact. But, as exigencies of space were exacting, I left out, on sound advice, these perhaps too exclusively descriptive pages. Nevertheless, though there is no rigid canon for a book of this kind, the little space devoted to the Spanish background is a serious deficiency, and one which I hope to remedy when the time comes to describe subsequent travels through the Central American Republics. It would be idle and impolitic to prolong this catalogue of omissions.

About the political problems and the economics, which I also jettisoned, I feel no such compunction, for there are many works on these themes. The scope of the book thus reduces itself to a personal, random account of an autumn and winter spent in wandering through these islands, and it has all the fallibility implicit in such a charter. Its ultimate purpose, if it must be defined, is to retransmit to the reader whatever interest and enjoyment we encountered. In a word, to give pleasure.

My companions, from beginning to end, were two friends: Joan, who is English, and Costa, who is Greek. Both of them, whittled now to shadows, are constantly present in the following pages. Joan was the Egeria, as it were, of our expedition, and Costa was not only its photographer and painter, but the motive force that launched it, its only begetter.

Nothing now remains but the pleasant task of thanking those who were kind to us on our travels and the friends who, before and afterwards, indirectly helped me to write this book.

Thanks are due to the Compagnie Générale Transatlantique (French Line) for much considerate help, and to M. Queffelian, the purser of the *Colombie*.

In Trinidad, our greatest debt was to the late Sir Patrick O'Reilly, K.C., of Port of Spain, whose kindness and knowledge and humour, as well as his professional eminence, will long be missed. We also gratefully remember Dr George Campbell, M.D., M.R.C.P., D.P.H., of the Chacachacare Leper Settlement. In Guadeloupe we would like to express our gratitude to Daniel Despointes, and in Martinique to M. René de Jaham, Dr Rose-Rosette, and the Vicomte d'Aurigny; in Dominica to Mrs Lennox Napier, the results of whose kind offices extended far beyond the island; and in Barbados to Mrs Nicolas Embiricos. I also record our gratitude to Sir Arthur Grimble, K.C.M.G., the Governor of the Windward Islands at the time that we visited them, and his daughter Rosemary; Mr Stowe, the Administrator of St Lucia, and Mrs Stowe; Mr Edward Challenger of Basseterre, St Kitts; in Haiti, M. Lorimer Denis, Mr DeWitt Peters, Mr Horace Ashton, former cultural attaché at the U.S. Embassy, and Selden Rodman; in Jamaica Miss Esther Chapman (Mrs Hepher), Colonel Rowe and Mr Emmanuel Rowe of Accompong, and Hélène and Wilfredo

Lam in Cuba. I would also like to thank James Pope-Hennessy who initiated me, before we set out, to the pleasure and instruction that are to be found in the old chronicles of the West Indies. (The writers and diarists that I consulted are mentioned as they occur in the course of the narrative, and of these, Père Labat, the Dominican monk of Martinique, is the one to whom I am most heavily indebted. Sir Algernon Aspinall's excellent *Short Guide to the West Indies* was the modern work that we consulted most frequently while actually on the move.)

I owe many thanks, also, to Mrs Postlethwaite Cobb and Norman Webb of the Easton Court Hotel, Chagford, Devon; to Professor and Mrs Julian Huxley and the Rev. J. H. Adams, M.A., Vicar of Landulph, Cornwall; and lastly, with especial emphasis, to Lindsay Drummond and Peggie Matheson, Amy and Walter Smart, Cécile and Mondi Howard and Dom Gabriel Gontard, O.S.B., the Lord Abbot of St Wandrille in Normandy.

P.M.L.F.

CHAGFORD,
GADENCOURT,
ST WANDRILLE,
SAN ANTONIO, TIVOLI.
May, 1950

CHAPTER 1

Guadeloupe

The moment the anchor was raised, the *Colombie* seemed to advance down the gulf with unnatural speed. To port, pale green islands were floating on the water, but the main body of Grande Terre, a dark shape whose depths and dimensions were only beginning to be defined, lay in shadow on the starboard side between us and the dawn. It was just possible to descry the waves of black vegetation and the lakes of mist entangled in the treetops where the country dipped. In the space of a few minutes the sunrise melted from violet into amber, from amber into scarlet, from scarlet into zinc and from zinc into saffron. The dark vegetation became a line of giant, pale green parsley, which hovered a hundred yards away in a fluttering cumulus that nothing appeared to tether to either land or sea. For no land was visible. But where the trees should have joined the sea the green mass curled backwards into shadow. It hung some yards above the water, and the smooth ripples from the ship disappeared under the leaves without meeting any resistance. Then, as if another dark filament had been withdrawn from the daybreak, the shapes of the mangrove trunks, the flimsy architecture that maintained all this greenstuff poised in mid-air, advanced from the darkness into the sea like a million bowling hoops. Under their leafy canopy, the tenuous Gothic arches receded in a dark triforium. A dawn wind stirred the leaves of the insecurely balanced green labyrinth, and the pace of our movement altered the outline of the stage wings of leaves from second to second, so that our ship was suspended in the very centre of motion and change and instability.

We rounded a buttress of mangroves, and a town appeared, the roofs and warehouses, masts and cranes were interspersed with palm trees. The sun cast loose from the leaves, and drifted up into the sky. The wind died, the clouds came to a standstill, and the sea was drained at last of every colour but an uncompromising blue. Even the forest stopped moving, and sank into an inert volume of unchanging green. It was going to be a really hot day.

The waterfront of Pointe-à-Pitre was hung with flags, and on the quay a platoon of soldiers stood at ease. A large crowd gazed in silence through the iron railings of the port. Surely the arrival of the *Colombie* was not the only reason for this? The scene on the quay below us was heavy with expectation. Groups of officials and of prominent burghers – a few of them white, but most of them brown or black – conversed in important little groups. White-drill French colonial uniforms gleamed with starch among black coats sashed with the tricolor. The women, severely spectacled and tightly gloved, were encased in black satin and hatted with intricate confections of sombre felt, relieved by artificial flowers or bunches of celluloid grapes. On the crown of a cloche hat of the fashion of 1926 perched, as though it had just alighted there, a tiny stuffed canary.

All at once the reason for this air of expectancy became clear, for down the gangway a scarcely recognizable figure was advancing at the head of a uniformed retinue. It was one of our shipmates, the high pro-consular dignitary, no longer the colourless and larva-like figure we had known on the journey, but a superb metamorphosis in white and gold and brass, arriving here to take over his new appointment as Prefect. His hat and his cuffs glittered with bullion, and on his bosom alongside another decoration of bright green, the Legion of Honour made a red splash. It was difficult to believe that it was the same man.

The guard of honour presented arms, and the band played the Marseillaise while everybody stood at the salute. A series of presentations followed. The passengers leant over the bulwarks admiring the urbane technique with which the new arrival shook hands. His right hand pumped up and down three times as he raised his resplendent headgear with his left, and brought his heels neatly to attention. Lift; shake; click.

A Packard drove up at the head of a fleet of cars that engulfed him and the other officials. The band struck up again, the harbour gates opened and a cohort of coloured policemen shepherded the silent crowd back; and the cars sailed away towards the governor's palace in the west of the island. The crowd broke on to the quay and the lesser passengers crowded down the gangway.

Half an hour later the *Colombie*, that congenial ship, was preparing to weigh anchor, and we were sitting in the lounge of the Hôtel des

Antilles. We had followed the elderly Negro who pushed our luggage up the main street of Pointe-à-Pitre. The heat was so intense that our clothes had stuck to our arms and legs; nearly everybody, we observed, was wearing open shirts and shorts or cotton trousers. The brilliance of the sunlight made all the shadows appear black and profound, and the change of temperature when walking into the shade was as welcome as a waterfall. All the way to the hotel we had not passed one white person. This, and the dazzling robes of the older women, the hundreds of black faces, the sound on every side of the odd new language, most of whose words were French but whose tenor was incomprehensible, this, and the murderous heat, invested the place with an atmosphere of entire strangeness. Even at eleven in the morning a heavy tropical languor weighed on the air. The streets had grown emptier every moment.

With slow enjoyment we ate the fruit we had bought in the market. The bananas were gigantic but commonplace. The sour-sops were about the size of a child's football, tapering into the shape of a pear, and covered with dark rind roughened with innumerable little hooked briers. The fruit inside was semi-liquid and snow white, expelling an aroma faintly resembling peardrops, and wringing our dusty palates with a delicious and slightly acid astringency. The paw-paw, which we next opened, was roughly the same size, but the soft rind was a smooth, patchy gold in colour, mottled with green and rusty brown. We halved it lengthways, and discovered two deep oblongs of a dewy, coral-coloured fruit of a consistency miraculously poised between solidity and liquescence; much sweeter than the sour-sop, and, I thought, even better. Its sweetness is mitigated and, as it were, underlined by the faintest tang of something sharper – was it creosote or turpentine? – but so slight that one loses the identity of the taste while attempting to define it. Pushing the ruins aside, we each chose an avocado pear: dark green or violet globes the size of cricket balls, enclosed in a hard and warty carapace. The knives made a sharp tearing noise as we opened them. In the centre, loose in their hollows, lay big round stones, completely spherical and smooth and very heavy. I hated throwing them away, they seemed so perfect and neat, and somehow important, but except as embryonic avocado trees, they are useless ... The pale green fruit clung to the shell with a consistency half-way between butter and plasticine.

Our ejaculations of delight must have been unusual, for two wide-eyed Guadeloupean waitresses made occasional bird-like titters. They were a mahogany colour, barefoot, and dressed in white, with aprons and turbans of marmalade-coloured tartan. They talked to each other in the same lingo as our porter, but addressed us in a prim rather old-fashioned French mysteriously lacking in R-sounds.

The world outside the windows had by now become a calcinated desert from which the perpendicular sun had driven every inch of shade. The palm trees, overtopping the corrugated iron roofs, stood motionless in a pale blue haze. The two maids showed us upstairs to our rooms, large wooden barns with no furniture except the beds under their milky tents of netting. I climbed inside and began cutting the pages of the memoirs of Père Labat, a French Dominican who lived in these islands at the end of the seventeenth century, but even the lively prose of this extraordinary monk failed to keep me awake for long ... I was about to fall asleep when a metallic uproar in the street brought me to the window. It was the rattle of rain on the roofs of Pointe-à-Pitre. The street had become a river of slime, bubbling and swirling under a wavering wall of water. But it was soon over and in five minutes the sun had dried up every trace of moisture, and all was arid and dusty again.

I woke up at five in the evening and could not think where I was. Only when I walked in a drugged way to the window and saw that the street was full of Negroes did I remember. I was still half asleep, and for some obscure reason the situation seemed tremendously funny, and I was still laughing when I met my two companions.

Towns in the Antilles do not have much of a chance. Their purpose, when they were built, was to serve as a warehouse, a market for slaves and a barracks for soldiers; a harbour for incoming slave-ships and for outgoing cargoes of sugar and rum. Government buildings, comfortable houses, the trees and fine streets came as an afterthought. They were always at the mercy of hurricanes, fires, earthquakes and volcanic eruptions, and of invasion and sack by their neighbours. (The reciprocal violence of the English and French in the seventeenth and eighteenth centuries in the Caribbean islands reached unbelievable proportions.) As a result of all this, few Antillean towns possess any architectural merits. The larger ones are tram-haunted nuclei of shops, warehouses and nondescript public buildings flung up in the worst period of European architecture, with a periphery of garden suburbs for the rich and an inferno of slums for the poor. The smaller ones – and of these Pointe-à-Pitre is probably the worst – are little more than agglomerations of shacks.

Pointe-à-Pitre, then, is an overgrown urban village, dating architecturally from its last disaster, the earthquake of 1845. Old Negroes still repeat their grandfathers' accounts of this event, when chasms fifty yards wide, seething with boiling mud and even, according to one account, flames, split the town from end to end. The central streets have the raggedness of the more squalid thoroughfares of Salonica. Gazing down them, the eye is caught by one or two buildings of reinforced concrete, a general store, a bank, a post office. Their unpleasant symmetry blinds one to the neighbouring houses which, though unsuccessful as units in a whole, are often either charming, or strange. They are made of wood which has been subjected to every kind of treatment: nailed on in overlapping boards like American colonial houses, woven into criss-cross trellises like the windows of harems, stencilled with complex patterns, or built up into Swiss gables and turrets and fretwork mansards. All the roofs are of corrugated iron, usually painted dark red, and their sides are pierced by little wooden belvederes and turrets in a romantic mid-Victorian style. The windows are large and they always open on to iron balconies, where old men and women sit in rocking-chairs gently fanning themselves. Brighton-Pavilionish shades overhang them in a flimsy line. Deckle-edged cornices of whitewashed tin, as complicated as cake frills, decorate these projections and the houses are sometimes painted Greek blue, ochre, yellow or ox-blood; the undersides of the balcony-shades are washed with cool and restful grey, pale blue, mauve, or Nile green. Many are built entirely of corrugated iron, with only wooden planks along the seams, and they are still a success. Alas! the extremes of sun and rain bring only dilapidation, and the general impression is one of abandonment and decay, and their aspect as a whole is utterly depressing.

Now and then we passed a wall or a railing with showers of hibiscus and bougainvillia tumbling over it and gazed at them with delight, unconscious yet of the hatred we would develop for the latter plant after a month or two. In front of the Bishop's palace we had a long moment of pleasure. It is a dignified eighteenth-century building lying back from the Cathedral square, behind ironwork and trees, built of wood and painted yellow and grey and with a gracious flight of columns and a triangular Greek pediment. A crocodile of school children was emerging from the Cathedral under the care of a beautiful black nun. This neo-Gothic building is made of iron, and riveted together against earthquakes by nuts and bolts and staples, inspiring one with the feeling of being inside a boiler, or a vast religious tramp steamer. We found ourselves in the outskirts of the town in a maze of shacks with the architecture, and almost the size, of derelict confessional boxes. The streets and the cabins grew smaller and more broken down as we advanced, and the population more ragged, dirtier, more miserable and shambling; a kind of Tobacco Road. 'Eh bien,' a young woman shouted, 'qu'est que vous regardez par ici? Vous êtes blancs et nous sommes noirs. Et alors?'

A few minutes after this we lost our way. Deep in the speculations that this Negro woman had opened up, we had passed a large white hospital, and, continuing along a grass footpath, found ourselves all at once in the heart of a tropical forest. No buildings were in sight, and we were surrounded by wooded hills. The change from town to country had been as sudden as if Pointe-à-Pitre had been lifted up and carried away by a team of djinns. The hills succeeded each other in a soft interlock of curves and all the outlines were blurred by the shapes of trees. Palms and bananas opened their heavy fans overhead, and here and there tall, thin, bare and twisting trunks wavered upwards, to balance in mid-air small blobs of leaves. These low hills are called *mornes* in the French islands, and as we advanced farther among them, isolated huts appeared in clearings on their flanks. Small cream-coloured cows grazed near them on patches of grass that looked softer and richer than velvet, and in the undergrowth black pigs rootled; long, swart creatures armed with snouts that were almost incipient trunks and almost two-dimensional in their leanness. Sugar-cane rustled round these huts, giving way, now and then, to patches of yam and cassava plant with their tendrils trained up bean-poles. Reed-fringed swamps were covered with a mantle of lilac flowers over which great butterflies beat their yellow wings. The grass tracks were vaulted by giant rushes. Breadfruit trees were everywhere, their leaves growing like spatulate hands joined at the wrists and opening in splays of fingers that hide in their shadow the soft round loaves. Under fleshy cartwheels of leaves the fruit of the paw-paw clustered round the perpendicular trunks as thickly and symmetrically as the breasts of Diana of the Ephesians. Funereal mangoes spread their dark, ilex-like and evergreen curves with the ampleness of oaks, and the pathway was carpeted with sensitive plants which shrank and closed with the slightest pressure, so that a footfall touched an entire miniature landscape into motion.

The African desert has the property of dwarfing everything. A figure only a hundred yards away is an insect lost in an overwhelming immensity. The rolling *mornes* achieve the opposite effect. It is as if this damp atmosphere acted as a lens that abolished all feeling of distance. We looked back from a hilltop and watched a Negro crossing a sloping green glade about a mile away. He was wearing a broad-brimmed straw hat, and held in his hand a bare cutlass, and appeared as distinct and out of proportion as a figure in the background of an early Italian picture. This giant strode slowly across the grass and disappeared into the sugar-cane. There was a note of momentousness about the immediacy and magnitude of this distant figure.

These green slopes, hemmed in by their Garden of Eden forests, have an almost miraculous beauty. In the extending shadows of the late-afternoon sunlight they appeared as idyllic and eternal as the clearings in a rather sad heaven. Purple shadows collected on the grass under the mangoes, and the infinity of greens was broken in places by the pale golden showers of cassia, or by the crimson of hibiscus. Somewhere, lost among the opposite line of hills, a solitary Negro practised the trombone, and the gloomy, inexpert notes reached our ears through the heavy air with a grotesque and almost delphic solemnity.

From the height of the *mornes* a new world appeared. The fronded landscape curled down to the sea and expired in a network of mangroves. The outlines of Marie Galante and the Islands of the Saints hung on the horizon, and the blue-green sky was piled with a monumental accumulation of pink clouds. In their midst, somewhere over the bay towards the sunset, was hidden the peak of La Soufrière, the volcano that dominates the whole of the west of Guadeloupe. Below us, huddled behind the masts of sailing vessels, Pointe-à-Pitre looked little more than a hamlet. The low tin roofs and the intruding palm trees were already in shadow, and as we watched, the sunlight died from the white façade of a bank, and then died from the hill and the air above us. Night descended all in one piece, like a shutter.

We followed a tunnel of leaves downhill to a stagnant pool and a derelict small-gauge railway that ran through cane-fields into the town. The croaking of millions of frogs and the scraping of crickets seemed to increase as the darkness grew more intense, and an odd feeling of desolation and remoteness infected us all. What on earth were we doing here? Sunset in the tropics is one of the most melancholy events in the world, a moment of sudden and all-pervading sadness.

An electricity strike had condemned the town to darkness. The Place de la Victoire was full of people promenading, all of them invisible except for the occasional blur of a white suit moving through the shadows without either head or hands. Cigarettes floated through the air of their own volition, glowed momentarily brighter in a void under the whites of eyes, then grew dim and sank again in a ghostly parabola. Now and then a match was struck, and a black mask would materialize for a few seconds and vanish. There was the sound of voices everywhere, and of whistling and humming, and sometimes a clap of laughter exploded in the dark and the hot air became full of ownerless teeth.

Invisible, too, were the enormous sand-box trees that surrounded the square. They owe their name – they are called *sabliers* in French – to their seed pods, which, in the eighteenth century, were filled with sand

and used as sprinklers for the blotting of parchment. Three sides of the square are enclosed by buildings and the fourth is a waterfront where sloops and schooners lie at anchor. During the French Revolution, the Place de la Victoire was the scene of a battle between the invading English and their French Royalist allies against Victor Hugues, the envoy of the Convention. The English were defeated, and the Royalists massacred, and not far from the marble bust of a late nineteenth-century governor – a mild torso on a pedestal with an imperial beard and huge epaulettes – the Revolutionary guillotine was erected.

The Hôtel des Antilles is a disaffected seminary, a cool, spacious building of wood, whose timbers, beams, balustrades, pillars and twisting staircases give it the air of an old galleon. The nautical atmosphere was augmented now by the hurricane lanterns that were its only lighting. The owner is a Frenchman who retired here from the Vichy Navy, a stout young man with a blond *barbe en collier* like Count d'Orsay, and an elaborately carved pipe. The proprietress, a blonde, middle-aged Parisian, complained bitterly about the way the French West Indies were run, and hinted regretfully that all was far better in the British possessions, especially with regard to sanitation, roads, public works and discipline. I felt there was an unspoken corollary that the blacks were 'kept in their place' better in the British possessions, and that, as a result, all were happier. Her conversation had an undercurrent of disillusionment that was to become increasingly familiar throughout the Antilles.

The wooden dining-room was sparsely occupied by a handful of French colonials who had been here too long – engineers, architects, government servants – by a great-grandson òf Fromentin, one or two coloured lawyers, and a Negro sergeant with a French wife. The heat, the lugubrious acoustics, the sudden silences and the rain falling outside were the stage properties of a Somerset Maugham scene that was all set for tragedy. Something ought to have happened. Nothing did.

Returning next evening from a beach at Gosier, a few miles outside the town, Costa and I must already have developed a kind of immunity to the gloom of sunsets. The day had been wonderful. The only possessors of the little bay, we swam for hours under the overhanging trees, and then lay smoking and talking until it was almost dark. The water had been as warm and as smooth as silk, and the only Negro we had passed as we were walking back had waved and shouted *bonsoir* in a friendly way. Returning to the Hôtel des Antilles, we found, waiting for us with Joan in the lantern light, a friend who was to prove our benefactor throughout our stay in Guadeloupe. We had sent off our only letter of introduction as soon as we landed, and the results had been almost instantaneous.

Raoul was twenty-one, and belonged to a Martinican family that has been established in the Antilles for centuries, part of that tiny white minority which formerly owned the sugar plantations and were the undisputed oligarchs of the island – the Créoles.

I must explain exactly what this term means, as it is one that will recur continually throughout the book. It derives from the Spanish word *criollo*, and applies, in the French Antilles, to a European born in the West Indies of pure white descent. In the time of the slave trade, the term *nègre-créole* was in use to describe a Negro born in the islands, as opposed to a *nouveau-nègre* fresh from the African forests; but with the suppression of this traffic, the term became superfluous and has disappeared. The opposite of a Créole – a Frenchman from France – is *un Français de la métropole*. For the past hundred years, the white families have tended to leave the islands and settle, after their long absence, in Metropolitan France, so that the remainder of this Créole squirearchy becomes every day a more compact and isolated body.

'Créole', when not applied to human beings, means anything (irrespective of colour) that is specifically West Indian, like the cooking and, above all, the extraordinary language of the Negroes: the Créole patois. During the early days of the colony, Raoul explained to us over dinner, the slave ships unloaded blacks in the Antilles who had been bought or kidnapped all along the western seaboard of Africa in the territories of a score of different native kingdoms, so that the majority of them were unable to communicate with each other; except, in time, by learning some of the language of their masters. But they only learnt the nouns and the verbs, which they maimed out of recognition and cemented into phrases with an *ad hoc* African syntax. Many of the French words they use – *bailler*, for instance, instead of *donner*, and now by Créole adoption *ba'* – have become obsolete in French, and the tenses are differentiated not by the verb endings, but by placing the three words *té*, *ka* and *ké* – indicating, respectively, past, present and future – between the unchanging verb and its subject. Nouns that begin with vowels very often preserve, even in the singular, the S-sound they would have when elided after *les*. A pin, in Créole, is *une zépingle*. The complication of these mutilations, and the amazing order of the words, are too intricate to discuss without launching into a whole thesis. *Je vous crois* in Créole is *Moin ka coué ou*, and *Donnez-moi mon épingle* would be *Ba' moin zépingle à moin*. The vowels lose all their Gallic crispness, especially the letter

'A' which is always pronounced as though it were roofed by a circumflex, and *moin* for *moi* indicates the essentially nasal quality of the language. If the reader repeats the two phrases I have written, in as deep a voice as he can, but through the nose, and opens his mouth as wide as possible, it will give him some idea of the sounds that would ring in his ears all day long in the Créole-speaking islands of the Caribbean. With the passing of time, one or two English and Spanish words have been absorbed. It is a childish and primitive language, but it *is* a language, not merely pidgin-French, or *petit-nègre*, and it has been almost static in its present form for two hundred years. It is spoken in all the French Antillean possessions; Martinique, Guadeloupe, St Barthélémy and French Guiana, though for some reason, the Negroes of the French half of St Martin speak English; and in most of the British Windward Isles, Dominica, St Lucia and St Vincent, that were formerly French colonies. The Créole spoken in Haiti is almost the same, and in Mauritius, too, it has developed and solidified on similar lines, and it is even spoken, I believe, in the tiny French island of La Réunion in the Indian Ocean; the easternmost point of that peculiar journey on which Baudelaire was packed off as a young man, *pour lui changer les idées*. It is an excellent language for the Negro songs of the Antilles, and is said to be a good medium for humour and epigram. Its sound is, above all, comic, a succession of heavy labial noises, nasal inflections and loud quacks. I found that its difficulty gave it a sort of tantalizing charm – I always thought I would understand what I heard, and scarcely ever did. It is, at any rate, full of life, and twenty times preferable to what Coleridge's nephew, in his *Six Months in the West Indies*, calls the 'yawny-drawly way' in which the Negroes in the British West Indies converse.

Even the Créoles themselves have been influenced by one strange characteristic of this slaves' lingua franca: the complete omission of the letter 'R'. It is replaced by a W-sound, and is the same curious distortion as that affected by pre-1914 English 'Nuts' in *Punch* jokes ('I say, Wonny old Fwuit, this is a wegula wamp,' etc.), and goes one step farther than the mere omission of an 'R' as affected by the Incroyables – *'C'est incoyable, ma paole d'honneu'* – in the Paris of the Directoire. But here it is quite involuntary. Many of Raoul's words and turns of phrase had a charming antique flavour, and his French was notable for the almost total lack of the mildest contemporary slang, as though the language in these remote islands had remained immovably lodged in its eighteenth-century mould. His colloquialisms were all old-fashioned, and the 'R-W' substitution lent his conversation a singular, faintly macaronic distinction. The Créole pronunciation, he told us, had long been a source of amusement in France.

'*Quand un de nous autwes Cwéoles se met a pawler a Pâwis, c'est la wigolade généwâle.*' I wondered if the Empress Joséphine, who was a kind of remote great-aunt of Raoul's, carried this quaint mannerism to France with her other Antillean foibles.*

Raoul asked us endless questions about Paris, while we were busy questioning him about the islands. We had all three been in Paris recently and told him all that we knew. I do not know why we were so surprised to learn that, although he had travelled as far as New York to buy machinery for a sugar plantation, he had never visited France. He was on the point of going to school in Paris when he was thirteen, but the outbreak of war had held him in the islands, and since the liberation work had kept him a prisoner. (He was manager of a sugar estate in the east of Guadeloupe.) Paris had to be postponed until the next year.

We sat talking until everybody in the hotel was asleep, and made plans to stay with him for a day and a night as the prelude to a series of excursions. He drove away in a jeep at about midnight through the downpour and slush of a particularly awful monsoon, and left us with the feeling that our stay in Guadeloupe had taken a turn for the better.

Like the population and the language, the costume of the women of the French Antilles is a fusion of Africa and France – in this case eighteenth-century France – and it is, without qualification, magnificent. A multiplicity of underskirts and of lace petticoats of various colours is surmounted by an overskirt – *La gwan' wobe* – of silk or satin or brocade. This is caught up at the waist on one side, or sometimes on both, in a voluminous salient of pleats that derives with the utmost legitimacy from the panniers of Boucher or Watteau. The top part of the body is enclosed in a tight bodice that admirably displays the slimness of the waist. The sleeves either come right down to the wrist, or end at the elbow, where they burst into a cataract of lace, or descending tiers of stiff accordion-pleated frills. Round the shoulders a silk *foulard* is arranged with a studied, formalistic abandon and fastened on the breast with a big gold brooch. This complicated finery is brilliantly coloured, and made of rich stuffs that have long vanished from the shops. A load of gold

---

* Another eccentricity (or survival?) in the pronunciation of these Créole squires is the flattening of the French *oi* sound into the equivalent of the English *aw*. Can this be the explanation of Barham's seemingly arbitrary rhymes in the *Ingoldsby Legends*? e.g. –

> 'And no poet could fancy, no painter could draw
> One more perfect in all points, more free from a flaw,
> Than hers, who now sits by the couch of St Foix ...'

> (The Black Mousquetaire)

jewellery hangs round the neck, triple chains with gold tassels and barrel-shaped clasps, necklaces and collars of large hollow balls of gold or little golden cockle-shells and medallions that clink against elaborate *agrafes* called '*zépingles twemblantes*'. Round the wrists hang chains and bracelets, and large ear-rings completely cover the lobe of the ear. The latter are called *chenilles*, and consist of globes of gold encircled by a thick gold, caterpillar-like cable from which a spiral projects that is flanked by two outward branching leaves.

This splendid attire is crowned by the *madwas* – Madras – a tight, stiff silk turban made of stuff which came originally, no doubt, from the French colonies in India. It is tied with a complexity and a tautness that turn it almost into a pillbox, tilted at a challenging angle over the forehead, with the ends spreading overhead in stiff and brilliant spikes. These are the feminine accoutrements that are catalogued in the famous Antillean song of the beginning of the last century, paraphrasing the adieux of a Martinicaise to her soldier-lover who is leaving for France,

> Adieu foulard, adieu madwas
> Adieu, gwain d'or, adieu collier-chou
> Doudou* a moin li ka pa'ti
> Hélas, hélas c'est pou' toujou' ...

The number of ends projecting from the Madras are ciphers of an unambiguous, amorous sign-language comparable to that of the hibiscus behind the ear mentioned in Rupert Brooke's letters. It was explained as follows: *Un bout = Je suis libre, coeur à prendre. (Porté par les jeunes filles.) Deux bouts = Coeur déjà pris. (Tu arrives trop tard.) Trois bouts = Doudou. (Il y a encore de la place pour toi.)*

Unfortunately, except at national fêtes and fancy-dress balls, these ravishing clothes are now only worn by the older women. We had the luck to see them once worn by a young woman, Mlle Paulette-Jean, a beautiful coloured girl of Fort-de-France, who was kind enough to put them on for Costa to photograph. The result was delightful, and gave us an idea of what the streets of Pointe-à-Pitre and Fort-de-France must have looked like fifty years ago when Lafcadio Hearn described them. This girl seemed the epitome of Antillean beauty, and of all the grace, charm and elegance for which the islands are so celebrated. She had that soft Créole voice which is characteristic of the French islands – a sort of bubbling sweetness. Her skin was about the same colour as a dark Greek girl's or a southern Italian's, and there was a round

---

* *Doudou* in the vocative means, exactly, darling, but in any other sense is the mild French-Antillean equivalent of *poule*.

patch of vanilla on her cheek, a vestigial *mouche* that is another survivor from the reign of Louis XVI.

Fortunately, almost without exception, the old women cling to these clothes, even if the semaphore of the turban has no longer any practical application. Their faces and bearing are often superb. Their features are aristocratic and gaunt, with piercing eyes embedded in a haggard bone structure that might have been hacked out of obsidian or blackthorn. These fierce and glittering matriarchs walk with a ruffling *amour propre*, a *prestance*, and a carriage of the head that achieve the dignity of the bearing of African queens. But the girls, often so pretty with their enormous smiles and great deers' eyes, are cheated of all their natural grace by horrible white silk or cotton dresses and worse hats, and high-heeled shoes that seem as long and pointed as skis; all their charm is turned into prinked-up leggy awkwardness. Negro women ought always to wear bright colours and compact, dashingly tied turbans. Mulatto girls should affect a sort of Italo-Iberian swank.

The male counterparts of the splendid old women of these islands wear dull black clothes, awkward butterfly collars and straw boaters or trilbies, and often metal-rimmed spectacles. Their dark, wrinkled faces and white hair make them look gentle and benevolent, but they seldom achieve the grand air of their wives. The young men are nearly all beautifully built, and look their best when they are working without their shirts, and displaying magnificent shoulders and torsos that taper down to flat stomachs and phenomenally narrow waists. Their bodies have the symmetry and perfection of machines. Muscles and joints melt smoothly into each other under skin which shines like a seal's or an otter's. But when they put on their best clothes, all this gracefulness vanishes. They suddenly acquire a clumsy, gangling look, and their wrists seem too long or their sleeves too short. Their hands hang purposelessly swinging, and under these garments the ease and looseness of their gait degenerates into a shuffle. We had to wait till Trinidad to see the right way for Negroes to dress.

A hundred years ago, the women wore practically the same clothes as those I have described, except that their turbans on great feast days were often rigid cylinders two feet high with enormous bows down the front. Père Labat, writing at the end of the seventeenth century, remarks that any money the slaves could save was spent on apparel for Sundays and holidays. This, for the men, would consist of tight white knee-breeches and a white shirt. Round their waists they tied like a kilt a length of brightly coloured cloth that came to the upper curve of the knee. This was secured on either hip with bunches of coloured ribbons.

Their torsos were encased in a tight-fitting bolero, that reached half-way down the back. Between this and the kilt-like cloth, the shirt puffed out. At the wrists and throat they would attach silver buttons, coloured stones, or bright tufts of ribbon, and if they wore a hat it would be a new straw sombrero. In rich houses the clothes of the slaves were basically the same, but carried out in the colours of the household livery, and the jackets would be covered with gold lace. Gold pendants hung in their ears, and, round their necks, emblazoned silver plaques. A large and dazzling turban was the crowning touch to this magnificence.

Guadeloupe is composed of two triangles of land linked by a narrow isthmus through which winds a sinuous and sluggish limb of sea called the Rivière Salée. The western part, La Basse Terre, is, unexpectedly, an intractable, precipitous and forested country climbing up into the clouds where the volcano of La Soufrière hides its cone, while the eastern part, La Grande Terre, is a low, rolling country of cane-fields and pasture-land. Driving across it from Pointe-à-Pitre, we passed through an undulation of *mornes* into a wide savannah, where the cattle grazed under the breadfruit trees; on, through the village of Abymes and the meadows and sugar-cane and banana plantations to the town of Moule.

The afternoon was baking and shadowless, and the town seemed only with an effort to remain upright among its thoroughfares of dust. It was as empty as a sarcophagus. The French guide-book describes it as a great centre of elegant Créole life in the past, hinting at routs and cavalcades and banquets of unparalleled sumptuousness. Acts of God must have fallen upon it with really purposeful vindictiveness, for not by the most violent manhandling of the imagination could one associate a chandelier or a powdered wig with this collection of hovels. Not even a dog was to be seen. But behind a tall crucifix stood a cemetery of such dimensions – Père Lachaise and the Campo Santo gone mad – that, opening their cameras, Joan and Costa slid from their seats with sharp gasps of delight. For hours I trudged behind them round this blazing necropolis, down avenues of stucco vaults and tombs, Parthenons, temples of Vesta, and Chartres cathedrals, past urns and weeping angels, mourning marble Lucreces hung with brown wreaths and even shaded sometimes by hardy evergreens white with dust, till they had seen and photographed their fill. These acres inhabited by the dead, these miniature halls and palaces and opera-houses, were, it occurred to me, the real town, and the houses falling to ruins outside the railings were in the nature of a negligible suburb. Joan had finished her third film with a photograph of an ochreous Aztec pyramid built round the faded photograph of a very old Negro in postman's uniform, and we left this city of mausoleums like three pillars of fire. The leather work of the car was as hot as an electric iron to the touch, and the dust that settled on our steaming faces turned us into a trio of zombies. It penetrated every orifice of the head and temporarily robbed us of all our faculties.

We ate our picnic in a belt of palm trees where a river ran under a bridge into the sea. A silent boy brought us a pitcher of water from a near-by well, and watched us as we slept and talked and bathed all through the afternoon. Moule, its distressing detail tamed by distance, projected into the sea on a tongue of sand. Now and then the water was ruffled by a series of faint splashes. Some mass-resolution had prompted an army of little silver fish to leap out of the water in an infinity of shallow trajectories. Almost before the eye could register this sudden glitter, they vanished and the water became smooth once more. Each time this little miracle occurred, it evoked the same spasm of pleasure. Half in and half out of the sea, we idled the afternoon away until the sun slanted under the branches and drove us towards St Marc, where Raoul was waiting for us. We just had time before dinner to drive with him to the easternmost point of Guadeloupe, La Pointe des Châteaux.

The jagged rocks were tufted with sea-grape and on the eastern skyline lay the island of La Désirade. It juts perpendicularly out of the water and then becomes as flat and elongated as a floating coffin. Its isolation – about seven miles to windward of Guadeloupe – and its inaccessibility were the reasons for its choice as the leper-colony of the French Antilles. It reminded me as I looked at it of Spinalonga, that other leper-island that I used to gaze at from the mouth of a cave in Crete. Several hundred lepers live on the Désirade, and as visitors are allowed to call, we planned to sail there next day. Its name – Desirada, the longed-for – was bestowed by Columbus, as its low silhouette was the first glimpse of land for the Spanish navigators on their way to the new world. *Quand bleuira sur l'horizon la Désirade?* The symbol of this long journey's ending is echoed by Guillaume Apollinaire.

As we strained our eyes towards the flattened outline, rain began to fall, heavy, ice-cold rain that soaked us to the skin in a couple of seconds. The car was some way off, so we hid our clothes under rocks, and ran to take shelter in the sea. We continued our conversation up to our necks in the blessedly warm water; but the rain, instead of abating, doubled its force and turned into hail. The sea grew rough, and treacherous under-currents were wrenching our feet from under us. It was also growing dark. There was nothing for it but to get out, and expose ourselves to the icy fusillade. It took us some time, stumbling about in the dark with our arms crooked over our heads for protection, to find our clothes again. The white pellets were rattling on the leaves of the sea-grape as we ran to the car, and bouncing all round us. What evil wind could have penetrated the kindly Trades with this awful present from Spitzbergen? The drive to St Marc was a shuddering nightmare. Chimneys of the sugar refinery and the sheds and barns and wagons, appeared faintly through the falling rain. Then we were inside the dry shelter of Raoul's house.

We dined in dressing-gowns, in the middle of the big central room of this rambling one-storeyed building, after warming ourselves with several glasses of *punch martinicais* that Raoul prepared with considerable care. This drink is made of rum and syrup with a sliver of lime or lemon peel, and sometimes a sprinkling of nutmeg. In bars, only the syrup is paid for. The rum itself is free, and left on the table as indifferently as though it were water. The mixture is stirred up with a white swizzle stick called a *lélé* that is sometimes two feet long, cut from an island tree and ending in a wheel of amputated concentric twigs.

Raoul, who is a Martinican, was lonely in Guadeloupe, and eager to talk of the life in his own island, where all, he maintained, was gayer, more established, more civilized. We spent the evening listening to tales of house parties from plantation to plantation, races, picnics, cock-fights, duels, old love affairs, Negro celebrations and contests between mongooses and snakes. Guadeloupe is free of poisonous snakes, but the woods in Martinique teem with a terrible reptile called the *trigonocéphale* or, in Créole, *fer de lance*, that lurks in the long grass, or lies along the branches of trees, to shoot through the air like a javelin when its prey approaches. Many theories have been put forward to explain the presence of this snake in Martinique, for it is unknown in the neighbouring islands to north and south. The most likely explanation is that the ancestors of this wicked swarm were carried on floating timber down the Orinoco from the Venezuelan hinterland (where they are very common) out into the Atlantic with the rest of the alluvia of the river, washed north-wards by the currents and finally cast ashore on Martinique. To counter-act this menace, mongooses were imported, and the struggle continued in the bush for decades. The ranks of the *fer de lance* were thinned, but the mongoose multiplied at such a pace that it, too, has become a problem. An uncle of Raoul's has the rare gift of handling snakes with complete immunity, and this attribute has surrounded him with the fame and the awe of a sorcerer. Some years ago he inherited an estate in Trinidad (where, during the French Revolution, many Royalist families escaped from the Jacobin ferocity of Victor Hugues). He now lives there alone in the high-woods in a house where snakes circulate as freely as kittens.

Under the mosquito net in a big shadowy bedroom, I fell asleep looking through old photograph albums by the light of an oil-lamp. The pictures had faded to a pale khaki, in which one could just make out the Martinican seigneurs in straw boaters, the Créole beauties in their feathers and their sweeping Boldini hats. Many of the photographs recorded picnics under palms or shady mango trees. Negroes in livery in the background carved cold fowls or drew the corks from bottles, while the horses waited patiently between the shafts of the assembled victorias. What remote and Elysian scenes!

A cat crept under the netting and curled up on the pillow. The rain rattled on the roof without ceasing, and from time to time lightning zigzagged through the rain, followed by thunderclaps that seemed to blow the night in half.

La Sainte Marie de la Garde, the tiny skiff that we found waiting for us next morning at the beach of St François, looked disturbingly small. She was manned by two elderly Negroes wearing odd Chinese hats like the tops of toadstools. The weather had cleared up magically and a strong wind sent us skimming in the direction of the Désirade.

Many of the Antilles are hemmed in by a nimbus of coral reefs that lie from a furlong to several miles out to sea. We crossed the smooth, sheltered waters to a ruffling causeway in this barrier, and the moment we had emerged, felt the boat tossing and pitching with a sharper motion. The shore became a delicate green line, and the misty quadrilateral of the Désirade began to appear in greater detail. The boat was only about eight feet long, and was propelled by a disproportionately large triangular sail that was ribbed like the canvas of a junk. This, and the strange headgear of the sailors, in the pearly morning light gave the world around us the appearance of a Far Eastern print. We were sailing through a sea-picture by Hiroshige.

But we had not been more than two hours on our way before a storm blew up. Clouds blotted out the sun, and in a few minutes rain was falling on a grey and turbulent sea. Soon we were shipping so much water that we had to bale continually with halves of calabash. The sea grew rougher and rougher, and I caught a glimpse of Costa in the stern vomiting genteelly into a scoop. It became much darker, as though night were about to fall, and suddenly I noticed that the little fleet of fishing boats that had been hovering in a scattered circle all round us had disappeared from view, and that the two grey blurs of Guadeloupe and

La Désirade had vanished too. The skyline had contracted to a close and jagged circumference of vast triangular waves that rose and tilted and sank with hateful deliberateness and recovered and rose again all round our little tossing pivot. The wind had almost reached gale force, and just in time the sailors hauled down the sodden sail, and piled it into the foot of rolling bilge water in which, huddled, baling demiurges, we were sitting waist deep. It was a dangerous moment. The motion of the vessel at once grew quieter, and its insane motion was reduced to a sickening climb and fall over the mountainous waves. The whites of the sailors' eyes had been treacherous tokens of alarm, but not once did the timbre of their deep incomprehensible Créole change, and even while they hauled the sail down they shot reassuring smiles in our direction. *'Ce n'est wien, Madame – un petit gwain de vent.'* But the nose of the boat was dragged round in the direction of invisible Guadeloupe, and our journey to the Désirade had to be abandoned; as it turned out, for ever. A moment of sunlight exposed a watery vision of the distant rock. Then the clouds closed in again and effaced it.

On the way back to Pointe-à-Pitre a small cemetery caught our eye. The remarkable thing about it was its wretchedness, for even the poorest Negro village is flanked by a little city of monuments. Who, then, were buried under these mounds of mud, that only a few pebbles adorned, or a nosegay of withered hibiscus? One or two were surmounted by crosses or worm-eaten slabs of wood. The only names that I could decipher were 'Samuel Valiswamy' and 'J. Alicout'. They were, Raoul explained, the graves of *coulis échappés*, and he told us a curious story which he had learnt from his old black nurse as a child, to account for the presence, so many thousands of miles from home, of these escaped coolies.

At an undefined era in the past (Raoul said), presumably after the emancipation of the slaves, the planters, anxious to fill the hole made in the labour-market by the abolition of slavery, turned their eyes in the direction of India. Ships mysteriously left the Antilles, and, after two months at sea, dropped anchor in harbours off the Indian coast, either off British India or the shores of their own colonies of Pondicherry and Chandernagore. When night fell, the crew festooned the rigging with lanterns. Bands discoursed cheerfully on the deck, and all who cared to come were welcome aboard. Drinks flowed, little presents were distributed, a ball was organized, and the Indians fluttered on to the glittering decks like a swarm of moths. The ball continued, and when a sufficiency of guests were carried away in the dance or reeling under unaccustomed draughts of rum punch, the anchor was secretly weighed, the ship drifted out to sea, and armed guards began to mingle with the revellers ... In two months' time the ship would reach the Caribees, and there, Raoul's nurse triumphantly concluded, the Indians were marooned, and here, generation after generation, they have remained ever since.

A queer, cool tale, but apocryphal. I was never able to discover what, if any, is the origin of this piece of Negro folklore, or if it was fabricated in order to foist unhappy beginnings comparable to their own on the history of these Caribbean East Indians; out of jealousy, perhaps, at their superior skill in commerce. I had to wait until we reached Martinique and Trinidad to learn the true history of Indian indentured labourers. Meanwhile, these small graves and the occasional Indians we saw in the streets acquired a special significance.

Point-à-Pitre was still in darkness, and Costa and I fumbled our way through the streets to call on Madame Eboué. The late M. Eboué, whose white hair and distinguished African features became familiar through their presence on the stamps of the Antilles, originated in French Guiana, and acquired considerable and deserved fame during the war when he was governor of the Chad, by being the first governor of a French colony to rally to the cause of the Free French. Madame Eboué, a Paris acquaintance of Costa's, was the M.R.P. deputy for her native island of Marie Galante, and was standing again at the impending elections. She was plainly a woman of great energy and acumen. Her glittering spectacles, massive figure and downright, no-nonsense way of talking, combined to present a dark replica of any of the few women M.P.s I have ever met.

But our conversation was obviously not going too well. She seemed a little distraught, and anxious, I thought, for our visit to end; so after a civil period we said good-bye, and left. Once in the street we discovered the source of a noise that both of us had heard in a vague way all through our visit, and which, we understood at once, must have been the reason for our hostess's slight distraction. An elderly dandy in a high collar and a boater was striding up and down outside the house shouting and waving a malacca cane. *'Tout le monde,'* his message went, *'doit voter communiste. Vous n'avez pas honte, Madame, de demander nos suffrages?'* We felt disturbed lest our visit should in any way have impaired her election chances, for colour questions (*à bas les blancs!*) are vigorously exploited by the Antillean left wing. It seemed curiously inappropriate, however, to hear these particular sentiments coming from such a heavy swell. The mystery was never explained. *'Vous n'avez pas honte, Madame ...'* As we turned the street corner, we could still hear his elegant peripatetic diatribe.

35

Rumours were abroad that the electricity strike had been specially engineered by the left. Most of the polling, and all of the count, takes place after sunset, and it was thought that total darkness or candle light might be more propitious to funny business than if the electric lights were functioning; a precaution that seemed redundant, as it is quite a normal manoeuvre to organize the smashing of the ballot urns and the consequent nullity of the poll. The post-war Antillean vote had been overwhelmingly left. But the islands follow the political trends of the Metropolis with a curious fidelity, and the recent swing to the right in France was causing concern.

We promenaded once round the Place de la Victoire on our way home. This island forum had been the theatre, the year before, of an awe-inspiring event. A quarrel had sprung up between a white bar proprietor and a coloured client which had resulted in the ejection of the Negro on the grounds that he was drunk. After a time he reappeared at the bar, accompanied by a large number of cronies. The proprietor was hauled into the square and literally torn limb from limb and then cut to bits with cutlasses. The participants, after this outburst, sank back again into normal life. They are all at large still, and the whole affair passed off like an inside-out lynching scene in the deep South.

We grew to loathe Pointe-à-Pitre. It was hard to choose between the day – the dust and mud and the vacuity of the streets – and the night, those interminable hours of damp torpor under a mosquito net. These edifices of muslin give to all sleepers the appearance of tented heroes on the Dardan Plain, and underneath them, lulled by the falsetto of thwarted insects, one hovers between sleeping and waking till dawn. *On se réveille*, states a French guide-book to the western tropics, *lourd et endolori*. Heavy and dolorous, we would descend to explore the dwindling charms of Pointe-à-Pitre.

Our last conscious sight-seeing expedition was a visit to the Musée Schoelcher. It was a small derelict building. Inside, we gazed at a plaster cast of the Venus de Milo, and another of the Apollo Belvedere, two turtle shells, a faded engraving of a mango tree, and our visit was over. There was nothing else. Except, in the railing-enclosed dust outside, a colossal plaster head – larger than a man – of Schoelcher, the French Wilberforce: a white Roc's egg with Louis Philippe whiskers, beaming into the suffocating Antillean emptiness. We determined there and then to make a getaway.

CHAPTER 2

Guadeloupe Continued

As the faded photographs in Raoul's albums had hinted, picnics are an essential part of Créole life, and their technique has become highly specialized. Raoul was continually improvising them at a second's notice, and of these one in particular stands out. After an hour in the sea, we had run on tiptoe across the fine grey sand – the sun heats it at midday to an intolerable temperature – to the shelter of the forest's edge. Up above, the branches climbed the mountainside in a wild, unbroken amphitheatre of green. We were encamped among dark, shady rocks. Drinks lay on a large slab of ice, and Raoul was cooking on a little fire. First we ate a delicious fish, then a chicken cooked with rice in the Créole way, and then mangoes, avocados and paw-paws. Coffee followed punch, wine and liqueurs. Half asleep, Costa asked the name of the beautiful and exceptionally shady tree under which we were reclining. 'Ah,' Raoul said, 'I meant to tell you. It's called the manchineel. One drop of its juice on the skin is almost certain death ...'

I woke up to find two pairs of eyes gazing down at me. Two young Negroes, naked except for a cloth round their middles, were standing under the branches with their backs to the sun. They were as lean and hollow-cheeked as Solomon islanders. Each wore a naked cutlass at his side and held in his hand a primitive crossbow, strung with a dozen twisted thongs cut from the inner tubing of a motor-car, and a long fiercely barbed harpoon. Home-made goggles for underwater fishing hung round their necks. They accepted cigarettes and smoked them in silence, then, saying good-bye, ran over the sand and into the water, and were soon swimming out of sight into the next combe, leaving the beach as bare once more as the shore of Robinson Crusoe's island.

On the way back we passed through Bouillante, on the western roots of the Soufrière, whose crest had so far remained obstinately hidden in cloud. Boiling water wells out of the sea here in little geysers, and the shore is pock-marked with grey circles of boiling mud. Many of them are covered with a brittle crust, but a poke with a walking-stick stirs up an angry bubbling noise, and a stench of sulphur fills the air. These places are scattered round the volcano like sores. The surrounding country is peppered with lumps of igneous rock, some of them many tons in weight, black and infernal-looking missiles nestling in green beds of forest and creeper, which have shot from the centre of the earth and landed among the trees after miles of flight through the air.

My growing aversion for tropical flora would be confirmed or exorcized, I knew, by climbing to the top of the Soufrière, and as the ascent began I started to feel, with the slight pang that always accompanies the surrender of a prejudice, that it would be the latter.

The tunnel of the pathway swung up the forested side of the volcano in long loops, roofed in by a green arcade of great height and of such denseness that the sky was often invisible. Under this high ceiling, our progress resembled the ascent of a shallow winding staircase through wavering and aqueous gloom, often illumined by only a single slanting shaft of sunlight. Scarlet and pink and purple hibiscus cascaded from the forest walls on either side, and yellow cassia and the fragile papery white bugles of datura. The mangoes and paw-paw of the slopes were replaced, as the path mounted, by thickets of bamboo and elephant-ear, *chou sauvage*, and the *balisier* plant with its long thin stems ending in ribbed and spatulate leaves ten feet long and the shape of Zulu shields. Tall, smooth palm trees overtopped the denser jungle growth, and, most beautiful of all, there was an abundance of tree-ferns of great size. The young ones grow like a sheaf of identical bishops' croziers. But when fully grown, the stem is straight and slender, and every few feet a corolla of branches expands from it, fanning upwards, outwards and then down in the most gracious of curves. Each branch is equidistant from its neighbour, and grows to exactly the same length, and each circle of branches is larger than the one below. The tree is crowned by the largest of all these circles, a delicious pale green cupola that is symmetrically and perfectly ribbed by a dark spidery masonry of branches from which, like a network of veins, the twigs thread their ancillary leaf-systems, curving and drooping and tapering away into points of the tenderest green. These frail umbrellas are as faultless in detail as an architect's compass-design for the building of a dome, and as light and fluttering and delicate as a Valentine made of peacock's feathers.

All this vegetation was far overtopped by the acomas, enormous trees that climbed to great heights and blotted out the sky. The boles, which were larger than any I had ever seen, sprang from roots that seemed webbed to the trunk by massive membranes of wood projecting like rudders whose apexes diminished and melted as they gained height, into the huge fabric of the tree. The trunk and the branches were so over-grown with parasites – by tree-ferns that had lodged in hollows and opened their green tents in mid-air, by elephant-ear and by *bois d'ananas* with its bristling armoury of spikes – that the tree looked like a dozen different kinds of tree climbing upwards in massive and insane confusion. Cataracts of creeper and convolvulus trailed from the branches and spiralled their way down the lianas which, like organ pipes, clung to the trunk, or hung loose, thicker and softer with moss than the grips of bell-ropes. Lianas of all diameters were looped and suspended every-where. Thin strands as tough as bootlaces hung dead straight from branches one hundred feet overhead, like the solidified trajectories of a downpour of rain. This huge green underworld was lighted by a sunlight somewhere overhead that only spilt an occasional beam through the opaque criss-cross of leaves. We did not hear a single bird.

The forest that confined our path on either side was as dense as some green fibre composed of undergrowth and creepers and young trees, and the rotten detritus of old ones. Many of these existed still only in shape, and would collapse when struck, with a sickly smell of decay.

Raoul had taken his shoes off, and mounted the green slopes with an ease that can only be the result of his family's three centuries in these forests. His alert and squire-ish figure led our little procession all the way, past a pool called Les Bains Jaunes, and then for a few curious furlongs of stepped and cobbled pathway laid out here by French sappers in the eighteen-sixties. The way grew steeper and more tortuous, and Raoul and our guide plied their cutlasses more frequently on the encroach-ing vegetation. All at once the forest stopped, and we found ourselves at the foot of an abrupt cone. A fleet of clouds, sailing from the east on the current of the Trade Winds, hung at anchor, as it were, level with the obstructing crater.

The last part of the ascent was almost as steep, but not nearly as easy, as climbing a ladder. Stunted trees projected in exclamatory gestures from the rocks, most of them seemingly a kind of magnolia tree, with shiny, saucer-shaped leaves. Spiky scarlet flowers grew on the ground, and flowers of deep violet, and plants as angular, hard and porous as coral. The rock was covered with moss of every imaginable colour, but pre-dominantly marigold or primrose, or of a green as deep as that of submarine foliage. At the very moment that we hoisted ourselves through the crater's toothy machicolations, bathed with sweat and with our hearts thumping, a furious blast of wind drove a reek of sulphur up our nostrils, and the clouds broke from their moorings and obliterated everything.

We were in a world of mist and wind, as remote from the tropics as an Irish bog in midwinter. The volcano has not erupted on a large scale since the period of the French Revolution, at which time it caused considerable damage in the neighbourhood of Basse Terre. The crater is now choked with scoriae and black basaltic rock, but so thickly muffled in rainbow-coloured moss that every inch of ground is damp, resilient and treacherous. Deep crevasses are roofed by a thin layer of spongy growth, so that it is very dangerous to leave the paths which traverse this wilderness. Even when the moss is torn away, the rocks themselves are less substantial than they look. For yet another layer of vegetation clings to them, far denser and more deceptive, but so compact that it appears as firm as a millstone. The guide drove his cutlass into it up to the hilt, meeting only the resistance of plasticine, and then, with cunning twists of his sharp weapon, removed firm cones and cubes and prisms of stinking and glutinous mauve stuff.

In clear weather the islands of Marie Galante, the Saints and the Désirade are visible from the crater towards the south-east, and the large British island of Dominica; and to the north, Antigua and Monserrat, and a faint indication of the smaller British Leeward Islands trailing north-westwards towards the horizon like a distant line of battle. But now the swirling mist obscured all but the spurs and cliffs that lay close to us. So we lay down on the moss like Niebelungen, and opened the bottle of red wine that Raoul had thoughtfully brought with him, and talked – or rather persuaded Raoul to talk – about Créole life, and the history of the French Antilles.

Raoul's family was among the earliest to settle in Martinique after the French laid claim to these islands in the person of the Norman sailor and colonizer, Pierre d'Esnambuc, governor of St Christopher, in 1635. This action on the part of France was a direct result of the expansionist policy of Cardinal Richelieu. The islands of Guadeloupe, Martinique and Dominica were to be exploited by the newly founded Compagnie des Iles d'Amérique, under the command of the Cardinal's namesake du Plessis, and of Lyenard de l'Olive. The Spaniards who had discovered the islands over a century before had made no effort to colonize them: the resistance of the Caribs was too fierce to make their capture worth while, compared to the glittering goals of Mexico, Peru and Eldorado. Since then the history of Raoul's family is typical of the landed proprietors of the French islands. An uncle later showed me in Martinique the grant of arms and the title-deeds to their Martinican estate, signed by Louis XIV, 'in recognition of his brave services in command of a regiment of Martinican grenadiers against the English and the savages of the islands' – a war of extermination that over the space of centuries wiped out the whole Carib race, except for a small number still surviving in Dominica. They grew rich with the importation of slave-labour in 1650 – a traffic that began fortuitously when a Spanish slave-ship was captured by French filibusters – and poorer with the emancipation of the slaves in 1848. They now live in moderate prosperity. The history of this family, with its affiliations scattered all over the Antilles, and even as far away as the valley of the Mississippi and Nova Scotia (for which Raoul used the obsolete French name of *Accadie*), is also a reminder of the sad fortunes of the great French Empire of the New World. Raoul's ancestors were the sort of Frenchmen that accompanied Champlain to the Great Lakes, and colonized Canada and Louisiana and Guiana. But Quebec fell to General Wolfe, Sainte Dominique – Haiti – revolted and won its freedom at the time of the Revolution, and Louisiana was sold by Napoleon to the United States. The lesser Antilles changed hands between the French and the English again and again, but most of them finally remained with the British: pawns won on the chessboard of the great European congresses and treaties. All that now remain under French domination are French Guiana, Martinique, Guadeloupe and its satellites, Saint Barthélémy and half St Martin in the Leeward Isles, and St Pierre and Miquelon, those two minute, icebound islets off the Newfoundland coast whose inhabitants eke their existence from the cod-fishing industry.

The bulk of these French pioneers were Normans, Bretons or Gascons. Raoul's first ancestor in the islands was, oddly enough, of Irish descent from a still remoter forerunner, perhaps in Elizabethan times, of the general exodus which later on was to sprinkle the courts and armies of Europe with names like Dillon, O'Rourke de Brefni, O'Kelly of Kallagh and Tycooly, Taaffe von Ballymote und Correu, O'Donnel of Tyrconnel or Tetuan. Through some romantic atavistic allegiance, his curiosity about Ireland was almost as strong as his more normal preoccupation with Paris. What was Dublin like? and Mayo, Sligo and Roscommon? *'Toute la province de Connaught, enfin? Comme je voudrais y aller ...'*

On our way down we passed a minor crater. Bright yellow sulphur heaved and hissed and rank fumes came curling upwards like corkscrews of smoke out of the nostril of a sleeping dragon. Half a mile below, a ghastly stone ravine of grey and white and mauve was littered with dead bleached branches that resembled the bones and antlers of calcinated fauna. A reek of sulphur, growing stronger as we climbed to the brink of the three Chaudières, blew down this horrible valley. Grey water boiled and spouted and bubbled in cauldrons of rock and a noise went roaring and echoing along the gorge louder than a hundred exhaust pipes in full blast. Extreme heat and a poisonous cloud of vapour hung over these holes. The wan colour of the rock, the heat, the smell of brimstone, and the desolation and the remoteness of this place, lent it the aspect of a backwater of hell. It was too sinister to remain long. We turned at last, and descended the haggard boneyard until the roar was only a distant sigh; and plunged down through the willow-pattern trees into the refuge of the forest.

There was nothing that suggested an old-established or a patrician way of life in the first Créole estate we visited. Our host and hostess were aggressively European in appearance, and in their conversation, disappointingly parochial. Every question was measured, and accepted or discarded, by the yardstick of conservatism, ultra-Catholicism and the interests of family life; usually discarded. Disapproval was expressed of a new official in the island administration. 'What do you expect,' our host said, 'from a government like the present one? Of course their nominee is a scoundrel. And what's more,' he lowered his voice as if he were about to pronounce the most dreadful enormities, 'they say – they *say* mark you! – that he is divorced! Then, take the roads in Martinique. Why are they in such a disgusting condition? *Je vous demande pourquoi?* Because,' he said with lugubrious triumph, 'the people responsible for their upkeep are a band of free-masons, sir, whose only interest is to fill their own pockets and destroy the state! *La Dissidence a fait beaucoup de mal dans les îles.*'

'*La Dissidence?*'

'Yes, the de Gaullist movement. A terrible mistake! What these islands need is a firm hand, and that's what they got, during the war, under Admiral Robert. Whereas now –' He raised his hand, in a gesture of helplessness that seemed to embrace his little timber villa, the mango trees in the garden, the descending tiers of banana trees and the sea. His opinions are by no means representative, but there is a section of the Créole world in the Antilles for whom the revolts and massacres of the Revolution have almost retained the cogency of a living memory. This ultra-conservative minority whose background is one of centuries of slave-owning, privilege, *blason*, the Church, and *cousinage*, was almost inevitably pro-Pétain during the war, and with the advent of reform, the presence of a Prefect instead of the former semi-independent governor, the spread of Leftist ideas and the islands' complete parliamentary integration into the Chamber in Paris, they feel their position growing weaker every day. For some of them, the return of the Comte de Paris to the throne of France is the only panacea.

We made a tour of the banana plantation. The trees were just ripening to harvest, huge 'hands', as they are called, dangling from the trunk, terminating in great purple heart-shaped buds. These profitable plants are one of the ugliest of trees. Their sagging, unwieldy branches are always battered and split, as though they had been unpacked from crates; unpacked, damaged in transit and improperly assembled after being torn from flower-pots in suburban greenhouses, and allowed like their fruit on the return journey, to reach maturity on the way.

La Joséphine, another Créole estate to which Raoul escorted us, lay farther along the leeward coast of the island than we had yet ventured. The road followed a serpentine course through the heavily forested *mornes*, crossing, every now and then, slender bridges that spanned gorges of great depth. These bridges hung poised above the tops of great trees, and through the leaves and the tangled spiders' webs of parasites, glimpses appeared of streams rushing downhill in a doleful penumbra. Again, seen from on top this time, the pale green parasols of tree-ferns appeared, fastidiously architectural and alien structures among the huge arboreal bruisers of the forest.

The frequency of hurricanes seems almost entirely to have abolished any attempt at beautiful building from the French islands. Most of the Créole families live in large wooden bungalows, or in modern flats in the towns – but the garden of La Joséphine was enchanting. It was a wilderness of overgrown rose trees, hibiscus, cassia and tall palmistes, dominated by a single araucaria. A little Créole cemetery, with graves of Doroys, Hucs, le Dentus, and Médards de la Farce, mouldered on the edge of the banana plantation.

Those Chinese hats the sailors wore on our abortive journey to the Désirade had intrigued us all. When we asked about them, the sailors looked blank, and said, 'They come from the Saints.' It was true, for, landing in the little port of Terre d'en Haut, we were surrounded by these spreading headgear, as by a grove of mushrooms. Here, in the Saints themselves, we learnt that a Saintois sailor had 'brought one back from Indo-China or Annam a number of years ago' (how long? I wondered) and the fashion had caught on at once. The Saintois now wear nothing else. The basis of the hat is a circle of white linen, two feet in diameter, tightly stretched across a radiating framework of split bamboo slats whose outer ends are bent down and attached to a thin hoop of bamboo. The middle of the underside of this cart-wheel is fastened to a shallow cylinder of bamboo, into which the head is inserted. Two tapes tie in a neat bow under the chin to keep it from blowing away. It affords perfect shade, and is wonderfully light. The Saintois call it *'chapeau annamite'* or *salaco*. It looks as curious in this part of the world as a deerstalker would in Bali. Eccentricity is the predominating character of the islands of the Saints. There are eight of them – Terre d'en Haut, Terre d'en Bas, Ilet à Cabrits, Grand Ilet, Paté, Les Persées, Redonde and La Coche – lying about three leagues from the Guadeloupean village port of Trois Rivières, on the southern bank of the Soufrière. Terre d'en Haut, the largest, is only about three miles long, the others diminish in size till they are little more than projecting rocks or reefs. They are more arid and spare than Guadeloupe and the rocks are overgrown with organ-cactus and prickly pear. The Trades drive their moisture unshed across the low hills of the archipelago.

The little ship approaching Bourg des Saintes, the capital of Terre d'en Haut, sails under the lee of a castle of cyclopean appearance called Fort Napoleon. It was built there on a promontory by slave-labour out of huge hewn stones, by the Emperor's orders. During the late war it served as a concentration camp and political prison for enemies of the Vichy régime. The rock sinks steeply to the sea, where a phenomenon occurs that made us rub our eyes and look again; for a large white liner seemed to be sailing straight out of the rock-face. She glittered with paint and reflected the brilliant sunlight from her hull, her anchor and all her portholes, and her rigging was gay with flags. But only the bows were visible. The stern and all of her aft of amidships was seemingly embedded in the leaf-clad matrix of the island. It turned out to be a large villa, built by the owner in a moment of furious and wonderful marine enthusiasm. A detestable modern villa dominates the little village-capital, a gathering of timber houses that otherwise has all the charm and simplicity of a European fishing village.

The café above the quay is a long chamber of planks painted in cool and watery colours. Sipping Pernod – or rather a cunningly labelled opalescent drink called Père Noel, which is brewed in Martinique – we covertly took stock of the other occupants.

The population of these islands – the Poor Whites of the Saints – seem to me as unusual as any of the odd ethnological rock-pools of Europe. It is difficult to discover who were the ancestors of this population. Most of them, no doubt, were *engagés*, humble white colonists and sailors who accompanied the various expeditions in the seventeenth century; some may have originated in the penal colony that was once established in the archipelago; a few filibusters, perhaps, and here and there a *cadet de famille* who had gone downhill. There is no cut-and-dried explanation, as there is for the Poor Whites of Jamaica (Cromwell), or the Redlegs of Barbados (Judge Jeffries). They refer to themselves as Bretons, which is probably pretty close to the truth, as large numbers of the early colonists came from Brittany. Bretons indeed still seem to expatriate themselves more easily than any other Frenchmen. They certainly look like most of the sailors and fishermen who one sees in Brittany. Till very recently, they remained rigorously white, and so the majority still remain, but a small minority have intermarried with their African neighbours during the last generation or so.

The remarkable thing about them is that they have turned themselves into Negroes in all but colour, and if all the races of the Caribbean sea were to be repatriated to their countries of origin, the Saintois would now feel more at home in the African jungle than in Brittany. They have long ago forgotten the French language, and speak nothing but the Afro-Gaulish patois of the Negroes, and are more inexpert in correct French and more illiterate than the humblest black inhabitants of the Guadeloupean savannahs.

They sat round us in the café, drinking rum at lightning speed. Their strange hats, shoved back like dilapidated haloes, framed heads which, though some had Negro characteristics, were mostly pure European in colour, texture and contour. A conflicting strain was visible in a few of the children who stood about among the grown-ups' tables, in the jutting bone structure under hair that was often lint-white and straight. The skin of most of the fishermen, under a heavy tan and the pickling effects of wind and brine and rum, was fair and florid. Their eyes were blue or grey, set in features of a fine aquiline cut of Latin or Celtic affinity. Their hair was brown or fair, wavy or straight, and bleached by the sun. Many were good-looking but most of them, on closer inspection, displayed degenerate physical traits that were plainly the result of centuries of inter-breeding. Some were large and brawny and sunburnt, but far too many were ravaged by alcoholism and disease. Their clothes were the same sordid rags as those of the Negroes. Their conversational tone seemed extraordinarily violent. The nasal quacking of Créole, the flailing gestures and the constant childish cachination appeared to separate these queer folk from Europe not by centuries, but by thousands of years. There is something disturbing, at first almost frightening in this strangeness; but something rather engaging too. Undertones of squalor, disease and brutality are mitigated by a timidity and a fecklessness which are far from unattractive. They are all fishermen and accomplished boat-builders. The quay was crowded with skeletons of half-built vessels and, in the morning, the waters between the Saints and Guadeloupe are white with their light craft, flying across the waves under their own Saintois rig. The masts are placed well forward, and the bows are shaded by primitive spinnakers, while the mainsails, vast triangles of ribbed canvas, swing out far beyond the stern on long booms of bamboo.

After a short time in the island, compassion is the predominating feeling that these people evoke. Evidence of disease, advanced and terrible, is visible on every side. A great number of the inhabitants suffer from elephantiasis. Necks and shoulders are afflicted by huge goitrous tumours, arms are converted into bolsters, and legs into bulbous monstrosities of vast proportions. Some of the women's legs are enlarged into the semblance of pumpkins that dwindle to the normal size at the ankle; so that the extremities of mammoth limbs disappear with a ghastly coquettishness into minute high-heeled shoes. The men are prone to this affliction in the region of the pudenda, which swell to such proportions that the wretched patients have to wear aprons or, in extreme cases, when their pendent tumours reach the ground, are condemned to an elaborate harness attached to their shoulders. It is pathetic to record that this particular form of the disease, propagated by a microbe that is indigenous to these regions, is incurable. The stigmata of hereditary syphilis are often discernible in the wreck of features and limbs.

An official of the island pointed out to us the marks of leprosy, which usually took the form of white patches on the skin, within the circumference of which the flesh had lost all sensibility. They could be pricked or cut without feeling pain or, indeed, anything at all. He explained that a recently discovered treatment can render the disease uncontagious, though it cannot actually cure it. This is held to be a great boon on the island, as its victims can thus sometimes escape the dreaded verdict of lifelong sequestration on the Désirade. It was fairly easy to tell lepers, he said, by a certain sweetish smell that followed them.

The heavy local incidence of insanity struck us during our first couple of hours on the island, in the persons of three men whom we encountered on the road at different points; croaking, stumbling, and cursing the empty blue sky; and in the voice of a very old man seated in a rocking-chair in front of his door. Alternating wails and giggles, or sudden spells of anger, sailed through the afternoon air.

It was in these waters that Admiral Rodney, with Hood as second-in-command, defeated the French fleet under the Comte de Grasse on the 6th of April, 1782, delivering Jamaica from attack and capture by

the French, and putting an end to a serious French threat to the whole
of the British West Indies. The battle lasted from dawn till sunset. The
forces engaged were 36 ships and 2,640 guns on the English side against
34 ships and 2,500 guns on the French. The English lost 261 men killed
and 837 wounded, while French losses amounted to as many as 14,000.
De Grasse was fighting stubbornly on the upper deck of the *Ville de Paris*,
beside the only other two unwounded men on board, when he was forced
to surrender. He was at once taken aboard the *Formidable*, Rodney's
flagship, where the two admirals dined together. It is permissible to think
of the two sailors, with Hood looking on, sitting over their port with
the lantern light on their gold lace and powdered wigs, shifting the
decanter, the pepper-pot and the salt-cellar about the table in a reconstruction of the day's action, while the flagship lay at anchor on these
tropical waters dark with wreckage. The Duc des Cars (whose brother was
killed in the battle) writes admiringly in his memoirs of Rodney's generosity and good manners to the French. He had often visited Versailles
before the outbreak of the war, where he was something of a favourite.

In the hope of discovering the graves of English or French sailors killed
in this action, I asked the way to the cemetery. A lane ran inland past
a green mound surmounted by a crucifix. Elder trees shaded the footpath
and rolling meadows lay on either hand; a tame, untropical landscape
more like a country lane in Brittany or Cornwall.

There were no heroes' resting-places from the battle of the Saints;
no graves, indeed, earlier than the first decades of the nineteenth century.
It was a small overgrown and almost derelict marine cemetery built
in a hollow of the hills and shaded by oak-like mango trees, full of a
romantic melancholy in its abandonment and decay. The elaborate
mausolea that make the cemeteries of the Caribbean so extravagant and
bizarre were replaced here by a forest of worm-eaten wooden crosses
which leaned at every angle among the long grass. The weather had half
obliterated the names and the graves themselves were bordered, sometimes completely covered, by the beautiful conch-shells that are scattered
over every Antillean shore, planted in rows on their broader ends, with
their cones pointing towards the sky. These lovely shells are often over
a foot in length, white and chalky in texture, twirled in spiralling volutes,
and opening spiky lips to reveal grottoes of the palest pink. A large number
of the graves symbolized the hazards of the sailor's and fisherman's life:
black wooden crosses with the legend inscribed in flaking white paint
on the cross-bar: ICI GIT UN MARIN, with no name, date or nationality.
Again and again the message was repeated, marking the burial-places
of bodies washed up on the island shores, with all their features and

47

identifying documents obliterated by their watery sojourn, and sometimes half eaten by sharks. Now and then a tattooed anchor would be just decipherable, and this emblem, echoed in white paint, accompanied their laconic epigraphs.

Under a cactus-plant, a marble slab marked the grave of Marie-Louise Félicité de Gimel, Baronne Serindon de La Salle, who died during the reign of Louis Philippe. Who was she, and what brought her to this minute island? A small mound covered the remains of twins who perished at the age of eight: '*Ici reposent Yves et Germaine, deux anges.*'

Grass, salty and rank, invaded everything. Fragile anemones and periwinkles prospered here and there, and lizards, as motionless as though they were carved out of emerald, lay on the cracked and baking slabs. They stared with wide unblinking eyes at nothing, in slanting postures of petrified alertness. At an approaching footfall they scuttled along a cross with the rapidity of a missile, and stopped upside-down in the same frozen attitude with a suddenness as astonishing as their speed. Two red butterflies wove patterns round each other in the meridional blaze.

On the way back, vainly attempting to remember some lines from Valéry's *Cimetière marin*, I heard a tremendous shindy in one of the back streets. A remarkably good-looking and completely drunk Breton was reeling, inasmuch as you can reel with half a dozen people 'holding you back', and waving his fists, shouting '*Vive de Gaulle*' and threatening all comers. Nobody had come forward, but several minor fights were in progress on the outskirts of the crowd, mainly between children. An old woman was sitting on the ground screaming, quite unheeded, till her veins stood out, while a grave middle-aged man watched the scene sorrowfully, holding under his arm a large stuffed turtle. It was an eve-of-election row, and had plainly been going on for some time. Costa, who like me had been drawn to the noise a little earlier, had nearly had his camera smashed.

'It means nothing at all,' the curé told us later, 'absolutely nothing.' Father Offrédo's eager, kind little face was split up into a smile, as he carefully poured out four glasses of white wine. He was born in Morbihan, but had lived for thirty years in different parishes of the French Antilles without returning to Brittany, travelling sometimes for days on horseback across the Guadeloupean *mornes* and savannahs to administer the Sacraments in isolated hinterland villages. His wiry, hale little frame and cheerful face spelt nothing but well-being, although he had suffered again and again from dropsy, pneumonia and malaria. His spleen had been completely removed, and he had received Extreme Unction no less than seven times. He spoke with great affection of his island parishioners, and referred with a laughing tolerance to their drunkenness and indolence. Their fishing is over early in the afternoon, and when they get home they do nothing but drink. About a litre of rum a day. Their illiteracy is worse than any he had ever encountered in the Negro world, and their bad language is famous (*'Ils sont connus, dans toutes les Antilles, pour les gens qui se servent des mots les plus orduriers'*). Their laxity in religious duties also presented stiff problems for a priest. They certainly sounded a handful. 'They are complete children,' the curé went on. 'They just don't grow up.' But he lingered at much greater length on their troubles – disease, remoteness from all other influence or example but themselves, the fatal ease of the fisherman's life here; and on their qualities – generosity, charitableness, honesty, their gift for enjoying themselves, and their courage. During the Vichy régime many of them slipped away to Dominica and made their way from there to the Free French navy. He assured us that, in spite of appearances, the row had not been a political, but a purely domestic one, a protest against the preponderance of the numerous Sampson family in island affairs. Inasmuch as the islanders had any politics, they were all pro-de Gaulle, and the bawling of political slogans was only intended to underline and add force to some family argument. But Communism – or indeed politics of any sort – was virtually unknown in the island; 'which, considering their mental age,' Father Offrédo concluded, with a tolerant grin, 'is just as well.'

Listening to this fine old man as he sat with his hands folded in the lap of his soutane, and his biretta far back on his wrinkled forehead, I was able to take in the details of his little presbytery, the flowered Second Empire wall-paper, the crucifix, the small chandelier, the two shields on the wall with the lilies of Valois, the shells and hibiscus on the table, and the Annamite hat hanging on the back of a chair. As we left he cut and presented to us three bunches of grapes from a trellis in his garden, the first we had seen in the islands. Were we going to Haiti? Would Costa take a photograph of him in front of his church, and give it to his sister, who was the abbess of a convent in the north-west corner of the Republic? *'C'est ma vraie soeur de sang,'* he explained, *'pas seulement ma soeur en Dieu ...'*

Four poor whites were hoisting the sail of the fishing boat that was to take us back to Guadeloupe. After rowing us clear of the bay, Terre d'en Haut withdrew into the middle distance. Its western cape and the little hillock of Goat Island were outlined against the contours of Terre d'en Bas, which is inhabited by Negroes. We asked what it was like. 'No good,' the sailors answered. Why? *'Pa'bleu, question de couleur,'* three of them answered. *'Ils sont noirs.'* *'Non pas ça,'* cried the fourth; he was several shades darker than the others. *'Plus bêtes.'* The sheet was made fast and they resumed their oars in a cloud of banter.

After a while one of them began singing a biguine, beating time with his feet on the bottom of the boat. The song grew faster until in his excitement he let go of his oar to clap out the accelerating rhythm with his hands. The words sounded like some alliterative gibberish but it obviously had a meaning, and clearly an improper one, as it launched the other two oarsmen into such paroxysms of mirth that they had to drop their oars as well. The ship was abandoned to the sail, while they held their sides and fought for breath and even rolled about helplessly in the bottom of the boat. Without understanding a word of the song, we were gradually infected by their laughter until we were also gasping and aching and wiping the moisture from our eyes. The helmsman had let go of the tiller and sat huddled in the stern with heaving shoulders, while the tears of laughter streamed down his face.

It had begun to rain, evening was coming on, and there the boat rocked about in the grey water with its seven occupants impotently doubled up in the throes of collective hysteria. Still the clapping and stamping continued and the rapid alliterative jingle of words. The singer was hypnotized by the spell of his song –

> Zoum! pa' dewie'! Zoum! pa' devant
> C'est l'amou' comme on dit!

went one chorus. When a song seemed to be dying away, and we were able to recover slightly, the tune would change, and a new song would begin with an agonizing and long-drawn-out wailing bellow that contorted us all into new knots of hilarity. We somehow managed to reach Trois Rivières, carried there by a swift and kindly wind. Weak, helpless, drenched with rain and tears, we climbed ashore at the little ruined mole. The boat turned about at once, and headed for the Saints, the four sailors waving their queer hats and shouting affectionate farewells.

An old colonial cobbled road climbs the mountain-side from the little port, to join the main road that connects Pointe-à-Pitre and Basse Terre. Not far from this old causeway, in a clearing in the forest, are some rocks adorned by pre-Columbian carvings by the Arawaks or Caribs – *'des monuments colossaux, ornés de sculptures caraïbes'*, as a French guidebook says. A little boy led us to the spot through the twilit forest, and there, in a little glade, stood a lump of rock. By the last rays of the sun we were just able to descry the shapes of three golliwogs. They had circles for heads, bristling with half a dozen wiry strands of hair

Two holes represented eyes and their mouths were turnip-lantern slits. An arm like a forked stick projected from one of the heads. *'Twès vieux,'* the child said reverently, and so they were. Their authenticity is beyond question, but they might have been scratched there yesterday by a backward child with an old nail. They are very comic and were the cause of fresh transports of philistine laughter. As it was too dark for a photograph I made a pencil sketch of this gem of pre-Columbian art –

It had been a long, strange day.

Guadeloupean buses, like battleships, all have names. These ramshackle torture-chambers hoot their way through the *mornes* and savannahs under names like *Le Tigre*, *Le Terrible*, *L'Ogre*, or, more modestly, *Rodolfe*. Their names are painted in bright colours on boards attached to the front of the vehicles. The fearful old diligence that we boarded at Dolé to take us to Pointe-à-Pitre was *L'Indomptable*. It broke down several times on the way, and at last decisively. Costa wisely unpacked his bed and went to sleep under a breadfruit tree.

We finally entered Pointe-à-Pitre at walking pace in the wake of a funeral. Scarcely a day goes by without one's catching at least a distant glimpse of a funeral, and *Pompes Funèbres* is a shop sign that seems as common as those of butchers or grocers. Coffins are constantly being bundled into monumental hearses, rattling black arks with chipped drapery carved out of wood, the roof piled high with carved scythes and skulls and hour-glasses. The letters *A* and *Ω* are sometimes painted on the panels to remind passers-by that every beginning has an end. The plumed horses amble slowly down the street (or a recalcitrant engine is cranked up) and the long procession shuffles after them in the direction of the cemetery. One coffin I saw being loaded up was shaped like a cannon-shell, as though its passenger was determined to cut out the red tape and hurtle direct to his bull's-eye in Abraham's bosom.

Depressed as we were to be back in Pointe-à-Pitre, we were buoyed up at the idea of leaving, almost at once, for Antigua, in a little steamer called the *St Laurent*. We soon learnt, however, that her crew was on strike. Indefinitely.

The Palais de Justice was as good a place as another to wile away a few of the innumerable hours of waiting until the strike on the *St Laurent* came to an end. Costa had disappeared into the outskirts of *La Pointe* with his painting-things under his arm soon after breakfast.

A Negro girl was sitting half a yard in front of me, so I was at last able to inspect at close range a method of hairdressing that had fascinated me for days. The hair is parted from forehead to nape, and from this central canal twin contiguous partings radiate at different but always symmetrical angles, which in their turn multiply into a sub-series of enclosures until the entire scalp is honeycombed and reticulated with lozenges, quadrilaterals and polygons. Then a mother or a sister plaits the segregated hair into tight clumps – it must be an almost impossible feat – and fastens them down flush with a whole arsenal of hairpins, so that the owner appears to be wearing a tight and elaborate cap of black wool. It is very sensible and, above all, very becoming, as it preserves the shape of the head, which is often very fine. Nor does it interrupt the splendid neckline of the Negro girls – a polished bronze column that melts into firm shoulders, and ends an uninterrupted line which, in profile, springs from the eyebrows to the shoulder-blades in a long, question-mark-shaped arabesque.

The girl in front of me wore large gold ear-rings, and a necklace of gold balls the size of chick peas, which, against the glittering smoothness of her skin, burnt with deep fires. There was scarcely a peasant woman there who was not weighted down with these gold ornaments. The men were peasants from the deep savannah, tired-looking elders with grizzled white moustaches, vestigial beards, wrinkled foreheads and nostrils so splayed that they spread half-way over the cheek. They had come in here to follow some lawsuit in which they were involved, or just to rest from the glare of the market-place. This was more or less our object too.

The judges and lawyers were seated beneath the fasces and the Phrygian cap of the Third Republic. All of them were coloured, some of them that matt obsidian that seems almost darker than black, and in their silk robes trimmed with fur and their white linen bands, they looked superbly dignified. We saw a lawyer friend from the hotel, sitting beside a robed and sable Mussolini: Maitre Lara, the best pleader in the Antilles.

Most of the cases were conducted in Créole (although French was used as much as possible), as they dealt with questions of land-tenure or infringement of boundaries between peasants. But one of them was concerned with a razor fight, another with wilful wounding with a cutlass. In the last case, the prosecution made great capital of a raffish-looking old man, half of whose ear had been cut off with a razor by a young neighbour. The voice of his lawyer shook with forensic indignation as his forefinger traced the outline of the remaining part of the ear. Thumping damages were demanded. If he had produced the severed lobe, there are no grounds for thinking that the judges would have proved less easily swayed by such corroborative detail than the British Parliament in the eighteenth century. But he didn't, and soon, in a swirling pillar of silk, Me Lara rose to his feet, and in accents that echoed through the tribunal began the best pleading I have ever heard. (I must excuse myself for the fragments of French that follow; I noted down some of his discourse, and it would lose a lot in translation.)

He began with a clear exposition of the case, and then warmed gradually into an accusing Buzfuz. He pointed at the old man – *'Sa gorge, monsieur le Juge, est aussi ouverte que sa poche est plate – à cause, evidemment, de sa fainéantise. Son alcoolisme est redouté par tous ses voisins ...'* He proved not only that the old man had damaged his own ear by falling down on his cutlass when he was drunk, but also that he had been abandoned, because of his intemperance and violence, first by his mistress and then by his daughter, who had taken refuge with *'ce jeune homme sobre et travailleur – mettez-vous debout, monsieur'* (a sort of simpleton grinned for a moment and sat down) *'merci – avec lequel elle vit maintenant maritalement.'* He won his case.

It was an illuminating glimpse of life in the *mornes*. There is something terrifying about these razor or cutlass fights in lamplit cabins.

Me Lara next defended a young man who was charged with rape. Here he became humorous, tolerant, detached. '*Que voulez-vous, monsieur, ce n'était qu'une idylle – la sorte d'idylle que nous connaissons tous – qui a pris une tournure un peu vive. Regardez-la, messieurs; merci, mademoiselle.*' (A very embarrassed girl stood up.) '*Elle est jeune. Elle est belle. Elle est latine. Maintenant, regardez le jeune homme, mon client*' (a young peasant clattered to his feet). '*Il est jeune, joli-garçon, vif, latin également. Ils sont tous les deux latins, messieurs. Ils vivent à la campagne, il y avait une lune,*' he waved, towards the spot on the whitewashed wall where that luminary would have hung, '*et il se peut que l'ardeur de ce jeune Tityre s'est exprimée en gestes où nous ne devons voir que de l'entrain, de la fougue et de la jeunesse. Et, au lieu d'aigrir, par un verdict trop peu pondéré, les rapports entre ces deux jeunes gens; au lieu de flétrir une fleur qui est en train de bourgeonner – que dis-je? – qui s'épanouit déjà, nous devons les congédier de ce tribunal sans haine, sans rancure entre eux, et suivis par nos voeux pour leur bonheur futur, et par notre espoir que la Sainte Eglise bénira bientôt une union que ne saurait être qu'heureuse et féconde.*' He won his case again, subsiding after his peroration like a weary Othello. The boy and the girl clumped down the aisle, looking slightly bewildered, but not ill-pleased. I was very much struck by the use of the word '*latin*'.

The coolest place in the *Hôtel des Antilles* was a vaulted drinking-hall on the ground floor, the foundations on which the old monkish super-structure had been built. I used to escape here to write during the afternoon when the atmosphere in my room, under a mosquito net, became unbearably hot. (Joan's plan – still, alas! as I write, no more than a plan – of sleeping chained to a chameleon seems to be the only practical way of neutralizing the unceasing siege of the insect world. With this alert little basilisk camped on one's bosom suitably camouflaged to melt into the slumberwear; prepared, at the faintest buzz in the surrounding ether, to fire half a yard of tongue at the foe, and swallow it without blinking an eye, one might snore the night peacefully through. Not otherwise.)

This afternoon the cool vault was empty of customers. Streaming with sweat, I settled at a table and opened my diary. As usual, the three rather pretty waitresses were sitting in a row, looking avidly through ancient, dog-eared copies of *Marie-Claire* and the Paris *Vogue*, gazing at themselves in the looking-glass, interminably tying and retying their tartan madrases, and giggling and quacking quietly to each other. One of them brought me a glass of beer, and said:

'*Vous écwivez toujours, Monsieu'?*'

'*Oui.*'

'*Vous aimez écwiw'?*'

'*Oui, merci.*'

'*Vous connaissez Helena, Monsieu'?*'

'*Non. Qui est elle?*'

'*C'est la twoisième jeune fille là.*'

'*Et alors?*'

'*Elle vous aime. Est-que vous l'aimez?*'

'*Enfin, j'aime tout le monde . . .*'

'*Alors, moi aussi?*'

'*Je suppose, oui.*'

At this stage she danced back to her companions, squeaking and clapping her hands.

A few minutes later Costa, in a state of liquefaction, came in from the street, threw his paints into a chair, and ordered a glass of beer. As soon as the waitress had retired, I repeated – with, I must confess, some complacency – the colloquy that had just taken place. Half-way through I noticed that Costa's enormous lettuce-green eyes were straining from their orbits with astonishment. When I had finished, he said: 'B-but that's extraordinary. I had exactly the same c-conversation half an hour ago.' We gazed into each other's eyes, first with amazement, then with rue, and finally burst out laughing.

The three waitresses, meanwhile, after eagerly following our conversation from a distance, were in convulsions of laughter, as though a long fuse had at last detonated some explosive. The arches rang with a sort of high scream, followed by a gasping sigh of indrawn breath and a powerless rocking of the head as, bent almost double, and helplessly striking their knees with their hands, they prepared for a fresh outburst.

H'm.

The *St Laurent* was still on strike and Pointe-à-Pitre had become as hateful to us as a plague-town. Dredging the guide-books of Guadeloupe, I discovered – how could I have missed it before? – that the Schoelcher was not the only museum of Pointe-à-Pitre; there was also *le musée l'Herminier d'Art Pré-columbéen*. I set off at once.

It was opposite the Lycée Carnot. There was nobody there. The door was wide open, all the glass was broken, and everything was coated with the dust of decades. Apart from half a dozen shapeless arrow-heads, there was nothing pre-Columbian. The walls were surrounded by glassless show-cases filled with stuffed birds and eggs, all of them broken, and fish. Everything was falling to bits. One of the fish looked rather unreal, so I reached into the case and took it out. Not only was the straw coming out of the tail, but it was made of cotton and sewn together with pack-thread; the scales were symbolized by crescents of red and blue paint. I thought for a long minute of slipping this treasure into my pocket, but, overcome at last by conscience, I laid it reverently back into its place.

A flamingo standing on a tree stump was being strangled by a python. The head of the snake had dropped off with decay, and lay glaring on the floor. Several pelicans with their wings closed hung on wires from the ceiling. Whether they had originally represented pelicans in flight whose wings had gradually shut with the passage of time, or whether they were just suspended in mid-air to save space, it was hard to determine. There were two fine armadillos whose shells were miraculously intact, and, in a back room, a two-headed calf which had been so badly stuffed that its front legs had spread outwards till its chest touched the floor, while the hind legs had bent double at the knees. A contemporary perambulator reposed under a dozen years' accumulation of dust.

There was something delightful about this museum, and I often think of the Herminier still. In a much mellower mood I strolled back to the hotel to tell Joan and Costa of my discovery, and visit it again with them in the capacity of an old habitué and cicerone.

But when I got there, all sorts of other questions ousted it from my mind. The *St Laurent* strike would go on indefinitely; but, my companions said, a plane was leaving in half an hour for Martinique; what about it? I ran up to my room to pack.

CHAPTER 3

Martinique

Everything below and around us was rapidly changing shape, and the only stable point was our shuddering condemned cell. Here we hung, enclosed in strident aluminium plumbing. Guadeloupe was drawn from underneath us and the coffin of the Désirade floated to the surface on the east. An infinitesimal chaplet of islands slid northward, slowly writhing and changing position and form as it travelled: the Saints. Marie Galante, a basking and wallowing turtle already far below, swam slowly after them, ruffling with its muzzle the still Caribbean. How could one connect this bald tropical convexity with Versailles? Yet Madame de Maintenon lived here for many years as a girl. She was then the poor and Protestant Mademoiselle d'Aubigné, the daughter of a gloomy crown official in the colony. Soon after she left the Antilles, her grand connections in Paris married her off to the invalid Scarron. This was the first step on her long journey from this tiny island to the Royal bed, from which, as wife of the ageing Louis XIV, she was able to abet, with a proselyte's ardour, the hounding of her former co-religionists from France. It is difficult to think of a more un-Caribbean character.

The windows were suddenly smothered with damp cotton-wool; we were in the middle of a cloud; and when we dropped out of it, the smooth blue gulf of Fort-de-France – sprinkled with shipping and guarded by lighthouses on promontories at the bottom of a glittering urban amphitheatre – was sliding up to receive us. A rush of spray flattened against the window pane, and we were in Martinique.

How irrelevant and deceptive most first impressions are! When I think of Fort-de-France, all, for a few seconds, that my inner-eye registers is a vast metal advertisement for Coca-Cola; plucking, in flesh-colours and pastel shades, at the four deep chords of hygiene, patriotism, snobbery and sex. For the mammoth beauty reclining on the sand is nothing if not healthy. It is a vision of pneumatic bliss newly pumped up and fitting as resiliently into the white swim suit as an inner tube into a tyre; Kolynosed, depilated, Mummed and varnished. The parasol, the expensive accoutrements, and the sunny dunes of Palm Beach indicate her income-group. There's money there, and lots of it. Her face is lighting up, dimples are burgeoning in her cheeks, and her smile sparkles as though each tooth were encased in cellophane. Optrexed pupils melt into surprise, delight and *attendrissement*; for something wonderful is happening in the foreground.

A naval sleeve advances into the picture from the lower edge, the forearm of a brave boy in blue, and, better still, an officer's forearm, for the star and circle of braid are the insignia of a sub-lieutenant in the U.S. Navy. (This, with allowances, means quite a lot of dollars a year, and he's probably got private means. There is money on both sides.) A brown wrist and then a brown hand – a strong hand, but capable of great gentleness – emerges from the blue cylinder, and muscular fingers are closed round a fluted and waisted bottle; but not so closed as to obscure the lettering on the offered gift. *Coca-Cola*, you read, and at the same instant the ejaculation above the recumbent girl bursts on your awareness: 'Mind Reader!' It's a walkover! The air resounds with invisible wedding-bells.

Thanks to Coke ...

The first time I contemplated these great eclogues in tin, the triumphant arm connected not only with a secret socket in my own *alter ego*, but with those of half a dozen Negroes (for Art and Commerce know no Mason-and-Dixon line) in the outskirts of Fort-de-France. Their bare feet shuffled in the dust as they gazed at the picture in morose cogitation, all sucking Coca-Cola through straws. (This has a happy ending, especially for the shareholders.)

The local manager, a relation of Raoul's, was a friend of mine. 'It's wonderful stuff,' he said. 'The locals adore it. It keeps them off the rum.' It's true. An increasing number of the inhabitants of Fort-de-France circulate the capital in a permanent state of stone-cold sobriety, their insides awash with this strange brown liquid. The propaganda drive of this firm has been so intensive and so ruthlessly efficient in its execution, that never for a second are the words Coca-Cola out of one's sight. It is on a scale that nobody who has not crossed the Atlantic can hope to grasp. They are printed on almost everything you touch. Everywhere the beaming heroines of these giant advertisements smirk and simper and leer. It becomes the air you breathe, a way of life, an entire civilization – the Coca-Cola age, yoke-fellow of the age of the Atomic Bomb.

The bottles, when they are emptied, are sent back to be refilled, but the tin capsules that seal them are littered everywhere. They clatter against your shoes in the dust and pile up in rusty drifts in the gutters. Bit by bit they will form a metal humus all over the western hemisphere, so that centuries after the bomb has done its work and made way, perhaps, for a nobler detritus, archaeologists will be able to put a date to our buried remains with the help of this stratum of small round lids.

The proximity of the United States to the Antilles is a thing that one constantly feels; perhaps disproportionately so, as it is chiefly apparent in the glittering external symptoms of modern life: Coca-Cola advertisements, frigidaires, wireless sets and motor-cars, especially the last. For the dusty streets of Fort-de-France are filled with shining and silent bolides so streamlined and purposeful that they give the illusion of an impending massed flight to Mars.

In former times (and still, though less frequently, today) the inhabitants of the French Antilles used to speak of the *Bons Gens de la Guadeloupe* and the *Grands Seigneurs de la Martinique*; and the atmosphere of Fort-de-France is certainly less enclosed in feeling, less parochial and remote, than that of Pointe-à-Pitre or Basse Terre. The political problems of Martinique, though they are exactly parallel to those of Guadeloupe, are intensified by the more urban character of a large section of this most densely populated country. As in the sister island, the years of disciplinarian rule under the Vichy régime, and the repressive nature of the governorship of Admiral Robert, provoked a swing to the Left; for the coloured community, which had borne most of the brunt of these bad years, is the section of the population from which is drawn almost the whole of the electorate. Again, like Guadeloupe, the intensity of this feeling has recently undergone a modification, in reflection of the political changes in Metropolitan France. Nevertheless, Communism still enjoys a majority vote. The deputy and the mayor of Fort-de-France, Aimé Césaire, the remarkable coloured surrealist poet and friend of André Breton, carried his political conviction to the length of flying the Red Flag on the same flagpole, above the Hôtel de Ville, as the Tricolor: an action which evoked from an opponent the words of Josephine Baker's song reshuffled into *'J'ai deux amours, mon pays et Moscou ...'* There is, however, nothing startlingly violent in his views on the problems of the island. He had always been one of the foremost agitators for the conversion of the colonies into prefectures with full parliamentary representation in the mother country, and he considers the recent realization of this project – first advanced by a Baron de la Reinty in 1880 – an important historical step, and one which will exclude the personal sway of a governor, often proved to be arbitrary in the past. 'Assimilation with France,' he maintains, 'is the only way to true democracy in the Antilles.' He opposes the idea of a union between all the Caribbean islands – a sort of international island federation, which is sometimes discussed – on the grounds that it would automatically fall under the economic and political domination of the U.S.A., and evolve into what he terms an 'execrable false democracy'; as the Caribbean islands merely juxtapose, without in any way complementing each other. He is an advocate of 'pluralist solutions': separate solutions, that is, for each of the colonies. There is no golden rule or panacea that can be applied to them wholesale. French colonial problems must be dealt with piecemeal, he insists, starting with the granting of dominion status to the French colonies in Africa.

M. Césaire has a consciousness of his colour which goes, as his poems illustrate, far farther than a complex or a persecution mania; it is a constant and burning sense of the sorrows and injustices of the African race in the Antilles, that is reminiscent in a more civilized way of the sentiments of the Haitian leaders of the early nineteenth century.

The colour question is wielded as a political arm by agitators with some success, by reviving and exploiting the bitterness that existed in the time of slavery, by automatically identifying White with the capitalist and tyrannous rich and Black with the downtrodden poor. This oversimplification is not exact, for in no island where the same conditions prevail are there fewer evidences of a colour bar or of racial discrimination to be observed. It is true that scarcely any intermarriage occurs between the Créoles and their coloured neighbours, and that the landowners are still mainly drawn from this white minority, or 'plantocracy'. This is an inevitable heritage of the old order which, under new conditions and the spread of education, is changing fast. The richest plantation-owner and rum- and sugar-factor at the moment is a coloured man; and the prosperous shops of the capital are owned by coloured men of African descent, by grandsons of indentured Indian coolies or by the ubiquitous recent arrivals from Syria and the Lebanon. The doctors, lawyers, professional men, mayors, deputies, police and the government officials who are responsible, under a white prefect nominated from Paris, for the internal conduct of the island are all coloured, as are the intelligentsia upon whom, more than any other group, the future of the island depends.

So complete has been the mixing of races in Guadeloupe and Martinique – in fact, it was nearing completion in the days of the observant Père

Labat two and a half centuries ago – that the authentic ebony shade of the Congo and the Guinea coasts is now extremely rare; much rarer than that of the pure whites who originally bought their black contemporaries from the slave merchants.

The overwhelming majority of the Martinicans are descended from both slaves and slave-owners. Sometimes there is only the faintest white admixture, or so little black that its presence would be quite undetectable to a European. But whatever the proportions may be, the prejudice in the past has forced all these elements into the same 'coloured' camp from which are drawn the bourgeoisie and intelligentsia, who, after studying in the universities of France, now represent in the French Antilles the world of art, medicine, law, letters and ideas.

Schoelcher abolished slavery in 1848, just over a hundred years ago. Since then, time has been slowly doing its work, and if the scars of ancient bitterness were not, for political reasons, kept open artificially, they could have healed in a generation. Metropolitan France which, in spite of her many mistakes, has an uncanny flair for the right course in these particular matters, herself led the way by granting, at once and under no pressure, and in practice as well as theory, equal rights to all citizens of every colour. This wise policy is furthered by the recent assimilation of Martinique, Guadeloupe, Guiana and La Réunion as integral prefectures of France, with exactly the same privileges, status and representation as the Bouches du Rhône or the Seine Inférieure. It is a significant tribute to France's management of her Empire that her distant territories should consider this to be the highest compliment and benefit they could receive.

A letter from the same friend in Paris – the Vicomte d'Aurigny – who had opened for us in Guadeloupe the gates of Raoul's companionship and munificence, performed the same kind office in Martinique with one of Raoul's many uncles; and within twenty-four hours of our arrival in the island we found ourselves travelling eastwards across Martinique by motor-car with Monsieur de Jaham and half a dozen other guests. Our destination was a little house on the windward coast of the island which was used as a kind of holiday house for fishing and bathing; *perdu dans le bled*, as our host termed it; and our expedition was really a vast picnic. A truck followed our two motor-cars, laden with ice and food and drink and two servants whose enormous and permanent grins showed that they enjoyed the prospect of this departure as much as we did. The charm and gaiety of our host, and his tremendous high spirits, augured well from the start.

The first part of the journey ran through the plain of Lamentin, a low, undulating country almost as tame and familiar as Kent. But as the day waned, it ascended into a wilder region. Our caravan rattled through the streets of Bourg under a deluge of rain and out again into a country of steep, tufted *mornes* in the foothills of Mount Vauclin, where the road turned into a river of mud. Dark and rainy corridors of sugarcane met over the tops of the car. We rounded a small hill, and stopped beside a clump of trees under which sheltered the shape of a house. A hundred yards away, the sea murmured quietly.

Lights appeared in the windows, like the eyes of a sleeper opening, a flicker first and then bright streams of golden light that poured out over the grass as the wicks of petrol lamps were turned up. A large Negro woman and two lesser servants emerged with joyful quacks of welcome, holding lanterns in their hands. It was quite dry again, and soon we were sitting in deck-chairs under the trees in the warm night, while, by lamplight, Monsieur de Jaham, with the benevolent officiousness of a Cheeryble brother, peeled limes and cut into the nutmeg for the *petit punch*. In went the lemon-peel and lime and nutmeg, the water, the sugar, the white rum, each addition accompanied by a flow of entertaining discourse that was only silenced by the sound of the long wooden swizzle-stick. After long and delectable libations, Modestine, the cook, called us indoors for dinner. This meal is memorable, apart from its other charms, by a first encounter with sea-eggs, the contents of smooth, hard white globes like spineless white sea-urchins, whose contents – a kind of reddish-brown roe – are scooped out and fried in butter. Afterwards, with roast pork, we had *beignets* of breadfruit, the first time we had encountered this vegetable. It tasted, in this form, lighter and better than any imaginable potato. Bottle after bottle of iced Riesling accompanied this journey of gastronomic discovery.

Dinner finished about midnight. We rose from the table to fish for lobsters, singing as we walked down to the seashore, with our cigar-smoke lingering about us in the still air. Under a little spinney of manchineel trees, the boat was tethered to a jetty. The weather was warm and mild, and the water was so phosphorescent that a hand in it, or the darting of a fish, shone like silver, and a diving figure was plumed with a blazing whirl of subaqueous fire. But as we sailed out into the bay, a pale moon rose through the milky clouds and drowned all this phosphorescent glitter with its greater radiance. A little way out, we found two Negroes walking knee-deep in the shallow water, pacing as warily as Mohicans, and gazing at the weedy floor of the sea, every detail of which stood out in the glare of a flaming torch that one of them held: a cylinder containing some bright-burning chemical that they call a *serbie*. The other was armed with a long forked stick. Every now and then he would stop and raise his hand. Our strange procession would halt, and like lightning the forked stick descended to imprison a lobster as it peered from the weeds at the unaccustomed light. Then the torch-bearer would seize the struggling captive by its middle and fling it into the boat which we were urging through the water behind him like tow-path horses. The procession wound on in a silence that was broken only by the flailing of the prisoners' tails and claws against the planks. After two hours of this, the bottom of the boat was a tangled mass of lobsters, and we had to avoid their claws as we climbed on board and sailed out through a gap in the reef to swim in the deeper water. We got back to the house and drank some brandy and a tisane, *'pour nous réchauffer la poitrine'*, and fell asleep the moment our heads touched the pillow.

Miraculously, none of us felt next day a trace of the potations and fatigues of the night before. The morning passed in a nepenthean coma under the poison-trees reading and talking, or gliding off into sleep. Towards noon we sailed out into the lagoon again and dived and swam in the warm green water, or lay half in and half out of the little yawl as she skimmed about the bay. Across the coral reefs and the lagoon, how dreamy and tropical the land looked! the gentle grassy hills and shadowy trees surrounding the house with its wooden-pillared and arcaded verandah; the sloping crests of coconut palm, a wavy vista of sugar-cane, and the spiky *mornes* beyond ascending into the little grass-green Matterhorn of Mt Vauclin. To north and south along the coast, pillars of rock and headlands enclosing quiet crescents of sand succeeded each other in fainter and still fainter shades of blue.

Only the steering wheel of a cutter and a model of a sailing-vessel decorated the white planks of the dining-room; a dark, airy chamber, in the depths of which, when we returned, another feast was being prepared. This again proved to be an unforgettable banquet, ushered in by many punches, and escorted as it slowly progressed from dish to dish, first by freezing Alsatian wine, then by excellent claret. Between the courses, we hurled little glasses of brandy down our throats. I am still unable to determine whether this was a good idea. It was done, I remember, on the same principle as Norman peasants practise what they term the *trou normand* – that recurring pause in their Gargantuan meals when they swallow stiff draughts of Calvados in order to revive a flagging appetite; to burn a hole, as it were, for still more food. We ate some of the lobsters we had caught, and then *Lambi*, the inhabitant of the Caribbean conch-shell. It tastes not unlike the octopus and ink-fish of the Mediterranean, but is ten times better. It has a dark, marine, mysterious taste which is incomparably good. The plates were removed, and our host began carving a shoulder of *pré-salé* lamb ...

My neighbour was a commandant in the French Air Force and was one of the first people after Lindbergh to fly across the Atlantic; a tall grave man, heavily spectacled. By the time we were drinking liqueurs, he and Costa and I, I recollect, were singing *Buvons un coup, buvons en deux, Jeanneton prend sa faucille* and *Chevaliers de la Table Ronde.* It was already beginning to get dark. When we had finished, the Créole gentleman who was sitting on the other side said: 'How I wish I had learnt some songs when I was young ... !'

'Why,' I asked him, 'did you never learn any?'

'I never had time,' he answered sadly. 'My life was so taken up with women. I had eyes and ears for nothing but them.' He sighed deeply. Half a dozen vociferous conversations that were already engaged round the table gave our colloquy a certain measure of privacy. Emboldened by the turn it had taken, I asked him under what auspices these romances had blossomed; who had been his companions in them? 'Because,' I said, 'such things, in a small and closed world like Martinique, cannot be easy ...'

'I used to live half the year in Paris,' he said, 'where I had an apartment in the rue de la Pompe. And then, of course, numbers of foreign ladies used to visit the islands – French from the Métropole, English, Dutch, German, Austrian, *que sais-je?*' He lowered his voice as though he were about to impart some hermetic secret of the alcove. 'And then, of course, there were always the people of the country, and the half-castes, and the Hindu world, especially the coolies. We would meet out in the country, you know, among the sugar-cane. It was remarkable, I assure you! Or better still, under the cataracts up in the *mornes*, drenched to the skin. *J'aimais beaucoup les cataractes ...*' His long, ringed hand described the arc of a waterfall.

It was soon pitch dark, and time to return to Fort-de-France. The streets of François were so full that it was necessary to slow down, and finally to stop. A fair was in progress, and the whole of the central square was ablaze with *serbies* and acetylene flares. Every inch of space was filled with villagers all singing and laughing and arguing, or shaking dice at the gambling booths, or shooting at clay pipes. One side of the square was lined with tombola booths – minute, dazzlingly-lit cubes of rushwork and carpet from which a wall had been folded back to reveal, among an undergrowth of ribbons and tinsel, decorated bottles of Vermouth and bogus Sèvres vases and celluloid thumbs-ups, and, for some reason, entire families of Negroes sitting amongst them in mournful silence, as if they, too, were waiting to be won. But everywhere else the hubbub was deafening. Somewhere in the background, the ear could just detect the thud of tom-toms.

We worked our way through the crowd, moving from booth to booth. All at once I saw Costa's hand being wrung by a towering Negro sergeant whose breast clanked with medals. *'Nom d'un nom, qu'est que vous faites ici, mon lieutenant?'* It was a war-time comrade-in-arms of Costa's from the Free French forces in Africa. We were soon sitting in his little dilapidated living-room drinking Triple-Sec, and talking to his wife. She was a Greek girl from Aleppo, very dusky, and plainly had some Arab blood. She spoke a queerly garbled and corrupt Greek of the type one hears in many towns of the Levant seaboard and hinterland, interspersed with guttural sounds that have never passed Athenian lips. She seemed to be very happy with her husband – a big, kind, gentle person who gazed at her with great pride as she talked in her strange language. Two children huddled against her skirts, addressing her occasionally in a mixture of French and Greek and Arabic, their eyes fixed on us in a bewildered stare. Yes, she was happy with Hyacinthe, she said, looking fondly at him; he was very good to her. But the Martinicans! She made the orthodox sign of the Cross three times and struck her forehead; wild, wild people! *Agrioi anthropoi!* If only she and Hyacinthe had stayed in Aleppo ...

It was a very sad and empty little room – an unmade bed in which they obviously all four slept, some household utensils, one chair and a few stools, all, in the wavering rushlight, appearing even shabbier than they really were. In the middle of the floor, placed there, one felt, for display as much as for use, stood a sewing machine of obsolete make. She placed her hand lovingly on its rusty back, and told us that it had been her dowry. How she had cried when, on the journey, they thought it was lost! But it had turned up as they got off the ship. We made plans to meet again in Fort-de-France, when they both went in on market day. (But they did not appear.)

Outside, in the torchlight chiaroscuro of the market-place, the noise, the shouting and the music seemed to have grown; amplified in my ears, perhaps, by the effects of the Triple-Sec, which had fallen like petrol on the embers of our midday celebrations inside me, and rekindled them into a generous blaze. At any rate, all seemed suddenly exciting, and almost magical, especially the roundabouts.

These were ramshackle contrivances, and the circus of galloping horses, gaudy wooden mounts decorated with rings and spots and stripes, was propelled, not by machinery, but by the exertions of an army of little boys who pelted round and round clutching some part of the framework, screaming at the top of their voices, shouting and laughing and fighting for a chance to help in the pushing. For, instead of being paid to do the work of the absent machinery, free fights for the privilege radiated from the merry-go-round over quite a large area. Some of these tiny boys were rolling on the ground and pommelling each other in their baulked eagerness. It was all that the proprietor could do to persuade them to stop now and then to allow for a change of riders. All was mud, shadow and darkness outside the ring of riders, but within that cavalcade of galloping silhouettes, crouching like jockeys and cowboys and curvetting round and round at breakneck speed, lay an enchanted circle of noise and light.

A sheaf of *serbies* sent wild shafts of light and darkness through the galloping but motionless legs of the horses. I fought my way on to the back of a zebra, and was at once carried clattering through space. Joan, with her fair hair streaming, was mounted on a sea-horse in front of me, with the commandant caracoling gallantly beside her on a dragon. Some places behind, a unicorn carried Costa. Immediately below, a Negro hammered like a madman on a tom-tom – a *qua* – that had been made by stretching goat-skins over the two mouths of a bottomless rum-keg. One end he struck with his hand in an unbroken tattoo, the other with a drumstick, now and then jumping astride it and pounding away with both hands at one end, only, after a few seconds, to leap back into his first position. Another wielded a shack-shack, a cylinder of bamboo about a foot long, filled with pebbles or heavy seeds. He grasped it at both ends and jerked it from side to side over his head like a bar-tender with a huge cocktail shaker, producing that rattling, clanking, fluctuating, swinging noise that is the background of all rhumbas and sambas; only, in this case, ten times louder. A third, with his head flung back and pointing it into the air, blew through a clarinet and defined the course of the tune that his comrades underlined with their clattering rhythm. But these three instruments were dominated by a fourth: a section from the trunk of a bamboo tree, about a foot in thickness and over eight feet long, lashed to two of the uprights of the merry-go-round. Three Negroes, naked to the waist and armed in both hands with two heavy bamboo clubs apiece, hammered away at it. Deafening reverberations at an unbelievable speed pierced the air. The rhythm was faster and more concentrated than anything I had ever heard. CRASH! bang-*bang-*

bang! CRASH-CRASH! bang-*bang*-bang! CRASH!... The momentum of the six simultaneous blows all fell at the same fraction of a second that the accent of the shack-shack and tom-tom struck the ear. This instrument is the bamboula, and against this mass of percussion the clarinet tore and screamed and zigzagged its path through biguine after biguine. Every now and then one of the clubs, striking the bamboula, would break or split, and, with no hiatus in the rhythm, another would be handed to the striker from a reserve pile at the side. The three players were soon surrounded by broken sticks, and the ferocious bastinado seemed to grow more intense each time they swung below and past us. There was something disturbing about these three men. Their activity had none of the jauntiness of musicians in a jazz band. Taut and intent, with their teeth bared and the sweat streaming down their black torsos, they stooped forward flogging and bashing their wooden victim like Ethiopian executioners. One of them would fall out exhausted from time to time, throwing his two clubs to one of the waiting substitutes. There was a moment of decrescendo as he caught them, and moved into the other's place; then as he brought them down with a fresh access of violence, the noise almost split the eardrums.

We raced round and round this extraordinary disc of light, unable, as though petrified by the din, to tear ourselves from the backs of our steeds. We managed to wrench ourselves away at last, and as we drove out of the little town, the truculent sounds died down. The thin scream of the clarinet was audible for a long time above the impact and boom and rattle of the other three. Then that too fell silent as the darkness and the sugar-cane swallowed us up.

Half asleep in the back of the car, I could just hear the voice of the Créole gentleman talking to Costa about the funeral practices of the villagers. Some of them sounded similar, in their milder forms, to the customs that still prevail in the villages of Rumania, and they were based on the same neighbourly desire not to let the corpse feel out of it during the vigil period. Friends and neighbours, he explained, sit up all night round the coffin, telling funny and often improper stories, dancing, and drinking rum, and even, after concealing small objects in the mouth or the other natural hiding-places of the corpse, playing games of hunt-the-thimble. If the corpse has been a heavy drinker during his lifetime, bottles of rum are poured down his throat; if a dancer, his body may be removed from his coffin and whirled round the room in a lively saraband, changing partners every few seconds. Sometimes he is propped up on a chair among his cronies, as though he were participating in the convivialities of the evening. 'You can't imagine,' the speaker concluded, 'how very curious this looks. *C'est un spectacle fort bizarre ...*'

The headlights scooped a long tunnel out of the night ahead of us, a leaf-fringed and mysterious cavity. We crossed several bridges, and I noticed that occasional solitary figures squatted on the parapet, with their broad-brimmed hats held in a peculiar fashion against their faces. It was some time before I was able to make out the purpose of this precarious position, and its intimate nature ... The moment the headlights of a car destroyed the privacy of the darkness, they achieved a simple incognito by clapping to their faces, in the manner of the Venetians of Longhi, these improvised masks, which they held there until the danger was past, and then replaced on their heads. There was something very satisfying about the economy of gesture and the foolproof efficacy of this device.

Walking down the passage of the Vieux Moulin – the Air France hotel in which we lived – I was arrested by a strange astrological injunction hanging on a little placard outside the door of one of the bedrooms: FAVOR NO MOLESTAR. I puzzled over the identity of the molestars all through breakfast, and wondered why none of them should be favoured. The Pole Star? The Great Bear? The Dog Star? It was obviously, judging by the spelling, a bit of advice from America. I could bear it no longer, and ran upstairs to see if a closer examination would shed any further light. In the corner, in minute Spanish print, was the name of a printer in Mexico City. Turning it over, the words 'Do not disturb' appeared. Of course! I replaced it on its hook, but only just in time, as the door opened a second after and I found myself suddenly two inches away from a pair of tired Aztec-Iberian eyes ... It was the same kind of language error that prompted the tongue-tied Polish forces to buy up, soon after their arrival in the Middle East, every single copy of *Polish up Your English* to be found in the bookshops of Cairo ...

The Vieux Moulin has a singular charm. It is perched high on a ledge of the Didier plateau, built round the massive stone cylinder of a windmill that some former decade has plucked of its sails. The windows from this tower look out over a swimming pool and a delightful flower garden and a long avenue of palmistes leading to the main road, where the ground begins to fall to the hollow in which lies Fort-de-France. The roofs of villas interrupt here and there the descending ledges of green. Across the blue haze that hides the capital, the dim peaks of Morne la Plaine and Morne Constant hang in the air; in their lee, on the other side of the gulf, are hidden the town of Trois Ilets and La Pagerie, the home of the Empress Josephine. The country behind the hotel climbs northward in a green jungle to a series of peaks called the Pitons de Carbet and the Gros Morne; steep and improbable green cones, ending in bare pencil-points of rock. In middle distance a white building appears, a dazzling structure whose faintly Moorish, faintly Gothic and Romanesque lines leave the observer at a loss. It turns out to be an exact replica, in the depths of the forest, of Sacré Coeur, and it is designated by the proud islanders as the *Montmartre Martinicais*. The Trade Winds blow here blessedly cool all day and all night. The French name for this wind – *Les Alizées* – evokes far better than the English this gentle and zephyrous benison.

The hotel shares the drawback which is possessed by many of the island houses: the room walls, in order that the inside of the house may catch any breath of wind, stop about a foot short of the ceiling, so that movement and conversations in the next room, and even several rooms away, are plainly audible; an arrangement that makes one, willy-nilly, an initiate of half a dozen private lives, and which fills the watches of the night with sighs and coughs and snores.

Martinique is an important cross-roads of the various air lines of the Antilles and the Americas, and many of the guests who stayed there a night had come from enormous distances. Once a week a French trans-atlantic seaplane called the T.K.R. alighted in the bay, its enormous white bulk making everything within sight look grotesquely small and out of proportion. Its arrival is an event whose wonder never stales for the less sophisticated inhabitants of the capital. They assemble on the quays and drink it in for hours. It has even passed into the island folklore under the name of *Gwos gibier*. Towards sunset every day a truckload of pilots and officials arrived, and the air was suddenly full of the clatter of ice in their punch glasses and of their uninhibited laughter. The food was so outstanding that the bell that announced mealtimes really did become the soul's tocsin.

The only real disadvantage of this retreat was its distance from the town. It is perched in the heart of the béké* garden-colony which always occupies the coolest region near these West Indian towns. The villas that lie on either hand as one descends towards the town spring from a wonderful variety of inspirations. Every house echoes a different archi-tectural style: Kephissia, Sinai, Zamalek, Pierrefonds, Hamburg, New York, South Carolina, and Ann Hathaway's Cottage. With each

---

* *Béqué* or *Béké* is the Negro name for a white in the French Antilles; a term which is said to derive from the reiterated question *Eh bien, quoi? Eh ben, que?* of the early colonists.

descending step, the air gets hotter, seeming to surge up towards one from the open door of an oven. The villas peter out and the humbler wooden houses begin with the first Coca-Cola advertisement – outposts of what is to follow. A glimpse is caught through a window of a congregation of Seventh Day Adventists who always seem to be in session and singing their hearts out; and then the town is reached.

The wooden houses, perched on the hillside among palms and breadfruit, lean dramatically over the waters of the two rivers between which, like Baghdad, the town lies: the rivers Monsieur and Madame. Though there is much in the town that is shabby and squalid, it has infinitely more grace than Pointe-à-Pitre. There is an iron cathedral built out of Meccano, and fine pillared law courts where tall palms thrust their feather-dusters up through a cool well of grey masonry. But in the centre of the town something very imposing occurs: the *Savane* – not, here, a plain, but an enormous and spacious quadrangle, that at once calls to mind the *maidan* of an oriental city. In the centre a statue of Josephine stands, surrounded by a square of slender palmistes, and the rest of the *Savane* is shaded by sandbox and tamarind. It is bounded on its western extremity by the seafront. Here, facing a gesticulating statue of d'Esnambuc, the sloops and schooners congregate, some of which ply as far afield as Jamaica or Haiti or even the Spanish Main. A long tongue of land juts from the southern corner of the *Savane*, the narrow platform on which is piled a massive old fort that has many times withstood the attacks of the English and the Dutch. It has a dank, solid appearance. The towers and machicolations are green with creepers and plumed with foliage, and once inside the gates – no easy accomplishment – a formidable system of flèches, redoubts, moats, glacis and barbicans appear, woven into an inexpugnable labyrinth possessing all the complexity of an engraving by Vauban.

An amazing building occupies the opposite corner of the *Savane*: the Schoelcher library. I often used to visit it to read memoirs of Martinique, by the travellers and settlers of former centuries, and the works of Lafcadio Hearn. It was with astonishment, and then with delight, that I discovered that he had lived for two years in Martinique, and written about it with the same enthusiasm and sympathy which he later brought to bear upon Japan. (We had been warned about the Bibliothèque Schoelcher by a local lady. 'Don't go *near* any of the books in the library; they are all infected with leprosy germs ...') This building too is entirely built out of metal; not, this time, on the anti-earthquake principle, but because for some reason it was constructed out of this lasting material for the Paris Exhibition of 1918. It was then taken to bits and shipped to

Martinique and reassembled here, where it now offers to the gaze a great cube whose iron fabric has been twisted and drawn-out and tormented into the architectural mould of ancient Egypt, relieved by elements of Norman and Gothic and *art nouveau* among the pillars of Luxor and lotus petals, and decorated with inset plaques of turquoise majolica. Inside, it is a skeleton which is spanned and arcaded by lengths of metal which, bristling with rivets and bolts, inspire the reader with the feeling of being some rare bird of paradise in a most ornate cage. My fellow-captives were nearly all students in spectacles, taking copious notes from textbooks.

It is strange – and a pity – that there is no tradition of the open-air café in the Lesser Antilles. This is understandable during the rainy season; it would involve endless gymnastics. But the dry season? The Martinicans are forced into the clubs or the rum shops that cluster round the centre of the town, instead of being able to sit at their leisure under the palm trees, and, as they talked and sipped their *petit punch*, to observe, through the palmistes and the masts of the schooners, the never-failing beauty of the sunset. When one thinks of the strong Parisian influences that prevail in Martinique, this is an astonishing gap in the amenities of island life.

There are so many of these gaps. But in spite of the disadvantages, the town has an inalienable charm. Round the *Savane*, the streets are laid out with depressing regularity, block after block, not, fortunately, of cement, but of wood, with jutting balconies and *persiennes* and high mansard roofs, trooping away to the rivers and the wooded foothills in dusty and animated vistas filled with the same variegated population as that of Guadeloupe. The same dowdiness of the girls, the same magnificence of their mothers and grandmothers. The men in the street seem more alert and friendly and cheerful than those of the sister island, and, in talking to white people, far less reserved. Under the walls of the fort stretches an avenue of mangoes and flamboyants called l'Allée des Soupirs, a shady thoroughfare ending in the region of the docks and back streets into whose battered precincts a pom-pommed sailor can now and then be observed disappearing in search of the afternoon of a faun.

'*La danse est leur passion favorite,*' writes Père Labat, describing the life of the slaves of Martinique at the close of the seventeenth century; as on every other subject concerning the Antilles, the indefatigable Dominican has much to say: '*Je ne crois pas qu'il y ait peuple au monde qui y soit plus attaché qu'eux.*'

Their favourite dance was the *calenda*, which he supposed originated in the Kingdom of Arada on the Guinea coast; but the movements of this dance were so equivocal, so opposed to all *pudeur*, that slave-owners who cared for the morality of their slaves, and incidentally for their own peace and security – the Father always has some eminently practical corollary for his precepts – put the *calenda* under an interdict. But it was no good: 'Their passion for this dance is beyond the imagination; old, young, even little mites who can scarcely stand. One would have thought they had danced it in their mothers' wombs.'

The rhythm of the *calenda* was given by two tom-toms made of hollowed sections of tree trunk. Both were about four feet long, but one was a foot and a half in diameter, the other nine inches. They were gripped between the knees or straddled. The big drummer played a measured rhythm, and the one who played the smaller instrument beat as fast as he could go, producing a noise without marking the cadence of the dance or the movements of the dancers.

The participants were drawn up in two lines opposite each other, the women on one side and the men on the other. One of them improvised a song, of which the refrain was taken up by dancers and spectators alike, and scanned by universal clapping. The dancers held up their hands in the position of castanet players, leapt and pirouetted, and shuffled towards the opposite rank and retreated interminably, only to advance again, until a change in the tempo of the drumming gave them the signal to strike their thighs against those of their opposites, dancing round and round each other, withdrawing and advancing and repeating the hip-striking, as many times as the drums beat that particular rhythm, *avec des gestes tout à fait lascifs*. Sometimes they danced round each other slowly with their arms interlocked, kissing their partners, with thighs touching, then recoiled once more. This dance, the monk continues, became such a favourite among the Spanish Créoles of the Americas that they seldom had thoughts for anything else. 'They dance it in their churches and their religious processions, and it is even performed by the nuns on Christmas night, on stages specially erected in the chancel behind an open grille, so that the people can share the joy to which these good souls bear witness at the birth of their Saviour. It is true that no men are admitted to join them in so devout a dance. I am even ready,' he concedes, 'to admit that they dance it with completely pure intentions. But how many spectators must there not be who judge less charitably than me?'

Negroes of the Congo danced in a completely different way. Men and women formed a queue all facing in one direction, and the two ends joined in a circle. Then, without moving backwards or forwards, they bent double, and, for hours on end, beat a shuffling rhythm on the ground with their feet, 'mumbling some rubbish' that was led by the voice of one of the dancers. The rest answered in chorus, while the spectators beat time by clapping. The Mine Negroes also danced in a ring, all facing outwards, while those from Gambia and Cape Verde practised their own tribal steps. 'But these dances, though more decent, are very dull, and all, no matter where they came from, prefer the *calenda*. To drive the idea of this infamous dance out of their heads, their masters taught them various French steps, the minuet, the coranto, the *branle* and *des danses rondes*, which many of them learnt with infinite nimbleness and grace, often better than Europeans who plume themselves on being fine dancers.'

Apart from the astonishing vision of the dancing nuns, the Father's account of these dances is important for several reasons. Firstly, because the addiction of the Spaniards of America to the dances of the jungle indicates a common ancestor to all the Latin-American dances that evolved in the ensuing centuries. Surely the earliest begetter of the rhumba, the samba, the son, and even the tango, can be none other than this *calenda* from the coast of Guinea? Even if its authentic African origin were not known, the description of the dance of the Congolese at once suggests to anybody who has seen it the Conga of the Negroes of Cuba. More important still, Father Labat's two main classifications – which, of course, subdivide into as many tribes and kingdoms as existed in either region – the Arada of the Guinea coast and the Congolese, were the same influences that dominated the formation of Voodoo, the Negro religion of Haiti. The dark mysteries of the Pétro rite grew up in the Antilles long after the slaves were first established there, but the two purely African rites of Haitian Voodoo, *Rada* (originating in Allada and Dahomey) and *Congo*, come from exactly the regions that the Father names, and the striking similarity of the *calenda* with the shuffling *yanvaloux* of the Voodoo temples will become clear in a later chapter.

Those minuets and *branles* which the slaves learnt from their French masters have plainly left their mark on the dance in Martinique, and the biguines that Costa and I were watching seemed to have descended straight from a marriage of those two dances with the abhorred *calenda*. For the dancing, for minutes on end, would be precise and almost formal. The two partners held each other in the customary gesture with considerable gravity. Then they would gradually unite in a clinch which shook and rippled in time to a new and complicated shuffling of their feet. Seismic waves passed up the legs and trunks of the dancers, setting their hips and loins and buttocks jerking and gyrating, then pausing for an instant and unwinding in the opposite direction with a jungly, spasmodic movement that would in a few seconds have set the room booming with the anathema of Père Labat.

The Select Tango, where Costa and I had made a bachelor descent to catch a glimpse of the Bal Doudou – an Antillean *bal musette* frequented by *doudous* – was a great barnlike place in a back street, agreeably tropical with its lattice work and wooden balconies and rickety staircases and the Calypso-like rattle and swing of the biguine band. The bar swarmed with youthful Negroes, and groups of young Negro women sat at tables, chattering and giggling and pouting. The air was afloat with the soft quacks and Z-sounds of their conversation as though the room were filled with birds and insects. When one of them said something funny, all their teeth would be bared at once, as they kicked their feet out and sunk their heads to the metal table-top in that infectious Negro laughter. They were all violently made up, and dressed in flaming best clothes that reminded one of little girls' party dresses. Large ear-rings hung in every lobe, but only one or two wore turbans. The rest were bareheaded; or hatted, for some reason, with men's trilbies, which they wore severely tilted over their noses. One girl affected a blancoed sun-helmet several times too big for her.

A friendly cry made us both turn our eyes from the floor. It was Sosthène, whom we had met on the *Colombie*. We joined him at a table in the corner, where he was sitting with two Negro friends. He looked as if he had been moving fast since landing, and had acquired a wonderfully raffish and beachcomber appearance: several days' beard, tousled hair, crumpled white clothes, jovial and bloodshot eyes. He was working as a welder in a factory near the docks. He introduced the others – *'Mes deux copains, Jacquot et Charlemagne. C'est des gentils types, très corrects.'* Charlemagne, who had been to Swansea and to U.S. ports in the Gulf of Mexico, New Orleans, Galveston and Mobile, spoke, or so I thought, a little English. His answer to every sentence addressed to him was an enormous display of teeth, a rich chuckle and the words, 'Well, for heaven's sake!' Then he rolled his head from side to side, and chuckled again.

'Have a drink, Charlemagne?'

'Well, for heaven's sake!'

'Pretty hot in here, eh?'

'Well, for heaven's sake!' and a pregnant chuckle.

'Nice band ...'

'Well, for ...' etc.

Sosthène was talking about black women. They were a terrible handful. He had already become engaged to two, but had discarded Marie-Thérèse, the first one, in favour of Françoise – *'Vous comprenez, mon cher, elle est plus logique, plus correcte, quoi.'* I remembered from the ship those two words of his, which for him were synonymous. Costa was soon biguining across the room with the most expert sinuosity, glued to a girl in a straw hat. There was an attractive mahogany-coloured girl at the next table in great ear-rings and a Madras. I asked the girls who were now sitting on either side of Sosthène what she was like.

'*Qui? la Fwancine?'*

'*Oui, celle-la.'*

'*Elle est twès, twès mauvaise.'*

'*Mauvaise? Pourquoi?'*

'*C'est une espionne.'*

Costa returned with his straw-hatted girl. In the middle of the dance she had pressed something into his hand. A key! ('Well, for heaven's sake!') This, it appears, is not so much for actual use as for a conventional token of complaisance. I danced with the spy, who at once slipped into a strangle-hold of such un-Dominican *impudeur* that, coupled with my inexpert attempts at mastering the complexities of the biguine, it was miraculous how we maintained our balance. Sitting down, after a few minutes, was a distinct relief.

There was something curiously engaging about these girls. Except for the one next to Sosthène, who was a terrible chatterbox, the rest were rather quiet, sitting relaxed upon their chairs with their hands folded in their laps, gazing solemnly at nothing; or else, if one's eyes crossed, smiling with the most transparent ingenuousness and benignity. They seemed to be extraordinarily unmercenary. When offered drinks, they quite often refused, or ordered a *punch martinicais*, which costs well under a shilling. Very different from the platinum blonde blunt instruments that would be their equivalents in a European bar of the kind. They had an extraordinary aura of rather comic integrity, and seemed miraculously to have escaped any feeling of vice and guilt, considering their status to be not so much discreditable as extremely humble. This stubbornly incorruptible innocence is a quality that, if it ever existed there, has vanished from the whole of Europe except Greece. A long and erudite essay could be written to explain exactly why the descendants of jungle dwellers and of the most civilized race in the world should have won this bloodless and permanent victory over the sense of sin.

Charlemagne accompanied us some of the way uphill (feeding the conversation at well-chosen points), and also Sosthène. We made an appointment to meet him at the Sourire de Venise later in the week, to be introduced to Françoise, '*ma fiancée – une jeune fille vraiment logique'.*

*

We were talking of ghosts. I had heard a diverting story about the deputy for a constituency in the west of the island. According to a local tradition, an ordinary hen's egg, if it is kept warm in the human armpit during the whole of Lent, hatches out on Easter Day and reveals a manikin three inches high, who at once prostrates himself before his foster-father and swears eternal obedience to him. He is invisible to all but his master. The deputy in question, owing to his adroitness at amateur conjuring tricks, already enjoyed a great reputation as a wizard, and did not bother to make glowing promises or to attack the opposition in his pre-election speech. He informed the electorate simply that he had posted one of these Easter-egg myrmidons inside the electoral urn with instructions to destroy any voting slips in favour of the opposition. The opposition, hearing this, knew that the game was up, and he was elected unanimously.

The road that led us northwards into the steep heart of the island soon reached a watershed. We were able to look westwards through the treetops at the quiet Caribbean Sea, and eastwards over the Gros Morne to where the jagged Caravelle peninsula intruded its long and intricate outline into the Atlantic. We gazed at this promontory with interest, for it was the home, in the eighteenth century, of the heroine of a singularly romantic story.

A beautiful Créole girl called Aimée du Buc de Rivry, the daughter of a nobleman with large estates in the neighbourhood, when walking one evening in the *mornes* with her favourite cousin, encountered an old Negro woman sitting under a mango tree who was famous in the region as a kind of Sibyl. They asked to have their fortunes told. The old woman made them sit beside her on the grass and gazed thoughtfully at the palms of their hands for a long time. 'You,' she said, after a long pause, pointing at the cousin, 'will be an Empress. You, my girl,' pointing at Mlle du Buc, 'will be more than an Empress.' After this Pythian pronouncement, she hobbled off, refusing to answer any more questions; and after a few days, the girls are reported to have forgotten all about it.

Shortly afterwards, as the custom then was (and often still is), Mlle du Buc was sent to a convent in France to be instructed in all the *arts d'agrément* suitable to her position. When her education was finished, a passage back to the Antilles was booked for her in a brigantine sailing from Bordeaux. A terrible storm blew up in mid-Atlantic, and the vessel was driven back towards the east and, as it soon appeared, far to the south of their home port. The captain managed to avoid shipwreck by steering his craft through the Pillars of Hercules. They were no sooner in the Mediterranean than they were attacked by the Barbary pirates who still plagued these waters, and the ship was taken as a prize to the Bey of Tunis, who kept the cargo and sold the passengers as slaves. But he was so struck by the beauty of Mlle du Buc that he withheld her from the general auction, and sent her – he was an old man – as a gift to his distant Suzerain in Stamboul, the Grand Turk. Once inside the Grand Serail, she contrived to mollify or annihilate the opposition among jealous co-wives and suborned eunuchs, and to penetrate without disaster the deepest intrigues of the seraglio – poisons, we know, the bowstring or the Bosphorus were the punishment of the most trivial false move – and to attain the sole occupancy of the imperial alcove. The vapours of legend now obliterate a decade or two of her life; at exactly the moment when Byron's hero, torn from the arms of Haidée, and dragged by the Turks from his Aegean island, is flung into a Constantinopolitan jail; escapes; and steals by night down the labyrinthine corridors of that very harem ... Do these insubstantial figures collide in the dark? For Mlle du Buc de Rivry is now scarcely more solid than a myth. The Turkish annals make no mention of her, and alas! Prince Cantemir, the historian, had died years ago. Suddenly, half a century later, she becomes three-dimensional again in the pages of history as the Sultana Validé – empress-mother of the Emperor Mahmoud II. But only for that bald line and a half of print; and then vanishes for ever.

Her cousin, of course, was Josephine Tascher de la Pagerie.

The eruption of the Montagne Pelée and the total destruction of St Pierre on the second of May, 1902, was one of the worst volcanic disasters of modern times. This is how one eye-witness describes it: 'The whole side of the mountain seemed to gape open, and from the fissure belched a lurid whirlwind of fire which wreathed itself into vast masses of flame as, with terrible speed, it descended on the doomed town. Before the true extent of the peril could be grasped, the fiery mass swept like a river over the town, and, thrusting the very waters of the sea before it, set the ships ablaze.' The entire population was wiped out, with the exception of a man called Syparis, a convicted murderer who owed his life to the resistance of the massive walls of the condemned cell to the tide of lava. The eruption had announced itself for days in advance by minor outbursts and showers of ash and an increase of heat, but the governor, thinking these were transitory manifestations, had bolstered up the morale of the citizens, many thousands of them, by cheerful speeches ('Now above all, don't panic'), and although the symptoms became every hour more ominous, the inhabitants remained in their capital with pathetic and completely insane courage, till the disaster broke on them with such devastating completeness and killed them all.

The inhabitants of Martinique still ascribe to this event nearly all the handicaps under which the island now labours, for all that was precious morally, materially, intellectually and politically had been centralized in the old capital; and all obliterated in the space of a few minutes. Everything that the colony boasted in the way of fine buildings, private houses, pictures, furniture, silver and works of art – for the houses on the plantations were often little more than temporary places destined more for administrative than domestic ends – also vanished in the conflagration. The only hints we can glean of this vanished magnificence are a few broken pieces of sculpture, and one or two twisted and half-melted bits of cutlery in the *Musée Volcanologique* in the outskirts of the town.

I felt surprised and, I suppose, disappointed at the aspect of the town. Our eyes were prepared for a total ruin, a West Indian Pompeii, a landscape of the moon. But below us, on a flat terrain between the spurs of lava and the leaf-covered scoriae, lay a thriving little town. The houses were sparsely placed, it is true, among shapeless masses of green. Tall, well-grown trees were everywhere, and over their branches a building appeared which might have been a young New York skyscraper. It was only when we were actually inside the town that we were able to descry the great heaps of weed-grown rubble; but it is possible that an uninformed stranger, wandering through the few crowded and shop-lined streets and the populous market-place, might have gathered no hint of the catastrophe. But, hidden and scarcely discernible under the breadfruit trees, lay the charred ruins of the old theatre, which, quite plainly, had once been a graceful eighteenth-century building. Now we were just able to locate, among the lianas and the tumbled masonry, the shallow and elegant ellipse of two curving staircases which joined in a horseshoe at the pedestal of a statue, continued as one for four or five steps and then ceased. We gazed with wonder at the cell which had saved the only survivor from the hecatomb.

The fact that a new and populous town has sprung so soon and so gaily from the wreck of the old is baffling. Is it dauntlessness, insane fecklessness, or a cautious reckoning on the law of averages? I asked an old man in a rum shop if he thought the mountain was no longer dangerous. He shrugged his shoulders, grinned, and said: *'Espéwons.'*

It is hard to reconstruct from the ruins and the new houses the beautiful old capital that novels and memoirs describe. It was founded by d'Esnambuc, and after his death became the headquarters of his nephew, le Sieur Duparquet, who owned the island as his personal domain, along with St Lucia, Grenada and the Grenadines. He administered this enormous property with great skill, patching up quarrels between settlers, quelling mutinies, fighting the Caribs, and laying out towns, among them Fort-de-France, which is still sometimes called 'Fwoyal' after its pre-Revolutionary name of Fort-Royal. However, his widow, during the minority of the heirs, was less fortunate, and the island was on the brink of ruin when Louis XIV bought it from her for 120,000 pounds tourney, and turned it into a Crown Colony. Thanks to the importation of sugar-cane in 1654, by a Brazilian Jew called Benjamin da Costa, and the later arrival of coffee and cocoa trees and indigo, the island became, in the eighteenth century, the most prosperous of all the French king's possessions overseas. For over a hundred years St Pierre was the market-place and sorting-house for all the French Antilles, and the town grew correspondingly in grandeur and wealth. During the reigns of the last two Louis, Martinican fortunes were as famous in Paris and Versailles as those of the East Indian nabobs in London.

The Martinican world at this period was roughly the following. The leading section of society were the colonists and landowners, many of them descendants of old French families, who owned large estates and paid a yearly levy on their crops to the government in tobacco, cotton or sugar. These were the people who built the large houses, imported the slaves, advised the governor on the conduct of the colony, officered the local forces, set the tempo of life in the Antilles, and echoed in their remote island the fashions and thought of Paris. Immediately below these were the bourgeoisie, who descended from the former *engagés* or employees whom the early colonists brought with them from France. They served them for a number of years, and then settled on their own account on concessions that were granted them in payment for their service. Next came the Freedmen, the manumitted Mulatto slaves who had acquired their freedom owing to their white blood. Intermarriage between white men and black women – the reverse seems to have been virtually non-existent – became so common that the privilege of automatic manumission was withdrawn. Mixed marriages were forbidden by law round 1700, but unions between slave-owners and Negro women still continued on a wide scale. They were based on a kind of willingly conceded *droit de jambage et cuissage* (as the correct old French term describes the *jus primae noctis*) of a temporary or occasionally of a permanent nature. As the extraordinary range of colour and characteristics in Martinique testifies, this was a custom that legislation was unable either to suppress or mitigate.

79

The last, and by far the largest group, were the slaves themselves, either those born in the country, *nègres créoles*, or Negroes from Africa brought to the islands in the slave-ships at the rate of tens of thousands yearly. Slave-owners who were proved to be the fathers of Mulatto children were compelled to pay a fine to the Crown of 2,000 pounds of sugar, and their concubines and the children in question were confiscated and presented to the monks of the Charité, of which institution they became slaves for life. Their former owners were forbidden ever to buy them back.

Naturally the monks, eagerly helped by the white wives of the delinquent planters, became expert at searching out these windfalls. Each case was tried in front of a judge in the presence of the woman, her child, the supposed father, and a monk, usually the same one, representing the interests of the Hospital. The usual excuse of the women was that they had fallen victims to unknown, drunken sailors who had inflicted the last outrages on them in the cane-fields and then sailed away. Occasionally, however, more original defences were discovered. One of these, set on record by Labat, I find impossible to omit. I translate him word for word:

I have often witnessed these debates, and, on one occasion, a woman belonging to a settler from one of our parishes [i.e. administered by the Order of Preachers of which Labat was a member] maintained to Brother —— that he himself was the father of the Mulatto baby of which she had been brought to bed. Unluckily for this cleric, he had visited the master of the Negress between nine and ten months previously, and had spent the night in his house. The master, remembering this, had instructed the Negress so well in what she was to say that it was the drollest conceivable scene (a priest or a monk ought to find such a sight deplorable) to hear the evidence that she brought forward to prove that she had never known any other man but the monk. The judge did everything in his power to trip her up, but without success; she stuck to her story, and, as she was carrying her infant in her arms, she presented it to Brother —— with the words '*toi papa li*' – the Créole for 'you're his father' – and then held it up to the whole assembly pretending it was as like Brother —— as two peas. The latter, accustomed as he was to these sessions, was so discountenanced that the gathering was almost expiring with laughter. It was difficult to say which was more comic – the effrontery of the Negress under the guise of extreme *naiveté*, the embarrassment of the monk (who was a very good man whom everybody knew to be incapable of such a backsliding), or the wavering gravity of the judge, who, despite all his efforts, would also have succumbed had he not put a stop to this scene by sending the Negress back to her master, and reserving his decision until more satisfactory evidence could be produced.

Like Guadeloupe, the island was attacked and occupied several times by the English, who each time set up their ephemeral headquarters in St Pierre. Their last sojourn covered the period of the Hundred Days, and since then Martinique has remained unmolested. The Revolution brought the usual series of upheavals, the donning of the Tricolor cockade at the fall of the Bastille, emancipation, repressive measures, battles against the Royalists and their English allies, British occupation, and the re-establishment of slavery and the slave trade by Napoleon.

Memoirs are rich in accounts of the social life of St Pierre, and descriptions of balls and governmental receptions and carnival. Earlier chronicles are also filled with descriptions of mass hangings in the central square, of burnings at the stake and breakings on the wheel. Both kinds of scene are equally difficult to reconstruct in the new mushroom town. Lafcadio Hearn gives captivating descriptions of former carnivals, of the songs and balls and firework displays of St Pierre, the beautiful *capresses*, and the dancing in the streets, when blacks and whites, dressed as dragons or tigers or demon kings, mingled freely for three strange days.

The old rum-drinker in the bar told a curious tale about these festivities. Some years before the eruption, the last time that carnival was held, a number of patients escaped from a local leper colony and evaded pursuit and recapture by disguising themselves in dominoes and losing themselves among the other masques and fancy dresses. Among the humbler classes in the islands, monogamy is seldom adhered to with much austerity; and at carnival time rum-drinking and the atmosphere of rejoicing lend an even greater latitude. The eight escaped lepers were, it seems, violently affected by the prevailing mood and, under cover of their disguise, managed to leave the imprint of their disease on a very large number of people. When the carnival was over they were apprehended by the very device that had enabled them to escape, as they were the only people among a population dressed with lenten sobriety who were still in fancy dress . . .

'*Apwès ça,*' the old man concluded, '*plus de carnaval. C'était dommage . . .*'

CHAPTER 4

Martinique Continued

These northern reaches of Martinique are scattered with small *gentil-hommières* belonging to the old French squirearchy of the island: rectangular, verandahed and lawn-encompassed houses of wood and stone standing in clearings in the forest, and shaded by tall trees: Pécoule, belonging to the Vicomte d'Aurigny, Potiche, the house of Madame d'Assier de Pompignon, and Beauséjour, a fine house built on a ledge of the northern slopes of Montagne Pelée. The details of an hour or two spent here, on a fortuitous visit while the rain splashed on the shutters, remain in my mind with great lucidity: the miniatures hanging on the wooden walls; a jar that enclosed in spirits a tangle of poisonous snakes; a great case of turquoise-coloured butterflies from Cayenne; the backs of books; and the light from the oil-lamp caught and refracted in the golden depths of my punch-glass. Above all, the lively voice and the witty and civilized discourse of our hostess, Madame de Lucy de Fossarieu. We rose to leave when the rain abated, and found that the moon had broken through the clouds. The garden was a faint constellation of flowers that were only distinguishable by their pallor from the darkness. Under the dripping mango trees, tier on tier of lawn descended into the darkness. The air was warm and scented, and the forest, faintly rimmed with silver, completely surrounded this high, sloping world. The singing of some Negro women floated up from the village with the echo of the falling waves and the faint gasp of the shingle.

Moments like this fill one with gratitude; not necessarily so much because of their incidental beauty, but because of the understanding they bring; they act as Rosetta stones to whole systems of hieroglyphics. That house, those lights and voices and flowers and smells and sounds, I felt, gave me a better chance of grasping the atmosphere, the scope and the mood of Créole life in the Antilles than a library full of memoirs and chronicles.

Soon afterwards I experienced another such rewarding fraction of time. French literature and poetry of the last two centuries are full of references to beautiful Créoles, and I had in my mind a clear picture of what such a lady ought to be: pale and dark-haired, a hammock-dweller, compound of languor and sprightliness, attended by worshipping black slaves, suggesting to the imagination at the same time an orchid and a humming-bird.

> Au pays parfumé que le soleil caresse,
> J'ai connu, sous un dais d'arbres tout empourprés
> Et de palmiers d'où pleut sur ses yeux la paresse,
> Une dame créole aux charmes ignorés.
>
> Son teint est pâle et chaud; la brune enchanteresse
> A dans le cou des airs noblement maniérés;
> Grande et svelte et marchant comme une chasseresse,
> Son sourire est tranquille et ses yeux assurés.

That was almost exactly my mental vision, though perhaps Baudelaire's heroine was a little too tall, too svelte. *Comme une chasseresse* ... I felt that was too athletic to tally exactly with the image that already existed in my mind; but the general lines, and above all the *ambiance*, were exactly right.

We had spent the morning visiting a sugar refinery belonging to a close relation of Raoul's at Basse Pointe. It was an enormous affair, full of great boilers and ladders and furlongs of piping and tanks brimming with molasses and huge vats of rum, and tubes that emptied brown and white sugar into sacks. Negroes unloaded sheaves of green sugar-cane from carts and carried them indoors on their heads and flung them on belts; and the belts ferried them to the first stage of destruction. Our host explained everything and his wife entertained us between this more technical talk with stories of village life, and a Negro called Gentilien gave us various samples to taste. Luncheon afterwards had been another of those milestones in Antillean gastronomy: roast sucking pig, which is a great island favourite, cooked on a barbecue in the open; and *chou palmiste*. Heart-of-palm – called, in the French islands, *chou palmiste* or *chou coco*, depending on the tree of its origin – is a delicious vegetable of which the taste is indefinable; 'vegetable', in fact, seems almost too ignoble a name for anything as rare or delicate as this. The texture is that of ivory, and one meal of this astonishing food involves the immola-tion of an entire tree. The palm is felled and split open by skilful cutlass-blows just below the beginning of the leaves; then, with the same care that would be observed in the handling of a codex, the precious parcel of the core is slid from the trunk.

We were sitting in rocking chairs in a cool white room whose arches framed a prospect of tropical trees. A black girl put the coffee things on a table and pattered away.

Our hostess was a great beauty. She had lustrous black hair parted in the middle, a complexion like a camellia-petal, and her violet eyes, which seemed to devour the rest of her face, possessed all the luminosity and depth of a heroine of the Romantic era. She talked and laughed in a warm, singing and fluttering voice, bringing her long and tapering hands into play with an almost Iberian flexibility and precision. Listening to her conversation with its charming Antillean vowels and the Créole omission of the letter 'R', I realized, all at once, that it was she, *la dame créole*, and a very rare and perfect specimen. Nothing was lacking. The colouring, the alternation between lassitude and gaiety, the gestures, the shady trees, even the *Incroyable* accent. '*Si vous alliez, Madame,*' I repeated slowly (but under my breath),

au vrai pays de gloire,

Sur les bords de la Seine ou de la verte Loire,
Belle digne d'orner les antiques manoirs,

Vous feriez, à l'abri des ombreuses retraites,
Germer mille sonnets dans le coeur des poëtes,
Que vos grands yeux rendraient plus soumis que vos noirs,

or rather, would have repeated, if I could have remembered it by heart.

An old colonial road followed the coast in a cobbled switchback, down into combe after combe, clambering up between them on to thickly wooded headlands and finally running level for miles high in the air along the lip of a cliff. Peering down through the overhanging network of forest, we could see the Atlantic breaking far below in long and sluggish scrolls.

The day had started in brilliant sunshine, but huge boxing-glove clouds had collected along the slopes of the volcano, and the rain soon came hammering down on the flat leaves like the fists of pugilists; leaving everything smashed, sodden, steaming and inert. But the rain stopped, the air was clear and windless and watery, and almost Nordic. As we gazed northwards, the Trade Wind revived, and sent a steady breath along the water. The clouds began to move ponderously towards the west. Only the British island of Dominica remained static.

This was the point, our companion explained, from which the Martinicans have been accustomed to make their escape to the English island to join the Free French. They usually went there by oar and sail in dug-out canoes, a good forty miles over very rough sea. Dominica became inundated with these volunteers, and the capital, the little town of Roseau, was for a time a kind of Gaullist reception camp and depôt, where they sometimes had to wait for months till they could find a passage to Europe and the theatre of war.

Travelling eastwards from Grande Rivière, we passed through innumerable valleys, down each of which a stream rushed into the sea. Arcades of bamboo closed over our heads. Their stems shot upwards in hundreds of dark, diverging jets, and wound away in mazy and glaucous tunnels.

We reached the little town of Macouba at nightfall. It was the parish of Father Labat. All students of the history of the West Indies owe a great debt to this extraordinary monk. And, as one reads his voluminous memoirs,* it is the personality of the author, quite as much as the subject of which he treats, that prompts one's admiration and gratitude and one's amusement. He is a sort of monastic West Indian Pepys. He has the same devouring curiosity and sense of humour and practical flair, and, above all, the same lucid and indefatigable garrulousness. Nothing is too important or too trivial for him to set on record in his vigorous and entertaining prose. France has a rich Antillean bibliography, but none of them approach the Dominican in value, except Father Du Tertre, who is the first of these monkish private chroniclers of the West Indies on whose writings one's knowledge of the early days of the islands is based. The others – Rochefort, de la Bare, Fueillée – fall a long way behind.

Jean Baptiste Labat was born in Paris three years before the great fire of London, of a bourgeois family from the Landes, near Bordeaux. He entered Holy Orders at the age of twenty-two, and took his final vows as a monk in the Order of Preachers. For a while he taught mathematics and philosophy in Nancy, and then accompanied the French army as a regimental chaplain to the wars in Flanders, and in 1693 he joined a mission leaving for Martinique. His memoirs open just before his departure for the New World, where he remained altogether about twelve years.

Few pages of his voluminous memoirs are concerned with the religious life of the West Indies, unless it has a bearing on some more pressing

* *Nouveau Voyage aux Isles de l'Amerique par le Rev. P. Labat*, Paris, 1722, 6 vols.

topic, like the sovereign rights of the French crown, or the way to handle slaves. The things that really interested him were the flowers, trees, animals and insects of the Antilles, the wars against the English, the personalities of the islands, economical and agricultural problems, the life and customs of the English, Dutch, Spanish, Africans and Caribs, and their history and language. Any excuse was sufficient to get away from his cure of souls, and he contrived on the flimsiest of pretexts to visit a large number of the Windward and Leeward islands and even some of the greater Antilles far away in the west; talking, arguing, quarrelling, observing, and, fortunately, making notes.

A contemporary portrait depicts him as a fleshy, full-faced Rabelaisian divine with a humorous curl to the mouth, and an expression in his large bright eyes that is a curious mixture of coarseness and subtlety; a kind of Friar Tuck with the grossness leavened by intellect and learning. His gastronomic inquisitiveness is boundless, and he never omits to give a full catalogue of the provisions – *les munitions de bouche* – with which, for the slightest departure, he equips himself; the kegs or demijohns of canary, the cold boiled capons and guinea-fowls, the patés, the baskets of fruit. He emerges from his pages as a gluttonous, intelligent, voluble, practical, pugnacious, argumentative and, above all, immensely likable busybody.

His picaresque and resilient spirit carries him safely through every kind of activity. At one moment he is bargaining for a dozen Negroes from an African slaver, at another he is chastising a sorcerer from the Guinea coast; laying out plans for the fortifications of the French islands, manning and firing a cannon during the English invasion of Guadeloupe, building sugar mills and refineries, expostulating and winning his way with the governor and the generals on questions of strategy or tactics, dining with filibusters and buccaneers and haggling over the price of their loot; wandering through the hinterland of Haiti, hunting wild hog in the Virgin Islands, arguing about religion with the captain of a Spanish galleon, helping to capture an enemy ship as a member of the boarding party; being himself in turn captured by pirates. We find him learning the Negro dialects of the Guinea coasts, or living in the High Woods of Dominica with the Caribs, making collections of their jewels and bows and arrows; scribbling down the names of tropical herbs and flowers and their medicinal properties, describing how a turtle should be cooked, or how the manicou carries its young ones upon its back with all their tails looped round the parent-tail to prevent them from sliding off.

The prints that illustrate his memoirs are amazing. The tropical flora, already strange enough, here goes mad. Shapeless monsters nibble and wallow under giant rhubarb leaves, pterodactyls blacken the sky, corkscrew-snouted swine gimble and gyre in gloomy equinoctial wabes.

But whatever else he was doing one factor is always constant: his insubordination and restlessness keep him at loggerheads with his ecclesiastical superiors. He was for ever having battles of words, from which, to judge by his writings, he always emerged the winner.

But when he finally left the islands to represent the interests of his order in Paris, he was not recalled. He had made things too hot for himself there, and the local authorities were glad to see the back of this stormy petrel. We find him as confessor to Vauban in the War of the Spanish Succession, or later, wandering through Spain and Italy on mysterious errands, eating enormously, drinking, talking and always writing. In 1706 he was travelling from Genoa with another Dominican, 'who, for his sins, was escorting to Paris, for the Archbishop of Rouen, a musician with a clear voice who had undergone an operation to prevent his voice breaking'. He died at last in Paris, in 1738, at the age of seventy-five.

Père Labat is the best of the writers on the background of this book, in any language; and, as his travels took him to a number of the Spanish or English islands, he is almost as rewarding a source on these as on his own French ones. I have introduced this ribald, perceptive monk at some length as his name, like the robust shoots of a tropical creeper, will appear many times among the branches of this traveller's tree. It is noteworthy that another monk, an English one this time, the amusing renegade Father Gage, should fill the same gap for the Central American republics as his French colleague for the Caribbean islands.

A friend was waiting in the hall of the Vieux Moulin with a queer little figure by his side. As soon as we were sitting in one of the arbours of the garden, the stranger put his hands on his knees and, leaning forward, said:

'And how are you getting along with these animals, sir?'

Thinking he was referring to the insects or possibly the snakes, which, although we had not seen any, infest the island, I made a suitable comment, which was interrupted by a noise like a faulty soda-water siphon. 'No, sir, no, not mosquitoes or the *trigonocéphales*. I was referring to the blacks.' He pointed to the old gardener, and a small boy who was hosing a flower bed. I thought the old man had looked up from his weeds at this explosion, and hinted to the stranger that he ought to talk a little more quietly. His voice went up several keys, and he almost shrieked, *'Quoi? Je m'en fous! Qu'ils m'entendent!'*

He was a civil engineer from Lyons who had served many years in Martinique. He was so small as to be almost a dwarf, and his rimless glasses and colourless toothbrush moustache gave him momentarily the anodyne appearance of the Little Man so beloved by caricaturists. But when one looked closer and observed the angry knot of wrinkles on his forehead, the hollow cheeks, the insane eyes and the ferocious twist of the eyebrows, one saw that the first impression was entirely illusory. It was impossible to believe that this tiny frame could harbour so much savagery and passion. He was soon embarked upon a hymn of hate against the Negroes, saying not only how idle and stupid and wicked and dangerous they were, but how absurd and ugly and smelly. His little fist, as he drove home his points, nearly smashed the flimsy wicker table.

Our friend had called to take us for a drive to see the mineral water works at Didier, and this little madman climbed in just before the car moved off, so that all the way through the forest and the dank, echoing tunnels cut through the heart of the tufa the bitter philippic continued. At the factory we had a little respite as we watched the water bubbling out of a rock in the side of the canyon. The jet was captured and steered into a jungle of pipes and tanks and filters, and finally into a revolving fountain of steel that poured it, as it turned, into bottles. Machine-like Negro girls removed and replaced them; belts carried them in an endless file to another girl, who seized them and stuffed their necks into another piece of machinery that sealed them with a capsule. They were then replaced at the end of a second procession which carried them to another brisk automaton who equipped them with labels and piled them into crates. All these operations were performed at breakneck speed. Workmen in shifts hoisted the crates on to their shoulders and loaded them on lorries which carried them clattering through the forest to the thirsty Martinicans all over the island. It was a hallucinating spectacle; terribly slow, I was informed, and antiquated – 'You should see the Coca-Cola factory. They've really got things moving there ...'

On our way back, after this pause, the civil engineer's passion came effervescing to the surface once more. The momentary well-being promoted by the sight of the Negroes grinding away at their various tasks had died down. To make a break in the continuity of this theme, attention was drawn to a grove of giant breadfruit trees. It had the reverse effect. A noise that was at the same time a bellow and a hiss pierced the air. 'How can you talk so calmly,' he cried, 'about those accursed, those iniquitous trees?'

'Why don't you like them?'

He appeared to be on the brink of apoplexy.

'Like them? Like them?' The afternoon was filled with fine saliva, as though the speaker were a watering-can on to which the rose had just been fitted. 'I'd like to see them all cut down, every one of them, and burnt. It's the bloody breadfruit that keeps the black alive without working. It lets them grow fat without doing a hand's turn, takes away all their incentive to work. That's what puts them beyond our control,' he held up two hands, with the fingers crooked like claws through which the whole of the Negro world was slipping. 'And who's to blame for *that? You*, sir.' A claw was placed on one of my shoulders in a conciliatory gesture. 'Not you directly, but your Bligg!'

Bligg? It took him some time to make it clear to us that the real villain of this disaster was the captain of the *Bounty*, none other than Captain Bligh, who first brought the breadfruit tree from the East Indies and planted it in the Caribbean. *'Bligg est le coupable, messieurs, de tout ça. Ne me parlez pas de l'arbre à pain!'* The car stopped and, after punctilious farewells, this minute phenomenon walked springily down his garden path.

The iron shutters of the *Sourire de Venise* were down and locked, and no amount of rapping on them produced any response. A dock-hand sitting in a barrow explained that the police had closed it two days before because of a fight *entre deux de ces dames*. We wandered down the street past a number of humble dens with evocative names – *A l'Instar de Paris, Bar de l'Enthousiasme, Caprice Antillais*. At last, in one with the signboard of a great staring eye, called *L'Oeil qui voit tout*, we found Sosthène in a neat suit and the shirt with the pattern of bleeding hearts that he had worn on the *Colombie*. He was full of complaints about the illogicality of the *Sourire de Venise*, where the fight, it transpired, had been about him, between Françoise and Marie-Thérèse. He had now settled in the hotel above the *Oeil*, maintaining – though it looked exactly the opposite – that it was more serious. He then introduced his new friend, Jeannine, who was much prettier and quieter than either of his other two fiancées. She was slim and coal-black, with a lot of shiny straight black hair piled in a bang on her forehead. She had a deep and gentle voice, but most of the time seemed content to watch us in happy silence. Sosthène complained bitterly about the conduct of his ex-fiancée. *'Vous savez, la Françoise, quand je n'étais pas là, passait son temps à monter avec d'autres types, surtout avec d'autres gens de sa race. Eh bien, moi, je n'aime pas ça, c'est pas correct, pas comme il faut.'* He took a long drink. *'Eh, quand on pense aux maladies qui circulent, ça vous donne la chair de poule.'* Same story with la Marie-Thérèse. *'Tandis que la Jeannine,'* he continued, patting his neighbour's hand, *'c'est tout à fait autre chose, ah! tout à fait! Elle est logique. C'est une dame, quoi, on peut la sortir n'importe où!'* Returning to the subject of Françoise, he maintained she was a savage. During the course of a single night – after a hard day's work, too – he had been compelled no less than three times to eject her from his room by force; but each time, by prising the lock or shinning up a drainpipe, she had contrived to sneak back and curl up while he was asleep, until out of sheer fatigue he had to tolerate her presence. 'Look at my cheeks,' he said, 'they're hollow. I'm a walking corpse. It couldn't go on ...' What was worse, she had been trying to persuade him to go to her village in the *mornes* and settle with her parents; once there, he continued, they poison you slowly with the juice of the manchineel tree, or with small chips of bamboo stirred into the food that they whittle from a stick that has been driven into a pauper's grave. It penetrates the coffinless corpse, and after remaining there for a week it is withdrawn for the purpose of doing in poor chaps like him. 'And they cast spells on you, too.' Sosthène really was looking haggard after all these vicissitudes.

After a while a young Frenchman appeared, who had arrived a few days before from Radio-Paris to visit the wireless station of Martinique, and we all went by taxi to a rather pretentious road-house outside Fort-de-France. There were a few French people, but most of the clientèle were the palest of Mulattoes, all elaborately dressed. We were in an atmosphere of stilt-like heels, diamond wrist-watches and popping champagne corks. The uncompromising ebony of Jeannine's complexion, her quietness and composure were in sharp contrast to the surrounding noise and the spuriously sophisticated atmosphere. She had lagged behind us as we left the *Sourire de Venise*, and there had been the sounds of a minor row behind us in the dark street. She told us that it was Françoise and Marie-Thérèse, who had lurked in the shadows to threaten her with vengeance if she went out with these three *békés* without asking them. She laughed gaily as she explained this, saying that she had nothing to fear; she could defend herself. Not, she continued seriously, that she approved of young women going armed. Sosthène patted her shoulder proudly and said, 'Quite right, Jeannine.' I asked her what sort of arms. Many of the girls, she said, carried scissors and hat-pins in their bodices; never for use against men, she reassured us; only against rivals. She disapproved of it strongly, 'Though, mind you, if another girl stabbed me, I would arm myself when I got out of hospital, and go round and wound her, at least.'

As we walked down to the capital by starlight after a good but ruinous dinner, Jeannine sang biguines in a thin, pretty little voice, just a fraction off the note. The only words I could catch among the patois were the ones with which the refrain ended: *joli lavabo*. The valley outside the town was illuminated by brilliant patches of light in half a dozen places, as though by huge colonies of glow-worms. They were caused by thousands of candles burning on the graves, for it was the vigil of the *Jour des Morts*. As we reached the town we could see, over the walls of the Cemetery of the Rich and the Cemetery of the Poor, families clustered round the tombs for the fateful night that divides All Saints' Day from All Souls' Day. The great white cubes were laden with flowers and lighted candles. Relations of the deceased knelt on the grass saying their rosaries, or sat on the edges of the tombs, quietly talking and laughing or dabbing their eyes with their handkerchiefs, their faces all glowing in the light of the candles. They stay there keeping the dead company till the dawn.

A short time after our arrival in the island, we met and made friends with Dr Robert Rose-Rosette. It is an encounter for which I will be eternally grateful, as not only did this meeting act as an introduction to intellectual Mulatto circles, and in a sense to much of the non-white world of Martinique, but the doctor himself is a man of outstanding quality and charm. The more I saw of him and his friends, the more convinced I became that the happy future evolution of the islands, and the slow exorcism of the cures that still linger from a miserable past, depend on such people as these.

The attitude of Dr Rose-Rosette and his friends is very different, for instance, from that of the Mulatto world of Haiti. The latter forms a separate élite who attempt, in exact proportion to the colour of their complexion, to deny and expunge from their minds all that links them to their African origins and the dismal centuries of slavery. Their attitude is, if not admirable, at least understandable in a world organized by whites. But it is a private and anti-social solution. It is no more help to the problems of these islands than the intransigent conservatism of some of the whites, the violent colour-consciousness of Césaire or the illiterate rancour of the Negro masses; attitudes which can only prolong the deadlock or, in time, precipitate the islands to disaster. The Rose-Rosette outlook seems to me to be the only dignified and constructive one. It is the result of much thought and of a conscious choice; a philosophy of tolerance founded on the mental extirpation of the inherited grief of a past of slavery, and on absolution for the inherited guilt of slave-owning. This philosophy, if I may call it so, adopts the opposite mental stance to that of the Haitian Mulatto élite. For, though its adherents have decided to drop their age-old lamentation, they find a source of pride and inspiration in the African past, and everything that concerns the customs and traditions that have survived the last centuries. This is accompanied by a corresponding abandonment of the age-old grievance against the whites for the sins of their ancestors; an acknowledgement that slavery was the accepted custom, and that this being so it would have been a phenomenon if the colonists had behaved otherwise; an acknowledgement, too, that the slave trade was in many cases merely the extension of a thriving institution that already existed among the Africans themselves. It is an outlook that the phrase about letting bygones be bygones adequately captures. *Les vieux temps sont les vieux temps.*

This may sound an impracticable and over-sanguine hope, and one which overrates the virtue of humanity. But it is the only solution, and one which has indeed good chances of success if its development is not vitiated at every turn by prejudice and the partisan exploitation of grievances which should now be moribund. For the Mulattoes form the largest proportion of the population, and the liberal traditions of the French government and its complete lack of colour prejudice do at least offer – as opposed to colonies like Antigua or Barbados – a psychological climate in which this better state of things could prosper. The Mulattoes to whom I refer feel that their black and white blood, instead of warring in their veins and leading to unhappiness and frustration as they have so often done in the past, should combine to equip them for appeasing the discord that history has left them; and that the intuitions they derive by their descent from both slave-owner and slave equip them psychologically, as much as their numerical preponderance designates them electorally, to tackle and solve their island questions. 'It's our task,' Rose-Rosette affirmed, *'vraiment une mission sacrée* – to try and uproot all the old bitterness, and build up some sort of harmony.'

It was the first reasonable solution that I had heard put forward, and one of immense importance; because harmony and a lasting solution in these islands can only come from the heart. Home governments may legislate wisely and humanely, but it is the passions on the spot, the hangover from the days of slavery, that queer the proper implementation of their measures. For every single one of the inhabitants of these islands had grandparents or great-grandparents that were either owner or slave; often both; and the few generations that have elapsed since the emancipation have not yet been sufficient to blot out the effects of those three hundred abnormal years. The white Créole world is on the defensive, and feels an understandable desire to remain white and maintain its own traditions of family life. This is backed, too, by a feeling of misgiving and hopelessness at the vast preponderance of the coloured race. The present situation tempts many of them to pack up and go, and, if they remain, limits and inhibits their actions. 'Why begin anything in this atmosphere of uncertainty?'

The rancour on the coloured side is equally understandable and more justified; and both of these outlooks are exacerbated by politics. There they are, black, brown and white, destined, if things continue as they are, to live side by side throughout eternity. The situation errs from the original foundation, and, unless an attitude such as that which has been outlined becomes general, the future looks very dark indeed, though perhaps a shade less dark in the French West Indies than the British.

Rose-Rosette is in his early forties, tall and fine-looking, with a rich coffee complexion, and features notable for their regularity and strength. He lived and studied in Paris for a number of years. He is infectiously cheerful and unbelievably kind, and it was obvious that he is liked and respected equally by whites and blacks. He and his brother, a friend called Dr Midas, who owns the *Echo des Antilles*, and M. Villeneuve, a young Frenchman, took us on several expeditions to the south of the island. Of these one especially sticks in my mind.

We stopped at the house of a cousin called Madame Chevalier de la Salle for ices and drinks on the way eastwards round the bay of Fort-de-France, and then struck south. Undulating *mornes* were succeeded by green volcanic slopes until the road was running through mud flats by the sea. Here, at the approach of the motor-car, scarlet and black landcrabs galloped away sideways over the surface of the dried swamp, and took refuge under the bamboo trees. East of here lies the Morne des Pétrifications, a rocky and treeless district given over to sea birds, cactus and prickly pear, and shards of wood that the nature of the water in these parts has completely petrified, giving them the appearance of jasper and agate. But westwards on the road we followed lay a village among shady trees, that clustered round a church. The volutes of the façade manifested, in a fumbling and infantile way, the first gestures of baroque; which, as we were later to understand in the Greater Antilles and Central America, is, with the huts of aboriginals, the only really suitable architecture for the tropics.

The car was hidden in the shade on the outskirts of this village, and we wandered barefoot along a wide beach shaded by coconut palms that stooped westward under the prevailing wind. Conch shells were scattered on the sand, and dug-out canoes were drawn up in little congeries, and here and there lay those giant wicker labyrinths that the Negroes use instead of nets for catching fish. A young Negro, black and glistening in the sun, was lopping down a branch with his cutlass, which he proceeded to trim, in order to replace the broken boom of his fishing boat. Then the jungle flowed right down to the water's edge. We struggled through its green glooms on to a glittering patch of shore enclosed by the forest and the glittering sea. A mile to the south lay the aim, or the excuse, for our journey: the Diamond Rock.

This island is a great block of stone about a mile in circumference. It rises perpendicularly out of the water a dozen furlongs from the shore, and resembles the emerging head and neck of a vast St Bernard dog in profile. On the south-western skyline, only just detectable through the afternoon haze, hovered the outline of the British Windward island of St Lucia.

British naval records have much to say about the Diamond Rock. Admiral Hood, who knew these waters well from the days of the War of American Independence, was back again among the islands during the Napoleonic Wars. Observing that large tonnages of French shipping were eluding him by sailing between the Martinican mainland and the Diamond, he ordered the frigate *Centaur* to sail to the rock. A hawser was rigged from the deck to the summit, on which five naval cannon were hoisted and placed at strategic points along the bare rocky crest, so that their fire raked the narrow straits through which the French ships were accustomed to ply. A party was landed, consisting of a naval lieutenant and a hundred and twenty men and boys, with large supplies of powder, shot, victuals and water. Perched on their lonely stronghold, which naval records thenceforward refer to as 'H.M.S. Diamond Rock', 'they defied and harassed the French navy and merchant ships for seventeen consecutive months. Only when their powder kegs were empty did they surrender, and then to a French squadron of two 75s, a frigate, a corvette, a schooner and eleven gunboats which they had severely mauled before surrendering; wounding seventy men and sinking three gunboats. Their own total losses were two men killed and one wounded.'

We lit a fire in a small clearing under the shade of an enormous *fromager*. We drank rum-punch and cooked excellent steaks in a buccaneerish way over the embers of a camp-fire on the end of a cutlass. A curious bone was discovered in the undergrowth that could only be, it was decided, the shoulderblade of a missionary abandoned here from some former banquet ... Afterwards we lay for hours on the hot sand, letting the sun sink through to our bones; then floated on the sea like bits of flotsam, utterly relaxed and rising and then falling with the swell, poised spread-eagled a couple of yards above the sea's floor, where our shadows repeated our lazy motions on the clear sand and shingle. A blue-green and transparent mattress buoyed us up. Close to the shore we dived through the breaking waves, or feigned dead in order that we might be flung, inert victims of an imaginary naval catastrophe, upon the shore; sucked back a few inches, and then hoisted farther inland by another wave until we lay on the dry sand again, once more comatose targets for the sun. Later the sky grew dark, and, opening our eyes, we saw a phalanx of black clouds advancing from the south. They covered the whole sky and then, heralded only by a few isolated drops, burst in a grey deluge. The Diamond Rock disappeared in an instant, and the contours of the trees half a dozen yards away wavered and disintegrated in the downpour. We adopted our old Guadeloupean stratagem of hiding in the sea, standing with our bodies encased in warmth and only our hair and cheeks exposed to the cold falling arrows. The rain stopped with the abruptness of a tap being turned off, and the clouds heaved away into a distant and harmless ring. Looking inland, I saw the brown forms of our hosts moving under the trees that the raindrops had turned into high baldachins and pagodas of glittering green. Beyond their crests, the mountains which a moment before had been obliterated were now uncannily clear in detail, suddenly close, impending, about to lean over and topple.

The country through which we were travelling rolled away from the road in the growing darkness. Clean, independent and sad. We were heading, for the second time, for Josephine's girlhood home of the Pagerie, the site and the remains of which Rose-Rosette had bought in order to save this relic by keeping the jungle at bay from the few shards that remained, and to have somewhere to retire from the dust of the capital.

The first time we had approached it through Trois Ilets, the nearest village: a collection of pleasant eighteenth-century houses built of brick and tile opening into a little square with a grey church at one end. The interior is more ornate than that of most of the churches of the island. Several fine chandeliers hang in the aisle, and a large slab in the north transept marks the resting-place of Josephine's mother, Madame Tascher de la Pagerie. The rustic track from the village passed through acres of sugar-cane that narrowed into a valley, and then rose and sank into the windless green hollow of La Pagerie.

Beyond the rambling farmhouse lie the remains of Josephine's house. The dilapidation is almost complete. Scarcely two stones of the original house remain standing, and only the quadrilateral of the foundations, which are nowhere more than three feet high, still stand. The rest has vanished, and its place has been taken by grass and weed and bramble. A few yards beyond the house lies a circle of truncated walls that were once the sugar mill, with a flowering tree growing in the heart of its crater. The tall rectangular chimney of the refinery is still erect, and the walls are intact, though unstable, as high as the second storey. Part of this was used as a dwelling-house during Josephine's visit after she had become Empress of the French. It is built of great blocks of hewn stone, and the lintels of doorways and the carved architraves of windows are on the point of falling from their sockets. The interior of the house is a wilderness of trees and creepers. Rusty hinges projecting from the masonry of the first storey, just discernible through the leaves, mark the entrance to a room where one of the Beauharnais children was born, but neither door nor walls nor floor remain. The roots of an enormous tree, fanning out in the tentacles of an octopus, hold the ruins in their grip. Creepers and parasites of immense girth reach through gaps in the stone, like the intruding forearms of burglars. They prise the walls out of their symmetry, as though the tensing of a single fibre would fling them headlong.

This shell is backed by the out-houses, the barns, the laundry, the rambling and rush-roofed barracoons where the slaves lived. All these meaner structures have outlived the seigneurial dwelling. Geese pecked and gobbled among the thick grass by the farmhouse, and cream-coloured cattle grazed across the sloping meadow that curved from the ruin to the edge of the forest. Below the sugar mill, under an archway of *savonettes* and hibiscus, the waters of a river lie in a dark sheet dappled by the shadows of leaves. They fall in a little cataract and meander away down a leafy tunnel. La Pagerie is at the bottom of a green bowl whose sides are heavy with vegetation. Tree-ferns and bamboos rear their plumage, and as the evening comes on, deep shadows collect under the mango trees. Fireflies hang in the air and dart backwards and forwards in angular patterns, brightening every second as the night falls and the cicadas and the frogs become more strident, and the woods are full of the cooing of pigeons. Downhill into the dusk winds the track along which the Taschers and the Beauharnais drove to church in Trois Rivières. Black coachmen and diminutive tigers in livery several sizes too large for them were perched on the boxes of the antiquated but armigerous equipages that swayed down the groves of sugar-cane and of hat-doffing slaves.

For it is plain that the Pagerie, though prosperous, was never a very resplendent establishment. But time, which had dealt so harshly here with bricks and mortar, has spared, in its entirety, the atmosphere that must have dominated the childhood of Josephine. For a kind of lovesick sloth, a heavy languishing drowsiness, prevails among the palms and the hibiscus and the mango trees. It clings to the liana-grown stones and the branches that trail their wild-vine over the water. It relives here as perceptibly as the mood that unfurls at the sound, on a hot afternoon, of a single note struck on a spinet in a disused room. And in this warm Martinican air, it becomes at once apparent why Josephine, shivering in the boreal climate of Europe, organized the heating system of Malmaison so that the rooms maintained all the year round the same mild West Indian temperature.

It is symptomatic of cultural orientations in the islands that Dr Rose-Rosette, although not a rich man, should have been the person to buy La Pagerie. He has a passion for it, and, walking among the leaves and ruins, listening to his enthusiastic voice as it traced and reconstructed every detail of history and conjecture about the former inhabitants of his house, the spell of the place became doubly real. He and his brother spend days slashing away at the invading vegetation, amputating parasites, propping up stones that the creepers were about to dislodge, and searching through old books and papers for yet another atom of relevant knowledge or corroborative detail.

My purpose, on this second visit, was twofold: one, simply to see this place again before leaving Martinique; the other, more specifically, to look through the copy of an inventory of the Pagerie, at the time of Madame Tascher's death, which is in Rose-Rosette's possession. We got there after dark. Some French friends of the doctor's were staying in the house. Two shy and unusually fair children were curled up on the floor, surrounded by picture books of Babar and Bécassine and *Images d'Epinal*, and another book I had never seen called *Les Aventures de Lord Ping-Pong*. I looked over their shoulders at this splendid English-man: a walrus moustache, an eyeglass, protruding teeth, a deerstalker, an elephant gun, a valet, a private aeroplane and a wonderful accent ('Ô, *il n'est pas de la gibier ici?* Good gracious, *je fiche la camp*, yes, yes ...').

I spread the Inventory out under the lamp. 'The year eighteen hundred and seven,' it began, 'and the third of the Emperor Napoleon ... The deceased lady, Rose du Verger de Sauvis, widow of messire Gaspard de Tascher, chevalier, Seigneur of the Pagerie, and mother of Her Majesty the Empress of the French, Queen of Italy ...' and went on, 'the Inventory of goods, furniture, slaves and cattle, jewels and silver of the late lady ...' The witnesses were Alexandre d'Audifrédy, Auguste Chasteau de Balyon, Georges Cacqueray de Valmenière and Thomas Villaret de Joyeuse. (The last two of these romantic names are famous ones in the history of the English as well as the French islands, during the wars of the eighteenth century.)

She did not seem, considering her position, to have a great deal to leave in the way of precious heirlooms; a few jewels, portraits and caskets painted with portraits of the Imperial family, and 'secondly a snuff-box in gold that was in the daily use of the late lady', a bundle of 'Imperial correspondence', a portrait of the Queen of Holland, 'the late lady's grand-daughter', some linen; and *'trois mauvaises malles et une cassette'*. Then comes 'item, thirty barracoons for the Negroes, roofed with palm branches, built and palissaded with reeds, estimated value 1,320 *livres'*; a *manio-querie* – a mill for the preparation of cassava-bread for the slaves; a row of tile-roofed rabbit hutches; a sugar-mill, a refinery and a workshop for making rum-barrels.

These are followed by a long catalogue of 'heads' of slaves – *'Vente de têtes d'esclaves'* – with their numbers, names and estimated value. The first on the list is 'Item, *le nommé Petit Médas, âgé de 38 ans, infirme, non estimé'*. There are five other slaves 'unestimated and infirm'. The first slave with an estimate of value is 'No. 6, Théodule, 70 years, 3,000 *livres'*, followed by a string of other names, male and female, of which many are odd or characteristic; their value varies between 1,000 and 4,000 *livres* a head: Apolline, Zabeth, Désirée *dite* Dody, Pierrette, Léocade, Victorine, Gertrude *dite* Yaya, Mignon, Hyacinthe, 'Guillaume, incommoded by a rupture', 'Eloi *dit* Gros-Jean', 'Lucette, the mulatto-girl', Uldarix, 'Frederick the cooper', *'La Petite Scholastique*, aged 20', Modestine, Eulalie, Charlemagne, Ulric, Ovide, 'Olympe aged 14', Radégonde, Bibiane, Simeon and Narcisse, aged 11 and 15, Angesse, Chrysostome, aged 7 (1,200 *livres*), Laurencine aged 5, Sabine aged 2 (400 *livres*), and finally, cheapest of all, poor little 'Franchine, *en nourrice*, 100 *livres'*. The list is ended by Zachary, Siriaque, Clovis, Grise and Sévérine, 'five new Negroes aged 20, priced at 3,300 *livres* per head'.

These must have been jet black and brawny newcomers, kidnapped on the African coast and freshly shipped to the Antilles, probably from different tribes and thus unable to communicate with each other or their new associates; they were certainly ignorant of Créole. The strangeness and misery of their predicament comes to one even after so many years. They were some of the early fruit of Napoleon's re-establishment of the slave trade, which had been abolished by the Convention. It is recorded that this measure was put through at Josephine's entreaty, in order to stabilize the revenues of her mother in the distant islands rather than have her clamouring for cash in Paris. That may be so, but Napoleon's bias against the coloured race is well known. He broke the military career of General Dumas, the novelist's father, because of his black blood (Dumas was the son of a Negro woman and of a French marquis from Sainte-Domingue); he sent his own brother-in-law, Pauline's husband Leclerc, to quell the Negroes of Haiti, and behaved towards Toussaint L'Ouverture, the Haitian hero, with extraordinary cruelty and perfidiousness.

It will be noticed that the list contains no surnames. These were adopted arbitrarily after the emancipation of the slaves. Unfortunately, no records remain of the system, if any, that dictated the choice of the strange and charming Christian names. Slaves were often separated from their parents as soon as they could walk, and bought and sold, as the beginning of the inventory indicates, with the same indifference to ties of blood as poultry or livestock. Even small boys and girls worked in the fields all the daylight hours under the surveillance of mounted overseers who wielded the whip without mercy. French and English chronicles tell horrifying tales of punitive floggings for the most trivial faults: punishments which, not infrequently, were the cause of death. Slaves with professions – carpenters, barrel-makers, blacksmiths, gardeners, etc. – were, of course, in a better position. The easiest jobs, and the most coveted for their advantages in respect to food, lodging and clothing, were those of the slaves employed around the persons of the planters in their houses. The 'Da', in particular, a French Negro equivalent of the English nanny, or the Mammy of the Southern States, occupied a position of great prestige, and even of authority. One feels, somehow, that 'Mignon' can't have had too bad a time ...

The slaves are easily the most valuable items in the inventory. The old lady left 132 in all, estimated at a total of 267,000 *livres*.* They are followed at once by 28 mules (34,320 *livres*) and five horses and a mare (5,320 *livres*).

The last item in the document is a special legacy to 'Messire Seigneur Rose Tascher de la Pagerie, my young nephew and godson', of a 'little Negro named André, aged 4, son of the slave called Marthe', and of a two and a half year old foal. It sounds as though he were destined to act as a mixture of servant and playmate.

There are one or two mentions of the estate of 'la Dame Catherine Brown', widow of Joseph du Verger de Sauvis. This was Josephine's

*The *livre tournoi* had been officially abolished by Josephine's day, but no doubt they still circulated in the Antilles. The value of one *livre* was a fraction more than that of the franc, of which, at that time, there were twenty-five to the pound. Compare with those on page 342.

maternal grandmother, who was of Irish origin. (French empresses seem to specialize in Celtic ancestry. Eugénie's mother was called Kirkpatrick of Closeburn.) Her paternal grandmother was a Mlle de Jaham de Vertpré, an aunt, several generations back, of our kind host at Vauclin, and of Raoul's.

I returned this absorbing document to Rose-Rosette. It had supplied exactly the extra detail to the illuminating moments, days before, on the steps of Beauséjour, and in contemplation of the beautiful Créole lady, that had been lacking in my mental reconstruction of the Créole world.

The *St Laurent* was in action again at last, lying in the harbour of Fort-de-France, bound for Guadeloupe, and calling at Roseau in Dominica on the way. The ugly quays grew smaller as we churned round and headed westwards out of the bay of Fort-de-France. The lights dwindled to starboard and then vanished and all was dark. As we sailed out of the shelter of the leeward coast into the full impact of the Trade Winds, the sea grew wilder. The *St Laurent* pitched and rolled, and we went below and stretched ourselves in the bunks and hoped for sleep. I opened the pages of Père Labat.

CHAPTER 5

Dominica

The mountains of Dominica rose from the sea in spikes, and the clouds that overhung their summits were loosened into a gap, through which, over a pale disc of the sea, the moon spilt a silver cone that looked like another ghostly outcrop of the inland ranges. The *St Laurent* was already sailing on northward to Guadeloupe as the dug-out canoe carried us across a quarter of a mile of water – for there is no natural harbour – to the few flickering lights that marked the meeting-place of the mountains and the sea and the little capital of Roseau. It was 1 a.m.

A magnificent black sergeant-major of police, the only figure on the quay, advised us to try to stay at Kingsland House for the night. He was wonderfully Britannic in appearance, standing as straight as a guardsman, with his cap-badge, boots and buttons and the knob of his swagger-cane glittering in the moonlight. His blue serge uniform was brightened by a scarlet cap-band and a broad red stripe down the side of his trousers. Three little boys appeared out of the shadows and, arranging most of our luggage on their heads, trotted before us through the empty streets. The wooden houses with their projecting first storeys, in not one of which a light showed, might have belonged to a village in the Balkans, or to the outskirts of Yannina or Monastir. This impression was heightened by the moonlight on the warm dust, by the chirping of insects and the croaking of frogs. When we knocked on the door of Kingsland House, a substantial building in a beautiful garden with lawns and mango trees, an elderly West Indian woman answered the door with an oil lamp in her hand, surprisingly dressed in all the starched and goffered and pleated severity of a mid-Victorian parlourmaid. Behind her, in the lamplight, a strangely English interior materialized. Polished mahogany gleamed darkly, and the panes of rosewood cabinets full of china and cut glass reflected her burning wick. But no, there were no rooms, and Miss Maggie was away in London. The door gently closed on the world of beeswax and starch and soft lamplight, and we were back again among the frogs. We had the same bad luck in the Hotel de Paz, and settled finally in Sutton House, wondering, as we fell asleep in our brass bedsteads, how the capital of our first British Colony would appear next morning.

It appeared enchanting in the early light (for it was impossible to stay in bed long with every noise of resurgent Roseau coming through the thin wooden walls). It was pretty, simple and innocent, and utterly different in feeling from the sultry, brooding, rather wicked atmosphere that hangs over Fort-de-France. The houses were built like chalets, and some had jutting, pillar-supported gables of trellis work, but most remarkable were the wooden houses built throughout of overlapping dark grey wooden shingles in the style of Bukovina. Little Union Jacks fluttered from carved roof-trees, placards marked the homes of the Bible Reading Society and the Gospel Mission, and the Arts and Crafts of Dominica displayed a windowful of swizzle-sticks and tasselled shack-shacks and Carib basketwork. Not far off, the brass plate of Barclays Bank gleamed in the morning air. A clean, sloping road climbed the hill past the windows of Ayoub Dib the Syrian, and every shop appeared to be called Shillingford. Window after window displayed cheeses, rope, bass, scythes, gym-shoes, shirts, straw hats, hams, and whisky, we noticed with pleasure, at pre-war prices. The covered market was crowded with old women selling vegetables and fish, wearing a less resplendent version of the *gwan' wobe* and the *madwas*, and talking to each other in Créole. The quay was lined with schooners and dug-out canoes, and, in the outskirts of the town, I discovered the cigar factory of a firm called Hillsborough, and bought a box of fifty from an old Spaniard there for what seemed almost nothing. In a side-street an undertaker advertised coffins, both ready-made and to measure, at cut-throat prices.

The central street climbed past a Catholic cathedral and a Wesleyan Methodist chapel, whose Gothic masonry towered above the wooden roofs and the tree-tops like the freestone towers of Westgate. An Anglican church, built in the style of the Regency, slumbered on the airy hill-top opposite a massive whitewashed police barracks: an old French fort, whose walls are pierced with breaches for cannon and musket. White uniformed convicts worked in the grounds, and from the white battlements and ravelins, cannon cast with the crowned ciphers of the earlier Georges aimed their stoppered mouths over the falling tree-tops and the white-sailed fishing boats that were skimming across the bay. Farther on, tall iron railings, a flagstaff with another Union Jack, and a sentry-box guarded the leafy expanses of grass at the end of which lay the grey bulk of Government House. On a headland over the bay the Free Library stood, a large, airy, balconied building. Two young Negroes sat in the reading room, deep in the *Bystander* and *Horse and Hound*. In the garden a giant banyan tree overshadowed, with its deep foliage and manifold stems and falling cables, an elegant and romantic fountain of painted metal.

The gathering of buildings on this hill-top, the clean whitewashed walls and the trees, the flags and towers, and the few acres of the roofs of Roseau possessed an engaging and a rather disarming quality. Altogether, the capital was scarcely more than a village, an Antillean Cranford clustering gracefully on the edge of a blazing extent of water, and overshadowed by steep and enormous hills fleecy with every excess of tropical vegetation. If they escape the gloom and the ungainliness which is so often their lot, there is something delightfully comic about many of these little Caribbean towns. The fact that there is a town at all, especially an almost European town, in the middle of such violence of flora and the elements, seems as unnatural an effect as a swimmer remaining for long periods under water.

A shady road, running along a wall like that of an English park, led out of the town for about half a mile in the direction of the hills, and a gate opened into the most beautiful botanical gardens I have ever seen. Lawns as perfect as the most ancient and august in England rolled in gentle slopes shaded by clumps of enormous and, for me, still unknown trees, except for another banyan under whose convolutions I lay for an hour or two and watched my cigar smoke drifting through its many trunks. Next to it a huge cannon-ball tree every now and then loosed off its ammunition, which fell with a dull thud upon the grass. It was a casual and empty paradise, with no other purpose, it seemed, than to furnish a solitary refuge for the Marvellian reveries of the wisely recumbent gardeners and me.

Returning to the lower town, I wandered into the High Court, near Government House. It was in full session and, in spite of the fans, so hot that everybody was mopping their brows. An old peasant woman was being tried for murdering her husband with a hoe. As I came in, a court official was holding the weapon out for the inspection of the jury. As she spoke only Créole, all her evidence had to be given through an interpreter. Under the Royal Arms, two ancient drums and a panoply of banners sat the Puisne Judge of the Windward Islands in his scarlet robe and bands and wig, while the barristers, in spite of the heat, were as heavily gowned and perruqued as they would have been at the Old Bailey. The white vault echoed with legal coughs. 'But m'lud ...' the defending counsel was beginning in the rarified tones of Balliol and the Inner Temple. It was a dignified and majestic scene. The strange garb of the law-courts always reminds me of the illustrations of *Alice in Wonderland*, and here the dreamlike atmosphere was heightened by the dark West Indian complexions which, under the powdered curls of the counsels and Judge, added to the Tenniel-like scene a more exotic eighteenth-century suggestion that might have derived from the pictures of Guardi or Zoffany.

We took advantage of an introduction from friends in England. 'If you want to see the Caribs,' Mrs Napier said, 'why don't you come and stay with me at the other end of the island? It's much nearer, and I might be able to help you. The boat leaves in a couple of hours.'

Owing to the mountainous character of the island, there are practically no roads, and the only means of communication between Roseau, which lies on the south-west coast, and Portsmouth, the other town in the north-west, is by launch: a journey of about twenty miles, which takes about four hours. It was a blazing afternoon, and we huddled for shade under the awning. Our fellow-passengers were fifty Dominicans, all talking to each other in Créole. The language took such firm root during the seventeenth century – when in spite of the usual changes of hand and the ferocities of the Caribs, French influence was predominant – that the following two centuries of English occupation have quite failed to oust it. Dominican English is still often hesitant and laborious, and, in some remote districts, virtually non-existent.

The mountains were wilder and steeper than any we had so far seen, all climbing up to the high, rocky spine of the island and the lofty mountain peak of Morne Diablotin. At the villages of Batalie and Massacre – named after a terrible slaughter of the Caribs in early colonial times – we bought coconuts and bananas, and reached Portsmouth, hidden in its refuge of Prince Rupert's Bay, in the late afternoon.

The village emerges from the forest to enclose three sides of a little market-place whose quadrangle is completed by the sea. Here, under the trees, stood a rectangular block of stone that resembled the empty pedestal of a former conqueror whose statue had taken wing for Valhalla. This is marked on ancient maps as the tomb of a military Lord Cathcart, who died at sea on some early expedition. No remains were found when it was opened in the last century. But it is known in Dominica as the

Tomb of Prince Rupert. For the Prince, when he could no longer charge the Cromwellian ranks across the shires, harried and sank the warships of King Charles's enemies in the Caribbean. He died, however, in England and was buried there. A French ship, disabled at the glorious Battle of the Saints – which the French call *La Bataille de la Dominique* – foundered on this coast and left her battered timbers to rot. Later on, Nelson would often put in at this little capital for supplies.

Darkening plantations of lime and cocoa and the remains of a rustic factory were soon replaced by the forest as the road led us uphill – into the interior, I thought, but really across the northernmost salient of the island to the north coast. It was quite dark when, turning downhill into a wooded hollow, we saw the windows of Mrs Napier's house gleaming through the tree-trunks. Walking across the grass, we came to a great airy room, with the golden light of the lamps shining on the backs of innumerable books. Drinks were standing on a table among vast sofas and chairs. The lamplight fell through the windows on to a balcony, and a tree-shaded expanse of grass which, after a few yards, fell away in a wooded cliff. The sound of the waves came up from the combe below.

Our stay at Pointe Baptiste prolonged itself into many more days than were needed for the preparation of a journey to the Carib country, and looking back on the whole of our Odyssey through the islands it remains, without question, the happiest part of it.

Mrs Napier was one of a very small number of people we met in the Antilles who have studied the colour question with sympathy and thoroughness; in which she may have had a more fortunate start than some of the white West Indians, in that she and her whole family are from England, or rather Scotland, and were thus burdened at the outset with none of the prejudices of colonials of island stock; though, indeed, many English people living in the islands adopt the local prejudices with pathetic docility.

In Dominica, fortunately, there is little of the colour feeling for which islands like Barbados and Antigua have such a bad reputation, as, apart from Government officials, bank employees and tradesmen, the static white population amounts to hardly more than fifty. The island, under the aegis of the Administration in Government House, is almost entirely run by Dominicans. 'So that,' Mrs Napier said, 'if anything like a colour bar existed in this place, none of us would ever see anybody.' She is a member of the House of Representatives – that is, the island equivalent of an M.P. – for the area through which we were proposing to travel.

It was a great delight to be, for once, surrounded by such quantities of books: the Encyclopaedia Britannica, which I had been longing to get at for weeks, books of reference about island history and politics, and, otherwise, exactly the sort of library one sighs for anywhere. It was equally pleasant to be in a lived-in house once again, with something more than the temporary patina of a holiday retreat so usual in the houses of English people in the West Indies.

Drinking equipment of almost Babylonian splendour and a pile of illustrated papers are, all too often, the only symbols of relaxation in Anglo-Caribbean houses. But this house, in its remote and forested mountains, was the result of half a lifetime of active pursuits – literature, politics, family, distant journeys and of a compendious and exhaustive range of interests. Here and there, among the accumulations of travel, appeared a print of a Scottish country house lying among misty hills, or of a member of the family in an obsolete and Ouida-esque uniform, bringing to this brilliant tropical world the faint memory of the Prince of Wales's court in Victorian times.

At last, after nearly a week of idleness and painting and reading and writing, we prepared to move south.

'It's terrible here, absolutely terrible,' the Polish doctor said, as, early next morning, he drove us through the rolling woodland. 'Nothing but malaria, congenital syphilis, and yaws.'

He was very civilized and urbane. He had lived in Paris for many years, had been in concentration camps in Russia and Germany during the war and subsequently escaped to England through France. Afterwards he had volunteered to take up a practice in the West Indies, expecting something very different from these remote fastnesses. We asked him exactly what he had expected. His white buckskin shoe trod on the brake as three cows strayed into the road from behind a thicket. Then, with a rather dismal laugh, he shrugged his shoulders and raised both hands from the wheel in an expansive gesture, and said, 'Tr-r-ropical l-life . . .'

We saw at once what he meant, and that he had, indeed, grounds for complaint. These damp, sad forests and volcanoes, the quick-falling night and the lack of company, for somebody who does not particularly care for reading and who finds solitude irksome, must be an appalling contrast to the bridge, the flirtations, the country clubs, the dozens of parked cars at drink-time, that the words 'tropical life' evoke in most people in Europe. There were, indeed, at this end of the island only a few isolated miles of road, leading from nowhere to nowhere, along which to drive the stupendous motor-car brought from Europe at great cost;

which, at that very moment, was reaching the end of its beat. There is no doubt that, without the adjuncts of a Lady Hester Stanhope-like hermitage such as Pointe Baptiste, life might at times seem mournful and lost. We pulled up at a Syrian grocery in a little collection of huts called Marigot, to buy some stores for the journey: bully-beef, tomato soup, cigarettes, matches, garlic and macaroni. The sound of a furious dispute in Arabic came out of the darkness. The white silken figure of the doctor waved as his glittering motor ploughed back through the slush, and the steaming leaves and the tangle of lianas that closed over it appeared a habitat more likely to conceal a diplodocus or a mammoth.

Our party, as it finally moved out of Marigot, looked formidable. Three enormous Negroes carrying on their heads our luggage and various essential impedimenta lent us by Mrs Napier, moved delicately along the narrow suspension bridge, setting the whole length of it swinging on its cables with each step. The ponies we rode through the pebbly river-bed below were scraggy little things, hired from different villages, each with a separate system of conditions and commitments. Only the first was shod. Seeing this, the owner of the second suddenly decided to have his horse shod as well, just as we were moving off, promising, as he led it away in the direction of a hypothetical blacksmith, to catch us up later. So our cavalcade was reduced to two. Joan mounted Misdemeanour, while Jockey Girl, who was barefoot, remained as a bone of contention between Costa and me. ('Go on, Costa,' I insisted, looking furtively at the first hill, and catching a glimpse of the still bigger one beyond, 'you have first go.' 'No, you have her. I feel like walking.' Then, with a sidelong glance in the same direction, 'P-perhaps in half an hour or so ...') The guide and head of our retinue was René Williams, a lean and gentle young man, who had studied divinity for a while. Our caravan had assumed the portentousness of an expedition of Mungo Park into the jungles of Africa.

The trees soon closed over the steep bridle path, dappling the soft, red clay with ragged stripes of sunlight. The road twisted as it climbed, and the thickness of the sodden leaves turned it into a dense and tortuous cavern. Each convolution hoisted our little procession higher into the foot-hills of Morne Diablotin, whose leafy cone pierced the sky miles away. From my position in the rear it was an impressive sight: René led the way, then came the porters, as slender and graceful as caryatids under their globular loads. Joan's horse ambled after them, bearing a figure that looked as purposeful in its dark glasses and great straw hat as a mid-Victorian lady heading for the mission-field in Uganda. She was followed by Costa riding dreamily through the shadows in his sky-blue shirt and shorts, or alternatively, at pleasanter moments, laboriously clambering up the glutinous pathway on foot. The path grew level at last, and through a gap in the trees we could gaze from our lofty headland into a deep gorge downy with tree-tops. The sea reached inland between the steep sides of the canyon to meet the emerging river.

All day long our path followed this long climb and fall. The island is so rich in rivers that it is rumoured to possess one for each day of the year. Another legend, which is applied in books to any of the islands which are at all mountainous, is that an early traveller – perhaps Columbus – when reporting his discovery, was asked by his sovereign to give a description of the new jewel that had been added to his diadem. The traveller crumpled a sheet of parchment in his hand and flung it on to the table before the king, with the words, 'Like this, sire.' It is a more apt description of Dominica than any of the other Antilles.

After the third horse had caught up with us, we rode for a long time encountering nobody. The road suddenly widened into a clearing, where a group of shingle huts lay back under the trees, and by the edge of the path a group of men were standing, as though they were expecting us. So sharp was the contrast of their complexion and bearing with those of the islanders, that I thought for a moment that they were white men. But they were Caribs.

We dismounted and walked towards them, and, as we met, hats were raised on either side with some solemnity. And we all shook hands. This meeting with the last survivors of this almost extinct race of conquerors was as stirring and impressive in its way as if the encounter had been with Etruscans or Hittites.

We were now able to see that they were either ivory-coloured in complexion or a deep bronze, with features that were almost Mongolian or Esquimaux except for the well-defined noses. Their straight black hair was cut across their foreheads in a fringe. They had a dignity of presence that even their hideous European rags could not stifle. A tall man in the middle, smoking a pipe and equipped with an elaborate walking-stick, took charge of us with a diffident, almost Manchu solemnity. This was George Frederick, the king or chief of the Caribs, and the elders that surrounded him were members of the Carib Council. He led us up a steep path through the leaves to a little green glade in front of his own shingle hut, where we sat down under a mango tree, and leaned our backs against a half-excavated canoe. An old man in a doorway was weaving a basket. These are remarkable things, accomplished with great intricacy and finish. Different coloured rushes and leaves are shredded into fine strands, and woven into complex angular patterns that give the effect of mosaic. The basket is composed of two deep oblongs open on one side that fit into each other as smoothly as the halves of a revelation suitcase, and grip each other so tightly that no other fastening is needed. The fineness of the mesh makes them completely water-tight. As we watched the strands overlap in the skilful fingers, a dozen coconuts came thundering from a palm tree, and a young Carib slid down the trunk with his bare cutlass in his hand. The king opened them deftly, and offered us the milk, saying that he was sorry Mrs Napier had not come with us, because, as her chief constituent, he wanted to have a serious chat about island affairs.

The presence of these men sends the mind winging back to the vague centuries before the November Sunday* in 1493 when, with a volley of poisoned arrows, the ancestors of these Caribs drove the sailors of Columbus back to their boats, forcing the Admiral to set sail again in the direction of Guadeloupe. How many centuries earlier, nobody knows, for the only traces of that dim pre-Columbian age are half a dozen lumps of stone scattered among the islands, incised with a few barbaric golliwogs, and all the rest is surmise.

Some writers speak of a prehistoric population in these islands, known, in Haiti and Cuba, as the Ciboneys, and in Martinique as the Ygneris. But about these shadowy figures almost nothing, barely the fact of their existence, is known, and they have left scarcely a trace.

The first really authenticated inhabitants of the Antilles were the Arawak Indians, who originated in Venezuela and the Guianas,† and sailed northwards in fleets of canoes at some remote period, stopping and settling on each island as they reached it, and then spreading farther north and finally peopling – several millions of them – the entire festoon of islands from Trinidad to Cuba. They seem to have been a sedentary, pacific people, hospitable and affectionate, living an almost idyllic life in the empty *Lebensraum* of the archipelago. They were ruled by Caciques and by a priestly clan, and they practised a primitive religion that is called by ethnologists Zemiism; a cult which was based on the worship of a supreme being in the form of Zemis, or idols. They were hunters and fishermen and farmers in a small way. Singing and dancing and

---

*Out of respect to the Lord's Day, the Carib island of *Wy-tou-koubouli* was promptly pricked down in the chart as Dominica.

†Arawaks are still to be found in British Guiana. It was the early reports of the pristine innocence of the Indians of the isles that inspired Montaigne and many subsequent writers with the idealized abstraction of the gentle savage.

lying in their hammocks, smoking tobacco through calumets were their chief recreations. The central tube of their pipes forked into two prongs, which were inserted into the nostrils, a method of smoking that put them into a state of semi-stupefaction and *kef* that played a certain part in their religious observances. Their usual pets were parrots and little dogs called alcos, which were unable to bark; ideal companions. They used to flatten the foreheads of their babies by binding a flat stone to their heads while they were still pliable. This process is said to have hardened the bone, so that in later life their skulls were proof against all primitive weapons, and even capable of turning or splintering the blade of a Toledo sword. In his plea to the King of Spain to forbid the continued enslavement and exploitation of the Indians lest the race should become extinct (a prophecy of which the truth was proved in very few decades), Father Las Casas described the Arawaks as the most naive and gentle of mortals.*

But long before the Spaniards burst into their quiet lives, the Arawaks were confronted by a far more terrible horde of newcomers. Again, no dates are known, and it is not even certain where exactly the Caribs came from. Some early chroniclers, notably Father Labat, thought that they must have reached the islands from North America, via Florida, the Bahamas and the Greater Antilles, but this theory must be abandoned owing to the absence at that time of all but Arawaks (and in western Cuba of a few surviving Ciboneys) in Cuba and Jamaica. Father Du Tertre – for it is to the monks, as usual, that we owe any inklings of knowledge – affirms that they were the descendants of the Galibis, who still live in a savage state between the Oyapock and Maroni Rivers, also in the Guianas. But the results of later researches, based on linguistic similarities, indicate that the original cradle of the Carib race lay much farther south; in Brazil, somewhere in the region of the Amazon. It is possible that they set out northwards from the mouth of the Orinoco, of which the currents still darken the waters of Trinidad with the effluvia of the Andes. From Trinidad their war canoes advanced northwards on exactly the same route as that of the Arawaks.

They made short work of their unwarlike forerunners. They massacred and sometimes devoured the men, and married the women; some of them taking root, while the others moved on, rapidly eating and marrying their way through the Windward and Leeward and Virgin Islands, and into the greater Antilles. They never, as far as I can gather from the

* Poor Las Casas's alternative – the importation of Negroes from Africa – was the pretext for the first shipment of black slaves and the cause of all the subsequent sorrows of the Caribbean. He soon bitterly repented his suggestion.

chroniclers, settled permanently in the western Caribbean. Cuba and Jamaica escaped them altogether, and Hispaniola and Puerto Rico lived in dread of their frequent invasions, but did not have to endure them as a permanent evil. Perhaps their arrival in these regions coincided with the advent of the Spaniards, or perhaps they preferred the forests and gorges of the Lesser Antilles to the sierras and savannahs of Borinquen. Or they may have felt that the time had come to pause and, as it were, digest their conquests. They became static.

When the Spaniards came to the Windwards and Leewards in 1493, Columbus dropped anchor at each of the islands, went ashore on some of them, and symbolically claimed them for his king. In nearly every case he was greeted by a fierce resistance; in Guadeloupe the men were reinforced by an army of Amazons who came down to the shore to loose off their poisoned shafts. He sailed away again, and on paper Hewanorra became St Lucia, Madanino became Martinica, Karoukera Guadeloupe, Wytoukoubouli Dominica, and so on, and that, for over a century, was all. There were brighter lures for the Spaniards in Mexico and Peru, and a long war with these savages for a handful of green tufted rocks was an unprofitable thought. Dominican monks landed occasionally to convert the Caribs and were massacred. The Conquistadors Ponce de Leon and Jerrando and even Sir Francis Drake, failed to dislodge the savages. The Caribs remained unchallenged masters of the Lesser Antilles. In the first decades of the seventeenth century, France and England started to settle in these languidly held possessions of Spain, and their wearisome two centuries of wars began. But the prolonged and ferocious resistance of the Caribs in some of the islands, and the impossibility of subduing them, prompted the English and French to agree at the treaty of Aix-la-Chapelle in 1748 that Dominica, St Vincent, St Lucia and Tobago should remain neutral, with the Caribs in undisturbed possession. De Rochefort and Fathers Du Tertre and Breton (who wrote a Carib dictionary, and translated parts of the liturgy into Carib) give us a clear idea of how these savages lived, but it is the pen of Father Labat that suddenly transforms these aboriginal phantoms into real and vivid people.

The wise monk realized the hopelessness of trying to convert the Caribs. Many Indian races, and notably the Caribs, are endowed with an inability to grasp alien ideas which is too total and grandiose a characteristic to be degraded with a word like stupidity. The Caribs were unable to count to higher than six, and, not surprisingly, the principles of Christian doctrine were beyond their grasp; no word existed in their

language for god, soul or spirit. They very hazily accepted the existence
of the principles of Good and Evil, but only the latter had a name –
Manitou; and Manitou, being the more dangerous and powerful of the
two, was occasionally worshipped. Labat's colleagues, after decades
among the Caribs, declared that they had not made a single conversion,
beyond the baptism of a few babies on the point of death. A number
of Caribs had wandered about the islands being baptized again and again,
in order to obtain the christening presents with which the governors
and magnates ratified these rare triumphs of the faith. Another mental
limitation was their inability to believe that anybody was dead unless
they actually saw the corpse. A corpse had thus to be kept for long
periods till all its family and relations had seen it. It was kept in a crouching
position in a hole under the floor of the hut, which was closed with
planks and covered with mats, and only filled with sand when everybody
had assured themselves, by sight and touch, that the corpse was no
longer alive. A stranger or a relation who died far away was believed,
even after a century or two centuries, to be still alive. Not out of any
superstition, but out of lack of sense of time, and the sheer inability
to understand death as an abstract idea.

No, Father Labat's interest in the Carib life was historical, ethnological
and, of course, gastronomic. There were Caribs in the other islands, and
pockets of them were dotted about his own island of Martinique; but
St Vincent and Dominica were their especial strongholds. He stayed for
three weeks in the hut of an old Carib woman known as Madame
Ouvernard, who was over a hundred years old, and had been, during
her youth, a great beauty, and for many years the mistress of an English
governor of St Kitts. (Labat stayed with her in 1700, and the great Sir
Thomas Warner died and was buried in his governorship of St Kitts
in 1648. It is generally supposed that Ouvernard is a garbled and gallicized
version of his name.) She was a cheerful old lady, quite naked and almost
totally bald, and a great brandy drinker. When he left her he travelled
all over Dominica, lingering longest in exactly the part of the island
where we were sitting with the last descendants of his hosts.

They lived in huts called *carbets*, high, roomy penthouses of woven
rush, bamboo or palm, whose eaves reached almost to the ground. When
out hunting they built themselves *adjoupas*, little lean-to bivouacs of leaves.
They struck fire by rotating a drill of hard wood in a socket of tinder,
and lived off fish, crabs, birds, yam, cassava, potato and sweet potato.
Their meat – they kept pigs, but mostly for trading – was always
'boucanned' – smoked in the buccaneer's way, over a slow fire. Labat
was astonished at the abundance of eels in the rivers which the Caribs

never touched. He immediately ate a dozen, and pronounced them capital, as well as the partridges and pigeons and ortolans with which the woods abounded.

The first action of a Carib's day was a bathe in a mountain stream or the sea. The men of the hut would sit on a stool to dry, and the women would then approach with gourds full of *roucou* dye, and paint them all over until every inch of their bodies was bright red. If they were preparing a warlike expedition, their faces would be adorned with great moustaches and their bodies with circles and lines, for which they used a black dye called *ganipa*. Many of them practised forehead deformation like the Arawaks, which made their heads appear strangely high and elongated. They anointed their long black hair with palm oil, and tied it in a clump on the crown of the head. Their only clothing was a cord round their loins, from the side of which hung a sheathless knife, while from the front suspended a length of cloth six inches broad, which reached the ground. From an alloy of silver and gold and bronze they hammered out their personal ornaments, the *karakoli*, or large crescents, which they suspended on chains from the lobes of their ears, and from between the nostrils and from the lower lip. A fifth, six or seven inches long, hung round their neck embedded in a slab of wood. These head decorations were sometimes removed, and the holes in nose, ears and lip were refilled by plugs of wood or blue stones or, more strangely, red, blue and green feathers from the tails of parrots, which had the appearance of multi-coloured whiskers and beards. The women were also painted, and their hair was caught behind with cotton. An exiguous apron, prettily beaded and fringed, was their only serious garment, but they wore, between the middle of their calves and their upper ankles, strange buskins or greaves of embroidered cotton. Blue stones embellished their ears, and six or seven necklaces of enamel and different coloured shells, and five or six rows of bracelets on either arm completed their attire. The general effect was charming, especially as the women, though reserved and modest, were gay, smiling creatures with beautiful hair and eyes and perfect teeth; while the faces of the men had, when it was possible to see them, a melancholy cast. The children wore circular head-dresses of bright parrot feathers.

The women lived as an inferior caste. Five or six of them, often sisters, were the wives of the same man. They would pound and prepare the cassava, which the men ate out of gourds in silence. The men would then squat for hours in front of the fire, gazing into the flames, whistling softly through their teeth, or blowing primitive and monotonous tunes down a reed pipe. Sometimes they would lie in their hammocks, smoking or gazing abstractedly at the plaited roof. Basketwork,* mending their bows, whittling arrows or carving clubs filled some of their time; but they would drop them the moment they were bored, and disappear without a word to hunt or fish for a few days, returning in equal silence. Or they would just sit or lie for further periods of cogitation. Their gift for impassivity seems to have been limitless. The only things that could disturb it were jealousy, revenge or drink. When several Caribs were squatting together, they would never interrupt each other. One of them would talk, and his words were invariably received with a deep hum of approval and a ponderous nodding of the head without a word being articulated. The following speaker, even if he flatly contradicted his predecessor, would be greeted by the same odd note of approbation. They never quarrelled. If one of them had any resentment against another, he would only remember it during one of their terrific drinking parties, and, rising, would walk round the outside of the ring till he was behind his rival, split his skull in two with a mace-blow, and then resume his place. If the friends or relations of the victim were in a minority, the party would continue without comment, but an unending feud would begin that in a few years' time might have annihilated the families of both sides.

Three languages were spoken. The men talked Carib among themselves, and the women Arawak: a survival of the ancient conquest when all the wives of the new owners were drawn from the defeated race. Arawak developed, as time passed, into a squaws' language of which, although they understood it perfectly from their childhood, the men never deigned to utter a syllable. The third language was a secret tongue of the elders, which was only used for palavers that involved weighty resolutions. As perfect equality reigned amongst them, this was a difficult achievement. Nobody was in a position to command, and obedience was a thing that had never occurred to anyone. Decisions, usually involving warlike expeditions, would only be made under the impulse of gregarious drunkenness, and the deadlock was usually resolved by one of the old women. She would burst into their indetermination, flourishing the smoked arm or leg of an enemy, and, haranguing them about the wrongs of their race, fling the trophy into their midst. They all hurled themselves upon it in a frenzy, gnawing and tearing it to shreds; then, inflamed with rum, *tafia* and *ouicou*, and at last decided, they gathered their weapons, and, blowing their conch-shells, ran down through the trees to their canoes.

* Of exactly the same kind as that practised today.

On the poop of one of these, which was roughly carved in the shape of a monkey's head, Père Labat once saw an arm tied with creeper, 'which they offered me, extremely civilly, saying that it was the arm of an Englishman that they had killed during a raid on Barbuda'. The Caribs, he says, in spite of their bad reputation as cannibals, devoured their victims as a warlike ceremonial, or in a rage, never out of sheer gluttony. A few weeks after leaving Dominica, however, in the library of Basseterre in St Kitts, I came across a magnificent old volume of De Rochefort,* who says that the Caribs of his day – half a century earlier than Labat – had very decided and discriminating views on meals of this kind. French people were considered delicious and by far the best of the Europeans, and next came the English. The Dutch were dull and rather tasteless, while the Spaniards were so stringy and full of gristle as to be practically uneatable. The taste of Arawaks had been forgotten long ago, and their own was too commonplace, it must be assumed, to warrant a mention. The victims were prepared while still alive, by cutting slits down the back and sides into which pimentos and other herbs were stuffed. After being dispatched with a mace, they were trussed to poles and roasted over a medium fire, while the women busied themselves turning and basting, and catching the lard in gourds and calabashes, which they allowed to set and then stored away. They would eagerly lick the sticks where the gravy had fallen. Often the meal was half roasted, and then half boiled. Some of the meat was eaten on the spot, the rest was cut up and smoked and also prudently put by for lean or unpatriotic periods in the future. But there was a symbolical aspect to these banquets. They were considered to seal a military victory, to put it for ever beyond question. De Rochefort reports that a Carib prisoner, while being made ready, would jeer at his captors, saying that, although they would soon be eating him, he had already swallowed so many of their family or tribe, and was so thoroughly nourished on their neighbours and kin, that they would virtually be eating one of their own people. This kind of language would continue until the final blow was delivered. It never failed to exasperate the company, and to cast an atmosphere of dejection over the whole meal.

As early as 1508 the geographer Juan de la Casa designated the Windward group as the Isles of the Cannibals. But, in spite of this custom, the chroniclers maintain that the Caribs were far more compassionate than the Indians of Darien, who ate without mercy everybody they could lay hands on; or than the Iroquois of the Canadian provinces with their

*Histoire Naturelle des Antilles de l'Amerique, Rotterdam, 1658.

scalpings and their protracted torments. They never harmed the women, but took them as their own wives, and then adopted the orphans and treated them as their own children.

They were skilful in building boats, which, as they do today, they hollowed out of the trunks of trees. They ranged from small canoes and pirogues to war boats, or *marassas*, over forty feet long, rigged with three masts and three sails, and propelled by oars and steered by a paddle. Little flotillas of these crafts would set out on expeditions of war and trade. If they were bent on warlike purposes, two women travelled in each boat to prepare the cassava and attend to the war-paint of the crew. Their skill as sailors was only paralleled by their wonderful powers of swimming, which was just as well, as they were frequently drunk on returning from their expeditions, and the boats often capsized. The women could swim as expertly as the men, even with one or two children in their arms, who soon learnt to swim round their mothers like little fishes. Their speed on the surface and under water was so great that they have been recorded to tackle sharks with knives and fight them under water until the shark floated to the top of the scarlet waves.

Father Labat never tired of admiring their skill at archery, for the children learnt to use bows as soon as they were weaned. He used to stick a wand into the ground and fasten a small coin to the top with wax. And children of ten, at a distance of fifty yards, would never miss, firing arrow after arrow at lightning speed, and yet with such nonchalance that they never appeared to aim. The grown Caribs would kill minute birds on branches so far away that they were invisible to the Father. For hunting small birds they affixed buttons to the ends of their arrows like those used on a fencer's foil, and so rapid was their fire that many observers thought that several arrows were loosed off simultaneously. Their bows were strung with liana, and their long reed arrows tipped with notched and iron-hard wood, which they poisoned by dipping into holes in the trunks of the manchineel tree. They shot fish from rocks and canoes, the string of each arrow being attached to a piece of wood to mark, like a buoy, the whereabouts of the captive. Their method of catching parrots was singular. They stole under the trees where the birds perched for the night, and laid burning brands sprinkled with gums and green peppers on the grass. If the parrots lived in the topmost branches, they would approach the trees on tiptoe with the burning drug in gourds attached to the ends of long poles. The fumes rose through the branches, and the dizzy birds fell half stupefied to the ground. The waiting Caribs quickly tied them up and revived them by throwing water in their faces, and carried them off to their huts to instruct them in one of their uncouth languages.

So violent was their sense of liberty that they jeered at the whites for their social hierarchy and their respect for rank, taxing them with having the habits and the mentality of slaves. On the rare occasions when they consented to become servants they were *indolents et fantasques*, and so touchy that the faintest slur on their dignity would drive them to flight or to hanging themselves or to swallowing earth until they died. Their hatred of coercion and their indomitable independence made it impossible for them to live beside Europeans, who saw no solution to the situation except in isolating or exterminating them. Until the latter solution could be enforced, both French and English were at pains to keep on good terms with the Caribs. *Compère* was the polite form of address in speaking to them, or, more formally, *Banaré*, a Carib word meaning 'He who has come by sea'. Their hostility was dreaded. Their method of attack on a wooden house was to loose off arrows, armed with burning cotton, into the thatch. When the house was on fire, the attackers, from the shadow of the trees, would shoot the inhabitants full of arrows as they tried to escape from the blaze. Their ambushes were almost more to be feared, for the Caribs would cover themselves entirely with branches, and tie a flat balisier-leaf over their heads, into which two eye-holes had been cut. They would wait beside the path for hours, and strike down their enemy as he passed; then, stepping backwards a pace, or falling flat among the bushes, they would be indistinguishable from the woods that surrounded them.

Father Labat, at the end of his journey, left the island with a collection of trophies, all bought in exchange for bottles of rum, of which he carried enormous supplies. It is agreeable to think of this massive, tonsured figure striding, in his voluminous black and white habit, along these green forest paths. Behind him trotted a couple of slaves with his luggage on their heads, urging a horse whose panniers bulged with bottles and demijohns and cold pork and ortolans and partridges, and with books and writing materials. Some bows and arrows were tied on top, a mace or two, and a fine bridal hammock. A set of carakolis rattled in his pouch alongside a number of green jadeite baubles which were sovereign against dazzlement, epilepsy and vertigo, and in his hands he carried a wicker Carib cage containing three magnificent parrots which screamed through the bars in protest against the violence of their motion.

The neighbourhood of two elements as irreconcilable as the Caribs and the white colonists could only end in the extinction of one of them, and by the end of the eighteenth century the Caribs had virtually vanished as a race from all the islands except Dominica and St Vincent.

The Caribs of Dominica remained the largest pocket of them – but not very large; Father Labat, at the beginning of the eighteenth century, reckoned that there could not be many more than two thousand in the island, though this number was certainly increased by countrymen fleeing from extermination in the other Antilles. In spite of the island's neutrality, many French planters settled there and imported slaves. It was finally assigned to the English in 1763, and, with short interregna of French invasion and occupation, it has remained in their possession ever since. Roseau and Portsmouth were suddenly full of Union Jacks and redcoats and powdered wigs. But the unofficial French period bestowed upon the Negroes (and those that were later imported by the English) the Créole patois and the Catholic faith. As the colony became organized and the population of slaves increased, the number of the Caribs shrank. Bit by bit, all three of their languages disappeared, to be replaced by Créole and, during the first decades of the nineteenth century, a more plausible and, at any rate in appearance, more deep-rooted conversion to the Catholic faith took place. Cannibalism had died out long ago, and many other customs, including their war paint and their dress, vanished one by one. Lost in the overwhelming Negro world, they had ceased to be dangerous. In 1903 the British Government, disturbed at their decline in numbers through miscegenation, and in prosperity through their inadaptability to alien ways, created by decree the Carib reserve where they now live. There are, in these few miles of mountains and forests, scarcely five hundred of them left, and of these many have a small amount of African blood. In the whole world there are now only about a hundred pure-blooded Caribs left, and the little rearguard is growing smaller every year. They are a doomed race lingering on the shores of extinction, and in a generation or two, unless some miracle of regeneration and fecundity intervenes, the black tide will have risen and swept them off the face of the earth for ever.

They are all, Caribs and mestizo-Caribs, consumingly proud of their race, and whatever their internal feuds may be, they are a stubborn and compact community in their attitude to the outside world. For the last few decades they have been presided over by a sort of elective voivode with the style of king, though the title is legally in abeyance at the moment owing to certain troubles with the authorities in Roseau. The present king or chieftain, George Frederick, whose office entails a civil list of ten shillings monthly from British Government funds, is the head of the Carib Council, which is responsible for the conduct of Carib home affairs. George Frederick owes his present position to his ability to read and write English as well as Créole. Most of the other elders spoke it imperfectly and all talked Créole among themselves. The only responsibility of the Caribs is to keep the bridle path open which runs through their territory, by cutting back the creepers and undergrowth.

The king and his council accompanied us from hut to hut of their little forest capital of Battaka. Most of the houses were built of shingle or bamboo and palm trash and scattered about singly in the woods. The women were pounding cassava in wooden mortars, sorting jute or cocoa beans on cloths spread out on the ground, or weaving baskets. Many of these Carib women were fine looking, with smooth blank faces of pale copper colour, and long gleaming black hair. In one clearing an elderly Carib lay smoking in a hammock stretched between the doorpost and a calabash tree that suspended above his restful figure half a dozen heavy green balloons.

No particular value is attached to virginity or technical chastity among these people, and bastards are always treated with kindness. Marriages in every degree of consanguinity except brother and sister, mother and son or father and daughter are usual, and the culminating step in a courtship is often a formalized kind of rape in the high woods. It is considered an indignity for the men to carry anything on their heads, in the manner of their women and the Negroes. They carry their loads lashed on to a shelf which is supported at the sides by ovals of basketwork, the whole being slung on their backs in the fashion of a haversack. Their little society is still a tangle of feuds and jealousies, and they frequently resort to their own sorcerers, who practise a survival of their aboriginal magic known as 'piai'. Belief in dreams and their interpretation plays a great part in their lives. One of their strangest customs is that of adopting a pseudonym, which they rigorously maintain whenever they undertake a long journey, so that all actions or gestures during their absences are considered to have been done by an unknown stranger. Death and burial are accompanied by elaborate wakes and fumigations which are often the occasion of celebrations and dancing and the swallowing of enormous quantities of rum, for the pleasures of drink are still as important to them as ever they were in the past.* When legally obtained supplies are too dear, shebeens are sometimes secretly erected.

Indifference to money, inaptitude or scorn for trade, and a total lack of ambition render them, for many of their fellow-islanders, a perplexing community. They have a marked distrust and contempt for laws and taxations imposed from without. Their purpose is to keep their own way

---

* See *The Caribs of Dominica*, by Douglas Taylor (Bureau of American Ethnology, U.S. Government Printing Office, Washington). King George Frederick verified almost every detail in this work, and knew the author well. Mr Taylor, who is married to a Carib, is certainly the best living authority on this race.

of life in the woods and on the sea unchanged, and with the minimum of interference from outside: a wish that seems, in spite of their many grumbles, to be fairly liberally indulged. Their food is mainly fish, and often, still, crabs, and, above all, cassava, yam and dasheen. They fish in the rivers at night by torchlight, and catch crayfish with cassava bait. Fish are also killed by poisoning the mountain streams with *larouma*, a vegetable whose venom is innocuous to humans. Lobsters are captured by divers, and elaborate wicker pots are woven to entice and imprison turtles. Iguanas, which are one of their great delicacies, are hunted with a technique as strange as their ancient mode of parrot-catching. The hunter steals under the leafy haunt of one of these reptiles, and whistles to it gently for hours, until it is hypnotized into a sort of aesthetic trance. The little prehistoric dragon is gently lassoed, and then, bound hand and foot, carried joyfully home. They cultivate vegetable gardens in the high woods, which they clear by felling the trees and burning the bush. When they have exhausted the soil they move on and repeat the same process elsewhere. (This is also a favourite practice of the country Negroes, and one which, in such a mountainous terrain threatens much of the island with serious soil erosion.) Little parties of them, laden with their garden produce and with Carib baskets for sale, climb the footpaths over the watersheds and ravines to the market in Roseau.

Many of them were hacking with adzes and cutlasses at the insides of canoes. When a Carib intends to make one of these *gommiers*, he chooses a tall *dacryoda hexandra* in the high woods and fells it at the time of the new moon. The shape is roughed out where it lies, and the centre excavated. The maker then summons his friends, and the hull is dragged to the rhythm of special songs down to the foot-hills with ropes made of liana. There, under a tree near his hut, he trusses the ends and splays it open by filling it with water and then stones, and finally expands it amidships over a slow fire, keeping the sides wide, like an alligator's mouth, with sticks. The sides of the craft are heightened with planks which converge at one end in a high blade; the seams in the planks are caulked, and when its two masts and a mizzen and lugsail have been prepared, the vessel is ready for launching.

Travel by sea is still a passion among the Caribs; for trade, for smuggling, and sometimes purely for fun. They have been known to sail their canoes far beyond their little archipelago, sometimes as far as Cuba, the Guianas, and the Spanish Main. They have cronies in all the neighbouring islands, and frequently they return from their expeditions in a condition of ancestral tipsiness, harmlessly capsizing several times on the way. They are accomplished smugglers, and load their pirogues with pigs and chickens and turkeys, which they exchange for the cheap untaxed liquor in Marie Galante or the Saints or even Guadeloupe, and then slip back to their creeks without paying the excise duty. The Government send motor boats to patrol the island waters and catch them red-handed, but as the Caribs work by night and have known every cove and rock and current for centuries before the Europeans arrived in the Antilles, it is usually a vain task. A serious smuggling incident occurred in the '30s. Five policemen penetrated the Carib territory and seized a quantity of contraband rum and tobacco. A battle with sticks began and a riot ensued, with two Caribs killed and two injured, while some of the police suffered injuries; it was only quelled by the Navy dispatching a ship to the Carib waters, which fired into the high woods with its heavy guns. It was then that, as a punishment, the kingship was abolished, and the royal mace carried away to Government House in Roseau.

It is a problem to know what course the authorities should take if a Carib commits a capital offence. For, being the last specimens of a race that is almost extinct, each pure Carib has a worldwide importance that transcends by far all legal considerations.

When the time came to leave the Carib capital, we sent the porters and ponies ahead to Solybia, and the king and his council accompanied us on foot. George Frederick is a dignified, rather melancholy grandee. As we came from Mrs Napier, I think he must have assumed we were in some official position, as, all the way up and down the ravines, his discourse was of minor vexations that he suggested we might have rectified in the island's Chamber in Roseau. This small Jeremiad was only stemmed by the diversion of one of his council killing a snake which was wriggling across the path. He drove the point of his walking-stick into the nape of its neck and pinned it to the ground. The snake lashed in the dust, straightening and shrinking to a tight spring, and finally coiling its length round the stick in a spiral. When it died, the elder raised his stick slowly in the air like the staff of Aesculapius.

During a rest on the mountainside, we produced a bottle of whisky which we had bought at the Syrian shop. It did one good to see the way their eyes lit up. We drank in turns, and the enormous swigs of the Caribs brought the whisky-level down two inches at a time. I took out Mr Douglas Taylor's treatise on the Caribs, which gives a vocabulary of the few dozen Carib and Arawak words that have survived the deluge of Créole. None of them had ever seen it, and they were flattered and excited when they heard us clumsily pronouncing the words of their ancient tongue: *Ahahoua* or *Twahleiba*, a snake; *Aotou*, a fish; *Canoa*,

Couriala, Oucouni, a boat; *Calleenago,* men; *Careepfouna,* women ... An impish elder, who seemed the brightest of the council, pronounced a word that doubled them all up with laughter. The king archly whispered the meaning. This was followed by other words that sent them all into paroxysms of hilarity. It is clear that the improper terms of the ancient language will be the last to die.

Our three porters looked substantial and normal after the Caribs, who, even after such a short time, began to seem as curious and unfamiliar as Martians. As we rode southwards we saw one or two more in the woods, a shade darker each time, but still straight-haired and Mongoloid, and the children, gathering sticks by the road, were as pretty as Japanese dolls. Finally the miscegenate fringe petered out and we were again in the heart of the Negro world.

Every few miles the porters sat down for a rest, and we dismounted and smoked cigarettes until it was time to move on. One of them was a good-looking young man, who sang Créole songs in a soft voice or whistled without ceasing. I asked him what he thought of the Caribs. 'Dey're maad people,' he answered, 'but dey got lovely, lovely hair.' His mouth opened in a large smile as he passed his palm over his own scalp: 'Not like me.'

The police station where we stayed that night in Castle Bruce was a verandahed bungalow perched on a smooth lawny hill with an old cannon lying on the grass. A police corporal, trim and martial in his blue serge and scarlet piped trousers, ran down the steps to meet us as we rode into the village.

The morning's ride brought us at midday to Saint Sauveur, a forest village with an old grey church, a massive presbytery, and a ruined and overgrown sugar mill. We tied the horses to a mango tree, and, settling among the sea-grape a few yards from the waves, peeled our avocado pears, and watched the children playing cricket on the green. The bats were made of the hard end of palm branches, and every now and then the soft ball would land in our midst, and we would throw it back. A schoolmistress appeared in the door of the school and blew a whistle, and they all fell into line and trotted along to the benches under the trees for lessons out of doors. The young schoolmaster took the older boys and girls on one side, and the schoolmistress led the kinder-garten class away to a clump of palm trees at the other end of the green. Looking out of the windows of the schoolroom into whose empty precincts we ventured for a moment before we rode away, we listened to the lesson. 'The Police Force was founded by Sir Robert Peel,' the schoolmaster said, 'and the policemen were colloquially known as peelers.' The air was full of the scratching of slates. A little girl, just under our window, whose head was covered with little blue bows, laboured away, her tongue sticking out of the corner of her mouth with concentration. Her slate pencil traced 'Colokwealy known as pillars'.

All the afternoon, sudden downpours alternated with bright sunshine, and we would halt in clearings for ten minutes to let our clothes dry during the sunny spells. In the late afternoon the clouds blew away and the denseness of the forest opened into a loosely connected system of dells and great clumps of creeper-hung trees, a vague, steaming and antediluvian world. The road was then enclosed once more between dank wet woods, heavy with melancholy, and full of the sad cooing of wood pigeons. Ropes of convolvulus looped their rainy flowers over our heads, and as we rode underneath them through the soft mud, a green and black hummingbird, no larger than a dragonfly, flickered almost motionlessly over the white trumpets, every few seconds plunging its needle-thin beak inside like a duellist.

The path brought us down again to the roar of the sea, and a long avenue of tall palms leading to the estuary of a river. The rain began, and our horses broke into a gallop through the slender trunks that brought us, after a mile, into the green pathway lined with stilted huts that is the main street of Rosalie.

Looking out of the window of the little police station, we saw a strange and wonderful sight. A brilliant lawn rose from the banks of the river to the forest's edge, where banana and palm, paw-paw, breadfruit and mango trees were glistening under the raindrops in a score of shades of green. In the middle of this smooth expanse stood a little grey Norman abbey, its architecture, in the sweeping rain, looking as authentic in detail as Iffley Church or Barfrestone. Sturdy pillars with heavy capitals blossomed into deep Romanesque arches jagged with herring-bone and dog-tooth, as though a team of seraphim had uprooted it from the yew trees and gravestones of an English village and flown it across the ocean to this tropical glade. The sun went down and the rain stopped, and the darkness filled with armies of fireflies.

Our ponies had been, all through the journey, a wearisome cause of change and debate and altercation, and when we set out soon after dawn next morning, only Joan's pony, Jockey Girl, remained from the original cavalcade. Costa and I mounted two newcomers called Fury and Guzman. After a mile or two of the scrub of the estuary and another slender suspension bridge, we ascended a pathway that climbed due westwards away from the coast up the sides of a tremendous canyon towards the central watershed of Dominica. One or two forest villages dropped behind us, and as the hours passed, the forest turned into something quite different from anything we had so far seen. The trees grew to enormous heights and locked us into a dank and desolate tube of a pathway cut on a narrow shelf out of the tufa. Everything dripped and rotted. Breaks in the trees revealed nothing but towering wooded mountainsides and rolling hollows and gorges roofed with millions of leaves. The green was only broken by hibiscus and convolvulus and the silver grey trunks of the Trumpet-Wood tree. This is a beautiful and delicate thing with thin silver boughs all curling up from the stem at the identically-spaced points in semicircles like the branches of Jewish candelabra, ending in sparsely growing leaves the same shape as those of the fig tree, but much larger; grey green on one side and on the other, silver white. In Créole it is called *Bois Canon*, because, according to one porter, its trunk, when broken, makes a report like a gun firing. The second said it was because it explodes if it is used as fuel, while the third maintained that it owes its name merely to its hollowness, which suggests the barrel of a cannon. This botanic argument carried us for an hour or two through the awe-inspiring high woods. The only person we met was a wild-looking Negro sitting on a rock with a flint-lock across his knees, the perfect image of a runaway Maroon in the seventeenth century. He showed us his pouch full of lead shot, an antique powder horn on a bandolier, and a set of spare flints beautifully shaped to fit between the screw-jaws of the hammer. He declared he was out after blue parrots. When we had left him behind, Antony, the tallest of the porters who sang charmingly most of the way in Créole, said he was a very bad man indeed, but would not enlarge on it. We saw none of these blue parrots, though we were eternally peering up into the branches. The only bird we heard all day was the Siffleur Montagne, which piped long lugubrious sounds, usually on one note, but occasionally on two; every few minutes; a noise so melancholy that it seemed the perfect emanation of these sad and beautiful forests. It haunts the high woods of Dominica and nowhere else in the world.

About noon the forest thinned and vanished, and the steep slopes were covered with low shrubs. The valley fell away for miles, sinking and winding down to the distant mouth of the river at Rosalie, which was just visible on the faint edge of the sea. The full force of the Trade Winds seemed to blow us and our little mounts up the last steep zig-zag of the mountain, and over the lip of a crater into an enormous windless punchbowl that was filled with clouds.

They cleared as we descended. At the bottom of this hollow lay a large pool, a cold and secret-looking stretch of water winding its irregular shape through water plants and weeds. Fragments of cloud lingered in the branches of the forest. The place was disturbingly still and impressive. It is, understandably, regarded by the islanders with superstitious awe. Oldmixon, the early eighteenth-century traveller, has set down a legend, current in his time, of a serpent that dwelt at the bottom of the Freshwater Lake, whose head enclosed a sparkling jewel of inestimable price. The jewel was usually concealed by a membrane 'Like that of a Man's Eyelid, and when it went to drink or sported itself in the deep Bottom, it fully discovered it, and the Rocks all about received a wonderful lustre from the Fire issuing out of that Precious Gem'. Other legends say that it is inhabited by a Lorelei that drags unwary travellers, Hylas-like, down to her underwater palaces. Sir Algernon records yet another tradition of a Carib chief who dived into the bottomless lake, and then, after swimming for miles through the dark entrails of Dominica, appeared again in the sea to the south west of the island.

When we climbed through the western edge of the crater, a different world confronted us. It was a clear, sunny, Arcadian land of falling wooded slopes and valleys and forested vistas that had none of the fierceness of the strange labyrinth through which we had ridden for so many hours. The sky was almost bare of clouds, and, miles away, at the end of the wooded valley, the Caribbean Sea flung back the sun from an infinity of brilliant points. Our height seemed to have lifted the horizon three-quarters of the way to the zenith. A peasant, climbing from Roseau, halted in the shade of a tree to mop his brow and ask us what it was like 'on windwardside'.

The watersheds of these islands are the boundary lines between different countries. Windwardside is the region of daybreak and morning, and of thousands of clouds blown up by the wind from the turbulent Atlantic on to the sodden mountainside; a country of terrible rocks and waves. Leewardside is the kingdom of the afternoon and sunset, of the clear sky where the clouds have shed their harm; of smooth reefs and lagoons and the glittering waters of a sea walled in by a drowned mountain range and machicolated by islands. An afternoon world.

Far beyond the horizon, fifty leagues due west of the mountain where we stood lay the little desert island of Aves. It floats there quite by itself in the empty Caribbean. The pleasant isle of Aves, celebrated by Kingsley and Kipling, played a great part in the time of the buccaneers. Père Labat was blown there on board a French corsair a hundred and fifty miles off his course. He found two English ladies, Mrs Hamilton and a friend, stranded on Aves with the crew of an English frigate that had come to grief, but for whom succour was expected daily. The monk gallantly rescued them, and carried them to St Kitts, as they were on their way from Barbados to spend Christmas in Antigua.

He describes it as a pleasant little island, looking, from a distance, like a sand-bank, but when they dropped anchor – 'in clear water, three and a half fathoms deep, with sandy bottom, half a pistol shot from the land' – it turned out to be plentifully covered with bushes and cashiman, soursop and guava trees, whose presence there was due, he presumed, to sea birds which had swallowed the seed in the Windward Islands, and dropped them here. Aves, and the little reefs lying nearby, were white with bird-lime, and the thousands of sea birds were so thick on the sand 'and so proud' that they refused to make way for him. Only by inflicting severe correction with his walking stick could he clear a passage through their midst. Gulls, plover, widgeon and all kinds of water-fowl, including flamingoes, abounded. It is a favourite nesting ground for the frigate or man-o'-war bird (a turbulent black creature with a white chest and a forty-inch wing span that we often saw flying restlessly along the shores of the islands). 'But if,' he says, 'orange and lemon trees are discovered there in later times, I take pleasure in informing the public that they will have me to thank, as I sowed a number of seeds of both of them, which might be of great relief to those that Providence takes thither . . .'

The monk stayed several days in Aves. They caught some of the turtles which swim round the island in scores, and he taught the Englishwomen to make a 'boucan' of turtle *à la Guadeloupéenne* which they washed down with draughts of cider, beer, canary and Madeira, of which they had salvaged several pipes from the English wreck. They in turn taught him to cook a breast of Irish beef in the English way, and how to make *pâtés en pot* and black-puddings of turtle-meat, 'and I know not how many stews, besides, with which I could fill an entire volume, if the yearning should take me to print an Anglo-American cookery book with instructions for serving a dinner of a hundred and twenty-five places magnificently, and without expense, on a desert island'. They became great friends, and, when they weighed anchor, the monk says that they 'let no opportunity slip of praising the politeness of our filibusters'.

The old woman who had been arraigned for murder was acquitted (to the general satisfaction) the afternoon we arrived back in Roseau, and condemned, I think, to a year's imprisonment. We were just in time to hear the fine summing-up of the Puisne Judge of the Windward Islands.

The food in Roseau was pretty bad. After Martinique it was incredible that such disastrous results could be attained with the same raw materials. Terrible pink soups appeared, and potatoes disguised with Daddy's Favourite Sauce, on whose awfulness it would be unpatriotic to enlarge. But the puddings were the most interesting, and as we laboured with them, washing down intractable mouthfuls with Big Tree Burgundy, we invented names for them; a game that, in a perverted fashion, made us look forward to their appearance. Carib Shape and Empire-Building Blanc-mange were followed by other marvels which only the names of Crimean battles seemed to fit: Inkerman Mould, the Redan, Sebastopol Pudding and Balaklava Helmet. These banquets were crowned by coffee that must have been made out of a bedstead which had been hammered to powder.

But these experiences were unable to break the charm of Dominica and the Dominicans, and of the little capital. The maid in Sutton House was tremendously old, kind and motherly in a starched cap, and appropriately called Nanny, whom the faintest suggestion of a joke on our part would send off into transports of delight. Seeing that we looked a bit hangdog over our meals, she brought us a plateful of fried frogs – *cwapaud* – which were very good indeed. It is a justly celebrated Dominican dish.

A strangely Victorian atmosphere pervaded the hotel. Heavy mahogany furniture filled the parlour, and a framed reproduction of Bubbles hung on the wall beside a calendar for 1882. Torsos of members of the Royal Family in ovals of laurel surrounded a faded and leafy prospect of Windsor Castle and the river. Only the yellow and insect-tunnelled music on top of the piano – *Hitchy-koo, Everybody's doing it*, and *There's a long, long trail a-winding* – suggested a more recent period. After dinner a coloured girl came in and sat down at the piano stool, and the room was filled with the sound of early rag-time. 'Every night,' this flapper-like figure sang, 'Mister Moon comes syncopating'; then after a pause –

> You can't get away from it (stop),
> Get away from it,
> You can't get away from it at all.

When she left, Nanny's hands were locked in rapture. She described to us Roseau in carnival time – the songs, calypsos and fancy dresses, when 'all young fellows, they run maasked'. But some of the songs were not fitting. 'The words, oh they make you blush!' she said, and gave her surprising squeak of laughter. 'The songs is *terrible*. But the Carnival Improvement Committee change that next year.'

It was our last night in Dominica, and hearing that there was to be some singing in a public hall, we hastened up the road, as there was an hour to spare before the *St Laurent* arrived.

Dr Chi-Chi was performing some conjuring tricks to a crowded audience. But after he had removed, to deep sighs of wonder, the last egg from his mouth, he put on a paper hat like a bishop's mitre, and took a shack-shack in each hand. The calypso band struck up. Dr Chi-Chi, who had a sad and distinguished face, was obviously of Hindu or Moslem origin. Flexing his knees slightly, and treading the measure of the brazen beat of the band, he began singing a song which was composed in Dominica by the Pottesville Calypso Bros. It was encored again and again, by an audience practically epileptic with laughter. At about the fifth repetition, I went outside, and heard the siren of the *St Laurent* wailing impatiently, so we had to run all the way down to the quay. But before leaving, a neighbour gave me a copy of the song. The atmosphere, the syntax and the scansion of this piece of folk poetry are so queer that I will repeat it word for word at its full length. '*Vigil convinced me gal,*' the Doctor announced each time amidst applause.

> Vigil convinced me gal in the palm of his hand-a
> By telling the gal I'm a rogue and a married man-a;
> And the gal with such a big explanation
> Told Vigil that I love your carnation.
>> But no, no, Vigil, you can't come here
>> And take my bacouta – I bet you that.

Each time the words 'but no, no, Vigil', came in, the Doctor spun slowly round two or three times, rattling his shack-shacks as the audience broke in with the chorus. Then –

> Vigil sat up a night, and kiss up the girl-a,
> And told the girl I love you like sweet banana.
> I want you to leave Georges for the sake of bananas.
> Come to me, you'll get mucho bananas.
>> But no, no, Vigil, etc.

> When I went into the room, I saw a kind of a something.
> I held my head and I started to bawl for Police.
> Oh, Police, Police, come and rescue me lover,
> My lover is under the cover.
>> But no, no, Vigil, etc.

> When the Police went, Vigil start to explain.
> Georges, my friend, I didn't try to put you in trouble.
> I just wanted to see how much banana
> This woman can eat in an hour.
>> But no, no, Vigil, etc.

DOMINICA

I shook my head and I say, We two are pals.
I bought me rum and we drunk it as to be millties.
But the woman without a bit of shame
Jump on me and held me radiator.
I say, Stop it, woman. I gone break
    this bottle on your Studebaker.

CHAPTER 6

Barbados

The only occupants of Barbados, when the English first landed there in 1605, were a number of wild swine that had been left there by the Portuguese on an earlier visit. Since then the history of the island has varied very little. The Arawaks and the Caribs, in their ascent of the Caribbean Chain, were either unaware of its existence or found that it lay too far from the route of their advance. Columbus also failed to discover it, and its records date only from the beginning of the seventeenth century, making it, historically speaking, the youngest of all the islands. It has been in uninterrupted British possession ever since, and, having been spared the conflicting occupations and cultures of the other islands, it has remained English to an almost unbelievable degree.

Barbados is geographically and geologically, as well as historically, different from the other islands, for it does not belong to the long volcanic mountain range in which the Caribbees are rooted. It is a coral island which has worked its way to the surface here fortuitously, rearing its mild contours above the water as a monument to the industry of many millions of zoophytes.

Arriving, as we did, straight from the precipitous scenery of Dominica, with the mountains of Martinique and Guadeloupe still fresh in our minds, the flatness of the skyline of Barbados came almost as a shock. But wandering through the streets of Bridgetown, we were both compensated and bewildered by the very familiarity of everything. It was a completely English town, a town on the edge of London, and the wide, clean streets appeared to be almost as full of white as of coloured Barbadians. All the familiar landmarks were there – the one-price bazaars, the chemists with well-known names and the multiplicity of teashops. We paused a long moment before the window of a dressmaker in Broad Street. The reader will understand the extreme English-ness of the Barbadian capital, and capture the exact shade of its identity with the Mother Country, by studying this advertisement of the Modern Dress Shoppe. 'The name of this Establishment,' it runs, 'was selected with a very definite purpose; namely, to enshrine an ideal. The employment of the designation SHOPPE may appear to be an anachronism, particularly when thrown into relief by its association with the term MODERN. There is no conflict of ideas, indeed the contrary is the case, for upon your first visit you will realize that, whilst every modern requirement can be procured, it is proffered with a gesture reminiscent of other days.'

The more one sees of the little capital, the more it resembles a London suburb. But, after leaving the thoroughfares of the centre – all of which bear homely names like Broad Street, Chapman's Road, Trafalgar Square or Lightfoot Lane – and when the region of the Women's Self-Help Association and the Ladies' Lyceum Club had fallen behind, glimpses are caught of fine wooden houses in the Regency style retreating from the road among groups of trees. A large savannah encircled by a race-course encloses a grandstand and a polo ground where grooms walk blanketed race-horses under the palms. The little contiguous towns of Hastings and Worthing faithfully echo in miniature the seaside resorts of England; and the Marine Hotel, the Windsor, the Ocean View and the Balmoral, bask placidly in the sunshine like advertisements of Torquay. Old gentlemen in tussore suits and panama hats sniff the ozone, and pink Anglo-Saxon babies, safe under their muslin mosquito nets, slumber in prams. The cricket pitches and golf links melt into the open country.

The rest of the island is a low, rolling panorama of cane-fields, 166 square miles in area – the size of the Isle of Wight or of a small English county which, in many ways, it closely resembles. For the omnipresent sugar-cane, sweeping and ruffling across the undulations, is wonderfully reminiscent of an English pastureland under a wheat harvest, and the turning sails of occasional windmills further an illusion which only the colonnades of palm trees belie. This gentle landscape, with the silver-grey arrows of the sugar-cane puffing and bending in the breeze, possesses a smooth and restful charm. The cool wind penetrates everywhere, for the island offers no obstruction to the westward blowing Trades, which ferry their cargo of clouds high overhead, sparing Barbados many of the terrible deluges of the other Antilles, and reserving their spite for the cones of St Vincent and the Grenadines. The air is clear and invigorating, and, at moments, almost European.

The little island is one of the most densely populated of the West Indies. Every inch of its surface is devoted to cultivation or sport – a factor which has drained from the scenery any wild or haphazard element that it may have possessed in the past. There are few points in the island in which houses and people are invisible. At every step one feels that this was the island where sugar-cane was first planted, and where its cultivation has attained the highest pitch of intensity and perfection. Barbados was, from the beginning of its colonization, one of the most profitable markets for the slave trade, and, with the labour of their well-stocked barracoons, the slave-owning oligarchy of the island, untroubled by foreign invasion or occupation, lived for many happy generations in solid and tranquil prosperity. Slave-management and sugar crops became their chief preoccupation and theme, and Trollope reports that the splendour of their cane harvests and the excellence of their rum and molasses were topics that ousted all others from the conversation of the white Barbadians. They were known then as the Bims: a syllable suggestive of solidity and security.* With such a record of well-being and authority it would be difficult for the Barbadians to escape the charge of self-satisfaction with which writers have so often taxed them.

Their conceit (if so strong a word may be used) has the curious obverse today of an extreme touchiness. In writing a book like this, one is often warned that all reference to the Colour problem must be made with the utmost circumspection; and it is true that the Negro race is often, understandably, sensitive to unintentional slights. But this readiness to take offence is the mildest of foibles compared with the touchiness of the white Barbadians, whose suspicion of foreign criticism goes to extravagant lengths. Unless one is prepared for the execration of a community from which one has after all received nothing but civility, one must think ten times before setting down anything about them that is not praise.

The term 'Little England' which the Barbadians apply to their home is no empty boast; and if the verdict of modern opinion has gone against the sort of English life on which the Barbadians have modelled theirs, it is not the Barbadians' fault. But it is hard to stay long in the island without feeling that Barbados reflects most faithfully the social and intellectual values and prejudices of a Golf Club in Outer London, for example, or of the married quarters of a barracks in Basutoland, which are not England's most interesting or precious contributions to world civilization. Many travellers find in the island a tropical exuberance

* It is interesting that the nicknames of the Negroes for their white masters usually begin with the letter B: Bim in Barbados, Béké in the French Antilles, and Buckra in Jamaica.

of exactly those values to which they had most joyfully bidden farewell in England.

But Barbados is pre-eminent in the Antilles for the beauty of its country houses. They excel anything which is to be seen in the French islands or, with the possible exception of Jamaica, in the other British West Indies. Labat, when he called here, was impressed by the appearance of Bridgetown, by the solidity of the buildings, the cleanliness of the streets, and the warehouses filled to the eaves with every kind of merchandise, but was stirred to greater wonder still by the plantation houses. 'They are even better built,' he writes, 'than those in the town. They are large, well ventilated, and all plentifully supplied with glazed windows. The layout of the rooms is commodious and well planned. They are almost all accompanied by beautiful alleys of tamarind, or by those great orange trees which we call Shaddock, or by other cool trees which bestow upon the houses a smiling aspect. The opulence and good taste of the inhabitants may be remarked in their furniture, which is magnificent, and in their silver, which they have in considerable quantities ... They eat much meat and little bread, and their tables are well served. They have excellent cooks and very fine linen, and much order and cleanliness. People of distinction have live partridges brought from Europe, which they keep in coops ... One can say that no people exist who spend more, or who go to greater lengths, to have all that is rarest and best from foreign lands, even the most distant. Their houses are well stocked with every kind of wine and liqueur and they are delighted if their guests are hard put to it to find their way home. It is to avoid accidents that might befall them, if the roads were bad, that they take special care of their upkeep.' All of this holds good today, except that the excellence of the roads, though they very often fulfil their original charitable office, may now be attributed to more general and prosaic causes. Every mile or so the sugar-cane is broken by a long avenue of trees leading to a manor house. A double flight of steps unites in a pillared portico, which leads into a splendid hall; and another flight of stairs ascends to a balustraded gallery into which the bedrooms open through finely carved and moulded doorways. None of these houses is very large, but some of them are, in their particular way, perfect. Here, at any rate, Barbados reflected all that England had best to offer, and indeed outlived her in architectural merit. For these houses, which an English observer would at once ascribe to the period of the Adam brothers, were built in the 1830s after the terrible hurricane of 1831, which demolished most of the old buildings and uprooted nearly all the trees in Barbados. But the island profited by an architectural time-lag of thirty years, and, while architecture at home was declining into less attractive forms, the manor houses of Barbados were rebuilt in the modes of one of the finest periods of English architecture. The cellars and the first floor are usually of stone and the upper storeys of planks in the American colonial style, with beautifully sculpted woodwork inside. The rooms are large and nobly planned and filled with beautiful furniture carved out of West Indian timber by Barbadian joiners and cabinet-makers in the designs of Sheraton and Hepplewhite. Miniatures and portraits of pleasant-faced, bewigged ancestors abound, and old English silver and all the agreeable amenities of life prove that, whatever may justly be said on other scores in detraction of the little colony, in architectural and domestic civilization it far excelled the other Antilles.

By great good luck we were redeemed from the usual squalors of our island sojourns to spend part of our stay in Barbados in one of these charming houses. For almost the most beautiful of them, Canefield House, is owned by Mrs Nicolas Embiricos, a cousin of Costa's, whose hospitality altered our whole life in Barbados. From mooching morosely about in one of the seaside hotels and growing bilious with rage over certain aspects of Barbadian life, we were transported to this refuge of great, cool rooms and, under the influences of Canefield and of our hostess's kindness and love for the island, we felt the acerbity of any future attack on the colony being gently blunted. Our days turned into a delicious sequence of bathes on the west coast and drives all over the island to look at the considerable amount of architectural beauties and curiosities; of visits to Barbadian and English neighbours or American compatriots of our hostess. There were days of reading and writing among the flower-ing trees in the garden, in front of a little pool bright with water-hyacinths; and in the evenings, memorable dinners in a long room where the walls were dimly resplendent, by the light of the candles in their enormous, cylindrical hurricane glasses, with replicas of the frescoes of Pompeii.

Our drives with Anne Embiricos resembled mild antiquarian rambles through a shire that had drifted loose from the coast of England and floated all the way to these tropic waters, its familiar fields having acquired outlandish flowers and trees on the journey, but never in great enough quantities to impair the deception. The roads lay in shallow ravines below the level of the surrounding countryside, crossing gullies on massive stone bridges, or sinking into hollows filled with a sudden damp profusion of undergrowth and trees. But they would always rise again, to continue their undulating courses through the fluttering grey-green dunes of sugar-cane as they lapsed in their gentle heave and fall to the rocky windward, or to the calm leeward, coast.

In a hollow beyond a spinney of tall mahogany, south of the township of Bathsheba, a beautiful Palladian building, reclining dreamily on the shores of a lake among lawns and balustrades and great shady trees, suddenly appeared, its columns and pediments conjuring up, in the afternoon sunlight, some enormous country seat in the Dukeries. It was Codrington College, founded at the beginning of the eighteenth century, and endowed from the revenues of his plantations, by Christopher Codrington,* the Governor-General of the Leeward Islands. A little farther on, the road climbed through an avenue of enormous cabbage palms, each of them between eighty and a hundred feet high. Their succession of smooth, grey trunks rose as straight and symmetrically as the peristyle of a Greek temple, bursting high in the air into a series of exaggerated Corinthian capitals.

Sam Lord's Castle, a curious house on the rocky windward coast, was the goal of one of our excursions. The roof is surrounded by machicolations that from a distance lend it the appearance of a fortress cut out of cardboard. The inside, with its pillars of mahogany, its carved trophies and cornices of stucco and chandeliers hanging from the centre of plaster cart-wheels, is strange and overpowering and convincingly grandiose. It was built, according to local rumours, on the proceeds of a certain Samuel Lord from the wrecking of cargo vessels which, like a will-o'-the-wisp, he lured to their destruction on stormy nights by hanging lanterns in the trees on the jagged rocks below the house. It is now a hotel (or a 'Club'). Its stout masonry resisted the 1831 hurricane, but the scaffolding that had been erected for some minor repairs was blown clean through the air and dropped in a yard three miles away.

On the way back to Canefield House we passed through the more hilly district of Scotland, and observed, working in the fields or sitting in the doorways of miserable wooden shacks, not the Negro figures to which the eye is accustomed in such settings in the West Indies, but ragged white men with blue eyes and tow-coloured hair bleached by the sun. This little population of Redlegs, as they are called, are descendants of the followers of the Duke of Monmouth, who, after their defeat at Sedgemoor, were deported to Barbados by order of Judge Jeffreys at the Bloody Assizes. They have remained here ever since, in the same humble plight as when they were first herded ashore. Labat and many

*This family, of which the victor of the battle of Navarino was a member, is one of those which owned vast estates in the West Indies, and whose name recurs again and again in the history of the Islands.

other writers talk of the presence in the islands of Irish deportees shipped here by Cromwell after Wexford and Drogheda, and it is perhaps due to them that the closest affinity of the Barbadian way of speaking is with the Irish accent. But this is now scarcely recognizable. Its nasal tone makes it resemble, for the first few minutes, the American accent, and it is further disguised by the 'yawny-drawly' delivery of which Coleridge speaks. If, as seems likely, this is the origin of the Barbadian speech, it has discovered the secret of purging every trace of charm from the Irish brogue. It sounds terrible. Some writers have succeeded in detecting West Country inflexions in the language of the Redlegs, miraculously surviving from the time when their ancestors were quiet country people in Dorset and Devon and Somerset, but to an unskilled listener there is nothing now to distinguish their speech from that of their fellow-islanders. For the Barbadian accent is the only thing in the island which is common, in some degree, to every stratum of society. Like the dialects of England a few generations ago, it is a regional, not a social thing.

Unruly Scots were also packed off to Barbados in the early days, and the numbers of the original Redlegs or, as they are alternately styled, the Mean Whites, were steadily augmented by the deportation of convicts from England to the West Indies, who lived here in the same loathsome circumstances as the slaves, and when their sentences had expired, often settled here. It is significant of the gulf that yawns between them and the other white islanders that even in this colony where a white complexion is considered to be of inestimable and intrinsic merit, they seldom rise in the world, or play, as the Negroes do, a rôle in island politics. These pale, Nordic people, standing barefoot in the dust with loads of sugar-cane on their heads and gazing listlessly as the trim limousines go bowling past, are pathetic and moving figures, and their aspect has none of the cheerfulness of the inhabitants of the Saints or of the pleasant solidity of the whites of the Guadeloupean hinterland. They look like poor devils and nothing else.

Owing to the smallness of the island, all the interesting things in Barbados seem to juxtapose each other with a gratifying abundance. At one moment we were wandering through the streets of the old capital at Speightstown, and a few minutes later peering through iron bars under a mahogany wood peopled by wild monkeys (for which we gazed in vain) into the dungeon where once the newly-landed slaves were locked. Soon afterwards we passed a gully choked with tropical vegetation which hides the entrance to a system of caves and a measureless subterranean river. These caves used to be a hiding-place for runaway slaves. During the night, with their naked black bodies invisible in the darkness, an old writer* records, the maroons would creep forth and range through the countryside, stealing pigs and potatoes and plantains, and then, safe in their grottoes, 'they would feast all day upon what they stole the night before'. This free life would continue until they were hunted down with hounds which had been specially trained for these occasions by the sport-loving planters.

Under the palm trees of a quiet beach in St James's Parish, in the west of the island, we beheld the arresting vision of three half-built Spanish galleons, their sterns climbing into high castellated poops, offering their new timbers to the sunlight like the breast-bones of whales. Negro shipwrights were sawing planks and hammering home wooden pegs. In a hut near by, a young Englishman unfolded the blue prints of the superannuated vessels and the heaps of canvas that were to be rigged to the castled masts and the spars. They were exact reproductions of the three ships in which Christopher Columbus first discovered the archipelago – the *Santa Maria*, the *Niña* and the *Pinta* – destined for use in an Arthur Rank film that was to be shot at some future date.

We encountered on the same day another spectacle that was, at first glance, utterly mysterious. In a clearing among the trees about a hundred yards from the sea, a group of young white Barbadians in bathing drawers was assembled round the mouth of a deep hole. It was several yards in diameter and, to within a yard or two of the surface, full of water. Pipes and ropes disappeared into this mysterious well, and a noisy pumping machine drained great quantities of water out of it, leading it away some distance down the slope of the beach. Young men, working away for all they were worth, replaced each other at a stirrup pump, and a constant circle of bubbles disturbed the surface. Every now and then a petrol-tin full of mud and stones was hauled from the depths, emptied, and lowered into the water again.

After a time an object like the head of a giant grasshopper appeared above the water, and was followed up the ladder by a plump and rosy middle-aged body. A gas mask, that had been turned into a primitive diving helmet, was unbuckled, and a mild-faced elderly gentleman confronted us. The helmet was fitted to the head of one of his colleagues who climbed slowly down into the water and vanished.

Mr Branch, whose appearance suggested that of a vicar with a quiet country living, gravely explained that they had only a few more yards to go, but that it might take some time as they could only work during

* Ligon.

the week-ends. 'But it's there all right,' he said. 'We're bound to strike it soon.'

'Strike what?'

His blue eyes opened wide. 'Why, buried treasure. There is gold down there and quite a lot of it. About so much.' He opened his arms to their full extent. 'Possibly a statue of the Madonna in solid gold or a chest full of pieces of eight or doubloons.'

This particular stretch of shore is well known to have been a hiding-place of the buccaneers for treasure captured from the Spanish Plate Fleet which sailed from Cartagena to the home ports of Corunna or Cadiz. It was invariably a target for the onslaught of French and English fili-busters based in the Windward Islands, and, as Barbados, except for occasional Portuguese visits (or, one record suggests, for Caribs, that came to the island from time to time to celebrate a cannibal feast and then sailed away again), was virtually uninhabited for the whole of the sixteenth century, there was no safer *cache*.

Mr Branch and his friends had no chart to work on. The gold had been located by means far beyond the scope of ordinary comprehension. Mr Branch is one of these rare people with the gift of divining, but he is not only a dowser for water, but for virtually any mineral matter lying below the surface of the earth or the sea. So far so good. But he is able to divine buried substances not only by standing above the actual stretch of ground that conceals them, but by suspending a plumbline from the fingers of his right hand over a large-scale map. The plummet, hanging on the end of its string, begins to rotate and draws his hand to a certain area of the map, and the cycle of the rotations gradually diminishes until the plummet is once more still, and pointing inexorably to a certain spot. If he is in search of water he holds between his fingers a piece of blue cloth an inch or two long; and if gold, yellow; and so on. He showed us the different pieces of material carefully arranged between the pages of a book like pressed flowers. He had located gold in British Guiana in this extraordinary way, though he had never been there. Prospectors had dug, and the gold was there in ample quantities. 'But, of course, this method only indicates the area roughly,' he continued. 'It depends on the scale of the map.' In the present case the map had indicated the position of the gold within a dozen yards or so. This called for more detailed work on the spot with the divining rod. But it didn't take long. The reactions of the rod were so violent that there was no doubt at all. He produced this instrument – two springy lengths of metal bound together at one end and spreading at the other into a fork. Placing the joined ends against his stomach and grasping the two prongs, with a piece of yellow stuff held between the fingers of his right hand, he leant over the hole. The rod dipped, and then recovered, and then dipped again, repeating the motion several times. He counted the movements and explained that each one indicated another yard's distance between himself and the gold below the surface. He gave us the rod in turn, placed it in position, and rested his right hand lightly on one of ours to preserve the magic touch, and, with each of us, the mysterious pull dragged the prongs and our hands down. There was no doubt about it. Without the touch of his hand, which exerted not the faintest pressure, there was no reaction at all. Could he divine, we asked, anything else except minerals? His soft eyes contemplated us for a moment. 'I can divine you.'

And he could. He asked Costa to give him something he was wearing. Costa gave him a handkerchief, and we walked to the water's edge. We bandaged his eyes, and placed him looking out to sea. Costa walked back a hundred yards and began to run across the beach. We told Mr Branch to begin, and he placed his rod in position and turned slowly round, holding the rod and the handkerchief, and slowly followed Costa's motion, swinging gently back when he doubled in his course, then forward again as he went straight on. Joan, leaving a book in his hands, went through the same process with the same results; and I finally gave him a belt, retreated a quarter of a mile away, and hid behind a long thicket of sea-grape; waving to Joan and Costa through a gap, so that Mr Branch could place his instrument and bring it into play. He turned slowly round and halted facing my hiding-place. I began to move slowly behind the cover, watching him through the leaves veer round into line, and then, as I ran at full speed in the opposite direction, gently follow the arc of my movements. I changed direction again and again, stopped, started again, and each time the distant figure moved in exact harmony with me as though we were two points on the same radius; he at the centre and I at the circumference. It was so unerring that I felt that he was almost commanding my movements. I returned slowly, moving round him in a circle three times, and three times dragging him right round. As I approached, walking barefoot and on tiptoe on the sand, I heard the blindfold figure saying: 'Very close now, very close indeed.' He held out the belt as I tiptoed up to him and undid the bandage and said: 'I think it's about my turn to dig again.' He bade us good-bye and walked towards the treasure-seekers' cavern. As we left, his masked head was just disappearing below the water level.

Anne drove us on with the feeling that we had seen something very close indeed to magic. We asked her, when we left, to let us know at once if they struck anything. But there has been no word so far.

These western strands of Barbados have a quality of reclusion and quietness that distinguishes them from the rest of the island. The woods of palm and casuarina enclose a scattering of solitary and beautiful houses which are a notable afterthought to the existing architectural achievement of the island. For these houses are new, though the coral rock of which they are built possesses, from the moment it is hewn, an almost miraculous patina, and the expanses of grass that surround them, though they may not have been planted a decade, appear to have been the preoccupation of gardeners for generations. They reflect, even more clearly than the old Barbadian houses, European nostalgia and allegiances. Sir Edward Cunard's house, lying aloof at the end of a tree-shaded vista of lawn whose confines are marked by pillared urns of the most Italianate and Augustan implication, authentically echoes the sobriety and the elegance of the Dutch seventeenth century. The tropical trees and the flowering shrubs that surround this beautiful building seem less a paradox than a docile approximation of nature to the feathery convention of landscape painters three centuries ago. At the bottom of the garden, a few hundred yards away among two mango trees by the sea-shore, the small pavilion of Caprarola rears its semi-circular arches over a balcony that opens as fittingly on these dark leaves and a panorama of tropical sea as upon the Roman Campagna. Poised on their plinth, on either side of the entrance, stone Cupids wrestle in the Caribbean afternoon.

Farther south, along the same deserted shore, not far from the friend's house from which we used to bathe, stood the half-built carcase of Mr Tree's house. This, too, was assembling in an architectural formula alien to the island, but which, by the same brilliant conjuring trick, seemed astonishingly appropriate and harmonious. For it was in the style of Palladio, suggesting the palace-villas of the Venetian plain: the Malcontenta, and still more, Maser. Owing to the porous texture of the coral, the great Vitruvian columns and pediment in the centre, and the two spreading wings arbitrarily but successfully warped into a shallow and colonnaded crescent, appear so antique and weathered that the building looks less like a house under construction than a Piranesi ruin. But instead of a minute three-corner-hatted figure pointing out to a companion an inscription with his malacca cane, a Barbadian fisherman, standing among his lobster-pots and the melancholy sea-grape at the water's edge, gazes up with wonder at the scaffolded façade. Its only drawback perhaps lies in its proximity to the sea. Properly to contemplate the noble proportions a helicopter would be needed, or the crow's nest of a windjammer lying a couple of furlongs out to sea.

*

The dispersal of the Jews from the Iberian peninsula which began with the edicts of Ferdinand and Isabella and which sprinkled the Low Countries, the Balkans and the Levant with Spanish-speaking Jews, once more set Jewry of the Latin world in motion. Maranos from Portugal were early settlers in Brazil, for the territory of the new world that lay to the east of the forty-sixth meridian of longitude (roughly speaking, east of a line running from north to south through a point to the east of the Amazon delta) was granted to Portugal in 1494 by a Bull of Pope Alexander VI Borgia at the treaty of Tordesillas. The rest, the Caribbees and all of North and the huge remainder of South America, fell to Spain. After the fall of Recife, enterprising Jews left Brazil and settled in likely trading points in the Caribbean, and many of the islands where the Jews are now extinct still shelter the cemeteries and ruined synagogues of these adventurous offshoots of the Sephardim.

A number of Jewish families took up their quarters in Barbados twenty years after the island was first annexed by the English, and the commerce and trade of the island prospered in their hands. 'Jews Street' in Bridgetown became the recognized commercial centre of the island, and names such as Lobo, Benjamin, Belasco, Elkin, Meyers, Danials, Samuel, Levi, Reuben, Massiah, Montefiore, Pinheiro and Da Costa – the last is still the name of a firm of Bridgetown merchants and of a monumental general stores in Broad Street – occur often in the history of the island. Some of these Marano families long ago adopted the Anglican faith, as the tablets in the churches prove. The Synagogue of Bridgetown fell into disuse. It was subject to the magnificent seventeenth-century Spanish-Portuguese Synagogue in the East End of London, whose fine Carolean panelling and gilding and sculpted festoons are such a surprise in those depressing streets. It is now the premises of the Barbados Turf Club. As they drive their motors into the garage, the members can still see the gravestone of an early rabbi who performed the rites of circumcision, according to the boast of his epitaph, 'with dexterity and to applause'.

Driving back from the coast of St James's Parish to Canefield, we would pass the old Moravian Church of Sharon. It is almost the earliest in the Western Hemisphere. Its massive white walls, deep arches and red roof, dominate fields of sugar like a small seventeenth-century *schloss* or a solid Hussite stronghold in the Czechoslovakian hills. The Catholic faith, owing to the unbroken English ownership of the island, is practically unknown, and Labat, rustling down the main street of Speightstown (where for several days he was the guest of a Church of England parson) in his Dominican habit, records the surprise of the burghers, who had never in their life before 'seen a bird of my feather'. But the island teems with Protestant sects. The wails of the Holy Rollers sail across the fields near Holetown; and through the windows of their churches glimpses can be caught of their ecstatic evolutions. Revivalism and rum are two important means of expression in a social system that affords few other outlets for the humbler coloured Barbadians. In more educated coloured circles a way out is often sought and found in disaffection.

In nothing is the illusion of England so compelling as in the Parish churches of Barbados. They stand alone in the canefields, their battle-mented belfries and vanes and pinnacles appearing over the tops of shelter-ing clumps of trees. Moss-covered crosses and headstones, or square hurricane graves embedded in the soil, scatter the turf inside the low walls with the haphazard charm of an English churchyard, and the interiors are full of the familiar and evocative aroma of hassocks and hymn-books and pews. Natural disasters have flung them down and the parishioners have built them up again and again, but no hint of these vicissitudes mars their peaceful solidity. Nothing but the mid-Victorian stained glass suggests a modification later than the earliest murmurs of the Gothic revival in the late eighteenth and early nineteenth centuries, although, like the plantation houses, they were nearly all rebuilt later than the great 1831 hurricane. But the shell always remained, and little differentiates them now from their English prototypes of a genera-tion or two earlier. It is the Gothic of the times of Beckford and Horace Walpole, not of the Victorian age. Occasional oddities, such as Regency fan-topped windows, arbitrarily placed among lancets and corbels that might have been modelled on the first illustrations of the works of Sir Walter Scott, or the juxtaposition of gargoyles and acanthus leaves, Corinthian pilasters and herringbone moulding, give the buildings a distinctive style, which, coupled with their green habitat of mango and paw-paw and palm, can best be evoked by the term of Tropical-Gothic. Memorial slabs on the walls and among the flagstones of the nave, bear the names and biographies of planters of former centuries – Hayneses, Challoners, Alleynes, Massiahs and a few dozen others that constantly recur – and those of former vicars and of soldiers and sailors laid low by fever or the fortunes of war.

The most pleasing of these churches is St John's. It rides high on the summit of an inland cliff which commands the eastern shores and a rugged palisade of coral reefs which break up the advance of the Atlantic waves and give shelter to a succession of lagoons. Canefields and trees embower it in tranquillity. But, apart from the beauty of its position it has a claim upon the attention of the traveller that makes it, in the recent world of the Antilles, strangely venerable. For, on a tablet in the churchyard, carved with Doric columns and the Cross of St Constantine, runs the following inscription: *Here lyeth ye body of Ferdinando Palaeologus, descended from ye Imperial lyne of ye last Christian Emperor of Greece. Church-warden of this parish 1655–1656. Vestryman twentye years. Died Oct 3. 1679.*

The implications of this brief epitaph send the mind spinning away to regions and to tremendous historical events remote indeed from the quiet parochial world of Barbados; back to the tragic morning of May 29th, 1453, when the Emperor Constantine XI Palaeologus, in full armour, sword in hand, shod with the purple buskins and crowned with the imperial diadem, waited at the head of his nobles for the last assault of the Turks on the walls of Byzantium. Historians have often repeated the terrible tale of the battle: the obliterating smoke of the artillery, the exhaustion of the defenders' ammunition, the Janissaries breaching the ramparts on a ladder of their own dead, the teeming thousands of the Turkish irruption and the desperate heroism of the Greeks. 'Amidst these multitudes,' writes Gibbon, 'the Emperor, who accomplished all the duties of a general and a soldier, was long seen and finally lost. The nobles who fought round his person sustained till their last breath the honourable names of Palaeologus and Cantacuzene.' The Emperor's body, surrounded by a mountain of Ottoman dead, was trampled out of recognition by the turbaned and stinking horde of Moslems, howling the name of Allah from a myriad throats, that surged through the Adrianople gate. The sacred town was given over to rape and massacre and sack, the Oecumenical Patriarchate was defiled, and the infidels were soon swarming in thousands beneath the great dome of Saint Sophia.

Later in the day the Emperor's body was singled out by the double-headed eagles of his insignia, and the victorious Sultan was able to expose before the barbarians the mangled head of the last of the Caesars. The Roman Empire, founded by Augustus almost fifteen centuries before, and Byzantium, that shimmering and iridescent thing, the inheritor and guardian, however corrupt, of the art and philosophy and learning of ancient Greece, had breathed their last. Gazing at the empty shell of the autocrator's halls, it was with justice indeed that Mahomet II thought-fully quoted an elegant couplet of Persian poetry: 'The spider has wove his web in the Imperial palace; and the owl has sung her watch-song on the tower of Afrasiab.'

A legend on the walls of Viterbo traces the origins of the Palaeologi to a certain Remigius Lellius of Vetulonia, but in authenticated Byzantine history, the dynasty emerges at the time of the Norman Conquest of Britain. What strange adventure ended in the burial of their descendant in this Anglican churchyard in the Barbadian hills? Did they settle in Rome, like Cardinal Bessarion of Trebizond, or gravitate, like Lascaris and Argyropoulos, to the court of the Medici? Or make their way north, like the Cantacuzeni, who were later to reign over the Rumanian principalities, and radiate powerful branches into the Russias? Nobody seemed to know. It was only on returning to Europe that I learned their strange history.

After the fall of Constantinople, two of the Emperor's brothers, Thomas and Demetrius, retired to the Morea, of which, as tributaries of the Sultan, they remained joint overlords. As they were constantly at war with each other, Demetrius treacherously appealed to the Sultan, who marched into the Morea and occupied it, taking the daughter of Demetrius into his harem. Demetrius died in Constantinople as a monk. Thomas fled to Rome, taking with him a precious relic, the head of St Andrew. There he was granted a pension by the Pope, and his sons were educated in Italy. Andrew, the eldest, married a Roman prostitute, sold his rights of imperial succession to the kings of France and Aragon and died in poverty. The second, Manuel, returned to Stamboul, where the Sultan maintained him and presented him with a couple of wives. 'His surviving son,' writes Gibbon, 'was lost in the habit and religion of a Turkish slave.' Thomas's shadowy third son, John, may have remained in Corfu, where, according to Chalcocondyles, Thomas left his family on his departure for Rome. He, states the memorial tablet of a descendant, was the father of Theodore, who begat Prosper, who begat Camilio, who begat yet a third Theodore, who is the father of the Palaeologus of Barbados. The family was by then established in the Tuscan town of Pesaro: subjects, like so many Byzantine refugee families, of the Medicean dukes. The preceding generations are more than vague, but if the authenticity of John is accepted, there are no grounds for doubting the succession. Among his compatriots and contemporaries, at any rate, his Imperial descent was never questioned. In 1593 he married Eudoxia Comnena, who also bore an imperial Byzantine name, in the Island of Chios. She died soon afterwards, and their only child, a daughter, married a member of the Chios family of Rhodokanaki.

The family then turned its face to the west and the north, for there is evidence that Theodore served the House of Orange as a soldier of fortune in the Low Countries. At the turn of the century he appears at Tattershall Castle in Lincolnshire as a gentleman rider to the ferocious Earl of Lincoln. He became acquainted here with the great John Smith of Virginia, who was living eccentrically as a hermit in the woods 'in a pavilion of boughs', reading Machiavelli and Marcus Aurelius. Theodore, as a scholar and a Greek, was sent by the Earl to 'insinuate himself into his woodish acquaintances'. At about the same time, he married, in an Anglican church, an English lady from Suffolk called Mary Balls. He crops up again as a correspondent of the Duke of Buckingham, shortly before the Duke was stabbed by Felton. His letter, written in excellent French, reveals that he was in poor circumstances, but it is pleasant to record that he lived the last few years of his life as the guest and friend of the family with Sir Nicholas Lower at Clifton in Cornwall. Lady Lower belonged to a race that was eminent for its great erudition. The family had already produced the learned Lady Burleigh and Bacon's equally learned mother, and it may be assumed that Theodore's friendship with the Lowers was based upon a common interest in European letters and the classics. He was buried in Landulph Church near Saltash in Cornwall, in 1636.*

He is reported (by a stranger who later inspected his coffin in the vault) to have been an immensely tall man with aquiline features and a long white beard.

His eldest son, John, is said to have taken part in the civil wars and to have fought on the Royalist side at Naseby; but little is known of him. Theodore, the second son, also fought in the wars, and was buried, through the influence of his commander, Lord St John, in Westminster Abbey. Ferdinando, the youngest, migrated to Barbados, where he settled with his wife on a small pineapple plantation in St John's Parish; dying there, as we have seen, in 1679. Of him, again, little is known beyond the modest parochial functions that he fulfilled. His son, another and final 'Theodore Palaeologus of Wapping, Kent', returned to England, settled in Stepney, and served in King Charles II's navy. He died at Corunna in 1692, leaving a posthumous daughter who was baptized by the strange name of Godscall Palaeologus. Whether she grew up and married is unknown. Nor is it known whether any other branches of the imperial family exist, and, for the time being, this oddly-named little girl in Stepney remains the last authentic descendant of the Palaeologi.

A hundred years ago, there lingered in Barbados a vague tradition of 'a Greek Prince from Cornwall', and a rumour, which appears in

---

*It is thanks to the generosity and scholarly research of the present Rector of Landulph, the Rev J. H. Adams, M.A., that I have been able to learn of the antecedents and descendants of his distinguished parishioner. The notes that I have included are the barest outline of a fascinating mass of unpublished material, the result of many years' work, which Mr Adams has kindly put at my disposal.

Bradfield and Schomburgk and Burke, that, 'during the late war in Greece, a letter was received in Barbadoes by the then existing authorities, from the members of the Greek Government, informing them that they had traced the family to Cornwall and thence to Barbadoes, where, if a male branch of the Palaeologi were still in existence, the Greeks, if requisite, would pay all expenses of the voyage, equip a ship for the illustrious exile, and proclaim him their lawful sovereign'.*

Such, then, was the destiny that scattered the bones of these exiled princes in Tuscany, Cornwall, London, Barbados, Wapping, and Corunna: a strange and rather inappropriate story. And rather sad. For nothing, after all, could be more remote in distance, or in feeling more alien to this little coral island, than the waters of the Golden Horn: waters that once reflected the vanished palace of Blachernae, the home of the purple-born; or the cypresses of Mystra, whose Byzantine parapets look down from the Taygetus towards the plain of Sparta and the wide valley where the Eurotas meanders through the olive groves of Lacedaemon to the mountains of the Peloponnese.

May the earth, as the Greeks say over the graves of their countrymen, rest upon them lightly,

καὶ αἰωνία ἦ μνήμη τῶν.

On the last day but one of our Barbadian stay, we paid a visit to the House of Assembly, which was then in session. After Westminster and the House of Assembly in Bermuda, it is the oldest parliament in the Empire. The debates take place in solid but rather characterless mid-Victorian premises overlooking Trafalgar Square, the statue of Nelson and the masts of sailing vessels.

But inside it was an impressive sight. Gothic windows surrounded the Chamber, paned with stained-glass portraits of the Sovereigns of England, including Cromwell, and their coats-of-arms impaling those of their consorts. The periwigged speaker was enthroned under the Lion and the Unicorn and a small gold mace, resting solemnly in its stand, symbolized the sitting. The members were seated facing the Speaker at a great semi-circular table, fanning themselves with round fans of dried palm leaves, for the heat was intolerable. Over three-quarters of the members were coloured Barbadians. The standard of oratory on both sides – for black and white seemed to divide naturally into the two sides

---

*I have not been able to discover any information of such a proposal in Greece. Anyway, on the existing evidence, the family had died out in the male line over a century before. At all events, the crown of Greece was given to Prince Otto of Bavaria.

of the house – was very poor except for the leader of the majority, Mr Grantley Adams; owing, perhaps, to the unrewarding topic under debate. The coloured M.P.s were protesting that they had been affronted by not being invited to a party at Government House to celebrate the Royal Wedding; while the white M.P.s explained that it had been a private party without any official character and that there was thus no question of an affront. The two cases were stated over and over again at vast length and in practically the same words for almost three hours.

We had tea in a huge teashop and bar above Goddard's general stores, which is a general meeting-place for the inhabitants of Bridgetown. We soon realized that, however absurd the debate might be, the ridicule was not confined to the coloured population, for the white people at the neighbouring tables were talking, in voices of blood-curdling gentility, exclusively of invitations to tea or to garden-parties at Government House, and with an urgency that amply proved the immense importance of these ceremonies and their charm as a conversational topic. We returned to the House of Assembly in a less critical frame of mind.

Nothing had changed. The same argument was droning on. But at last an elderly man with a white beard and a tail coat, whose sad eyes and ducal weariness of manner imparted to the room an aura of enormous dignity, placed the mace on his shoulder and, followed by the Speaker, loped slowly out of the Chamber. The session was at an end. We had been waiting for the proceedings to break up, as Mrs Napier had given us a letter to Mr Adams. Leaning on one of the window-sills, we sat talking with him until the light began to fail, and, all of us deciding to continue our talk over a drink, drove in Mr Adams's motor-car to Goddard's. It was almost six o'clock and the shop was shutting. As we turned away in search of another place, Mr Adams said that there was no other restaurant handy and that perhaps we had better meet, earlier, another day. We all shook hands rather sadly and Mr Adams drove away. It was, somehow, a rather disappointing end to a conversation that had been developing in the most friendly and promising fashion; and also slightly mysterious.

We had an hour or two to spare and decided to seek somewhere else. After wandering down a few streets and encountering nothing but some rather dismal rum shops for which we were not in the right mood, we asked a taxi to take us to 'some pleasant bar'. 'You won't like the bars, boss,' he said: 'I'll take you to a club.' He named half a dozen, and when we said we were not members of any of them he laughed and said; 'That's all right, boss, you just walk in. They's all white folk there.' We insisted that we wanted a bar that anyone could go into, not a club. He took off his cap and scratched his head. He was plainly bewildered. 'They don't have bars, only places for people like me – for black people. You wouldn't like them. The white people all go to the clubs.' He cheered up again. 'Don't be afraid, boss. You just walk in.'

The bar that we finally discovered, though he assured us that it was the best he could think of, was a lugubrious little den. Three or four Negroes were drinking rum, and the silence that greeted our arrival plainly showed that we were casting a blight on the place. There was none of the ease or the volubility (or even indeed any conversation at all) that would normally be found in a similar place in Martinique or Dominica; no reaction to the presence of strangers, except a rather alarmed and monosyllabic politeness. We were plainly breaking some unwritten rule by being there, and it was a thoroughly uncomfortable business for everyone. A Salvation Army band took up its position in the street outside and the Captain delivered a violent homily on the pitfalls of rum-drinking. At the end of his peroration, the drum and the bugles played a lively tune and everybody sang a hymn about booking a passage to Canaan's shore:

> I'm going for a trip
> In de Hallelujah ship
> And I'm not coming back any more.

A car drew level with us as we walked back through the town and a head, wreathed with a triumphant smile, stuck out. It was the taxi-driver. 'I knew you wouldn't like the bar, boss,' he said. 'Now would you like to go to a club?'

The situation became clearer. All the restaurants or places of amusement we had visited, either with friends or alone, were officially clubs; of which, thanks to the clarity of our complexions, we were automatically members. We had never been elected and it was impossible to resign, though I have not the slightest doubt one can be barred. In fact they were not real clubs at all, and could only become so at the rash approach of a coloured stranger (for no black Barbadian could make such a mistake), when their dormant legal status as a club would become for a moment real. The mechanism of exclusion would slip smoothly into gear. ('Let me see. Are you a member? Not? Oh dear!' And then with a rueful smile: 'I'm afraid only members are admitted ...') It has never had a breakdown yet. A Barbadian acquaintance explained the intricacies of the system with quiet pride, as though he was pointing out one of the natural beauties of the island. 'It's better that way all round.'

'But what do you do if you want to have dinner with a coloured Barbadian? Where do you meet?'

He looked faintly taken aback.

'But we don't meet – except on official and business occasions. They don't like it either. You say you didn't feel you were welcome in one of their bars. There you are. We each keep to ourselves. It's much better that way all round. Some of them are first-class chaps, of course, I'm not saying they aren't ...' Goddard's, he continued, was the only place frequented at a pinch by blacks and whites. It was in the middle of the business centre and came in very handy. There was nowhere else.

The club system runs all through Barbadian life and the cold shoulder and the open snub are resorted to only when no legal quibble is available. It segregates the two races of islanders just as effectively as the most stringent colour discrimination in the United States, and not half so honestly. There, at least, loathsome as the American colour laws appear to me, Negroes know exactly where they are. There is none of the mean juggling with the written word that prevails in Barbados, where, on paper, no colour bar exists. It is a pretty state of society when any white Barbadian or English pup can bounce in virtually where he chooses, while the elected head of the Government, who is the island's equivalent of the British Prime Minister, may have to hesitate and draw back. It must be one of the most disgustingly hypocritical systems in the world.

Except for Canefield and the kindness of our hostess, it was without a pang that we flew away to Trinidad. Looking backwards we could almost see, suspended with the most delicate equipoise above the flat little island, the ghostly shapes of those twin orbs of the Empire, the cricket ball and the blackball.

CHAPTER 7

Trinidad

Port of Spain. What a legendary and romantic town the syllables evoke! The mind overflows at once with a confusion of anchored galleons, caskets of moidores, silken-lashed girls in high combs and mantillas, swan-necked spurs, the sound of guitars under balconies, tree-shaded patios, and spires of water weeping in alabaster fountains.

On landing, this shroud of purple is blown to ribbons in a second. The ugly carcase of the Trinidadian capital is laid bare. Dismal barracks and Victorian red-brick public buildings appear, and churches built in servile imitation of English models of the time of Pusey and Ruskin. The bleak streets echo with the clatter of trams, and the prevailing weather alternates between damp and debilitating heat, when the glare scorches the eyeballs like quick-lime and the wind drives the dust along the thoroughfares in hot volleys of grape-shot, and a grey and all-obliterating deluge. At these moments the town and the lamp-posts and bricks and tramlines, faintly looming through the downpour, are indistinguishable from Glasgow in December. Suburbs and slums trail away for miles. They are replaced here and there by trim white blocks of workers' flats, which are healthy but hideous. Then the slums resume their sway.

And yet, after the gentility of Bridgetown, Port of Spain possesses a forcefulness and a vulgarity that are almost pleasing. It is a large and startlingly cosmopolitan town. The streets blaze with milk-bars, drug stores, joints and picture-palaces, and almost everybody on the pavement chews gum, for the American influx during the war – which was as large, proportionately, as that of the British Isles – has left a deep mark on Trinidadian life. The island is now the southern bastion of the strategic semi-circle which protects the eastern approaches to the Panama Canal: America's newly reared island-wall of defence from which only the two bricks of Martinique and Guadeloupe are missing. (When the United States made her deal with Great Britain for naval bases in the West Indies, the French Antilles were under the rule of Vichy France, and between them and the U.S.A. an uneasy truce prevailed which was an unsuitable atmosphere for bargaining.) American sailors still promenade the streets in great numbers, deambulating with that slow, rolling, muscle-bound, non-sissy-suspect gait which is such a singular and striking appanage of the U.S. armed forces.

The Negroes are dressed with great smartness or with a colourful and studied abandon and, one-third of the island's population being of East Indian origin, Hindus and Moslems abound. Songs in Hindustani – plaintive little tunes in the oriental minor mode – float into the air from upper windows which the flag of the Indian Republic adorns, while opposing windows fly the colours of Pakistan. The Moslem banner also flutters from the walls of a great snow-white mosque which raises onion-shaped domes and minarets and crescents high above the mean surrounding streets. Against the flamboyance of the Trinidadian sunset, these pearly cylinders and spheres possess the exaggerated orientalism of European illustrations to Omar Khayyam or the Arabian Nights. Peering through an Alhambra-like window whose stained glass panes had been left ajar, we watched the turbaned Imam chalk up on a black-board a neat line of Arabic writing. Underlining it, he turned to a row of little girls with saris over their heads, sitting cross-legged on the mats. '*Bismallah*,' they squeaked in unison, spelling out the words, '*ar Rahman ar Rajeem* ...' Seeing our inquisitive faces, the Imam walked over to the window and closed it, and the voices were drowned ... Between the Hindus and the Mohammedans, dormant hostility smoulders, in sympathy with the passions of the Indian peninsula. In grocers' shops and eating-hells in the tram-haunted Chinese quarter, flags bearing the Kuomintang star and portraits of Chiang Kai Shek hang on the walls, and Chinese shopkeepers, seated on chairs underneath hanging signs which are painted all over with beautiful white ideograms, chirrup to each other across the street. Guttural voices from Syria and the Lebanon haggle in the glooms of grocers' and drapers' shops, and Venezuelans with side-whiskers and narrow moustaches along their upper lips, covertly peer at the reflection of their profiles in the windows of tailors' shops. Dummies in tweed with nymph-like waists and Herculean shoulders posture back at them through the plate glass. *Vestidos elegantísimos*, the labels announce, *por los caballeros*. The atmosphere of this part of the town is pleasantly raffish.

But the tram carried us away from this region and across the Savannah to the mournful elegance of the residential district. The enormous expanse of the Savannah is girdled not only by a race-track, but by an electric tramline, 'affording,' as one guide book says, 'a pleasant evening drive'. Round and round the vehicles go, glowing, as evening falls more enticingly every second. Inside this magic circle lie cricket pitches and football grounds, a cemetery, a bandstand, tall clumps of palmistes, and a monumental monkey-pot-tree whose radiation of root crawls outwards from the great bole, and still above the ground, for over an acre. On the southern extremity lies the Queen's Park Hotel, a large and slightly dilapidated block of white plaster and nickel plumbing with faintly cubistic affinities. On the evening of our arrival, with its neon lighting beginning to prevail over the dusk, and with all its fittings a-glitter, it seemed to dominate this town-locked prairie like a giant dentist's chair for the painless extraction of dollars. The houses which surround the rest of the Savannah – except for the bleak Prince's Building, which was built in honour of an expected visit, in 1861, of Queen Marie of Roumania's father (which never happened) – are some of the most remarkable architectural phenomena in the world. The essential skeleton of these villas is the high-gabled, acute-angled, ginger-bread house of the witch in Hansel and Gretel, bristling with pinnacles and weathercocks, spiked and frilled along the coping like a stickleback, and with eaves that drip, as though they overhung the grey dwelling-place of the Norns, with icicles and stalactites of painted wood and tin. Pillars and caryatids from the Parthenon or Ankor buttress the fabric, and the mosaic of Byzantium, or turquoise-green majolica, or glazed porcelain tiles of panniered shepherdesses leading beribboned lambs, are framed in beams and half-timbering that pay silent tribute to Stratford-on-Avon. Georgian bow-windows, roofed like Chinese pagodas, suddenly bulge from the walls, and from the steep roofs grow the spires of Hohenschwangau, the turrets of Azay-le-Rideau and the domes and cupolas of Kiev. William Morris and Dante Gabriel Rossetti triumph over other influences in the stained glass of the windows. There, among giant celery, blessèd damozels dream in the poppy fields, and storks balance themselves on one leg among the petals of waterlily and lotus. Many of these houses were closed and silent. But in one of them, detectable through the brighly lit windows, a party of which the guests were drawn from Spain, France, Portugal, Corsica, Africa and England was brilliantly evolving among cocktail cabinets, fringed and tasselled lamp shades, pierrot-dolls, and the black and orange wall-paper of the Jazz and Vorticist periods. For long minutes, on this first voyage of discovery through Port of Spain, we remained spellbound, as every newcomer must, spellbound and riveted to the pavement by the terrible beauty of these buildings; turning at last reluctantly to the shadows of the giant cotton-trees and the tramline that carried us past the dark world of the Botanic Gardens and Government House to the forested hills where the suburbs evaporate. Descending into the sweltering dampness of the night, we walked to our small hotel. It was perched among the mosquitoes and fireflies of the hillside like a hunting lodge of the Emperor Franz Josef in the Tyrol. Here we were confronted by our first Trinidadian meal, with a description of which I don't want to afflict the reader. Hotel cooking in the island is so appalling that a stretcher may profitably be ordered at the same time as dinner. Fortunately, owing to the profusion of excellent Chinese and Indian restaurants in Port of Spain, it is a scourge that can usually be evaded; and the food in Trinidadian houses is excellent. The only danger that remains is the Cascadura fish, which has the legendary property, like the water of the Nile with respect to Egypt – *Qui aquam Nili bibit rursus bibet* – of casting a spell over anyone who eats it, making him, ever afterwards, unable to live far from Trinidad. So great care must be taken when ordering.

Drawing a comparison between Barbados and Trinidad is almost irresistible, and it is a contest in which, in spite of the beautiful churches and houses of Barbados and of the gracelessness and the sodden climate of Port of Spain, Trinidad, for me, wins, hands down. Trinidadians are free of the characteristics which, among the Barbadians, impair the quiet beauty of the coral island; and whatever the colour feeling in Trinidad may be, it does not fly at you the moment you arrive and lodge in your gullet for ever. The Trinidadians appear, by contrast, fantastically carefree and cheerful and definite, and the dominating attribute of the islanders, both black and white, is certainly their vitality.

For so large and, now, so rich an island, Trinidad has had an odd career. Columbus claimed it for Spain on his third voyage, and dubbed it 'the Trinity' after the three peaks in the south of the island. Then, after adventuring through the Serpent's Mouth and trading with the Caribs in the Gulf of Paria, he sailed away again to the north through the Dragons' Mouths, the channel which divides its north-western promontory from modern Venezuela. Sir Walter Raleigh, pausing here on his quest for Eldorado, sacked the new Spanish capital; and Sir Robert Dudley,* that striking and unhappy figure of the English renaissance, made a youthful argosy to the island, and landed here, like Jason on

---

* For a full account of this strange Elizabethan and his exploits in the New World, the reader is warmly recommended to read *West Indian Summer*, by James Pope-Hennessy.

the Colchian shore. Marching inland in full plate-armour, with drums beating and banners unfurled at the head of his little phalanx, he ceremoniously claimed the island for his Queen; and sailed away for ever, leaving no token of his quixotic pretension but a superbly magniloquent and challenging inscription nailed to the trunk of a tree. The island, during the following centuries, suffered the customary fortunes of the lesser Spanish Caribbees; Peru and Mexico, as usual, drew from the island all that was enterprising, and the swindling Spanish colony mouldered miserably on, unable to hear Mass, for lack of a priest, more than once a year; so poor that they were forced, for the occasion, to borrow each other's clothes, and reduced, by the middle of the eighteenth century, to only one set of small clothes, which was the common property of the entire administrative body. In 1783 the population numbered no more than three hundred souls. A policy of throwing the fertile island open to immigration was then adopted, and at the turn of the century the population had risen to almost twenty thousand. All kinds of people flocked to Trinidad. But the bulk of the new settlers were French. The British landing of a small force to back their countrymen in a street brawl between British sailors and French privateersmen was one of the reasons for a Spanish declaration of war on Britain in 1797. At the approach of a British expedition to invade the island, the Spanish admiral fired the Spanish ships in the harbour, and the Governor, Don José Maria Chacon, surrendered Trinidad to Abercromby and Picton. It was declared officially British at the treaty of Amiens in 1802.

Although the Spanish occupation of the island lasted two centuries longer than in any of the lesser Antilles, it has left little mark on the island either culturally or architecturally. A number of Spanish families still exist and one often hears Spanish spoken in the streets – usually as the result of the closeness of Venezuela. There are many French families, and many descendants of French Royalists, who escaped here from the French Antilles during the Revolution, still survive. There are small Portuguese and Jewish minorities and, rather surprisingly, a number of Corsican families, who (I was told) derive from supporters of the eighteenth-century Corsican patriot, General Paoli, the leader whose cause impelled Boswell to the eccentricity of appearing in the full Corsican uniform in the streets of London. All these curious threads in the fabric of the Trinidadian world invest the social life of the island with a colourfulness, a lack of inhibition and a dashing cosmopolitan atmosphere that turn the fading recollection of Barbados into something parochial and grey and fiercely Anglo-English.

We were sailing, a few days later, along the north-western peninsula, the mountainous contours of which define the northern side of the Gulf of Paria. The promontory seemed to continue straight into the Venezuelan range that stretched from the flank of the South American Continent to meet it. As the launch churned its way westwards, the sea appeared between the extremities of the two mountain ranges. Both of them subsided into the water to join hands, as it were, in a ravine beneath the channel of the Dragons' Mouths which separates them with its fifteen island-sprinkled miles. Trinidad was once a part of the mainland, and the subsiding of the dividing valley was an event which, geologists say, happened very recently; so few million years ago, in fact, that from their tone of voice it scarcely sounds older than yesterday's evening paper. The southern promontory of the Gulf loomed along the horizon towards the Orinoco Delta, from which the island is severed by the expanse of water known as the Serpent's Mouth. The dim coast of the South American mainland lay beyond the fringe of the interior where the phantom city of Eldorado lay. The sea here is discoloured by the water that the Orinoco carries down from its many sources in the Andes. It was exciting to remember that the faint sky-line was the rim of a continent containing colossal rivers and mountains, forests, and Indian tribes that have never been disturbed in their forests; swelling southwards to a great girth, and tapering then to the mountains of Patagonia and the Tierra del Fuego and then expiring at last on the rugged coast where Cape Horn points its crooked and broken knuckle bones to the Antarctic. Conversing of Amazonian forests and Inca cities and inland seas that were lifted above the clouds, we threaded our way through a collection of pale green islands which floated gently towards us, and then fell away behind, almost brushing the bulwarks with their drooping boughs: two lines of green plumage on the smooth water. The sea roughened as we emerged from the shelter of the mainland and reached the shores of our destination.

Nothing, at first, distinguished the lepers of Chacachacare from the other inhabitants of the West Indies. Some were working under the trees, and others were talking or sitting in the sun on the balconies of their little cabins. 'Good morning, Doctor,' they all said, as Dr Campbell led us along the village street. He pointed to a neat building between the pathway and the shore. 'That's the theatre they built for themselves. They've got a band, and they give concerts to each other there, quite good ones, and variety shows, and we manage to get cinemas from Port of Spain now and then to cheer them up.' There were sports for the lepers whose stamina and whose equal state of contamination with their fellows permitted it.

The disease, as we had learnt in the Saints, is very widespread in the West Indies, and little leper colonies, usually situated, like Chacachacare or the Désirade, on islands, are scattered all over the archipelago. The mysterious leprosy bacillus, the *Mycobacterium leprae*, whose effects may only in some cases be arrested or mitigated, but which, once it has attacked a victim in its severe form, can never be cured, is the cause of unimaginable misery; but not, thank heavens, of the ostracism and shame to which it once condemned its victims. After seeing Chacachacare and meeting Dr George Campbell (who has lived among lepers for years) and some of the nuns who devote their lives to the alleviation of the disease, one realizes what a gulf now exists between the bells and the clappers, the cries of Unclean, the outlawry, the official, and sometimes religiously solemnized, death-in-life of the lepers of the past. But the main curse of the disease, the segregation, lasting usually for the whole of the patient's life, still remains. And lifelong separation from the rest of humanity being as bad or worse than death itself for many people, a government is faced with the problem of discovering the lepers, in order that they may be prevented from infecting others. Many of them nobly forswear their right to a normal life, and, by declaring their disease to the authorities, condemn themselves to a life sentence of segregation. But many cannot bring themselves to do this, and official surveys have to be organized, backed up if necessary by the force and authority of the state; a hopeless task in India, where a million and a half known lepers exist, and perhaps an equal number of undeclared cases. The problem of detecting and segregating them is almost insoluble; but the smaller extent of the Antilles fortunately makes this task much easier.

But, painful as the segregation of an unwilling or of a crypto-leper must be, or of a victim who is unaware of his disease, once they are installed in a place like Chacachacare, all is done that ingenuity and humanity can invent to make their lives as normal as the circumstances allow. Unfortunately, the nature of the disease excludes complete normality even here. For the children, who are only slightly infected – some of them perhaps curable – have to be specially guarded from their elders. They live and sleep and eat in separate buildings. Schools and playgrounds are provided for them, and they are taught games and dancing and trained in professions, and in fishing and boating. Many find a pleasant and stimulating outlet in the Boy Scout Movement. The ones whom we saw eating in their little dining-room, chattering and laughing and interrupting each other, or sitting on a bench and talking to one of the nuns, appeared as happy and as normal as though they did not know that leprosy existed. On the arm of one little girl – separated, alas, from the other children – Dr Campbell pointed out to us the greyish-mauve patch that is the equivalent on a skin with African pigmentation of the almost mythical snow-white leprous colour that plays such a lurid part in literature.

The grown-ups, too, are not all able to mix freely, owing to the varying gravity of their infection. For some of them, who are afflicted with the mild variety of the disease which limits itself to certain parts of the body, are uninfectious. The complaint may heal up with treatment or even vanish of its own accord; or – for its nature is incalculable – it may prolong itself, and attack the larger nerves and limbs and deform the feet and hands. But the leading of a normal life is encouraged, to the very limits of possibility and safety. It is, unfortunately, an affliction that occurs most frequently among people with little education and few of the inner resources which would enable them to occupy their time by study or artistic activity; who are least able to put up a philosophic resistance to that apathy which is the worst enemy of recovery – a factor which sometimes drives incurable patients to chronic despair and melancholia.

One of the best antidotes to this frame of mind, and to that lack of physical and mental resistance which accelerates all diseases, is the provision of good and varied food. Many of the patients, Dr Campbell explained, as we walked from hut to hut, have become skilled tailors, carpenters and cobblers; some of them turn themselves into farmers and market gardeners for supplying the needs of the little republic or for sale outside the colony. Pregnancy is dangerous for women patients, and mothers must at once be separated from their children; and so sexual frustration contributes its misery to the other scourges of leprosy. But (and this is a great consolation to parents) leprosy is not a congenital disease, and so, although they may never again see their children, who are looked after by relations or government institutions, they know that they will grow up free of the disease which has ruined their own lives. Thus lepers can marry, and though it is not a perfect solution, it is certainly better than the mental ravages that would occur if the sexes were thrust apart. The problems and the anguish that beset a normal married couple outside the colony when one of the parties suddenly develops leprosy may be imagined.

The last house to which Dr Campbell took us was the infirmary for advanced cases of the disease's more violent form. It was a pathetic sight. The patients were most of them past middle age, but one or two whose malady had been neglected since infancy were fairly young. Here we saw distorted and discoloured members, fingers missing or swollen or twisted out of shape, and limbs with their truncated extremities tapering into a mass of bandages. Faces were distorted by nodules which clustered on the skin like clumps of oak-apples, and the features in some instances had fallen into a curious leonine cast, which Dr Campbell told us is one of the best-known stigmata of the disease. Some of the lepers were half paralysed, and others completely crippled. Three or four nuns in their white tropical habits were moving about among the beds, bringing food, dressing sores, changing bandages, and sitting talking to these poor people. Many of them brightened up at Dr Campbell's appearance. He stopped and talked to all of them, resting his hand on their shoulders, or making some quiet joke, or (to me, inexplicably) evoking a look of interest and pleasure by saying, 'Look, Mary (or Richard), I've brought some friends of mine to see you.' They all seemed to cheer up, and the atmosphere of the place, which might have been one of Stygian despair, was astonishingly cheerful, and imbued with a feeling of unforced normality which is noticeable in the whole of the colony. Contemplating those tragic distortions and mutilations, the apathy and melancholia which Dr Campbell had suggested were the greatest danger in a leper colony became doubly understandable; and the fact that it existed, or appeared to exist, so little, still more remarkable. We came out again into the prospect of the shining sea and the palm trees with feelings of admiration and sober pity and of a furtive, guilty relief.

As the boat sailed away from the island, we watched the white figure of Dr Campbell walk back to his little house at the water's side, on the outskirts of the leper village.

Leprosy has no specific cure. Until recently Chaulmoogra oil and its derivatives were the standard treatment. For the last five years, since treatment on new lines was started at Carville, the U.S. National Leprosarium, encouraging results have been reported from the use of various sulphone derivatives, such as diasone, promin and promizole. The last words on this theme I will leave to Dr Campbell himself:*

The discoveries made by chemists who have sought for drugs which will kill bacteria have been so remarkable that there is every hope that a cure for leprosy will one day be found. Meanwhile we can help the leper with all the resources which modern civilization can muster. If we cannot cure him, we can do everything possible to alleviate the sufferings of his body. The sufferings of his mind, which spring from the knowledge that he is, so far as human society is concerned, already dead, are not so easily alleviated. Yet much can be done to mitigate even this appalling knowledge. There have been many men for whom, for various reasons, the world has been of little account, and their lives have proved that,

* George Campbell, M.D., M.R.C.P., D.P.H., *Health Horizon*, October, 1947.

even for the outcast from human society, there yet remains a great deal that is exhilarating, valuable and satisfying to the human soul.

The Pitch Lake of Trinidad sounds satanic, and, indeed, it is; but not exactly in the seething, Phlegethontic fashion that one might suppose. It is the blankness, the emptiness, the boredom of this expanse that fills the observer with horror. It has the colour and texture of a gramophone record a hundred and fourteen acres in extent, channelled and broken up by a network of cracks, where the surface softens into black treacle treacherously covered by a thin wrinkled skin. It is one of the hottest places in the world. Into the middle of this broiling disc runs a miniature railway, and an army of dark navvies hack lumps of reeking black gruyère out of the surface with pickaxes, and load them into the trucks; the trucks are hauled to the lakeside, emptied and sent back for more. The lake being inexhaustible, the operation will presumably go on until the end of the world – a thought as appalling as anything in Aquinas or Dante. To punish the villagers for destroying some humming-birds that were really their ancestral ghosts, an Indian village is said to have been engulfed in this filth. Sir Walter Raleigh also caulked his vessels here on his way to the Orinoco.

It was a relief to leave this beastly place and motor away to Fyzabad through the trees, and on into the rolling country near Syparia. Here we contemplated the little Black Virgin of the parish. She is a grey-faced figure entirely clad in leather, standing above the altar in a church founded in the eighteenth century by Franciscans from Aragon. The image is thaumaturgic and possesses the faculty, not uncommon in Italian and Byzantine saints, of homing when she is removed from her shrine, like those wonderful ikons that embark on solitary Odysseys across the mountains of Athos: a feat of levitation twice as miraculous as the airy journeys of St Joseph of Cupertino. She did not hold us for long, however, and it seemed anomalous and wrong that, turning from such a figure from the Old World, we should be surrounded not by Tuscans or Calabrians or Macedonians, but by Hindus in saris, and even, here and there, in turbans. The entire district round Fyzabad was settled by indentured labourers who preferred to remain there when their contracts had expired, and swop their return tickets for ten acres of land.

What happened was this. After the slaves were emancipated on August 1st, 1834, the short period of compulsory apprenticeship to their old masters was abandoned everywhere by 1838. The Negroes in most of the islands, including Trinidad, moved into the fruitful interior, where they squatted and lived happy and indolent lives on their little plots under the breadfruit trees. When the ground was exhausted, they had only to move on and clear a fresh plot of ground. This flight from the plantations threatened to bring the sugar industry to a standstill, and free labourers, indentured to work for a number of years, were brought from many sources including St Helena and Sierra Leone. The scheme was abandoned as a failure. Then an experiment was made with labourers from India, which turned out to be so successful that in 1845 a regular flow began of Indian labourers, mostly from Bengal.* The greatest demand was in Trinidad, where they arrived at the rate of two or three thousand a year. They now form a third of the population, and in British Guiana they are the largest single element in the colony. The movement went on at this rate until the end of the First World War, when the Indian Government placed it under a ban.

There are some very unpleasant stories about the speculators in these movements of population, one of which, mentioned by the German writer Otto Kunze in a nasty little book called *Um die Erde*, indicates that, to increase the demand for labour in Trinidad, they thinned the ranks of local labour by spreading small-pox among the Negro population. (If this incredible statement is anything more than a slander, it also had the effect, according to Kingsley, of killing off large numbers of monkeys in the island, whose susceptibility to small-pox and cholera is, unfortunately, one of their anthropoid characteristics.)

When their time was up, most of these immigrants remained and settled on the land which was granted to them; some even went back to India, to return to the island with a host of relations and acquaintances. The majority were Hindus, but there were a large number of Mussulmans too, whose presence is signalized by the mosque in Port of Spain, and the occasional Moslem cemeteries – those little groves of turbaned monoliths – in the country districts. But wide tracts of Trinidad are now, for all visual purposes, Bengal. The same vegetation is here, the same villages of mud and thatch, a semblance of the same clothing, and everywhere little Hindu cemeteries with scarcely identifiable idols and epitaphs on the headstones inscribed in Urdu characters.

Not far from the Black Virgin of Syparia, we came upon a large temple of Vishnu, shaped like a jelly mould, standing under mango and palm trees. Little coloured flags fluttered from poles of bamboo, and the walls inside were frescoed with the figures of Shiva and Parvati and of her son Katri, and with the outlines of a lingam and the bull of Shiva.

But at Curepe, on the way back to Port of Spain, we beheld a much

*A similar system, but one which ended much earlier, accounts for small East Indian minorities in the French Antilles.

more imposing fane. Passant lions and tigers were painted on either side of the gate through the wall that enclosed the courtyard, and three towering white domes crowned a temple, on the pediment of which stood an effigy of Hanuman, the Monkey-God. A little club rested on his shoulder, and one knee was advanced in the first step of a grave religious saraband. Blue and blood-red peacocks unfolded their tails on the wall of the temple. Entering the inner chamber through a scalloped archway, we gazed with wonder at the profusion of expatriated divinities which were frescoed all over the white plaster. A young priest placed his fore-finger on them in turn, and announced their names. Here was Ganesh, all in red, with his grave little eyes and his elephant's trunk twisted into a question mark, and his multiplicity of arms, one of them grasping an ankus, woodenly gesticulating. Krishna was painted in blue, with a caste mark on his brow like an inverted horse-shoe, and a little beaded heart suspended round his neck; dancing, but not, for once, to the sound of his own flute; three peacocks' feathers were arranged on his forehead in a tiara. How solemnly all these gods displayed their emblems! Latchmi contrived simultaneously to hold, in the most hieratic of gestures a cup, a ring, a flower and a club. Opposite Sita, Hanuman attitudinized in a striped busby, and on Vashti's head a baby was perilously balanced. Mahadeo wore a cobra round his neck, and on a five-headed cobra next door, Krishna again appeared, abstractedly dancing. Brahma was gravely seated, and Rawan grasped a club studded with appalling spikes. 'This is Indra,' the postulant murmured, indicating a strange couple embowered in foliage, 'in the high woods with a Negro.' No, alas, he knew no more. His father had known, but he was dead; and the Saddhu, he continued sadly, was an away-fellow. An away-fellow? An absentee? A pluralist? He seemed unable to explain.

Under an arch, only a yard away, we came face to face with a live dignitary, dressed in a kind of thin yellow silk chasuble, squatting motion-lessly, peering vaguely into the ether. A chaplet of beads hung from one wrist, and in his hands was a brass vase holding a red and a yellow hibiscus. He made no answer when the postulant gently addressed him, but continued gazing into the afternoon haze. The young man smiled at us in a manner that seemed to beseech forgiveness. A possible inter-pretation of 'away-fellow' began to dawn upon us.

It was pouring with rain. The sea, which a few minutes ago had been dark with bathers, was empty, and the entire amphibian population was sheltering under the trees. Hopelessly ill-informed, we had imagined Maracas Bay to be a deserted beach, and felt disappointed on arrival to find ourselves swallowed up in the transports of a Trinidadian Lido. The lids of Coca-Cola bottles sparkled on the sand, and fastened their perforated rims into the soles of our feet with the viciousness of crustaceans. But once we were in the water, it was a different matter. The whole atmosphere changed, for the majority of our fellow-bathers turned out, at close quarters, to be Hindus, many of them dressed in shifts or in *dhoti*-like underpants instead of bathing dresses, and our ears were filled with the sound of Hindustani. A bulky old woman, heavily earringed, with silver bangles from her wrists to her elbows, and her hair uncoiling across her enormous back in a flapperish plait, wallowed and basked in the middle of her children and grandchildren like a matriarchal hippopotamus. There must have been several hundred people in the water, not so much swimming as wading slowly out into the sea with their arms akimbo, and standing, as far as the waves permitted, up to their necks in the sea and conversing. The water all round us was dotted with these severed Asiatic heads, whose features appeared delicate and frail after the robuster cast of the Negroes. We felt that we had wandered by mistake into the middle of a religious ceremony in Benares.

But the rain and, above all, the growing violence of the waves had driven us all helter-skelter to the shore, and the grey water was left alone to the pelicans. When the sea had been full of human beings, they had huddled at a safe distance on a rock in earnest conclave, but as the sea emptied of intruders they had taken to the air one by one, flying across the bay with the unwieldiness of pieces of luggage. They would suddenly stop dead in mid-air, as though they had applied a brake, and then collapse in a flurried spiral, to reappear floating serenely over the billows, still looking oddly unlike birds; more like Gladstone bags on to which badly rolled umbrellas had been strapped.

Trinidad made us understand how scarce birds had been in the other islands. One can travel for hours in many of the Windward Isles without hearing a twitter. But the reckless Elisée Reclus in his *Nouvelle Géographie Universelle*, of 1893, declares that the bird population of Trinidad once amounted to three-quarters of that of the whole of Europe, which, considering Trinidad is about the size of Lancashire, is a bewildering thought. But mankind has wrought terrible carnage among them. The chief victims were the humming-birds after which, in pre-Columbian times, the Caribs baptized the island. No less than fifteen thousand of these little creatures, M. Reclus states, were stuffed and exported weekly to the hatters and dressmakers of Europe; and, when one thinks of the fashions of the 'nineties and of the pictures of Boldini and Helleu, and of the old hats that one still comes across in cupboards, the number of these posthumous migrants hardly seems exaggerated.

The heart of the capital rings with the eternal questioning of the *Qu'est qu'il dit*-Bird, as though the branches were populated by deaf people at the theatre, and in the suburbs the telegraph wires are often black with scavengers: ragged, dirty and funereal birds, resembling cartoons of obscurantism and political bias. Flamingoes haunt the meanderings of the Caroni river, and the high woods – those wonderful green labyrinths so well described by Kingsley and Pope-Hennessy, which, alas, I never saw – are populous with parrots. Monkeys, whose ancestors survived the mythical plots of the coolie-shippers, still abound; for the trees and animals and flowers and birds, like Trinidad itself, belong, in a large measure, to the South American mainland. Green lizards gaze from the rocks with blue eyes of a Scandinavian depth and integrity, and the forests are inhabited by wild goats and fierce and predatory cats and by a little deer *d'une extrême douceur*. Apart from the dangerous cascadura, Trinidadian waters harbour the *hydrocion*, one mouthful of which kills the unwary diner stone dead almost before it has passed his lips. As though to atone for this, another fish puts its head above the waters, and makes a musical sound. Alligators, the descendants of the beasts that alarmed the sailors of Raleigh, are still numerous, and the west coast teems with timid little creatures, half-fish, half-insect, called Big Eyes. We saw them in quantities on the way from the south of the island to San Fernando. They are about half an inch long, semi-transparent, and each equipped with a pair of enormous projecting eyes. Standing motionless on the edge of the shallow water so that they should get used to us, we watched them gradually advance towards the land, swimming, leaping and wriggling in little troops, and all gazing upward so piercingly that the Argus-eyed water seemed fraught with accusation; a sort of fluid conscience. It was gratifying to remember that the slightest gesture would disperse this hypnotic legion and send them scampering back into the deep water.

Port of Spain, at the time between what the French call 'dog and wolf' – the moment the sun dips, when werewolves cast their human and don their four-footed nocturnal shape – for a moment resembles the outskirts of a medieval town. But only for a moment, before the light of the sun has completely vanished, and before the street lamps, gaining command over the thickening darkness, have exposed the town again in all its breath-taking ugliness. And only in one part of the town: the neighbourhood of the Dry River. The last Spanish Governor, Don

José Maria Chacon, deflected the Ariapita from its course, so that the former bed, a dry gully that soon became choked with filth, was left to wind, quite empty, through the town. It is now a deep, broad, rectangular trench, neatly cemented and balustraded, but in this peculiar light it might be the moat of a fortress, and the humble wooden shacks that overhang this dark gulf are just the kind of swellings that so often grovel, in southern Europe, at some great castle's foot.

Wandering beside it one evening, on my way back from another eaves-dropping session outside the mosque, I was stopped in my tracks by a deafening hullabaloo from the other side: a metallic clangour that slowly resolved itself into the tune of *The bonny, bonny banks of Loch Lomond.* Craning over the balustrade towards the source of the sound, I asked a young Negro, who was leaning beside me, what it was. 'It's a steel band,' he answered. 'The boys are practising for carnival. Would you like to call round?'

'Do you know them?'

'Sure.'

We jumped on to a tram that took us to the hotel near the harbour, to which we had shifted on our return from Tobago. Costa and Joan were resting in the bar after our half-mile tramp through the Botanic Gardens that afternoon. We all four took a taxi to the street called Piccadilly, on the other side of the dry river, and our new acquaintance led us down an alley-way between heavily populated wooden houses, over a wall and into a large pit built in a bay of the embankment. It was full of young Negroes hammering out, on extraordinary instruments, the noise I had heard. When we appeared with his friend, the leader rose, shook hands, and gave us four little rum kegs to sit on, and went on playing.

The leader, or Captain, was a Negro in his early twenties called Fish Eyes Rudolf Olivier. His face, of which the most notable feature were two great bulging eyes, was full of humour and sensibility and remarkably attractive. When the din had stopped, he made some introductions. 'This is Neville Jules, my second-in-command, and this is my managing director, O. Rudder.' The ease of his manner was admirable. 'Now I'll show you our yard.' He led the way into the centre with the air of a country magnate flinging open the double doors of the ballroom.

It was a piece of waste land, a-flutter with clothes lines, jammed between the embankment and the backs of houses, and the only way in and out was by climbing the six-foot wall we had just negotiated. The band was a little group of young men from the neighbourhood who had installed themselves here and turned it into a stronghold. A large blue banner, embroidered with the name of the group, was stuck in the ground, and, beyond the minstrels, half a dozen familiars were playing gin-rummy on a plank between two kegs. One or two of them worked in the docks, some of them were out of work, one was a mechanic's apprentice; all of them were between sixteen and seventeen and the early twenties. The little enclosure was illuminated by flambeaux – the Trinidadian equivalent of the Guadeloupean *serbies* – tied to the branches of a tree.

The instruments that produced the music looked at first like the rusty spare parts of motor-cars, and on closer inspection that is exactly what some of them proved to be. Fish Eyes Olivier played the most complicated of them all, the Tock-Tock, which has a range of fourteen notes. The Tock-Tock is the sawn-off bottom of a cylindrical kerosene tin, and the different notes are made by striking with a spanner or with a metal bar the different-sized triangles enclosed between segments of the rim and the two radii that enclose them. Each radius is hammered into a groove, to detach the resonance of the triangles from that of the ones on either side, and fourteen radii produced fourteen distinct notes, varying in pitch according to the distance between the enclosing grooves. Fish Eye struck them in turn with his iron bar and each one rang distinct and true; two notes short of two octaves, which is a pretty good range. The Tock-Tock is the dominating instrument. It is seconded by the Belly, another kerosene tin, divided into seven deeper notes. Then comes the Base-Kettle, which is made out of a large vaseline drum, and the Base-Bum, a vast biscuit container from a local factory. An unremitting clash is furnished by the 'steel' – a brake drum beaten with an iron rod – and by the shack-shack. Other lumps of machinery, manhandled into shapes that produce the correct notes, form the remainder of the orchestra.

'To please you, madam,' the Captain said, 'we'll play *Ave Maria*.'

The sound that burst on the ears was hallucinating. From a mile away it might be almost agreeable; but it was Bach all right, and without a single false note. The long notes were held, as with the clavichord before the pedals were evolved, by repeated blows on the same one until it was time to move to the next. After *Ave Maria* they practised a tune that Fish Eyes had just composed. Every now and then he tapped impatiently with his iron bar on the sides of the drum, and the others stopped while he hummed the passage over. At the end of the rehearsal, he pointed to our introducer and said, 'You shouldn't have come with Henry. He's terrible.'

'That's all right, Fish Eyes,' Henry said. 'I won't tell nobody.'

'What's the matter with him?'

'He's one of the Desperadoes. He's a spy.'

The Desperadoes are another steel band, and they are rivals. Each steel band, at Carnival time, roves the streets with banners flying, and plays the tunes they have been practising in secret; though how such a noise can ever be secret is a mystery. Lookouts are posted during the close season to keep spies at bay. The din when the Desperadoes, Fish Eyes' band, Sun Valley, Hill Sixty, the Crusaders and Destination Tokyo are all roving the streets at the same time does not bear thinking of. Each band is accompanied by a small army of partisans, and if they collide in the same street the adherents of opposing factions fall upon each other like Guelphs and Ghibellines.

The lack of inhibitions of the Trinidadian Negroes, their exuberance and brio, come out in many ways: in music and song, and, very noticeably, in their clothes.

In all the islands I had seen before (and in most of them that I saw afterwards) the Negroes were either dressed like tramps or town councillors. There was nothing in between. It was either the old white trousers and shirt, and the shapeless wicker hat, or black serge, starched butterfly collars and watch-chains. In Trinidad all this changes. It has nothing or very little to do with economics and the facility of supply, and I do not think it is entirely due to the size, compared to the other island capitals, of Port of Spain. It is just one aspect of a general phenomenon.

One reason for this general phenomenon of Trinidadian vitality is that, in a direct line, Trinidad's slavery lasted a very short time. If in 1783 the total population of the island was as small as my authority* asserts – 300, including the Governor, the administration, the white landowners and the garrison – there can have been, for practical purposes, hardly any slaves at all. This was probably the lowest ebb of Spanish power in Trinidad, but the shortage among the colonists, decades earlier, of underclothing and of ghostly comforts, and the absolute lack, today, of those architectural remnants which are such a remarkable and splendid heirloom in the poorest of Spain's other colonies, would seem to hint that such misery among the whites cannot have been accompanied by slave-owning on a large scale. So Trinidadian slavery before 1783 is too insignificant to be considered. The country was then flung open. New settlers arrived and new slaves were brought from Africa, and in fourteen years the population shot up to 18,000. In 1807, ten years after the island became British, the Slave *Trade* was abolished; which

---

* Sir Algernon Aspinall.

means that, apart from the illegal activities of the slave-runners,* and the remnant (perhaps 1 per cent?) of the old Spanish slaves, the ancestors of the present black population of Trinidad must all have come to the island from Africa between 1783 and 1807: twenty-four years. So assuming that eighteen was the likeliest age for a Negro to be enslaved and shipped to Trinidad, and that his normal span of life was the biblical seventy years, the oldest slaves would have survived the Emancipation Act of 1834 with exactly one year's grace, and the youngest of the slaves imported from Africa would only have known slavery for twenty-seven; only a little more than a third of his life. And most of the Negroes born into slavery in Trinidad came of parents who had known freedom.

If there is no basic error in this theory, the period of slavery in the ancestry of the coloured population of Trinidad today can virtually be limited to fifty-one years, and fifty-one years when the memory or the tradition of Africa and freedom was fresh in all their minds, and filled, for the latter half of its length (as the anti-slavery campaign gained momentum in England), with the growing hope of deliverance.† And brutal and oppressive as all slavery by its nature must be, it was certainly milder then in its application than during the preceding centuries.

The Trinidadian Negroes, then, have escaped the deadening effects of centuries of slavery in the same place, of generation after generation of it, with no hope of change till the world's end. It would be surprising if this terrible continuity had not in some measure quenched the natural ebullience of the African race in the other islands. (It is astonishing how much has survived.) A certain self-consciousness, the wariness of a man in a false position, has taken its place. Caribbean slavery was a double-edged weapon, for while it was steadily damping the spirits of the Negroes, it was also taking terrible toll of the intelligence and of the civilized virtues among the slave-owners; a loss which their descendants have not yet been able to make good. The art of combining the ownership of slaves with intellectual maturity and a high state of civilization must have vanished with Greece and Rome.

The Trinidadian population of African origin has now risen to well

* Slaves were smuggled from Africa to the West Indies for years after the Trade was abolished, and a cosy illicit commerce went on between the planters and these wretches. At the approach of a Government ship, cannon balls were speedily attached to the legs of the Negroes and the whole cargo was thrown overboard. When the ship was searched, nothing was discovered on board but a token cargo as a cover story.

† I have left out of the reckoning the Negroes of old slave stock which the French Royalist refugees brought from the other Antilles during the Revolution, because I have not been able to discover what the figures were; but I do not think there can have been enough of them, under the circumstances, to have made much difference.

over 200,000 – a growth that has taken place in the middle of a multitude of cosmopolitan influences, great changes in the economic and strategic importance of the island, and the rapid growth of the capital. A thoroughly stimulating atmosphere, in fact, and I suggest that these factors, and the short duration of slavery and a quick psychological convalescence, are the causes of Trinidadian eupepsia.

To return to clothes. At last we saw coloured people (who are physically, I suppose, the best built race in the world) dressed with befitting splendour, especially the slightly raffish, urban class known as the Saga Boys.* The term has definite implications of low life, and Saga Boys, as far as I can discover, live idle and happy lives on music and air and immoral earnings. They are, in fact, a mixture of wide boys, dead-end kids, fly coves and *garçons du milieu*; though, and this is important – in case some absolutely virtuous Saga Boy should ever read these pages with indignation – it can also be a purely sartorial term, implying nothing more than adherence to a certain canon of adornment. Not having been to America, I cannot say how much Harlem has contributed to Port of Spain fashions; obviously quite a lot.

The basis of the whole outfit is the trousers, the saga-pants. They are usually held up by transparent plastic belts, and pleats like scimitars run down to an unusual fullness at the knee, where they begin to taper, reaching almost ankle tightness where the turn-up rests on the two-coloured shoe; peg-top trousers, in fact, but so neat and clean and beautifully ironed that they are nothing like the floppy inexpressibles of *La Bohème*. The jacket, too, the Bim-Bim, or Saga-Boy-coat, has an eccentric and individual cut. There is no padding in the shoulders, a wasp waist, a vent up the back, and lappets that descend in some cases – and this is what gives them their distinctive character – as low as the voluminously trousered knee. They are sometimes cut square in front, so that the whole lower part forms a kind of elongated bell. A broad snap-brim hat is worn with this costume, absolutely straight on the head, or tilted rather forward. The shirts may be severely cut out of some pastel-shade material with a high collar and deep cuffs fastened with glittering links, or in patterns of crossed Coca-Cola bottles, mandolines, palm trees, hearts transfixed with arrows, peonies or masks of Tragedy or Comedy; or even of *toile de Jouy*, with quiet pastoral scenes of rustics and grazing cattle, against the background of a watermill or ivy-hung ruins. The ties, secured with gold pins or chains, have the splendour of lanced ulcers. A rare but notable affectation is the wearing of a long gold Cab Calloway watch-

* Pronounced Sagga.

chain, running from the belt in a loop that may fall below the knee before curving up again to the left-hand trouser pocket. The effect of all this on the Trinidadians, with their wide shoulders, long legs and diminutive middles, is flamboyant, certainly, but at the same time elegant and imposing beyond words. The magnificent Negro carriage comes into its own at last. The *ensemble* is, exactly as it should be, ineffably foppish and *voulu*, but worn with a flaunting ease and a grace of deportment that compels nothing but admiration; and like the authentic dandyism of Baudelaire and Constantin Guys, it is much more than a mere point of fashion. It is a philosophy and a way of life: the symbol, the outward and visible sign of the Saga *Weltanschauung*.

The disreputable side of this world has developed a jargon that is sometimes as lively and as difficult as the cant of Alsatia in seventeenth-century London, or the ballads of Villon. A 'Robust Man' – with the stress on the first syllable – is fairly simply, a tough guy. A 'Sweet Man' is the same as a Saga Boy, while a 'Smart Man' is a crook. The sympathetic word 'Mopsy' was translated to me as 'a girl, a little number', while 'Spoat' is a downright whore. A 'Mauvais' Langue' – only interesting as a survival – is a scold, 'Black as White' means 'anything goes', and 'Mattafix' is O.K. 'Mareeko', after the Spanish *Maricon*, and 'Mama Poule', both of which mean a pathic, hint that catamitish delights are not unknown in this easy-going society. These are the only words I managed to collect in the limited time at my disposal for linguistic field-work, but I believe that, with time and application, a large vocabulary of Saga words could be assembled. Perhaps it has been done. If not, it would be worth doing – it would take the student clean out of the study and the rut of a library research.

The distance from the lower strata of the Saga world to the world of razor-slashing and serious crime cannot be great, and, to judge by the Port of Spain newspapers and some of the Calypsos, this is pretty advanced. One Calypso has a dolefully recurrent chorus about 'Port of Spain alone, boasting a criminal zone', as though its existence were a source of sombre pride.

In the English-speaking Negro world of the Americas, Harlem is Rome, St Louis might be Athens or Alexandria, and Port of Spain is Byzantium: Jazz; Blues; Calypso.

These songs are supposed to have started about the time of the Emancipation, and they were composed at first in the Créole patois, which the slaves had learnt from their masters, at that time predominantly French. Trinidadian students of the subject attribute the tunes to a mixture of African tribal songs with the music of France and Spain. English words began to be used as the new language ousted the old some time before the turn of the century. French, it seems, must have been the dominant influence for too short a time for Créole to sink the sturdy roots that it grew in Dominica and other Windward Isles. But the English is extremely peculiar, and often incomprehensible to a non-Trinidadian; almost a very mild English equivalent of Créole.

Unfortunately, we came to Trinidad a couple of months too early to hear Calypso in its proper setting – in the tents where the Calypsonians rehearse their songs for Carnival. These are roofs of palm leaf or corrugated iron held up by wooden supports and filled by the admirers of the different virtuosi. We had to search for them in night clubs – enormous, rather exciting oases miles from the capital in the middle of trees, where, if one stays late, taxis become so scarce that one has to trudge all the way back in the small hours through what seems a limitless and virgin forest. But all the restaurants and dives are haunted by itinerant Calypso-players with enormous repertoires, who produce a faint replica of what Calypso must be like in its proper setting: strident, truculent and breathless tunes with words that are split up into a scanned and rhythmic wail, or which race along in a headlong and alliterative jumble which only the beat can marshal into some kind of symmetry.

Every year brings forth a fresh harvest of Calypso songs. Some of them comment on world events, like the famous ones about the Abdication or the Marriage of the Duke and Duchess of Kent, others deal with internal Trinidadian affairs. They are a vehicle for lampoon and political satire and hard luck story, and all of them are couched in the curious naif-grandiloquent jargon which has become the vernacular of Calypso. One of the best known, composed by Attila the Hun in the early 'thirties to celebrate the visit of the Graf Zeppelin, is an excellent illustration of the high-flown, almost euphuistic language –

> I gazed at the Zeppelin contemplatively
> And marvelled at man's ingenuity.
> To see that huge object in the air,
> Maintaining perfect equilibrium in the atmosphere,
> Wonderfully, beautifully, gloriously
> Decidedly defying all the laws of gravity:
> 'Twas the Graf Zeppelin which had
> Come to pay a visit to Trinidad.

Words with endings like 'tribulation', 'embezzlement', 'calamity' occur again and again in Calypsos, always with the accent on the last syllable: tribulay-shón, embezzle-mént, calami-tée. One, by the – for a Calypsonian

– democratically styled Reggie Joseph, is typical of the domestic-moralist school –

> They clever, they sly, and so tricky,*
> So they should 'cat' women who commit adultery.
> Hit them damn hard, make them understand
> That a woman must be true to her husband.
>
> Some women today get married just for so
> Live with their husbands a few days, then off they go.
> So when to keep marriage vows they fail,
> I think they should get the cat-o'-nine-tail.

'Madame Joe' strikes the same note of social admonition.

> You go straightening your hair
> And going on with strange doings most everywhere.
> Your age is about sixty-three,
> Yet you behave so disgracefully.
> And in the night you like rufus-vampire
> Going around the town as a British Spitfire,
> With your balloon-barrage.
> O Lord, Madam, do give up your badge.

Attila the Hun is the Calypsonian whose songs are most prone to slip into a type of vaguely metrical pamphleteering – a sort of Calypso that will provide precious data for Trinidadian social historians of the future. For instance –

> In this world I know there are millions of whites
> Who appreciate the coloured man's rights,
> And has a desire and willingness
> To aid in his pursuit of happiness.
> A white man would love a Negro to the core
> As a brother, but not a brother-in-law.
> So these mixed marriages, in my opinion,
> Is the cause of all this racial discrimination.

And

> Again and again I am forced to comment
> On what I call our most peculiar government.
> They said they were unable financially
> To help the West Indian University.
> To aid deserving cases they always fail
> Yet they can build a million-dollar jail.

*I have not attempted to transliterate the Trinidadian accent because I do not know it well enough to do it accurately. 'D' instead of 'Th' and the open, flat vowels as 'maan' for 'man', etc., are the most noticeable peculiarities.

There is something very impressive about the names of the Calypsonians – itself a superbly fustian word – many of them, like my acquaintance the Duke of Albany (to whose diligence in collecting old Calypsos I owe most of the ones quoted), remaining with them for life. They form a Trinidadian Debrett, Zoo and Valhalla: the Black Prince, the Iron Duke, King Fanto, the Cat, the Duke of Normandy, Attila the Hun, Lord Executor, the Lion, King Radio, the Tiger, the Mighty Viking, Lord Kitchener,* Lord Invader, Lord Caressor, Count Buckram and the Mighty Spoiler. Many of their songs express patronage and scorn for the neighbouring islands, treating them as provincial, poor and backward. Barbados, Grenada and Tobago get a very bad press –

> Small Island, go back where you really come from.†
> You came from Grenada in a fishing-boat,
> And now you're wearing a Saga-Boy-Coat.
> Small Island, go back where you really come from.

The presence of Americans is often reflected in war-time and post-war Calypsos, especially in songs like this –

> I was living with a decent and contented wife
> When the soldier came along and broke up my life.
>   And if I struck her
>   She bawl for murder,
> 'Find another mopsy, but leave me with me soldier.'

A curious one that was being sung when we were in the island went, at the speed of a gallop –

> Spoat! Spoat!
> Yankee sufferer,
> Chinee Spoat!
> They bawlin' for murder!
> Indian Spoat,
> Same sufferer!
> Rhythm in your body and you're bound to manoeuvre!

And another which ended –

> Jump on the land!
> Swing your body-line.
> Jump on the land!
> Swing your body in time.

* Who has moved to London.
† Some of the words may be wrong, as they are written down from memory.

But my favourite, which transports one into a region of absolute fantasy and ambiguity, was the following –

> I went to Donkey-City
> To circumcise my body,
> And on the way I met
> A donkey with a mule.
> And the mule said to the donkey,
> 'Saga-Boy, don't you tarry behind me.
> Donkey, woah!
> Take care of my junior commando!'

The chorus goes on, rather dreamily –

> Soft like jelly,
> Red like cherry,
> Sweet like honey,
> And you get it free.

and so on through a sequence of weird and equivocal adventures.

The reader may have concluded by this time that the Trinidadian Parnassus is not a very high mountain, and it is not fair, except for their interest as oddities, to print these lyrics without their accompaniment. For then every drawback of scansion and emphasis, every metrical sprain, seems to be righted by magic, and this splendid, jangling, essentially plebeian music combines with the verse into the most heady and startling songs that can be imagined. They must be the only living folk-music – at any rate, in English – in the British Empire.

CHAPTER 8

Grenada, St Lucia, Antigua, St Kitts

We left Trinidad, for some reason, in the small hours of the morning; driving, half asleep, to the aerodrome at Cocorite, through caverns of bamboo that the headlights summoned out of the darkness. There we waited a long time in the empty white halls, nodding among coffee cups until the unearthly voice from the loudspeaker roused us. Sleepy officials loaded us and our luggage into the plane, where we fell into a sleep whose surface was only ruffled now and then by the jolt of an air pocket. The ninety miles of flight into the north, the landing in Grenada and climbing, as dawn broke, into a motor, were incidents that affected us as remotely as though we had been sleep-walkers, and it was only in the middle of some mountains that we really woke up.

Nothing can be more mysterious and, in their sinister fashion, beautiful than these tarns in the craters of dead volcanoes. Here was another, lying high in the windy folds of the watershed; the water, in this early morning light, stagnant and smooth and steel grey. But the Grand Etang was even more unearthly than the bottomless lake of Dominica, because the forest, as it waded into the lake, seemed to have fallen under a curse which had killed it dead. The far bank was an unearthly wood of skeleton mahogany trees as white and exsanguine as though every single one had been separately struck by lightning and frozen in the moment of death into a demonstrative posture of horror. It was a forest in its agony, the pale, cold scaffolding of a wood, and as we watched the reflections of the trees in the lake they vanished. The surface of the water was broken up into millions of pock-marks as the rain began.

Dark green woods glimmered through the tracks of the rain-drops across the window-panes after we left this deserted place. Steep hills rose and fell and rose again in a final eminence before sinking into the sea.

Among the trees of the last apex a great Regency building appeared: Government House, the driver told us. Remembering a letter of introduction that Mrs Napier had given us, we dug it out and left it in the hands of a splendid-looking white uniformed servant who was standing among brass cannon under the portico, and drove downhill towards the sea and the outskirts of St George's.

The capital of Grenada and the pinnacled belfries under the rain, the steep streets and the wet stone columns and fanlights of Adam houses, the glimpses along the lanes of a grey and turbulent sea – all this resembled a beautiful eighteenth-century Devonshire town in mid-winter. The car drove into the yard of a small hotel that might have been a coaching inn. Dashing indoors through the downpour, we expected to plunge into a world of crops, goloshes, toby-jugs, superannuated advertisements for Apollinaris Water, and copies of Pears' Cyclopaedia; which was, indeed, more or less what we found.

By the time we woke up, the rain had stopped and the little capital wore a different, but no less charming, aspect. How dissimilar everything in Grenada was from the immensity, the trams and the ugliness of Port of Spain! The change in atmosphere, tempo, mood and scenery was complete.

Like Roseau, St George's is a large village that has evolved easily and slowly into a small country town, but the houses, instead of wood and lattice and shingle, are built of stone: fine, solid dwellings, with graceful balustraded staircases running up to pilastered doorways supporting fanlights and pediments. The burnished knockers and door-knobs and letter-boxes reflect the morning sunlight. So steep is the hillside on which the town clusters that the cobbled lanes and streets twist in many directions, and it was only by climbing to the top of the town that we could get an idea of its economy as a whole.

The coast is a succession of volcanic craters, of which one of the largest, the Carenage, is the harbour of St George's. The capital itself is built on the steep crater's rim, which is submerged at its outer segment to form a gap over which the ships can sail out and in; the broken circumference, emerging from the water in bluffs, ascends under its load of houses and churches, to unite with the forested slopes inland. Lagoons engrail the coast with pale blue crescents and discs, and from their landward circumferences the island soars in a steep and regular geometry of volcanic peaks. Old fortresses lie along the hilltops commanding the town, and, on the escarpment of the crater's rim that ends and completes St George's – rising into a final knoll before its steep plunge under water – the old

French Fort Royal (later re-baptized Fort George) rears its defences. The road along the waterfront follows a tunnel through the heart of this castellated tufa, and re-emerges under a little bandstand which rests on the sunlit slope like an empty birdcage.

Windward Islands sloops lay at anchor, and a long way below a schooner under full sail was gliding out of the Carenage into the Caribbean. From our point above the town we could see the law courts, the tower of the eighteenth-century parish church, the tropical-Gothic belfry of the Scottish kirk with its high finials and crockets, and the high roofs of the town, whose steep mansard-gables and beautiful rose-coloured and semi-circular tiles all overlapping like fish-scales must be an architectural device which has lingered here from the time of the French. The town was first laid out by the French Governor, M. de Bellair, in 1705, and continued by the English when it was granted them by treaty in 1763. It has remained British ever since, except for the four years after it was attacked by the fleet of Count D'Estaing and captured by a landing force under Count Dillon, the Irish Commander of Dillon's Regiment of the French Army. The French relinquished it again at the Treaty of Versailles in 1783.

But these roofs seemed to derive from an older tradition than the eighteenth century, and the first progenitors of these Grenadian roofs and gables may well be the steep summits of the Marais and the Place des Vosges. Of French origin, too, are the beautiful wrought-iron balconies on many of the older houses. Everywhere among the roofs and towers the tops of trees appeared, and hibiscus and bougainvillia and flamboyant overflowed the walls, as though the little town were built on an effervescent foundation of tropical flora which sprang foaming through every available gap, pillowing the upper storeys on a tide of leaves and flowers.

To the north of our elevation, the land dived down to a large circle of grass, another volcano's mouth, in the middle of which, far below us and overshadowed by the wooded peaks, a game of football was in progress. The striped jerseys of the players moved about the field in pursuit of the invisible ball with the purposeless motion of insects, and the ragged square of spectators swarmed in bulges, and thinned out and swarmed again with the fluctuations of the game. The rumour of their shouts came faintly to our ears across the green hollow. Our sylvan vantage-point was deserted except for an overgrown cemetery and a young Negro reclining Byronically on a tombstone, under a mango tree, reading *The Prose Works of Oliver Goldsmith*.

Grenada is only twenty-one miles from north to south, and twelve miles at its broadest point from east to west; but owing to the mountainous ridge running along its spine, and the deep valleys that radiate from it on either side, it seems very much larger. Our road along the west coast was overshadowed by the steep mountains of the interior, a towering geometrical organization of green volcanic cones. Valley after valley discharged their rivers under the bridges. They loitered in wide loops for a furlong or two by the waterside and joined the sea through shallow troughs of sand. These junctions of sweet and salt water were the emplacement of villages, each of them built in a little coppice, where Negroes sat weaving lobster-pots in the shade, and the women spread their laundry to dry on the boulders of their little estuaries. A forest of coconut palms stretched in a tenuous belt between the road and the smooth sea, and here and there we passed fishermen hammering away at their half-built sloops, standing under the leaves among their palisades of props. One of them was almost ready for launching, and the shipbuilder and his brother were painting tar on to the clean white timbers of the hull. By her side, all ready for use, lay the freshly cut rollers over which, a week or two later, the sloop would ride into the water. These vessels were the points of departure for the impressively expert colloquies between Rosemary Grimble and the shipbuilders, and we would sit and smoke on one of the bulwarks listening to our beautiful and Brontean companion and these elderly Sinbads as they conversed of tonnages and winds and currents and rigs. Most of these shipbuilders are from Carriacou, the little island half a dozen miles long which lies to the north of Grenada, where the majority of the islanders are engaged in the craft, and their vessels do much of the carrying trade in the archipelago. They are an industrious and thrifty race of Negro, Scotch, English and French descent. Their Scotch ancestry dates from the time when much of the land in Carriacou was in the hands of Scotsmen, and though they seem to have vanished now they have bequeathed to the islanders, along with their other characteristics, a Scots accent. Cattle and poultry raising, with shipbuilding and farming, form their main industries, and until recently Carriacou ponies were the best bred in the Windward Islands.

So close did the road run to the sea that twice we stopped while the path was momentarily blocked by teams of fishermen hauling in their nets; and waited until the final loop, with its agitated haul of captives, was dragged on to the shore. The fishermen dispatched the larger fish by grasping their tails and striking them against the sand, while the smaller ones were poured into rotund wicker amphoras, which were hoisted on to the fishermen's heads and carried away, still shaking and reverberating with the languishing throes of the fish.

A notice in the small township of Gouyave announced a sweepstake of which the first prize was a free funeral for the ticket holder or for any friend or relation. This, and the fact that the town (so Rosemary told us) was equipped with a lilac-coloured hearse emblazoned with the words *Bon Voyage*, seems to hint that the burghers of Gouyave have an individual attitude to death of which one would be glad to learn the secret. Reach-me-down coffins were advertised in the usual glowing terms.

We settled for our picnic in a grassy clearing above the sea at a north-eastern point of the island, called Sauteurs. An overgrown cliff lay on one side of us, and on the other the village green, and a spinney in the middle of which stood the pretty tropical-Gothic church of St Patrick. Carriacou was a long blur on the horizon, only just visible through the line of scattered inlets and rocks that lay due north of the bay. Rosemary, drawing on her fund of nautical lore, pointed them out and named them: Sugar Loaf, Green Island, Sandy Island, Mouche Carrée, Ile Ronde, Les Tantes, Isle de Caille, London Bridge, and the jagged spike of Kickem Jenny – a transliteration, it is believed, of *Caye* (reef) *qu'on gêne* or *qui gêne*.

Sauteurs – or Sotairs as it is alternatively pronounced – gained its name in a gruesome way. After the discovery of Grenada, Spain displayed her customary indifference, and when (except for an abortive attempt at settlement by a company of London merchants) the island had been left to the Caribs for well over a century, Richelieu claimed it for Louis XIII in 1626. Next year Charles I granted it, along with nearly all the Caribees, to the Earl of Carlisle,* but neither France nor England attempted to enforce their claims. The great buccaneer Longvilliers de Poincy attempted to land a few years later, but was driven off by the Caribs. The formidable Duparquet (whom I have mentioned in connection with Martinique) had better luck. For the sum of 1,660 *livres*, he bought Martinique, St Lucia and Grenada from the French 'Company of the Isles of America', settled in Martinique, and, landing in Grenada with a gang of adventurers in 1650, also succeeded in buying the island from the Caribs for (Father Du Tertre records) 'some knives and hatchets and a large quantity of glass beads, besides two bottles of brandy for the chief himself'. Leaving a relation of his behind as governor, Duparquet sailed back to Martinique. Le Comte had orders to exterminate the Caribs if they should attempt to go back on their bargain, which the poor wretches were not slow to do – they could not stop killing Frenchmen whenever they got the chance. The campaign of annihilation began, and the Caribs, who were

* The early history of many of the islands – especially Barbados – is a long catalogue of disputes and lawsuits about their possession by English magnates; notably Lord Carlisle, Lord Marlborough and Lord Willoughby of Parham.

powerless against the armour and the muskets of the French, were routed from the leewardside with terrible losses. Père Labat* describes their last stand, which took place exactly where we were eating our hard-boiled eggs. The savages withdrew to the summit of a steep *morne* surrounded by terrible precipices, which could only be climbed by a narrow secret pathway. Having at last discovered it, the French attacked them by surprise. A fierce fight took place, and those of the Caribs who survived the battle preferred to hurl themselves to death from the top of this rock rather than surrender. Father Du Tertre, who describes the same event, remarks that the victors marched home *bien joyeux*. The Caribs on the leewardside retaliated by killing every isolated Frenchman they saw, and le Comte (who, it appears, would have spared them if his orders had been less definite) surprised their headquarters, where the majority of the remaining Caribs in the island were assembled, and, without regard to age or sex, butchered them all. The last evidence of the race was recorded in 1705, when a handful of them still lived in a valley in the north-west of Grenada.†

As we rounded the north-eastern corner of the island, the scenery changed instantaneously. The smooth sand and water were replaced by the rough windward waves and a gusty shore from which the more luxuriant trees had retreated inland. The only growth on these bleak dunes was the sea-grape, that stubborn shrub which alone is able to resist the violence of the weather. The Trade Winds had twisted and topiaried it into innumerable fantastic shapes; growing normally on the sheltered side, the part of the bush which was exposed to the east appeared to have been shorn away in flat, slanting planes. These extraordinary contortions infect the whole coastline with a disquietingly harassed and tyrannized air, as though the landscape might all at once be blown away, leaving the traveller locked there knee deep in the wet sand like a scape-goat.

It took me some time to determine, as we travelled inland through the wooded hills, what it was that made the country so pleasant and so distinct from other tropical forests. There was none of that sodden and noxious splendour about these trees which in the past had moved us to admiration and rage, and when they made way for clearings, no monotonous sweep of sugar-cane broke loose. For we were driving through plantations of nutmeg and cacao. The straight stems of the cacao

---

* He spent a few days with the Governor de Bellair in 1700.

† The island was sold by Duparquet to a Comte de Cerillac, who sold it to the French Crown, under which it continued until it became a colony of George III's in 1774.

trees and their large, pointed and almond-shaped leaves were gathered in woods and groves which were filled with an unreal and filtered light, an atmosphere resembling that of a medieval tapestry or the mysterious background of a nocturnal hunting scene by Paolo Uccello. The cacao beans hung on the end of short stalks, like red and purple hand-grenades. Weeds, for some reason, refuse to grow under the cacao and the nutmeg, so the trunks are free of the choking tangle of undergrowth and creeper and parasite that muffles the shapes of nearly everything else in these latitudes. The architecture of the forest is unencumbered, and one can gaze among their trunks down glimmering vistas of luminous and variable green. A great luxury after a month or two of the throttling and claustrophobic underwood of the tropics.

It is a pleasure for which one can thank the Emancipation Act. For here, as in Trinidad and most of the islands, the freed Negroes preferred to settle on their own land, or just to squat; or, rather than work as paid labourers on the hated sugar estates, to earn their living as charcoal burners. Labour was imported from Malta and Madeira, but the scheme was a failure. A few of the Maltese became porters or wandering pedlars, but most of them emigrated to Trinidad, and the Portuguese settled down as shop-keepers or plantation assistants, but seldom as labourers. The cultivation of sugar had to be practically abandoned, and its place was taken by the nutmeg and cacao which have become the chief industries of the country. Their cultivation is many times less laborious than the back-breaking grind of the canefields, and much more suited to the character of the islanders; as it would be to anybody's.

In clearings by the road, we saw little farmhouses where solitary Negroes were superintending barbecues – flat trays that could be slid under cover at the approach of rain – on which nutmeg and cacao beans, and the frail scarlet network that covers the nutmeg, were spread to roast in the sun. This red substance is formed by a juice that oozes through the shell of the nut, which, when it dries, becomes a tight, russet lacy substance: the mace of commerce.

Moving through this beautiful forest, then, we blessed the events that had put down sugar from its high place, and made way for these spices, and for the limes and grapefruit and coconut palms, for coconuts and bananas are also an important cultivation. Palms, though they may be monotonous sometimes or inappropriate, are never ugly; and, among the civilized Grenadian flora, even the banana trees looked acceptable. But above all one must revere the memory of the early Spaniards who brought the cacao tree from the banks of the Amazon and the fastnesses of Ecuador.

Derelict sugar-mills mouldered among the usurping trees. Their chimneys were broken, and the semi-circular tiles were moulting from their roofs; and in the long grass by these surrendered palaces, giant cauldrons lay, in which the cassava-flour for the slaves used to be baked. These vessels are an essential part of the Antillean landscape. They are the exact shape of tin helmets in the British Army, but six or eight feet in diameter, and made out of cast iron. Covered with rust and moss, they are another reminder in the abandoned mills of the Antilles of the recentness of slavery and the ravished omnipotence of sugar.

Villages are scarce in the eastern reaches of Grenada. Now and then Rosemary would point out an old plantation house and occasionally we drove through a group of wooden cabins; but most frequent were the mills. Outside one of them in an alcove of the forest a lonely peasant was sharpening a cutlass on a grindstone; pedalling away, pausing every now and then to examine minutely the edge of the glittering blade, and then applying it once more to the screaming and spark-shedding disc. An oddly disquieting vision.

Sessions in the public libraries and, if they existed, the town museums of the different islands had long ago become a point of routine. They vary – many of the insular capitals have beautiful libraries which they owe to the munificence of the later Mr Andrew Carnegie – but they are invariably pleasant retreats, equipped with several thousand books, and always with the Encyclopaedia Britannica, the ordinary works of reference, and most of the books concerning the island in which they are situated. The British colonies are gratifyingly superior to those of any other Caribbean power in this matter.

Grenada, though it somehow missed the benevolence of Carnegie, is no exception. One of the most rewarding books I found there had an unpromising title and a prosaic official binding: *The Grenada Handbook and Directory*, 1946 – nearly four hundred closely printed pages of information about the little island. Much of it is dry, official stuff. But many pages are concerned with the animals, birds, reptiles, fish, insects, trees and flowers of the island, and, best of all, over seventy beautifully written, almost Gibbonian, pages (anonymous, alas) are devoted to the island's history. Wars, earthquakes, hurricanes, religious debates, civil disturbances, reforms, eclipses of the sun, presents of plate to retiring governors, epidemics of whooping cough – nothing has been forgotten. Turning back to the period of which I was in pursuit, I was arrested by the following incident:

About 8 o'clock p.m. on October 5, 1797, a large ship approached the town of Gouyave, showing no lights, whereupon the detachment of the 2nd West Indian

Regiment stationed there ... fired a gun at her from the battery, which was returned from the ship by two or three broadsides at the battery and the town. Believing the French were landing at Gouyave, the inhabitants of the neighbourhood began to fly to St George's. The next morning H.M.S. *Favourite* (Captain Lord Camelford) anchored at St George's, and it was ascertained that this bombardment of a peaceful town had been done at the order of Lord Camelford, who, without thinking of the suspicion his stealthy movements must have excited on the shore, considered himself insulted by the gun fired from the battery in the first instance, and had retaliated in the disgraceful manner described.

'Believing the French were landing ...' – this was the period I was after.

When Victor Hugues, the emissary of the Convention, had fought and overcome the French Royalists and their British allies, and had erected the guillotine in Guadeloupe, he formed a plan to recapture from the English the islands of Martinique, St Lucia and Grenada. Owing to tension between the English and French colonists, Grenada was the likeliest starting-point, and it was there that he dispatched his envoys to stir up revolt. A coloured planter called Julien Fédon was chosen as leader of the insurrection.

'At midnight on March 2, 1795, the storm broke; a body of insurgents under Fédon surrounded the town of Grenville and a horrible massacre of the British subjects ensued. Neither age nor sex proved a bar to the ferocity of the rebels, and by morning the town was a reeking shambles, from which the butchers retreated to the mountains, laden with spoil.' The rebels entrenched themselves on Fédon's estate on Morne Quaqua, near the Grand Etang.

The Lieutenant-Governor, 'instead of being at headquarters at such a time, was spending some days with a party of gentlemen at his estate, Paraclete', in the eastern foot-hills near Grenville. The party of fifty-one hastily embarked in a sloop and, sailing round the island, landed at Gouyave, which they did not realize was also in a state of rebellion. They were all promptly captured and marched as prisoners to Fédon's camp and 'subjected to every indignity that malice could suggest, and were further informed by Fédon that, if an attack were made on his camp, they would be slaughtered without mercy'. Reinforcements were rushed to the island, and siege was laid to Morne Quaqua. But the camp, owing to the incessant rain, the scarcity, to begin with, of troops, the fever, and the suicide, in a fit of delirium, of the English commander, was still untaken a month later. But more troops arrived and 'the assault was characterized by intrepid bravery on both sides. The difficulty had been underestimated of storming the crest of an almost inaccessible mountain protected by strong *abattis* of felled trees in the face of a galling fire and on ground so slippery from continual tropical rains that even a foothold was difficult to obtain.'

Inside the stockade, meanwhile, a terrible tragedy was taking place, a description of which I discovered in a narrative by Dr John Hay, who almost suffered the fate of his companions: 'A voice was heard saying, "The prisoners are to be shot." The guard ... appeared very much agitated, and trembling with impatience, and some seemed to have their guns cocked. A few prisoners called out, "Mercy!" No reply was made. Others, who were not in stocks, were on their knees praying. Not a word was exchanged among us ... The door was opened; two men appeared with hammers to take the prisoners out of the stocks. Those who were not in confinement were ordered to go out ... Fédon began the bloody massacre in the presence of his wife and daughters, who remained there, unfeeling spectators of his horrid barbarity. He gave the word *"Feu!"* himself to every man as soon as he came out; and of fifty-one prisoners, only Parson McMahon, Mr Kerr and myself were saved.' 'With one or two exceptions,' resumes the anonymous historian of the *Handbook*, 'where protracted suffering had affected their minds, they met their fate as became their race and station. There can be little doubt that the immediate cause of this execrable deed was the death of Fédon's brother, who fell early in the day.'

The rebellion took about three months to subdue. (No help could come from the neighbouring island of St Vincent, which was in the throes of the black Carib revolt, or from St Lucia, where Jervis was coping with an insurrection of the Maroons: distant explosions of the French Revolution, touched off on the spot by the agents of Victor Hugues.) But after the arrival of Sir Ralph Abercromby the rebel strong-points were reduced one by one. Morne Quaqua was the last to fall. 'No quarter was given to the rebels', as the soldiers were incensed by a last act of wanton barbarity on their part, twenty white prisoners, having just been led out and 'brutally murdered before the eyes of the advancing troops'. There were many fierce battles in the last phases – bayonet charges by the Buffs under a commander with the familiar name (in such circumstances) of Brigadier-General Campbell, sieges by the 57th Regiment, and assaults by Prince Löwenstein's German Jäger-regiment under Graf von Heillimer, 'whose troops were well accustomed to mountain and forest warfare'. After the capture of the governor, the Attorney-General sent letters asking for assistance from the neighbouring islands, among others to the Spanish Governor in Trinidad, none other than Don José Maria Chacon, who was the first to respond by sending two brigs, filled with soldiers. One cannot help wondering what must have been the feelings of this Spanish gentleman when, two years later, with his fleet still burning in Port of Spain harbour to save it from capture, he had to surrender the island of Trinidad to the British.

A special Court of Oyer and Terminer was called to deal with the rebels. Forty-seven were condemned without hearing to be hanged, on proof of identity alone. But Lieutenant-Governor Houston pardoned all except fourteen of the ringleaders. His clemency, though warmly applauded by the British Government, was bitterly attacked by the colonists, who so far prevailed that, in the end, thirty-eight were executed. But he succeeded in saving many others who were caught later. These, like the rank and file of the slaves – and like the Black Caribs of St Vincent – were deported to British Honduras. 'It is gratifying to record that the Legislators so far blended justice with mercy as to make a grant to some of the families of those who suffered the extreme penalty of the law in consequence of their treason.'

The strangest part of the story is the total disappearance of the villain – or the hero – of the whole affair. After hiding some time in the woods, Fédon was completely lost sight of; and nothing certain is known of his fate, 'although it is conjectured that he was drowned while seeking escape to Trinidad in a small canoe'. It was as though he had been lifted into the sky as unvestigially as Enoch and Elijah, and borne away to some Negro garden of the Hesperides.

Mount Moritz, an inland valley north of the town, is inhabited by a little colony of whites; transplanted offshoots of the Redlegs of Barbados, and so, most of them, descendants of the Duke of Monmouth's followers. They were shy, simple people, living the same rustic life as the coloured islanders – which in Grenada, and in comparison with the living conditions and the arduous labour of many rural populations in England, is not at all bad – and speaking the same difficult English. Strolling up the path of the scattered village, we again listened in vain for the accents of the West Country. They looked stronger and bigger than the 'Poor Whites' of Guadeloupe and the Saints and Barbados, and if their cotton clothes were changed into corduroy and tweed, indistinguishable from English country people. The darker colour of the children – almost non-existent among the older villagers – indicated that mixed marriages are becoming more frequent. One old woman we met said that her family was Scottish, or so she thought; probably one of the 'unruly Scots' deported to the Indies by Cromwell. In the village school I had a look through the list of the children's names. Several of them were Scotch – Alexander, Campbell, Kerr – and the others looked completely English, not at once noticeably deriving, I should have thought, from any specific region – Dowden, Edwards, Greaves, Medford, Searles, Winbush – but as likely to have originated in the south-western counties as anywhere. Two of the boys had the christian names of Aubrey and Taflin, and a little girl, I noticed with interest, was called Lilith.

The Government House of Grenada is a building suitable to the dignity of the Governor and Commander-in-Chief of the Windward Islands. For Sir Arthur Grimble's hegemony embraced not only Grenada, but Carriacou and the Grenadine islands, St Vincent and St Lucia, and, since 1940, it has flung out a long loop to the north to include Dominica, which until then belonged to the administrative unit of the Leeward Islands. The Government Houses of Dominica, St Lucia and St Vincent are the bases of three Administrators who, in the absence of the Governor in Grenada, preside over the affairs of the three colonies.

We spent pleasant, unhurried hours there, looking at Rosemary Grimble's beautiful drawings of Caribbean life, or talking with the Governor about Island life and, among other things, I remember, of religion and politics, and books and poetry and sonnet-forms; and listening to our host's accounts of Pacific islands: hours of singular charm that always came to an end too soon. The Governor was about to retire and settle in England after half a lifetime spent in helping to administer and, later, in governing different parts of the Empire. A note of valediction pervaded those large and beautifully proportioned rooms; and we also felt sadder at the prospect of leaving Grenada than we had felt anywhere else.

Half-way down the hill on our last night, we stopped to gaze at the Seventh Day Adventist chapel, a lovely classical building, built entirely of wood, with a pediment sustained by fine Doric columns; as cool and serene among the moonlit trees as though it had been built out of Parian marble on a headland in Attica. There must be something in the atmosphere of Grenada that prevents an architect from going wrong.

All the lights were out in the rectory, and the quayside was silent. The sea here is not relegated to a slum as though it were a magnified drain. It is right in the town, and the houses begin at the quay. The air in some of the back lanes is heavy with the smell of stored spices, and the shops on the waterfront are deep, cool caves of shade reaching back from a colonnade of rounded vaults. Grocers and ships' chandlers mostly.

As we strolled along the quay, hardly a ripple moved the reflections of the sloops and the street lamps and the moon. They hung drowned and immobile in the middle of the sleeping town. The stars shone like blue pendant balls, so close, in appearance, that an outstretched hand might almost pluck them down.

But the capital was not quite asleep, for the sound of singing came floating down the lanes. We pursued it to its source, and, climbing a flight of stairs, looked into a kind of parish hall. About a hundred Grenadians were lustily singing, and a white clergyman, with his mouth also manfully distended in song, played a harmonium. He accentuated the beat by swinging his head, in a semi-jocular fashion, from side to side. They were practising carols – a fact that made us suddenly realize how close we were to Christmas. 'Through de rude wind's wild lament,' they roared, 'and de bitter wedder.' The mixture of familiarity and un-familiarity was pleasing and strange. At first I could not understand why it should seem so odd. '... where de snow lay dinted,' they went on, 'Heat was in de very sod where de Saint had printed ...' Of course! the snow. We descended again into the hot night. The tops of tropical trees appeared above the roofs. How many conversations I had recently had about snow!

'Yes, but what's it like?'

'Well, it's light, like confetti. It falls out of the sky and blows about in the wind. It's terribly cold, and when it settles it resembles cassava or mashed potatoes. Your feet leave marks on it as though you were treading on sand, and you can make balls of it, or even snowmen. It is so heavy it sometimes breaks the branches of trees. It's deep and crisp and even ...'

'I'm sorry, I don't get it, maan. I don't get it at all. Not what it's *really* like ...'

The Christmas carols reminded us how quickly the time was passing. We determined all at once upon a drastic burst of speed through the Leeward Islands, in order to dawdle and still to have a little money left over in the Greater Antilles. This sudden rush meant travelling by air most of the time, and, for some reason which I have forgotten, cutting out St Vincent. Anyway, we thought, as we sailed up into the air over Grenada, we will be able to see it from above. We peered down through the dawn at the vanishing coast of Grenada. Carriacou paddled after it into the southern haze like an abandoned puppy.

As the air cleared, the entire archipelago of the Grenadines appeared: innumerable islets scattered across the sea from horizon to horizon, and seeming, as they slid slowly southwards, to writhe and change shape and turn over: violoncellos, scissors, earwigs, pairs of braces, old boots, cogwheels, armadillos, palettes, wishbones, oak leaves, boomerangs and bowler hats, all of them hanging mysteriously in a blue dimensionless dream. Haloed at the surface with pale green water, their pedestals, visible until they were obscured by darkness, sank sharply to the bottom of the sea. Solitary cones rose portentously through the penumbra, but no little wreaths of foam surrounded their crests; only a few yards of water separated them from the water-level. Pathetically, after so much uphill work, they had just missed being islands – 'Well tried,' one felt like murmuring – and scattered and sharp-toothed reefs combed the winding currents into parallel skeins of surf. Isolated clouds went bowling past like overblown cherubim, or languished, seraph-like, above their shadows. Then the clouds assembled in troops, and we were skimming over the summit of a bulbous mountain of vapour.

Something was going on underneath this great white heap, for the outline of its meeting with the water was marked by a sprinkling of sailing boats. A little steamer was even trailing its wake into one of the bulges. 'St Vincent,' the air hostess murmured.

It was very sad. And it was fantastic, too, that a British Crown Colony, half the size, as Sir Algernon Aspinall observes, of Middlesex, should be buried somewhere under that colossal tea-cosy. I thought ruefully of the hidden towns and villages; the cathedral; the hundred and thirty-three square miles and the fifty-seven thousand people; the Kingstown and the Aquatic clubs; the mountains and the forests and the rivers; the bronze chandelier presented by George III; the battlefields of the Brigands' War; the tombstone of Alexander Leith, a hero in that same war, 'The Carib Chief Chattawar falling by his hand'; and of the Botanical Gardens where Captain Bligh, after his second journey from the South Seas, first planted the breadfruit tree. I thought especially of the Soufrière, a volcano over four thousand feet high, whose eruption in 1902 wiped out two thousand of the islanders, and ash from whose crater had plunged Barbados, ninety-seven miles away, into pitch darkness ... all hidden under that big white blob, which, even as we stared at it, was moving off, still enshrouding its invisible contents. What a miserable way to travel! There was something thoroughly improper about the whole thing.

The sea, for half an hour or so, was bare of anything except, towards the end, our tiny shadow slanting slowly down towards a great wallowing island; a rhinoceros, it might have been, magnified millions of times, for two great horns came snouting up towards us through the sunlight. A blanket of cloud concealed the rest of its anatomy as though it had been packed for travelling purposes, or muffled against the cold. As we flew lower, the cloud became torn, revealing ragged vignettes of mountain-sides or forested plateaux, or deep gorges; and soon we were flying low over the sails of fishing boats, dozens of white triangles, all of them converging on an inlet and a town.

A few minutes later, as we were climbing into a little bus, an affable young Negro wandered up with his hands in his pockets. He had been an amused but quite unhelpful spectator of our struggles with the luggage. He gave us a pleasant smile and said: 'Give me ten cents, boss.'

'No.'

'No? No? You've let me down, boss.'

The Pitons, close up, were just as surprising as they had looked from the air: two lonely spikes jutting out of the coast of the island, each shaped like the Matterhorn, and one of them slightly taller than the other. Their perpendicular sides were coated with red, green and canary-yellow moss and creeper, and when, from our little boat in the gulf that they enclosed, we clapped our hands, a host of birds took flight from their nests on invisible ledges and gyrated clamorously above our heads. They are described in books as 'spires of lava forced out generations ago from the craters of two great volcanoes'. Being no geologist, this is not very clear to me, and I have not been able to discover, from works of reference, exactly what it means. The vision which immediately presents itself is of two pointed jets of lava shooting out of holes to a great height – 2,619 feet and 2,481 feet respectively – and cooling before they could fall to earth again: petrified fountains. There is plainly something wrong with this. The second (I cannot think of any other meaning) is that the two elongated lozenges were already solid, and lurking somewhere under the surface of the earth; and when the volcanic holes were blown in the coast, they both got caught in the upward motion, and jammed half-way out. If this is anywhere near the truth, creepers and forests have now entirely smothered their foundations except where their sides drop clean into the sea. The Petit Piton had never been scaled till late in the last century, after, it is rumoured, a party of British sailors had made the attempt, all of them falling dead at various points on the way to the summit, from the bite of the *Trigonocéphale*. This terrible snake has contrived to make its way here from the South American mainland, travelling, it must be supposed, in the same way as the ancestors of the Martinican brutes – by sea, on floating branches.

There is a low-lying volcano behind these peaks, called – it is the last one in this book – Soufrière. A pleasant little fishing town of the same name extricates itself from the forest at the edge of the water.

Our encampment among the coconut palms and dug-out canoes – for the old Carib art has been inherited by nearly all the Windward islanders

– was soon the meeting-place of a swarm of lewd village children who settled round us in a ring and commented on our appearance. A boy of ten, to put us at our ease, civilly offered us cigarettes, and then, lighting them with his own, expatiated on the backwardness of his home town. It was a dead-and-alive place, he affirmed. He broke off to ask if we would like some beer. It was a wonderful thought. He ran off into the village with one of our pound notes. The other children began chattering to each other in Créole. 'Herbert won't come back,' one of them said.

'Why won't he?'

'Herbert's a thief.'

As if to disprove this libel, he came running down the sand with the beer a few seconds later. We thanked him and, glaring icily at his detractors, ostentatiously gave him a shilling. He was off like a bullet, and back beside us in a few moments with another bottle for himself. Lying on the sand, thoughtfully smoking and drinking his beer, he continued his discourse. You could not make a career in Soufrière. 'That's a nice shirt,' he said, pointing to one I had bought in Trinidad, covered with agricultural scenes. 'A real saga-shirt.' He lay back and nostalgically sang us a song with a chorus about 'The two-coloured shoes, sir, the saga-pants, and the bim-bim coat.' When he had finished he said, 'But you can't be a saga-boy here, sir. Too poor. They put you in custody, sure bet.' After a moment of reverie, he said, 'Would you like to have a bath?' He explained that he did not mean the sea, but a real hot bath. Following him through the village, and a little way uphill into the forest, we came to the domesticated little crater of the Soufrière: a few patches of boiling mud among grey rocks. He threw some stones into the biggest cauldron, and stirred it up with a long stick to its hissing maximum of ferocity. Then he took a shilling, and buried it in the mud; when he dug it up again, the fumes had turned it black. 'There you are, madam,' he said. 'It's no Vesuvius, but that's all we got in Soufrière.'

The baths were a row of stone troughs in a wooden enclosure in the thick of the woods. Herbert roused an old man from his sleep in a little hut, who stopped up the holes in the trough with plugs of banana leaf. They filled up with warm sulphurous water, and we were able to recline in the leafy shade and converse at our leisure, with the craters hissing gently below us. These delightful baths were installed by a grant of Louis XVI, seven years before the taking of the Bastille. The *Médecins du Roi*, summoned from Martinique by the Baron de Labordie, the French Governor of the island, had examined the waters and pronounced them to be sovereign for rheumatic complaints and full of every kind of health-giving property; and the baths were duly built for the benefit of the royal troops in the Antilles. Lying in the warm water and looking up at the sky through a dozen strata of different-shaped leaves was so luxurious and agreeable that it was an effort to get out. When we climbed into our boat again we felt that we had accumulated considerable strength.

One of the children, a detestable sneak, asked us, in a loud voice, if Herbert wasn't wrong to smoke. 'That kid's right,' Herbert said, 'I got to cut down. Too dear. There's no money about.'

Our boat edged its way through a little fleet of incoming canoes, several of which, furnished with outriggers to keep their balance, were carrying enormous polygonal lobster cages. As we headed northwards towards the distant capital we looked back at the Pitons, and the diminishing silhouette of Herbert with his hat raised above his head in a grave valedictory posture. Like the grove of cauliflower-clouds along the horizon, the setting sun had washed the two rocky prongs a wonderful love-sick pink. The water was streaked with green and lilac, and every few yards there was the sound of a multitude of small splashes, as shoals of sprats leapt out of the sea in flight from our keel. It was quite dark when, three hours later, we sailed down the gulf towards the lights of Castries.

Architecturally speaking, Castries seems to be the victim of a curse. It is always catching fire and being burnt to the ground. The last holocaust had taken place in 1927, and since we left the island it has had another visitation. It seems to be a magnet for Acts of God, and the ugliness of the town has thus nothing intentional and perverted about it.

It looked, merely, as if the inhabitants, sceptical of the permanence of their handiwork, had got tired of building it up again. It is a brisk and shoddy piece of work and there is little more to be said about it. The Church of the Immaculate Conception may, as reference books aver, have been built by a student of Pugin, but by an unimaginative student who has succeeded all too well in bridling the extravagance of his master. It stands on one side of a large central square whose tree-encompassed bandstand is the only other detail that contrives to stick in the memory. The rest remains in the mind only as a mist of scorching streets running down to the waterfront, where the funnels of steamers appear; for Castries is one of the very few harbours in the Antilles where the water is deep enough for ships to drop anchor alongside the wharf.

And yet, in spite of its ungrateful appearance and the swarms of beggars that torture you as you trudge down those incandescent thoroughfares, it fails to leave a disagreeable impression. Perhaps because the mental blur of recollection so quickly takes shape again at the ends of the town, and faithfully recalls the beautiful wooded inlet that unwinds towards the sea, the reflected mops of palm leaves suspended on long threads of trunk from green headlands, and the mountainsides that fall towards it from the inland clouds. Also, perhaps, it was a change to hear everybody clucking away in Créole, and to see the panniered skirts and spike-ended turbans once more, and to feel the livelier Afro-Gaulish ambience of the French Antilles. St Lucia was the last of the Antilles to fall from French into English hands, and the predominant patois, the surviving French traditions and an important French minority, stamp it as the most French of the British West Indies. For Castries, if the names over the shops did not remind you that you are in a British Crown Colony, might be a part of Fort-de-France.

Standing under an araucaria planted by the Prince of Wales in 1920 on the lawn of Government House – a magnificently ugly edifice reared in late Victorian times – we were able to see the pale shape of Martinique and the small, solider dome of Diamond Rock, where (it seemed such a long time ago already) we had spent the day with Dr Rose-Rosette. For we had nearly completed the circuit of these southern islands.

The Caribs got rid of the first English settlers by the same stratagem which they used, according to Père Labat, for overcoming parrots: they drove them out with red-pepper smoke. When, later on, Duparquet bought it, his lieutenant wisely married a Carib girl; but his peaceful reign was followed by the murder of his three successors. Lord Willoughby of Parham, who also considered himself the owner of St Lucia, sent a party of settlers who captured the island in 1664; but three years later it was French again. The Marshal d'Estrées had a grant from the French King, the Duke of Montagu from the English; and so on, until the difference became a matter of conflict between the mother countries themselves. It was mainly French, however, until its final cession. The English took it several times, but had to hand it back at various treaties. Victor Hugues captured it during one of its British occupations, and the French held it finally until one year before Waterloo. Since then it has remained British. All the familiar Caribbean figures played a part in its fortunes – Rodney, Abercromby, Jervis, Grey, d'Estaing, and de Bouillé; and even the Duke of Kent, Queen Victoria's father, captured Morne Fortuné in 1794. It again fell to the French, and Sir John Moore, the hero of Corunna, recaptured it next year at the head of a bayonet charge of the Royal Inniskilling Fusiliers.

The extra decades (in relation to French suzerainty in the other Antilles which have since become British) during which St Lucia remained in French hands, and the large number of French landowners, cousins of the squirearchy of Martinique, who stayed on afterwards, meant that Paris was still the chief luminary to reflect its lustre on St Lucian life, and, though the French landowners are now in a minority, they form a society of their own with a most definite feeling of tribal solidarity. The smart life of Castries in the first forty years of the nineteenth century sounds extraordinarily sophisticated and lively. Mr Stow, the Administrator lent me Father Pelletier's and Henry Breen's books on St Lucia,* which I read with absolute mystification. All these routs and cotillions, these mazurkas and schottisches and quadrilles in these splendid ballrooms! These chandeliers glittering with hundreds of wax candles, and the brilliant performances of the comedies of Crebillon and Beaumarchais and Scribe – where did they take place? In dozens of houses apparently. The equipages and crinolines, the witty local press, the quarrels about precedence, the duels – why, it might be Regency London or Paris of Napoleon III! This is the sort of knowledge my brain is absolutely unable to deal with. It is not disbelief, for it is obviously true (though Mr Breen may have piled it on a bit), but a sort of mental disability, like the attempt to conjure up powdered wigs in the Guadeloupean town of Moule. One bit of Etruscan pottery, about which I know nothing, can, in a dark, vague and instinctive fashion, bring Lars Porsena of Clusium and all the ranks of Tuscany to life for me. But here? I got up and looked out of the hotel window at the miserable, rain-soaked street that straggled away into the trees. This glittering world existed only a hundred years ago, and there is nothing, not a grain of corroborative evidence, not the remotest clue to prove that it once existed. Absolutely nothing.

The climate of Castries may be relaxing in the normal sense of the word, but for patients suffering from the languors of over-imaginativeness it must be the most bracing and astringent place in the world. Soufrière for rheumatics, the island might announce on its tourist advertisements, Castries for romantics.

Wandering along the main street after dinner, I stopped in front of the cinema. But there was no performance that night, the posters said; the building had been taken over for the Speech Day and Prize Giving of St Mary's College, a school justly famous throughout the Antilles. The door was open, so I went in and found a seat at the back of the dress circle.

Here, at any rate, I soon saw, was a completely English atmosphere, of a very familiar and sympathetic sort. On the stage were the Headmaster,

---

* *St Lucia*, Henry Breen, Longman, 1844.

a few of the masters, and Mrs Stow, who was giving the prizes away. The names were shouted out, and each time a boy got up and climbed on to the stage, smoothing his hair, pulling down the back of his jacket and straightening his tie with a sort of stumbling gravity. Then the book, the bow, the handshake, stumble-stumble, and down. From the very rare occasions I ever had to go through this performance I remembered the agony. They had my sympathy. The inter-House trophies came next: Rodney had won the cricket and football, Abercromby the aquatics. The Swots, thin, spectacled boys, made way for the Bloods, who seized the handles of the great cups with a muscular grip. Abercromby had also carried off the Davidson-Houston House Championship. Then came the presentation of the new Colours: Bloods again. I noticed with interest that the island fashions had remained faithful to Oxford bags. These obsolete trousers were especially noticeable because they are the exact reverse of the Trinidadian mode.

When the last of the colours and prizes had been carried away, the curtain came down and, after a minute or two, rose again on the Forum scene in *Julius Caesar*. Brutus and Antony left less of an impression on the mind than the citizens, who were wonderfully violent. Bellowing for the Will, they galloped across the stage in a body, with their left hands upheld in a uniform gesture, suddenly stopping dead and silent in their tracks. Then, swayed by Antony's rhetoric, they slowly recoiled again, all snarling with scorn and hatred of the Senate; and finally, when the peroration reached its climax, they milled round and round as though Antony from the height of the rostrum were stirring them up with a spoon. A real uproar, and a thoroughly spirited performance.

The loudspeaker announced His Honour the Administrator, and Mr Stow, an elegantly dinner-jacketed figure in the blinding spotlight, rose and made an excellent speech, which was answered by the Head Prefect in words that struck me as far better than any head prefect's speech I had ever heard at school. After a series of hip-hoorays, the stage was filled by the school choir, which, like the actors and prize-winners and athletes, represented every variation of the St Lucian population; England and France and Africa in about equal proportions. In the programme, I noticed that English names outnumbered the French by almost two to one. The school song was rousingly delivered –

> Step together, play the game,
> Thus we'll bring St Mary's fame.
> Unity will make us strong,
> Love will guide our steps along.
> Love indeed our lives will frame,

> Love for God which cares not whether
> Foes smite
> Left, right.
> We Samarians work together;
> Steady, boys, and step together!

It was all very impressive and nostalgic. *God Save the King* was immediately preceded by the Neapolitan song *Santa Lucia*; and the proceedings broke up.

Santa Lucia seems to have been adopted as the national anthem of the island (whose name is pronounced St Loosha).* As the next day was the feast day of the Saint, and a great island holiday, I heard it sung many times. It came to the public rescue in notable circumstances in the evening, when a competition was billed to take place in the bandstand between rival jazz-band orchestras. The whole of Castries was assembled in the square. But an earlier item on the programme was the recitation of *The Lifeboat*, by Service. This contemporary poem, which I had never heard before, deals with the return of a prodigal son to his little village in Cornwall in the middle of a storm. His father, the lifeboatman, lies dying, and a ship is foundering on the rocks. The son, who has always been a waster, is greeted by the reproaches of his parents, and, stung by their scorn, he goes out into the tempest and rescues the whole crew, I think, single-handed. The story is told by an old sailorman at unbelievable length and in Cornish dialect. After about an hour of it, the St Lucians were plainly unable to stand much more, and the groans and protests became more frequent. The situation was solved at last by one of the musicians quietly playing *Santa Lucia* on the saxophone. Others joined in one by one, and the song was taken up by the crowd until the speaker was inaudible. Only his gestures and the movements of his lips hinted that the Cornish storm was still raging. I was rather sorry, because I wanted to know how it ended.

Perhaps the adoption of this song is not as arbitrary as it seems at first. After all, Columbus discovered the island on St Lucy's day, and she was an island saint – a Sicilian – and Neapolitan is fairly close to her own vernacular. '*Elle triompha à Syracuse,*' writes Dom Guéranger, '*comme Agathe brille à Catane, comme Rosalie embaume Palerme de ses parfums.*' She certainly came triumphantly to the rescue of her distant devotees on this occasion.

*

* There are several catches like this. Dominica receives the stress on the third syllable – eeka; Antigua is pronounced Anteega; Saba like a cavalry sword; Grenada with the first *a* as *ay*, not *ah*.

The line that the aeroplane followed through the air was a recapitulation of our earlier journeys: the Diamond Rock, Martinique, Dominica, Marie Galante, the Saints, the Désirade, Guadeloupe – they seemed to flick back like beads along a wire, and all that lay before us was unfamiliar and new; a different archipelago was obtruding itself towards us out of the north.

Caribbean towns are very surprising. St John's, the capital of Antigua and the seat of government of the Leeward Islands, sounds important enough, and I was mentally geared for an active little metropolis; bustling, commercial and proconsular, with traffic blocks, perhaps, in the busy streets. But the car drove past a village green into an empty street where low, white wooden houses were as closed and empty-looking as if they had been evacuated years ago. It was quite early, and yet there was nobody about, not even a figure in the distance to prove that the blank façades hid anything except sheeted furniture and cobwebs. It was like a bone-yard, the bleached anatomy of a flat fish washed up here among the sand dunes. The motor, although it had been creaking along at the pace of a tortoise, seemed unable to stop. The driver jerked again and again at the levers until it shuddered into immobility. We asked him where the centre of the town was. He told us we were right there.

The light in the streets of this necropolis burnt into the eyeballs pitilessly. It was with real relief that we found an hotel and escaped behind the plank walls into an interior as dim as a harem, and as quiet and shuttered. But seemingly an abandoned one, as there was no sign of life there except, at the end of a passage, a many-branched hat-stand adorned with an extraordinary profusion of superannuated masculine headgear – several trilbies and peaked caps, a reversible fishing hat that was covered with tweed on the outside and lined with leather, a faded straw boater, a solar topee, and the forage cap of some regiment that must have been disbanded for half a century. Thinking that we had irrupted into a private house, we were about to depart when an elderly parlourmaid appeared and led us in silence to rooms which were crammed full of beds, either assembled or leaning against the walls. She uncoiled a mosquito net in each room and vanished. There seemed nothing for it but to go to bed. The message of the town was imperious. We climbed therefore into our milky pavilions, and prepared for sleep.

A copy of *John Inglesant* had been forgotten by somebody on the table beside my bed. The print had faded to a pale brown, and the pages and cover were drilled full of tunnels by insects. I dozed off after half a page.

At the other side of the island, later in the day, a lugubrious Negro pointed to a worm-eaten four-poster, a chair almost in bits and a table. 'These aren't the real ones. They were sold when the Admiralty gave up the place in 1906. But this is where Lord Nelson lived. This was his bedroom.'

These sad and echoing chambers were decayed almost to the verge of disintegration. We tiptoed from room to room. One hard stamp, you felt, would bring the building down in a heap. The bedrooms, the dining-room, the office – these had been the daily background of Nelson for the years which, as Captain of H.M.S. *Boreas*, he had spent on the West Indies Station. A figurehead and a little cannon guarded the door, and all over the flat promontory that jutted into English Harbour stood the crumbling impedimenta of an eighteenth-century naval base. Capstans, for careening the men-o'-war, radiating long rotten beams, overhung the water's edge like enormous spiders too old to walk away. The Negro pointed out the emplacements of the batteries that had defended the harbour, the old powder magazine, and the massive pillars which had once held up the roof of the boathouse, standing above the water like a group of druidical monoliths. The galleried officers' quarters at the end of the spit had relapsed into a state of barn-like desolation. We followed our guide into a dark and enormous building of wood: the old sail loft and stores. The timbers were so eaten away that we had to step from beam to beam, for the boards between them had fallen to powder, or still hung from rusty nails in rotten fragments. He put his finger on the walls, and indicated the words 'A merry Xmas a Happy New Year 2 you all' painted there, it was formerly believed, by King George V when he visited Antigua as a young sailor. Clambering out into the sunlight again over mountains of mouldering nautical gear and anchors eaten by rust, we looked across the bay to the house where the Sailor King, William IV, when he was still Duke of Clarence, and a young officer in command of H.M.S. *Pegasus*, had lived in 1786.

A point on the quay was the scene of a strange exploit of the same Lord Camelford who behaved so oddly off the coast of Grenada. In the absence of their superior officer, there was some doubt as to whether he or a fellow-lieutenant called Peterson was in command of the station. Camelford ordered Peterson to patrol the harbour on the night of a ball, and Peterson, refusing to recognize his authority, dressed himself in his party clothes, and prepared to leave. But his way was barred by Camelford, who repeated the order and, when Peterson again refused, pulled out a brace of pistols and shot him through the breast. 'He fell a corpse to the ground,' a contemporary wrote, 'the deadly stream welling from the wound, and staining, as it flowed, the gay ball dress which he wore.'

After several other curious incidents, Lord Camelford was killed in a duel in London by a Mr Best of Barbados.

Just below the waterline at the end of the quay, the stones were covered with a wonderful foliage of rainbow-coloured sea-anemones, whose feelers gently wavered in the water with the motion of the current. We watched them for a long time, touching the tips of their tendrils every now and then with the end of a walking-stick, when they would at once shrink into nondescript lumps, only venturing to unroll again after several minutes. Walking back towards the Admiral's house, we lingered a while to watch a dozen Negroes in white dungarees and little white caps playing a primitive game of cricket on the stones. They were the only people we had seen in English Harbour since arriving. Convicts, the guide said.

Just outside the town there is a large water-catchment, one of those big stone quadrangles that is built on the slope of a hillside, and walled in so that, during the dry season, not a drop of rain-water is lost. We searched here for a long time for the letters 'ELS' carved near the name of 'H.M.S. *Boreas*' in the surrounding stone wall, reputed to have been scratched there by Nelson himself. Its presence is recorded by Sir A. Aspinall; but we failed to disentangle it from the quantities of names with which the stone is carved. This custom must have developed into some sort of tradition among the sailors in Antigua, for there are hundreds of signatures, many of them accompanied by the names of their homes in England: Winchelsea, Rye, Deal, Portsmouth, Rochester, Chatham or Gravesend. The oldest date we could discover was 1715. Like the whole of English Harbour, this was a queerly moving place, heavy with melancholy and the allusions of ancient fame.

All Antigua seems to be like this. We saw little of it during our stay, but in Aspinall's account of the island phrases like '... though ruinous, is of interest', '... the once prosperous town ...', 'a ghost of its former self ...', '... the ruins of the old military barracks emerge from the hush ...', '... the ruins of the old Great House ...', '... in former days ...', everything in the island speaks of evanescence and the lapse of time. On the way back we stopped at the parish church of the little town of Falmouth, whose decrepitude bears the same rueful message, and contemplated the grave of the Honble. James Charles Pitt, a brother of William, who died here, in command of H.M.S. *Hornet*, at the age of twenty. *'The genius,'* we read, *'that inspired and the Virtues that adorned the Parent were revived in the Son whose dawning Merit bespoke a meridian Splendour worthy of the name of Pitt.'* How very sad! It is such a dismal place to be buried.

We drove back over a bleak, undulating country that was disturbingly like an English heath, planted sporadically with sea island cotton. The sugar-cane only began as we got closer to St John's.

I have hinted before that Antigua is always mentioned in the same breath with Barbados, as a place where racial prejudice and the colour bar reach greater lengths of intransigence. In the light of all that has happened since our passage back, I bitterly regret not having stayed in the island some time. Alas, I can only just, after remaining there exactly twenty-four hours, claim to have been there; and I saw no evidence of it, perhaps because I scarcely saw anybody at all. I only set eyes on two white people during that time – the corporal and the owner of the hotel – and about twenty coloured Antiguans. It is a mystery that still puzzles me. Reference books speak of a population of thirty-four thousand; but there seemed to be nobody either in the town or the country. So not only did I see no evidence of discrimination, but nobody to discriminate or to be discriminated against. If Lord Baldwin's friction with the white inhabitants of the island sprang from a refusal to condone the same sort of situation that prevails in Barbados, my private reaction is to stand up and cheer; but as I say, I have no right to express an opinion about it. Instead of showing any signs of friction, the island while we were there seemed to be either empty of its folk like the village on the Grecian Urn, or locked by some spell in a state of catalepsy.

Much of the frontage of the white plank houses consisted of shutters that were fitted with slats like Venetian blinds. As the day grew cooler, many of the slats opened like gills, as though for breathing purposes, and some shutters were hooked back to let in the evening air; proving that pulses were beating somewhere in the recesses of those silent husks.

At the end of this broad street, which sloped slightly as it receded, from the shallow harbour, an Anglican but extremely baroque-looking cathedral stood among the trees. The twin towers that flanked the classical façade were topped by polygonal bronze cupolas and everything in the treatment of the massive stone fabric led one to believe that it had been built in the late seventeenth or the eighteenth century. Accustomed as we were becoming to surprises of this kind, we were taken aback by the information that it was built – on the exact lines, though, of its predecessor, which an earthquake had destroyed – in 1847. There was nothing inside to impair the illusion. The spacious and airy proportions, the Corinthian pillars, the panelling, the gilding, and the lettering of the Ten Commandments all belonged to the Augustan age of English architecture. And the presiding Godhead, one felt (as one feels in all the churches built between

Wren and the Gothic revival) is also a denizen of that prolonged and opulent afternoon. He is not the mysterious Presence of the Middle Ages, nor is He the avenging Thunderer of the Puritans, nor the top-hatted Puseyite of later times, nor yet the stoled and white-overalled Scientist of today. Gazing through the thin, drained atmosphere at the fluted columns and the acanthus leaves, the cornucopias and the formal flutter of the ribbons of wood that secure the carved festoons, our island Deity of the reigns of Queen Anne and the Georges slowly begins, like an emerging portrait by Kneller or Gainsborough or Raeburn, to take shape. The placid features assemble and the misty grey eyes with their compound expression of humour and severity; the heavy judicial curls of the wig, the amaranthine volume of the robes, and the soft blue of the Garter are unfolded in mid-air. A forefinger marks the place in a pocket edition of Voltaire; on a marble table, the tea-time sunlight rests on the vellum-bound Pentateuch and the Odes of Horace, and gently glows on the scales, the marshal's baton and the metal strawberry-leaves. A heavy curtain is looped back, and beyond, with the sweep of soft shadow and faded gold of a gentleman's deer-park, lie the mild prospects of Paradise, the pillared rotunda reflected in the lake, the dreaming swans, and at last, the celestial mansion built by Vanbrugh, rearing, against the sky of Sèvres blue and the whipped-cream clouds, its colonnaded entablature, its marble Graces and its urns ... This Elysian fancy paled all at once at the sight, on the cushion of one of the pews in the chancel, of the black pom-pom of a biretta. The Hanoverian vision grew vaporous and confused with anachronistic draughts from Oxford and Rome; and vanished.

Our attention was drawn from the old epitaphs in the churchyard by the goings-on of three little Antiguan boys. They must have been aged about eight. One of them kept climbing on to the end of a tomb, and then, when the second of them made a motion with his hand as though he were pulling a lever, jumped stiffly to the grass, and stood there with his tongue out and his eyes crossed; the third meanwhile, went through the motions of pulling a cord, and gloomily pronouncing the syllable *clang!* They repeated the performance several times, and there was eager competition for the position on the tomb. Noticing our interest in this game, they explained that it was called 'Hanging'. They seemed to have made a study of criminology, for they tacked themselves on to us, and described, in detail, all the murders that had taken place in late years, pointed out the prison where the executions had taken place, and told us the name of the hangman on each occasion. As they spoke their eyes popped out of their heads. It was profoundly macabre, a mixture of the Flopsy Bunnies and the Newgate Calendar. The gloomy recital continued as we looked at the fine lifesize metal images of St John the Divine and St John the Baptist, posturing on their pillars on either side of the church-yard gate. They were very baroque indeed, and the extravagance of gesture, the overstatement, and the whirlwind of draperies struck an unfamiliar note in the prevailing Englishness. Understandably, it proved, for they were both captured on a French ship bound for Dominica, and brought to Antigua as part of the prize.

When we left next morning, the three little boys appeared to help us with our luggage, and – rather surprisingly, for they were barefoot and in tatters – hotly refused to accept a small sum of money. They said they would much rather shake hands; an operation which was gravely performed.

The forty-five-mile journey westwards from Antigua seemed to be over in an instant. Up we went into the sky, and our extended range of vision only seemed to assemble the islands – Antigua with its satellites of Barbuda and Redonda; Montserrat to the south, and to the westwards, St Kitts, Nevis, St Eustatius and Saba – for a minute or two before they dispersed again into the distance, and we were landing in St Kitts.

St Christopher was not, for once, named after the Saint's day on which the island was discovered by Columbus, but either, some say, after the great sailor's own Christian name as a mark of especial esteem, or because something in the outline reminded him of his own hoary patron saint bowed beneath his sacred load. It was impossible to catch the likeness, as Mount Misery, the highest point of the island, was concealed by a sphere of cloud so perfectly round and so solid that it looked as if it had been impaled upon the peak. It was especially remarkable by being the only cloud in the sky. An islander, seeing our gaze directed towards it, said that the rainy season had come to an end. Ever since our first arrival in Guadeloupe we had been hearing this observation, sometimes when the very air seemed to turn into water every few minutes, and we had become case-hardened sceptics. But this time (although we had isolated days of rain after that) it was true. 'It's real Christmas weather,' the islander observed.

It was a period of change for us, not only in the weather, but in atmosphere and in the ground under our feet. We were still treading the summits of dead and drowned Strombolis, but the thuggish vegetation had vanished. Antigua, already, had been different – mournful and derelict, but, as far as tropical forests went, unjugulated. There was some-thing clean and spare about the declivities of St Kitts. The forests were there, all right, on the slopes of Mount Misery, but they had none of the suffocating and murderous immediacy of the other Antilles. None

of the menace, that, falling asleep at night in Guadeloupe, made us feel
like Princes in the Tower.

Unlike the steep and accidented charm of St George's, the beauty of
the capital of St Kitts lies in its level and graceful solidity; all, it must
be understood, on a village scale, or, at the most, the scale of a busy
and populous little market town.

Two minutes' walk from the quay brought us into a square which
was filled with great weeping trees whose tasselled branches all swayed
together with the least breath of wind. The fronts of noble Georgian houses
outlined this quadrangle, flanked by columned stone doorways surmounted by semi-circles and triangles and tablets, and grooved pilasters
which stayed the wooden upper storeys; buildings of great dignity and
grace, all of them weathered and time-nibbled to a state of infinite mellow-
ness. In one corner stood a Court House that serves as a chamber for
the sessions for the Island Legislature as well as for the administration
of justice: a grand barrel-vaulted eighteenth-century room, built so long
ago – a millennial span for these cyclone-swept islands – that the shield
which surmounted the throne between the prancing supporters still
quartered, with the leopards and the lion and the harp under a super-
imposed inescutcheon of the House of Hanover, the lilies of France. I
climbed a steep staircase into the Free Library of Basseterre, a room in
which I was to spend many pleasant hours. The windows overlook the
emplacement of the old slave-market where the planters of St Kitts
appraised the dark and bewildered strangers, most of them drawn, the
islanders maintain, from the warrior tribes of Ashanti and Dahomey. This
was the official place of exchange, where the agents of the Royal Company
that held the monopoly of the slave trade contracted their business. More
covert bargains were struck on the deserted beaches between the colonists
and the Interlopers who smuggled shiploads of slaves from the Guinea
coasts without the sanction of a royal warrant.

The library was a fascinating retreat. On the walls among the oil-
paintings of periwigged notables hung an old print illustrating the naval
action between Hood and de Grasse in the Roads of Basseterre in 1782,
three weeks before Rodney broke the frightening sequence of French
triumphs in the Caribees by his victory over de Grasse at the Battle of
the Saints. Old swords and chests lay among cases of Carib axe-heads,
and the drawers were stuffed with old maps and seals, indentures and
title deeds, and the shelves were filled with an absorbing collection of
old books on the islands, including, I discovered with delight, Father
Breton's French-Carib dictionary and the 1658 edition of de Rochefort.

Basseterre and the whole of St Kitts have an undeniably patrician air, and there is nothing in the architecture or the atmosphere of the place that hinders the evocation of its evaporated grandeur. Even in Labat's time, when the island was shared by the English and the French, it was considered – possibly because it was the earliest island to be settled – the grandest in the archipelago. The inhabitants, he says, had had more time to clean themselves up (*se décrasser*) and had become so polite and civil that one would have difficulty in finding greater polish in the best towns of Europe. A proverb of the day stated that the noblesse were to be found in St Kitts, the bourgeois in Guadeloupe, soldiers in Martinique, and peasants in Grenada. The early settlers were followed by members of great French families, and the children were regularly sent back to Paris for their education. The same circumstances prevailed in the English part. Labat mentions the Hamilton and the Codrington families (the latter, apart from their other estates, owned the whole island of Barbuda). The names of Cotton, St Clair, Boon, Napier, Reid, Wemyss and Berkeley, most of which have now vanished from the island, constantly crop up in old papers and books and on the monuments in the churches; and occasional French names, like Delisle, still survive. Staircases in the island of Nevis – whose abrupt silhouette lies only a couple of miles to the south of St Kitts – still exist, with the iron banisters so shaped that three ladies in panniered dresses could descend them abreast. It was here that Nelson was married to Mrs Nesbit, a doctor's widow, and daughter of Mr Woodward and granddaughter of Mr Herbert of Nevis. Not so very long ago there were five thousand white inhabitants in the daughter island; there are now exactly six – souls, not thousands – a minute rearguard of the flight from the islands after the dethronement of King Sugar at the Emancipation of the slaves. The population of the island is now fourteen thousand, and of St Kitts, where the same evacuation took place, eighteen thousand five hundred. In Antigua, the English settlers (who arrived there with a son of the great Thomas Warner of St Kitts) were governed by two successive Lords Willoughby of Parham, who held the lease from the son of Charles I's original grantee, Lord Carlisle; grantee not only for Antigua, but for nearly all the Caribbean islands – a private archipelago. The size and value of the property makes one's head swim. We met a lady of St Kitts who still remembers the last of the great receptions and balls given by the last remnants of this vanished island aristocracy. They sounded, from her description, magically dazzling. How I would like to have seen one! One is so often a century, a decade, or a day late for occasions like these.

*

Sugar-cane clothes the country that lies round the great fortress of Brimstone Hill, flowing and waving down from Mount Misery in the same beautiful sweeps, fold on soft fold of pale grey-green, which in Barbados make such a pleasing impression. These smooth planes of colour snap off near the sea's edge, and sink to the waves in a disorder of rocks and a sudden flaring green insurrection of tropical trees. Here, on forested beaches near little African-looking kraals of wooden houses, we swam all through the afternoons, and (always in vain) stalked fish with goggles and the underwater gun I had acquired in Martinique.

Not far from one of these retreats we searched a long time, without success, for some carved Carib stones which we had been recommended to look at. A village woman had pity on us finally, and led us through the cane to a large dark stone that must have been flung here from the volcano. Thrusting the stalks aside and recklessly lopping off a few with her cutlass, she cleared the sloping upper surface. It was another of those button-eyed, stick-limbed scribbles, but this time attached to a lozenge-shaped body; and the arms and legs were scratched with some semblance of a design. The drawing had resolved itself into some sort of glyptic formula. The ones in Guadeloupe might have been done by a three-year-old child; this perhaps by a four-year-old. Poor old Caribs! How many centuries, I wonder, spanned this enormous stride in plastic feeling and technique?

But in their real racial attribute they were always expert, and they fought with the utmost fierceness against Warner and his settlers and against the filibusters of d'Esnambuc, both of whom landed here on the same day of 1625.* But the Caribs were slaughtered in the end, and the survivors fled in their canoes to other islands. The curious thing about the occupation of St Kitts is that the French and the English settled down amicably side by side, and for a long time they shared the island, and threatened to take such firm root there that for once the Spaniards resented it, and sent an armada of thirty-eight ships to St Kitts that almost exterminated the settlers. This, as far as I can make out, is the only backward glance of the Spaniards from their drive westward through the colonies into the American continent.

D'Esnambuc was the originator and patriarch of the French colonies in the Antilles, and Warner was the Governor of the first English Antillean possession. A formidable figure, whose progeny – half-Carib, if Labat's bald and centenarian Madame Ouvernard is none other than Mrs Warner, widow, or rather ex-mistress, of the Governor – played a telling role in

* There is some doubt about this coincidence. Some authorities state that the Norman arrived two years later than Warner.

the formation of the colonies. Not far from the stones, we found the little churchyard, where, under a rickety wooden canopy, his moss-covered tomb stands among the long grass. A nest of giant hornets was suspended in the canopy, so that it was not without risk that I took down the words incised underneath his coat of arms.*

An Epitaph vpon The Noble and Mvch Lamented Gent Sir Tho Warner Kt Lievtenant Generall of Ye Carribee Ieland Gover^r of Ye Ieland of St Christ^r who departed this life on 10 of March 1648.

> First Read then weepe when thou art hereby taught
> That Warner lyes interr'd here, one that bought
> With loss of noble bloud the Illustrious Name
> Of a Commander Greate in Acts of Fame
> Traynd from his youth in Armes his Courage bold
> Attempted braue exploites, and Vncontrold
> By fortunes fiercest frownes hee still gave forth
> Large Narratiues of Military worth
> Written with his swords point but what is man
> In the midst of his glory and who can
> Secure this Life A moment since that hee
> Both by Sea and Land so long kept free
> At mortal stroakes at length did yeeld
> Grace to Conqueringe Death the field.
>   FINE CORONAT

The walls of this little church were hung with the Stations of the Cross, and various other pieces of Spike-ish equipment hinted that here, too, the official party-line of the national church had been left far behind.

An interesting little edifice of doctrinal casuistry surrounded, in former centuries, the spiritual matters of the slaves. The French planters only with difficulty persuaded Louis XIII to sanction the Slave Trade between Africa and the Americas. There was a French law that formally forbade the enslavement of any subject of the Crown, and it was only by assuring the king that slavery was the only means of bringing these lost sheep into the fold of the True Church that the royal veto was reluctantly withdrawn. Slavery, the planters maintained – as their colossal fortunes multiplied by dint of slave labour – was a method of proselytizing merely, an insignificant detail. What mattered was the salvation of the souls of these poor people.

---

* Quite unnecessarily, as the whole thing is down in Aspinall, including a few words which are broken off the slab, but discovered by Sir Algernon in an eighteenth-century manuscript, and which are here included.

The English, states Father Labat, through negligence or for some other motive, never baptized their slaves; they allowed them to welter in the error of their primitive cults, whether these were Mohammedanism* or one of the many forms of idolatry. He tackled an English parson about this in St Kitts, and the parson piously answered that it was improper for a Christian to hold in bondage his brothers in Christ; so they let them remain heathens; a piece of dogma, the Dominican goes on, that is promptly thrust into oblivion whenever French slaves, known to be Christians, were captured by the English. It is hard to decide which is the more devious and unpleasant of these two bits of sophistry. The English perhaps win by a very short head on the strength of absolute callousness. The French, however cynical and dishonest in their original argument, did attempt, by sending out numbers of missionaries, to give some faint corroborative tinge to their argument; and many priests, especially of the Dominican Order, worked all their lives among the slaves. Not that this mitigated the barbarous treatment of the Negroes, which was every bit as iniquitous as that of the English. These regarded their slaves, quite literally, as heads of cattle. It was very late in the day – only slightly earlier than the first agitation for the abolition of the slave trade – that evangelization began on any scale. The numbers of slaves in the colonies of both powers were so vast that, even then, they received little more than a veneer of Christianity, adopting the talismanic and, to them, immediately comprehensible side of the religion, and discarding the rest. The Quakers let both sides down by purchasing slaves, converting them and setting them free; a procedure that made the Quakers objects of abhorrence to Catholics and Protestants alike. The Jews bought slaves and circumcised them.

One very noticeable result of all this is the lack of importance that is attached to the rite or the sacrament of marriage. No rebuke or stigma clings to the loss of virginity or the birth of illegitimate children, and, like so many other things, the illegitimacy rate in the islands is very high. Children are usually the commitment of the mother, and it is not rare for a woman to have produced several illegitimate children before she settles down with her final mate. These she brings with her, and rears them alongside the offspring of her last and quasi-official ménage. Their adopted fathers find nothing incongruous in this, and they treat their wives' unusual dowries with great kindness. Indeed, a man may also bring one or two of his own, either because they have taken his fancy or because their mothers have died, and they are greeted by his wife

---

*There were only a few of these.

with the same impartial benevolence. Bourgeois yearnings sometimes overcome them late in life and they may, if they have enough money to spend on the social celebrations involved, treat themselves to a marriage. There are accounts of fifty or a hundred couples of old paramours being, at a single service, married *en masse*. But in the poorer classes of which I have been speaking, concubinage and illegitimacy is the general custom, and on the whole it works out very well, thanks to the good nature and charitable disposition of the Negroes.

The drawback, of course, is that nobody has time to look after these vast and heteroclite families. Often they run quite wild, and many Antillean towns seethe with children who range about the streets like little wolves, fighting, begging and stealing when they get a chance, and generally leading an undisciplined and uninhibited life. It must be due to some fundamental virtue in the Negro character that they are not ten times worse.

As a rule, with their enormous liquid eyes, amazing teeth and lithe and graceful movements, they are charming to look at, and sometimes funny, intelligent and entertaining conversationalists. Quite often, as the reader will have gathered, they turn themselves into unofficial guides and general managers if they discover a stranger wandering about the town, and by no means always in the hopes of a tip; out of interest and kindness, I think, and because it makes a change. Grown-up Negroes, collectively, usually give an impression of shyness in dealing with white people; sometimes of hostility – not incomprehensibly. Individually, they are practically always communicative and friendly.

Monkey Hill, a mountain some miles west of Basseterre, on the way to the fortress, was the scene of a sharp battle between the French and a Barbadian baronet called Sir Timothy Thornhill, in which the latter succeeded in defeating the French and in turning them out of the colony. Was it called Monkey Hill then? I have not been able to discover. If not, and if monkeys were not indigenous to the island, a possible, and at any rate attractive, explanation can be deduced from the pages of Père Labat.

When the French were driven from the island, their pet monkeys (brought from the Guianas, perhaps) left the abandoned houses of their masters and ran wild in the woods, multiplying with such speed, that by the time the French came back (seven years later) after the Treaty of Ryswick, they were roving the island in troops, pulling up the cane-shoots and sweet potatoes as fast as they were planted, and breaking into the houses and stealing whatever they could lay their hands on. The planters were driven to hunting down their former pets. Father Labat describes one of these monkey-shoots, near the house of his friend, M. Lambert, a captain of filibusters.

The monk and the filibuster, armed with fowling-pieces, lay in wait in a clump of bushes on the edge of a newly planted cane-field. They had not waited an hour before a large monkey appeared through the undergrowth. After looking on all sides to see if the coast was clear, it climbed a tree, had another look round, and then let out 'a great cry, to which more than a hundred voices responded at once, and immediately afterwards, a large troop of monkeys, all of different sizes burst gambolling (à gambades) into the cane-field'. They began pulling up the shoots, loading them on to their shoulders, and disappearing into the woods. Others put the cane-shoots into their mouths, and, making a thousand gambadoes, also retired. The monk and the filibuster, after watching their behaviour for some time, opened fire, and killed four. One of them was a female with a little monkey on its back, which even when they approached refused to let go. 'Il la tenait embrassée, à peu près comme nos nègres tiennent leurs mères. Nous le prîmes, on l'éleva et il devint le plus gentil animal qu'on put souhaiter.'

It was the first time he had tasted monkey and he owns to some twinges of repugnance at the sight of the four heads in the dish. They looked exactly like the heads of small children. But he soon got over this, and declared the meat to be tender, white, delicate, full of nutritive properties and equally good with any kind of sauce.

The baby monkey was given to a colleague called Father Cabasson, who brought it up.

The little animal became so fond of him that it never left his side; to such an extent indeed, that, having no chain, he had to lock it up whenever he went to church. Once, however, it got away and, hiding on top of the pulpit, only showed itself when its master began to preach. It sat on the edge of the canopy, and, watching the preacher's gestures, began to mimic them with postures and grimaces which set everybody laughing. Father Cabasson, unaware of the cause of such immodesty, reproved them gently at first, but, seeing that the fits of laughter were increasing instead of growing less, he flew into a holy rage and began, in the most lively fashion, to fling anathema at them for the slight respect in which they held the word of God. His movements, becoming even more violent than usual, augmented the postures and grimaces of his monkey and, at the same time, the laughter of the assembly. At last somebody told the preacher to take a look at what was going on above his head. He had no sooner beheld the conduct of his monkey than he began, in spite of himself, to laugh like the others, and as there was no way of catching the animal, he abandoned the remainder of his sermon, being himself in no fit state to continue, nor his congregation to listen.

*

We were determined to break the detestable series of aeroplane journeys, and began to hang about the docks to see if we could get a passage on a sailing vessel to St Eustatius, Saba and St Martin. But Christmas was approaching, and the large number of vessels lying at anchor had assembled there from all over the archipelago in order that the captains and crews could be with their families. It was beginning to look hopeless, and we were almost resigned to continuing by air when a sea captain from Anguilla appeared, saying that he would take us for a reasonable sum. A bargain was struck, and we arranged to set sail at two o'clock that afternoon, and reach St Eustatius, if the wind continued favourable, in an hour or two. Captain Fleming explained that his sloop had no engine, so we would have to rely on sail. His appearance – those deep black features of enormous length and the steel-rimmed glasses – had a strangely studious cast for a man of the sea. You would have taken him for a vicar or a professor.

CHAPTER 9

St Eustatius, Saba, St Martin, St Thomas

This, we were all agreed, was the proper way to travel in the Caribbean islands.

We weighed anchor at about three, and watched the pretty town of Basseterre slide slowly away to the south as, luffing and tacking, we beat up the leeward side of St Kitts. Then it seemed to slide back, for every breath of air was blocked by the cloudy cone of Mount Misery, and our laborious zigzag of acute angles was infuriatingly slow. All through the afternoon we wavered along the brilliant green line of palm trees that rimmed the shore. Fields of sugar-cane swept across the foothills in pale drifts, climbing and expiring on the flanks of Brimstone Hill, where, spiked with obsolete cannon, the fortress poised in its tiers of battlements. We were virtually becalmed. The outline of St Eustatius, seven leagues to the north-west, appeared impossibly remote.

About fifty Negroes from the island of Anguilla had straggled on board the sloop in Basseterre. They were festooned over the decks among their hastily-packed bundles in jubilant disorder. Our sluggish progress was soon cheered by a steady downpour of rain, and Joan and Costa and I crawled into a little deck-house the size of a dog's kennel, where we huddled with our chins upon our knees. At last, just about nightfall, the *Rose Millicent* slithered past the northern cape of the island, and the Trade Winds hit the sail with a satisfactory slap of tightening canvas. The skipper heaved the sloop's bowsprit round and pointed it at the fading silhouette of St Eustatius. The wind was piercingly cold, and as the ship leapt forward, we dug out a half-empty bottle and lowered comforting stalactites of whisky down our throats. Night fell, and the rain stopped. The heads of the Negroes, who had all taken refuge under a tarpaulin like some tremendous recumbent group of statuary before its unveiling, began to appear again round the edge. The two nearest to us were talking to each other in an incomprehensible language that was neither pidgin English nor Créole. Many of the words sounded like Spanish, but the flow of the language was suddenly thickened by noises that were guttural and uncouth. Seeing that I was listening, one of them whispered, *'Papia poco poco bo tende?'* and their voices dropped. But I understood, with excitement, that they were talking Papiamento, that almost mythical compound of Spanish, Portuguese, Dutch, French, English and African dialects evolved by the slaves of Curaçao and the Dutch islands of the Southern Caribbean.

The sky had cleared, and the mast and rigging, shuddering slowly backwards and forwards as the sloop rode over the waves, moved through a host of low-flying and brilliant stars, Orion, as usual, dominating all the other constellations. The boom, straining at the tug of its great sweep of taut sail, was lashed back almost parallel with the beam. So full of phosphorus was the sea that the bow-waves rose out of the darkness like wings of fire and the wake trailed away into the night in a dishevelled tress. It had become warm again, and I left the hut to sit on some rope and talk to Captain Fleming as he twirled the wheel. This tall and oddly scholarly-looking man with his long jet black features and steel-rimmed spectacles, was a Seventh Day Adventist and a native of the little island of Anguilla. The Anguillans live by raising cattle, by collecting and exporting salt, and by ship-building, in which their only rivals are the sailors of Carriacou, far to the south in the Grenadines. He was an expert shipwright, and he had built the *Rose Millicent* with the help of his brother and two friends and his great-uncle, who formed the crew of the sloop. This charming, ragged old man, Uncle Pete, was sitting in the top of a hatchway, with his feet dangling inside. They talked about the little archipelago for which we were heading; of the white French villagers of St Barthélémy and their own fellow-islanders of Anguilla, many of whom sail westwards to get work during the cane-cutting season in the American island of Puerto Rico and even, until it was forbidden by the dictator, in Santo Domingo. Many of them, for this reason, speak Spanish as well as English. One of the Dutchmen spoke of a small island on which, during the war, empty provision crates and fuel containers were found lying about on a deserted beach: a place of call for enemy submarines. Very much intrigued, I asked which island, but the Aruban said he didn't know, and it was only hearsay. Later, talking of personalities in the islands, the conversation veered round to the Captain's name-sake, Mr Fleming of St Martin and Tintamarre, whose buccaneerish reputation had reached our ears in London. According to the Captain, he was a millionaire several times over, but always lived quietly in St Martin, half of which he owned, among a fleet of schooners and speed-boats. At one time he had possessed a little flotilla of private aeroplanes run by a young pilot called de Heynen: 'He's about thirty-five,' the Captain said, 'and he's wild, oh wild. Always walkin' fast with his eyes burning. He let his hair grow long on the shoulders ... Education sure drove him crazy, so much education ... But Mr Fleming's a lovely man.' He repeated this in a sort of incantation. 'When St Martin was poor during the war, he keep and feed de whole island. If anybody touch him, dey touch de whole island; dey touch me.'

The two Dutchmen spoke of the days of prohibition in America, when liquor smuggling from the free port of St Martin to Florida and to all the Antilles was a flourishing industry. Uncle Pete had a moral tale of a three-masted schooner carrying thirty thousand dollars' worth of contraband liquor. The Captain and the crew broached their own stock and were soon drunk to a man. They gave up steering and just lay about the decks while the craft drifted south towards Venezuela, where she struck a reef and sank with all hands except one, who escaped, but did not dare tell the tale till years later. The schooner was only spotted after a couple of months by a passing aeroplane, with her masts sticking out of a lagoon whose waters were afloat with bodies and stove-in kegs. He had once seen two whales in the middle of the Caribbean, 'swimmin' along close, like they were two sweethearts', and as a young man he had been wrecked on the Spanish Main, two hundred miles east of Trinidad. He was nearly killed by savage Indians, who did not even speak Spanish – 'They no Christians, they never see no priest' – and had lived with them for months in mud huts built on a mountain-side that fell into the sea so steeply that no anchor could touch the bottom.

The stars were blacked out in a triangle that grew bigger as we approached the extinct volcano in the eastern end of St Eustatius. 'We comin' to Statia,' Uncle Pete said, knocking out his pipe. Soon, from the little island capital of Oranjestad, a single light appeared. We drew in till we were about two hundred yards off the shore. The sails came down, and one of the Dutchmen shouted through the dark in Papiamento, as he thought one of the police was from his island. But when we got ashore we found a policeman talking English (which is the language of all the Dutch Leeward Islands), who led us up a winding track to a vaulted police station, and stamped our passports. The lantern shone on his badge of the Lion of Orange and on his steel-scabbarded sabre. It was almost ten o'clock. The little capital was fast asleep.

The Deputy Governor sat up late with us in the dining-room of an annexe of Government House, where he had invited us, on the strength of our telegram, to stay. It was a massive white room, from the walls of which a crowned photograph of Queen Wilhelmina as a girl smiled benignantly down upon us.

The Dutch possessions in the Caribbean lead a life of their own, and one that is in many ways as detached from the life of Holland as that of Canada is from England. Our host, Mr Voges, was born in Curaçao of a pure Dutch family, but had never yet been to Holland, and though he would like, out of interest, to go there some time, he felt that the matter had no particular urgency. The beautiful little town of Willemstad in Curaçao is a real capital for the Dutch in the West Indies. They look no farther than those gables and spires and bridges – so freakishly reminiscent, in the paradoxical Caribbean sunlight, of Rotterdam or Delft – for home. The Dutch Antilles – Curaçao, Aruba and Bonaire in the Windward, and St Eustatius, Saba and St Martin in the Leeward Isles, form a quiet and aloof little galaxy, comparable, in the complicated relationships of the other Caribbees, to the pacific status of the Netherlands in the maelstrom of Europe. Each of the islands is administered by a lieutenant-governor, who is always a Dutch West Indian, under the jurisdiction of a central governor in Willemstad. These civil servants never take up appointments in Holland, still less in Java or Bali.

When Mr Voges said good night, we climbed to our rooms: spotlessly clean chambers with gigantic four-posters and substantial mahogany wardrobes, all pleasantly solid and Dutch. The beds were draped in cubic pavilions of muslin, accessible through beautifully made thresholds in the fabric fastened with bows of tape. Once inside, the sleeper was immured against the fiercest invasion. Trimming the wick, I installed myself with the security of a medieval burgher, and opened the ancient copy of Mr S. J. Kruythoff's *Netherland Windward Islands and a few interesting Items on French St Martin* of which the kind Mr Challenger of St Kitts had made me a parting present. The text is relieved by photographs by Mr Toppin and Mr Buncamper, and by Mr Kruythoff's own stirring Byronic quatrains:

> No more your spicy groves bewail
>   On soft Hesperian breeze set free
> The bloodstained pelf, the bloody tale
>   Of vile marauders of the sea.
>
> The hectic rovers of the deep
>   In mighty frigates lie at rest,
> Whilst pearl and pirate share the sleep:
>   The victim and the victim's quest ...

The island, whose total area is only nine square miles, was taken by the Dutch early in the seventeenth century, and though, like all the islands, it changed hands many times, it has remained steadily Dutch since 1816. During the first part of the American War of Independence, Holland remained neutral, but the sympathies of the Governor and colonists were on the side of the American States. An illicit arms traffic to the struggling rebels was connived at by the Governor. Statia, as the island is called by its inhabitants, was one of the first to salute the flag of the infant Republic; and the failure of the fort to dip its flag low or long enough when British warships sailed past called down upon the little island the thunders of Admiral Rodney when hostilities broke out between England and Holland. He appeared in the roadstead before the Governor was aware that the two countries were at war. The Governor surrendered. The account of the damage and plunder that the English inflicted on the island made me shift uneasily between the smooth Dutch sheets. Three million pounds' worth of booty and merchandise was carried away, and everything that was not portable was destroyed. 400,000 guilders' worth of dyewoods were burnt. A long line of warehouses and breakwaters were fired and destroyed, and the harbour was dismantled. The island has never recovered from this crushing blow. The population dwindled, and, in spite of countless efforts to restore its former prosperity, trade and commerce have steadily declined. The population today is not much over a thousand souls. Like the king of Lundy Island, two adventurers in the eighteenth century who made their fortunes on the island struck their own coinage, a few examples of which are still in existence. The coins of the first, Herman Gossling, bear the legend 'God bless St Eustatius and Guvn' on one side, and on the other a little goose pecking among the reeds. The coinage of the second, Jenkins, commemorates his way of life when he first arrived on the island, for on one side is stamped the image of a man sleeping under a canoe on the beach.

By the time I had finished the book and turned out the light, a storm had blown up. The wind was screaming round the walls. Looking down into the darkness of the bay, I could see the sloop's lantern tossing up and down, and wondered what sort of a time the Flemings and the fifty islanders were having. Somewhere in the building a shutter creaked and slammed all night.

Costa, the most logical and unsuperstitious of mortals, appeared pale and haggard at the breakfast table, worn out by haunting. Although he had locked the door after the first disturbance, ghosts had come into his room and moved about, shifting the furniture, colliding into things, and even striking lights and chattering among themselves, with the result that he had not had a moment's sleep.

It was a dismal day, and the sea was slate-coloured and turbulent. Leaden clouds covered the summit of the Venusberg, hanging over Oranjestad little higher than a ceiling.

The Governor accompanied us out into the capital, a village of which every other house was a ruin, except for a few shops, Government House and the trim little fort with its sundial and cannon, and a monument to commemorate the passage, in 1666, of Admiral de Ruyter. The hilly island is still as empty of wheeled vehicles as it was when Columbus discovered it in 1493, and even islanders on foot were very scarce in the streets. In the graveyard of the Dutch Reformed Church (which has fallen to an empty shell of masonry) hurricane graves – those mausolea built like cisterns to resist the wildest cyclones: great cubes of stone from the upper surfaces of which bulges a shallow barrel vault – mark the last resting-places of forgotten Jonkheers and Mijnheers. At one end of the churchyard lies the tomb of Joseph Blake, Esquire, born in the County of Galway in 1701. The synagogue of the Portuguese Jews from Brazil, who once ran the trade of the island, is a wreck of overgrown archways of brick. On a windy hillside beyond the Anglican cemetery outside the town lies the Sephardic Jewish burial-ground, where a dozen tomb-stones cover the graves of Solomons, Levis, Pereiras and da Leons; Caribbean cousins of Spinoza. They are broken, moss-covered slabs with epitaphs cut in Hebrew and Latin characters, and dates that are reckoned from the Creation of the World; only, according to these inscriptions, 5,500 years earlier than the digging of these graves in the eighteenth century. Neither Jews nor Anglicans are to be found on the island today. The majority of the Statians are Wesleyan Methodists, and there are a few hundred Catholics whose spiritual needs are supplied by a Dominican friar, of whom we caught a glimpse as he mounted the cobbled main street. There is also a stubborn little kernel of Seventh Day Adventists, about fifty strong.

The Governor accompanied us through the last wooden houses of the village. The dinghy, rowed by Captain Fleming and Uncle Pete, was pulling towards the shore. Before saying goodbye, I asked the Governor if people were ever bothered by ghosts in the island. 'No,' he said, after a pause, 'have you seen any?' I said no, and rather cravenly let the subject drop. As we walked downhill, Mr Voges regretted that we could not stay longer to meet one or two old ladies living in farms near Oranjestad who are the last representatives of the colonial families of St Eustatius. But

Captain Fleming was shouting that the weather was blowing up again, and that we ought to weigh anchor at once. We waved back to the Governor as our dinghy crossed the water towards the *Rose Millicent* past the wrecked stanchions of the demolished jetty. Uncle Pete made us look overboard at the walls and timbers of a drowned village that faintly loomed, yards below us, through the waves. He had no explanation for it, except 'It was dry once.'

The wind that carried us towards Saba blew the clouds off the blunted cone of the Venusberg. The crater of this volcano is a deep pit, entirely surrounded by the jagged walls of the mountain. It is densely forested, and as there is no side light, all the trees try to force their way up to the sun, and the cedars and eucalyptus attain enormous heights. The trees are caught in a vast cobweb of creepers and lianas, of which many, after having grown to a thickness of over four inches, have become semi-petrified. Mr Kruythoff states that some of this fossilized vegetation is over six thousand years old; thus, by Sephardic reckoning, slightly earlier than the Creation. A hurricane in 1928 uprooted large numbers of the trees, churning the imprisoned forest into a tangle of timber and torn lianas. A great ceiba tree growing in the bottom of the crater is carved with the names of hundreds of sailors, some of them dating from as far back as the middle of the eighteenth century. Brilliantly coloured birds fly between the branches in the half darkness, and the damp air is heavy with a smell of decay that rises from the rotting trunks and the many centuries' accumulation of fallen leaves. Night falls early and fast owing to the height of the crater-sides. One of our fellow-passengers had once lost himself among the trees. He had been forced to spend the night in the wilderness, and said that, by the time dawn broke, he was nearly out of his mind.

The shape of the island as we sailed to leeward of it lengthened into a high saddle stretched between two dead cones. At Tumble-Down-Dick Bay, which is possibly the only existing memorial of Oliver Cromwell's ineffective son, we turned westwards.

The sea grew rough, and great grey waves and then heavy rain reduced everybody except the crew to a state of misery. We all crept back into our shelters. A few hours later, when we ventured out into the sunlight, the sloop was sailing close under the side of Saba.

It is a round, absolutely symmetrical mountain ribbed by lava streams, rising sheer out of the sea, and climbing in a perpendicular wall to a height that, from below, looks enormous. The summit disappeared in the clouds and the sides were so steep and uncompromising that landing, or climbing to the top of the island, appeared an impossible feat. But

Captain Fleming pointed to a little gathering of houses, high above the clouds and the circling gulls, perched, like a Thessalian monastery, on the very lip of the crater. It was the village of Hells Gate, of which the houses, the Captain said, were secured to the rocks with chains lest the wind should tear them loose and scatter them over the sea; and the over-hanging rocks are braced back to prevent them falling and destroying the houses. The island gives the effect of the cylindrical keep of a fortress, several miles in circumference, rising from the sea, and tapering to a dome. We sailed under the echoing flanks of this enormous thing, while hundreds of mewing sea birds fluttered and wheeled round the sloop. The *Rose Millicent* was pitching and tossing in waves that broke all round the island's base in a girdle of foam. We came level at length with a ledge of black volcanic sand about thirty yards from end to end. Under a fluttering tricolor, a little cubic customs-house was perched. This is the only place where an anchor can touch bottom on the submarine shelf of rock; everywhere else the sides fall straight into the Caribbean to very great depths. As our boat carried us towards the beach, a jeep, the island's one vehicle, appeared on the mountain-side, threading its way down a steep winding road from the interior. It was driven by the brigadier of police, who told us, as we landed, that the Governor of Statia had signalled our arrival. He drove us up the ladder of a road which curled into the side of the mountain through a chasm of rock. A final twist brought us into the open, revealing the centre of Saba like the inside of a rotten tooth. It was the most unexpected sight.

The inside of the dead volcano's crater rolled down towards us in a hollow of green meadows and great leafy trees. It was a gentle European landscape of spinneys and wild flowers and cattle grazing in a mild, sunny atmosphere. In the centre of the plateau lay a woodland village of white-walled, red-roofed houses, with long threads of smoke rising straight from their chimneys into the windless air. And, as we penetrated this sylvan capital, the fair-haired, pale-skinned islanders lowered the hoes with which they were working their potato-patches, and cried good-afternoon over their garden walls.

The origin of the Sabamen is a mystery. The majority of them are reputed to be of Scottish origin, though how they came here none of the memoirs or travel diaries or histories state. There is certainly a fair amount of Dutch blood, and one or two of the Sabamen I spoke to seemed to think there might be a little Danish as well. Livingstone, Simmonds, Hassel and Laverack are the most widespread surnames.

They have always been a quiet, hard-working folk. When Father Labat came ashore, he found a prosperous, bourgeois community, every one of whom (including, he suspected, the Governor) passed his life making boots and shoes for export to the other islands. Many of them had Negro slaves, whose descendants still form a coloured minority. He lamented that the islanders were not Catholics, as they could have put themselves under the protection of St Crispin, the patron saint of cobblers. As a matter of fact, the Sabamen, though Dutch subjects, are half of them Catholic and half of them Anglican, except for a few dozen adherents to a sect known as the Pilgrim Holiness; and a point in the island known as Chrispeen does exist. The Father bought a couple of pairs of shoes in Saba, which, he records wore extremely well.

But the trade must have died out during the last two centuries. Most of the male inhabitants – about 1,600 souls inhabit the five square miles of the island – go to sea. They have a great name as sailors throughout the islands, and many of them rise to be captains of Dutch steamers plying all over the world. The oil-wells of Curaçao and Aruba have drawn many away from the rock; but they always return and always send their savings home. The Sabamen are now, as in the past, accomplished boat-builders. They fell the timbers for their crafts high in the mountains, and then carry them down, rigged and complete, on their shoulders, to launch them in the stormy Sabian waters. Old writers perpetuate in their memoirs a legend that they used to lower them hundreds of feet down the volcano side on ropes from the crater's edge to the sea. Windwardside is perched like a guillemot's nest high on the rim of Saba; a cluster of white houses lost among evergreen trees and giant ferns and the clouds that the Trades blow along the deep gorge that it commands. It is inhabited by about 600 villagers, and is one of the only completely white villages in the West Indies. When they retire from the sea, the older men spend the latter part of their lives farming and gardening, and the women of the island are famous for drawn-thread work. They are a hale, rosy-complexioned, quiet population, exactly what the descendants of Scotsmen and Dutchmen might be expected to be. Many times in the past they have been attacked by pirates and filibusters and predatory foreign powers, and their defensive stratagem was always the same, and always successful: they raked the attacking craft and the landing skiffs with cannon and musket fire, and, once the invaders were ashore, demolished them in the Thermopylean causeway up which we had come, by hurling down on them cascades of boulders, hundreds of which were always in readiness.

The island is far from the tracks of steamers, and even the schooners and sloops are rare and haphazard visitors; so travellers arriving there become the objects of a kind and generous hospitality. We were invited to luncheon by the jovial Dr Schokolaad, the town doctor of Bottom, the capital, who, during the temporary absence of the deputy governor, was managing the affairs of the island in his stead. It was a great meal, ushered in by draughts of Hollands gin, and followed by 'Spice', the drink of the island. It is made of cloves and cinnamon and aniseed which is first ground to a powder, then boiled in syrup. Rum is poured on the mixture and strained, and the rum is set fire to, quickly extinguished, and then bottled. All these islands have their own drinks. The inhabitants of St Martin drink guavaberry rum, while the Statians have a grog called 'Miss Blyden' which used to be a great favourite of the buccaneers.

Our plans to climb the inside of the crater to the village of Windwardside had to be cancelled, as an emissary arrived from the shore, saying that the *Rose Millicent* was dragging her anchor and was in danger, unless she put to sea at once, of being carried inshore by the waves and battered against the rocky side of the island. So we had to thank host and hostess hurriedly and go down to the sloop.

When we reached the little ledge of sand, the sea was so rough that the sloop was leaping about like a restless horse at its tether. Beside it lay the rusty hulk of a little steamer called the *Kralendijk*, also bound for St Martin, which had arrived with stores for the island. Captain Fleming said that the journey to the next island would take many hours in such a sea, as St Martin lay to NNW of Saba, and the Trades were blowing steadily westward. He advised us to take passage in the *Kralendijk*. The *Rose Millicent* had already collided against her side and damaged her bulwarks. We got on board the steamer just as the anchor was coming up. Captain Fleming went bobbing across the intervening waves towards the sloop.

We landed at Phillipsburg, the capital of St Martin, in the dark; and, like Statia, it appeared to be tucked up for the night, although it was only nine o'clock. The journey had been rough, and, feeling still slightly green, we sat drinking Bols gin in a sad little saloon where three English-speaking Negroes were playing billiards while an ancient Ford was being prepared to take us over to the French side. Nothing marked the change from St Maarten to St Martin except the imperceptible elimination of an 'a'. The car pulled up in the main street of the dismal little town of Marigot, capital of the French colony of St Martin. The single hotel looked as though it had been sealed up decades ago, but knocking at last produced light and movement inside. A wild-eyed young woman from St Barthélémy admitted us and showed us into our little hutches, all of which gave on to a bleak central room. Here, after an hour or two, we had a sad and tasteless meal. It was served by a young coloured girl called Bella, who giggled and mooned and pouted her way with exasperating slowness from dining-room to kitchen and back again, her progress marked by dropped rolls and plates and the drag of her slippers. We rejoiced at the idea of leaving next day.

The first person we encountered in Marigot next morning was the fabulous Mr Fleming; a plump, thick-set, fair-headed man of about forty-five, with shrewd eyes behind tortoiseshell spectacles. He spoke impeccable English and French, and radiated almost visible sparks of energy and efficiency. Our journey to the Virgin Isles was organized in a few minutes. The journey would take over twenty-five hours in a sloop, across an expanse of sea that was bare of islands and probably very rough. How much did the sloop-journey cost? Why, it would be much cheaper and quicker to hire a taxi-plane from the Republic Aircraft Co., a private firm of Americans in St Thomas. Where were we heading for? St Thomas? Fine. Mr Fleming wrote out a signal there and then, which was tapped out a few moments later from a private transmitting set in his office just opposite our hotel. That was that. He invited us to come for a drink that afternoon, and vanished without the faintest hint of bustle in an aura of cordiality and acumen.

Marigot is a miserable town. Two hundred yards of dust, lined with wooden houses that have none of the charm of those of the other island towns, and with grocers' shops, all of which are owned by Flemings, who vary from the deepest black to the palest *sangmêlé*, or, like our recent acquaintance, pure white, comprise the main street. At one end lay the quay, where a couple of fishing smacks lay at anchor, the other trailed off into rolling meadowland that might have been anywhere in Sussex, with cows grazing under tame European trees. Only a single palm tree, and a few Negroes hanging listlessly about, hinted that we were in the tropics. And nothing else. Listlessness, we were to learn, was the essential characteristic of the town; that, and an absolute characterlessness that was so extreme that it contrived to develop from a negative attribute into something destructively positive.

The plane, of course, didn't come.

After hours of waiting, a signal arrived saying that it was impossible to send a plane for four days. The *Rose Millicent* had sailed off to her home port, and all the other sloops had vanished during the night. No planes were calling from any other island. We were marooned.

How welcome such a delay would have been anywhere but here –

in Grenada, or Pointe Baptiste, or with Raoul in Guadeloupe! Even Pointe-
à-Pitre seemed an eligible stopping-place compared to Marigot. We
thought with nostalgia of the Schoelcher and Herminier museums,
the snakes, the birds, the fish made out of cotton and straw ... Here
there was nothing. Even the blazing sunlight seemed to have been
deadened and robbed of some essential component on its journey from
the sun to this island. Our picnics turned out to be flat little expeditions,
possibly because Bella and the girl from St Barthélémy prepared them
with such poor grace and, above all, so dismally badly. Costa found the
light unsuitable for painting, I found writing impossible, and Joan
languished over the pages of *Oblomoff*. We watched the sun go down
from a balcony from which a lump of concrete had fallen to expose a
rusty iron prong, part of the entrails of the building. The various Flemings
sat outside their stores, drawling tedious items of news to each other,
or shouting good-evening as the super-Fleming descended from his office,
climbed into his car and drove away. As the days dragged by we got
the impression that our presence in the island was becoming as much
a bore for the islanders as it was for us.

It rained without stopping all through the fourth day of our exile, so
we were compelled to remain indoors, talking listlessly and playing paper-
games. Soon after sunset I heard Bella talking about a film. Going down
to the street, I saw that people were splashing through the mud towards
an ancient marquee that had been pitched in the yard of the rum-shop.
I shouted up to Joan and Costa, but neither of them wanted to come.
So I joined a queue which contained the entire population of Marigot.
The only other European there was a Dominican monk. His black and
white habit and pale tonsured head looked quite extraordinary in the
African concourse. While the tent filled up, a cornet soloist played *Horsy
keep your tail up*. The film began. It was *Konigsmark*, a French picture
made at some very remote period; exactly the sort of thing I felt like seeing:
reviews of hussars in the squares of Ruritanian castles, with a grand-
duchess riding side-saddle in a plumed busby, a frogged jacket and a
dolman; duels between mediatized princes in moonlit gardens, chiefs of
police with spiked helmets and Kaiser-Bill moustaches; cloaks, sword-
sticks, poison and secret passages. The audience gazed at the small screen
in silence until a fight broke out. Then the marquee burst into a frenzy,
the spectators shouting advice and punching one hand deliriously into
the palm of the other. As the hero was a French private tutor at the
Grand Ducal Court, and thus far less apt at fighting than the spurred
and swashbuckling bullies that surrounded him, he usually got a pretty
bad time, and was frequently booed by the audience. Their sentiments

were all on the side of the monocles and uniforms, and when the hero was knocked spinning across a Louis XV library by the Count, all the spectators rose to their feet, bellowing 'Go on, maan! Hit him again! *Hit de maan!*' Rain, falling through patches in the marquee, added verisimilitude to the constant drizzle in which, on the screen, all the duels and love scenes were taking place, and at last one whole side of the tent, owing to the weight of the water in a hollow of the roof, or the snapping of a guide-rope, collapsed, and we were suddenly precipitated from the banqueting-hall of a baroque castle in central Europe into a pitch dark rain-storm in the French West Indies. But it was almost the end, and we were able to crawl back under the sodden débris for the finale. As we extricated ourselves and headed for shelter, many of the ticket-holders seemed, by their conversation, to be displeased with the final upshot of the film, and countless arguments about the plot grew fainter through the rain as I regained the hotel.

On our fifth morning on the island, a signal came from the Virgin Islands, saying a plane would call for us at midday. Our jubilation at the thought of escaping from this horrible island buoyed us up all through the morning. It was a cloudless, perfect flying day. We drove out to the aerodrome at a quarter to twelve, and found the KLM agent waiting with two men and a mobile petrol tank to fill the plane with fuel when it arrived, and a Dutch policeman to go through the papers.

We waited an hour, and still no plane came, and, in spite of our remonstrances, the policeman, agent and workmen went away and the offices were locked up. They promised to return if a plane appeared. We were left alone on the aerodrome. Our spirits were fast ebbing, but none of us dared to put our gloom into words. Costa and Joan bathed and I lay down on the asphalt, hiding from the sun under the big Guadeloupean hat. The hours passed, and nothing happened.

The whole of this stay had been rock bottom, the nadir of our fortunes on our journey, and these torrid hours, with our hope draining away drop by drop after our almost feverish joy at the idea of departure, was the worst of all. We strained our faculties to detect the approach of a plane; but nothing came. And after a long time gazing at the expanse of blue, it seemed impossible that anything ever should come. At last, after we had given up hope, a tiny speck appeared to the south, and the faint buzz of a plane's propeller, and in a few minutes a very small scarlet amphibian plane landed and taxied towards us. The pilot was a tall, cheerful young American. He had been held up in Martinique, he said, by the slowness of the staff in producing petrol. The policeman arrived on his bicycle, and the papers were put in order. But no KLM agent or workmen came to fill the plane up, so we sat down to wait. The policeman pedalled away. After waiting three-quarters of an hour, the pilot began to be disturbed about the light, as it was very dangerous landing at St Thomas after dark. Finally, in despair, I got a lift on the step of a passing bicycle, and wobbled into Phillipsburg, where the police-man told me the agent refused to come out because he had no guarantee that the car journey to the aerodrome – about a mile – would be paid for. By producing cash, this loathsome brute – a comatose Billy Bunter whose heavy lids were half closed over two minute, lack-lustre eyes – was lured into his own motor with his two attendants and away to the aerodrome. The moment the plane was filled he pocketed the money and they drove away again without a word.

We packed ourselves into the little scarlet plane, and plodded up into the air, heading north-westward. We watched Statia and the cone of Saba, St Barthélémy, Anguilla and the odious St Martin draw slowly behind us. The lonely island of Sombrero followed them, looking, appropriately enough, exactly like the floating Spanish Hat which has been for centuries its unofficial name. It was here that Robert Jeffreys, the armourer's mate of the brig *Recruit*, was marooned by the captain of his ship in 1807. Then the sea, for over a hundred miles, was quite empty, for the first time since our arrival in the Caribbean: a circle of blue, gleaming and creased with currents and freakishly bare, enclosed in a globe of sky, in which for once there was not a cloud. Our plane hung on tiny wings in a vacuum of blue. We were heading straight for the sun, whose sinking ball was our only fellow-occupant of all this emptiness.

After an hour of vacancy, the island of St Croix appeared far to the south, and then, one by one, the whole of the archipelago of the Virgin Islands advanced out of the western sky like a dark mountain-range: Virgin Gorda, a jagged spine of rock with its little satellite of Fallen Jerusalem; Tortola and, away to the north, Anegada and Jost Van Dyke, the water round their capes and creeks sprinkled with the innumerable brood of islets, and, as the plane sank lower, with the white sails of fishing boats. All these islands belong to Britain. But as we flew westwards, the larger islands of St John and St Thomas which came to meet us with their scattered escort of islets and reefs in a shadowy procession belonged, like St Croix, to the United States. The sun was dying fast as we approached St Thomas. We circled over a great, almost landlocked bay from the steep sides of which winked the lights of Charlotte Amalie, the island capital. The machine tilted over on one wing and, spiralling vertiginously down this mountain funnel, subsided on to the water. There, without stopping, the aeroplane thrashed towards the shore, and drove up the beach with the ease of a small motor-car. There seemed no reason why we shouldn't drive like this all over the island.

The Danes first took possession of St Thomas – after the Dutch colonists had sailed away to the little town of New Amsterdam (from which, when its name had been changed to New York, were to come its present owners, centuries later), and at the end of a transitory English colonization – in the year of the Great Fire of London. St John and St Croix – which the islanders pronounce San Croy – were annexed to the Danish crown during the next seventy years. St Croix was purchased from the Knights of Malta, whose passion for islands had brought them here, so many thousand miles away from their usual hunting ground; and all three islands, together with their lesser dependencies, were bought by the United States from Denmark, after decades of negotiations between the two countries, and protracted debates in the Folkething and the Landesthing in Copenhagen, in 1916. I heard nothing but English spoken, and have not been able to discover from books or memoirs whether or not a sort of Danish Créole has been added to the many lingoes of the Caribbean Islands.

But the Danish influence is felt everywhere. It is especially noticeable in the gabled and shingled houses and the clean white cobbles, the massive and brightly painted buildings, the statues and coats of arms, and the names of streets and towns. The capital has a childish and Scandinavian aspect which is very strange indeed. On top of this strangeness comes the American influence. Charlotte Amalie has been 'developed', as the phrase goes, for the tourist industry, so that the cleanness and brightness are just a fraction cleaner and brighter than is natural. Curio shops abound, and piles of knick-knacks which are either barbaric and Caribbean or elfin and Nordic are piled up under the ghastly lustre of neon-lighting. Striped awnings abound and shrubs bloom in gaily painted tubs – again a little too gaily painted – outside cocktail caverns that are not quite decided whether they want to be haunted by zombies or by trolls. The result of this compounding of elements is a fascinating elfo-African atmosphere: Santa Claus in robes of scarlet and fur, but equipped as well with a grass skirt and wreath of hibiscus, sipping, with evident relish, Coco-Cola through a straw.

The islanders were outnumbered in the streets by visitors from America who had come for their Christmas holidays to this very adequate replica of the Mediterranean, and our hotel, the Saint Anna, a delightful old Danish house where a great empty ballroom and long glasses and chandeliers are perched high above the falling amphitheatre of roofs, was inhabited by an exact American equivalent of English spinsters in Florence. Steep lanes of steps led us past the white walls of little gardens over which fell showers of bougainvillia, up and down the semicircle of the bay to Bluebeard's castle. There, in an atmosphere laden with the smell of syringa, visitors on the terrace of the buccaneers' stronghold drank their highballs with apposite emotions. Other lanes led through undeveloped parts of the town, where old Danish houses, built over white arches of great depth and span, lay back in the starlight behind palisades of wrought iron.

The evening of our arrival ended in a bar on the waterfront, where, in a setting of vaults, chintz curtains and indirect lighting, a number of sailors were clustered in silent homage round a jukebox. It was the first time I had seen one of these wonderful machines. The barman called it a Wurlitzer Nickelodeum. It was a shrine of steel and bakelite and glass, six feet high, and a queue of sailors were waiting to insert their nickels. At the drop of a coin, an unerring steel hand inside this tabernacle grasped the chosen record from the shelf and placed it on a disc that rose like a magic carpet. A needle-bearing arm descended and unleashed a muted throbbing and the voice of a crooner. The air was filled with an etherialized treacle. Glass panels were illuminated in shades of mauve and pink, and liquids that must have been orangeade and Chartreuse and Grenadine syrup bubbled and glowed softly through a maze of decorative glass-piping with the intention of attuning the listener's bloodstream to the mood of the music. Sailor after sailor slipped their coins into this engine, their eyes becoming every second mistier with *Sehnsucht* and *Heimweh*. The Nickelodeum is in its infancy. When it is perfected it is to be armed with slowly turning rollers of satin and fur and plush for the palms of the hands, and a battery of little scent sprays, while, from a bakelite orifice, an inch of barley sugar or Turkish delight, antiseptically sheathed in cellophane, will emerge, in order that all five senses, and not only two, may be simultaneously gratified.

BRIDGE PASSAGE

The enormous bulk of Puerto Rico on the western horizon had less the appearance of an island, as we had come to understand the word – an infinitesimal star in a straggling constellation – than of the beginnings of a new continent. We gazed at it almost with consternation. Everything had suddenly begun to change at high speed.

Except for the remote haven of Jamaica, the friendly world of sterling and francs was behind us for good, and only a precarious lifeline of dollars separated us from poverty. We were approaching an alien universe: the first outpost of Spanish America. We had seen the last of the small islands, with their easy and familiar values, and the emerging peaks of the sub-marine cordillera were slipping out of control, swelling into the Greater Antilles – islands comparable in size to Wales or Ireland, or even England, independent republics, some of them, whose populations are reckoned in millions – preparing to expand, after the ultimate giant of Cuba, into the mass of the American continent. It was a sobering notion, a caesura, a fundamental break in our journeys; a time to take stock of where we were and whither we were flying.

For once I was glad to be suspended in mid-air, and to observe, Daedalus-like, the scission of the two worlds; for the contrast of Culebra, Vieques and the retreating swarm of the Virgin Islands with the solitary approaching volume of Puerto Rico aptly epitomized the change-over.

The Yunque, the low, anvil-shaped mountain beyond our propeller, was, several million years ago, not only the eastern cape of Puerto Rico, but of a colossal island of which the four Great Antilles – Puerto Rico, Hispaniola, Jamaica and Cuba – were the mountain-tops; the valleys, some time ago, merely became swamped with sea-water. A few million years earlier still, Cuba was united to the Yucatan Peninsula and the North American mainland, and Puerto Rico to a dry and continuous Lesser Antillean mountain range that was a projection of Venezuela and the Guianas. But Puerto Rico was not only a terminal point, but a road fork, for the single line of the Lesser Antilles branches here – westwards through Haiti and Cuba to Mexico, and north-westwards over the high plateau, now submerged and studded by the coral reefs of the Bahamas, to join the Florida peninsula. The surface of the earth must have tilted, for at this remote epoch the wasp-waist of the mainland leading down to Panama was exactly what the Antilles are today: a series of islands. It was not over the isthmus of Panama, but through the sunny foothills of the Antillean Andes, now split up into a loop of archipelagoes, that the obsolete fauna of those times trotted from continent to continent: a traffic that is proved by the discovery in Guadeloupe of the bones of a megatherium. It is at Puerto Rico, too, that the smallest distance separates the greatest depth of the Caribbean and the Atlantic. We could see the great dark masses of water closing in on the pale coastal shallows. The Caribbean chain sinks, just to the north of the island, to a bottom nearly eight and a half kilometres deep; the greatest depth, in 1891, that had been discovered in the Atlantic Ocean. The height of the mountains of Cuba from their visible summits to their roots on the floor of the Caribbean overtops the snowy crest of Kanchenjunga.

But the valleys that separate the peaks of the Lesser Antillean chain nowhere sink deeper than a few hundred yards except round Martinique and Sombrero: a high sea-wall shelving down to the deep soundings of the Caribbean and the Atlantic. If the island sea is to be compared to the Mediterranean, these occidental Pillars of Hercules are multiplied into a colonnade through the many pillars of which the Atlantic everlastingly propels its trillions of tons of water. For the great equatorial currents of the Atlantic, sweeping from east to west, strike the Brazilian coasts and turn north-westwards, pouring through the open gateways of the Antilles into the Caribbean cauldron; travelling, at a leisurely walking pace – eighteen to thirty-three kilometres a day – and only breaking into a run through the tortuous funnel that lies between Trinidad and Venezuela. In the centre of the Caribbean they slow down or, striking other currents, revolve in maelstroms. But still travelling westwards, slowly over the submerged hurdles in the west and growing, on their long, sluggish journey, every second warmer and saltier, they move at a rush through the exiguous rapids between Yucatan and Cuba into the smooth amphitheatre of the Gulf of Mexico. There they slowly gyrate in three-quarters of a circle. At a point two-thirds of the way round, their smooth surface is smeared, as though with a long dyed lock of hair, by the turbid waters that the Mississippi has drained from half of the United States. It curls southwards and plaits itself into the current as it hastens its speed through the defile of the Florida channel.

The waters are sucked foaming through these narrows, shooting northward then to rejoin the huge volume of warm water which, ferrying northwards its meadows of Sargasso weed, had shunned the doorways of the Lesser Antilles and taken a short cut by following the edge of the coral plateau of the Bahamas. There the united currents turn eastwards across the Atlantic in a long tropical flux, streaming and expanding round the British Isles and carrying the warmth of the Caribbees as far as Spitzbergen and Nova Zembla and the Arctic Circle. Its itinerary, ending in this long stroke of the pen, evolves like a sentence of Arabic script; delicately unwinding among the islands and curving and repeating itself, and then trailing airily away.

At a different angle across this great map the Trade Winds eternally blow. Running straight as a railway-line from western Europe to the Caribbean, they flatten into a westerly course against the coasts of the

Spanish Main, and then, rebounding from the South American Sierras, fan the coast of Jamaica and Cuba from the south-east; leaving, like the sea, centres of stillness in the middle of the Caribbean and the Gulf of Mexico. The island we were approaching is in the middle of another more baleful thoroughfare, for when the overheated surface of South America draws to itself the cooler and denser air of the north in late summer and autumn, the atmospheric commotion turns into hurricanes – a Carib word – that roll thundering northwards from the Guianas, and, following a line drawn through St Vincent and Puerto Rico to South Carolina, turn off north-westwards to spend their fury over the Atlantic waters. Houses are torn up like trees, and, in the past, fortresses have been demolished, ships lifted out of the water and carried miles inland, and cyclopean rocks blown through the air; islands have been broken up into scattered reefs, and reefs, piled one on top of the other, turned into islands. The Great Hurricane of the 10th of October, 1786, swept whole towns away, sunk fleets, and even, by a community of distress, reconciled the French and the English, on the point of disembowelling each other. In 1685 the Guadeloupeans, creeping out of cover after the passage of one of these visitations, found the ruins teeming with dazed and innumerable pelicans – birds till then unknown in the island. Flurried and helpless parcels, a whole population of them had been whirled hundreds of miles across the sea, the pouches of their lower jaws blown taut by the wind like the sails of an armada.

The region of Antillia existed in the minds of Europeans long before the Antilles were discovered. In ancient maps it is represented as an archipelago or, alternatively, as a single mass of land, wandering in the Tenebrous Sea between the Canaries and the south-eastern confines of Asia. Sometimes they are set down as the Lentils, on account of their profusion and their size. As exploration expanded the Atlantic, the chart-ographers thrust the legendary region farther and farther towards the setting sun, and Columbus, landing on Guanahani and the northern coasts of Hispaniola, was convinced that the Arawaks were akin to the Indians of the Orient and the Chinese. Cathay and Hindustan, he felt sure, were not far off (oddly enough, time has lent some colour to his adumbrations; for now, after four centuries, Chinese and East Indians abound in Cuba. As he never circumnavigated it, he died in the conviction that it was a peninsula of the Asian continent.) But the Antilles they have appropriately remained: fore-islands, the outposts of America.

We were losing height, and the roofs and belfries and battlements of San Juan de Puerto Rico appeared along the coast. Due north lay the track of Columbus, and that of all the Conquistadors who succeeded him;

the highway to the new world, ruffling gently under the Trade Winds, *Los Vientos Alicios*. Heredia, himself the descendant of one of these paladins – of the founder, in fact, of that powerful but deleted Carthage of the Spanish Main, Cartagena de las Indias – conjures up, in elaborate Parnassian periods, their yard-arms stooping under the wind's impulsion.

> ... Les vents alisés inclinaient leurs antennes
> Aux bords mystérieux du monde occidental
> Chaque soir, espérant des lendemains épiques,
> L'azur phosphorescent de la mer des Tropiques
> Enchantait leur sommeil d'un mirage doré;
> Ou penchés à l'avent des blanches caravelles,
> Ils regardaient monter en un ciel ignoré
> Du fond de l'Océan des étoiles nouvelles.

CHAPTER 10

Haiti

We had travelled through the last two islands with scarcely less speed than that of thought. But the moment we arrived in Haiti this breakneck tempo slowed down to one of almost prehistoric sloth. Avoiding the taxis outside the aerodrome, we chose the solitary carriage and creaked off in the direction of Port-au-Prince. These black and obsolete vehicles are drawn by horses on the point of death and driven by very old men. They are to be found in all the islands. Recently, stunned by the haste of our movement, by aeroplane and motor-car through air and streets, and then up and down the skyscrapers of Puerto Rico in lifts, I had gazed at them hungrily. Sitting under the hood of these thinking-machines, the works of one's mind must surely unglue themselves after an hour or so and begin to function again in sympathy with the revolution of the wheels.

The cane-field and savannah turned into the outskirts of the capital. Thatched cabins straggled into the country under the palm trees, and multiplied into a suburb, through which the road ran in a straight, interminable line. For the first mile or so, the town consisted entirely of rum-shops and barbers' saloons and harness-makers. Hundreds of saddles were piled up in the sunlight. Bits and bridles and spurs and saddle-bags hung in festoons. There were horses everywhere. Our equipage churned its way upstream through a current of horses and mules ridden by Negroes who straddled among bulky packages, all heading for their villages with their purchases for Christmas. One or two were singing Haitian *meringues*, and several were carrying game-cocks under their arms, lovingly stroking their feathers as they trotted past. Old women, puffing at their pipes, jogged along side-saddle. They had scarlet and blue kerchiefs tied round their heads in a fortuitous, rather piratical fashion, half-covered by broad-brimmed straw hats against the sun. The sides of

the road pullulated with country people chattering, drinking rum, playing cards and throwing dice under the trees. The air was thick with dust, and ringing with incomprehensible and deafening Créole. I felt I might like Haiti.

We reached the centre of the town at last, where arcades of ochreous and flaking plaster intersected and vanished in vistas. Here and there this fabric of romantic dilapidation festered into an American drugstore or a milk-bar, and everywhere, in tin and plastic and cardboard, were symptoms of the Coca-Cola plague. Gutters four feet deep separated the pavements from the roads, and in the pavements occasional open man-holes gaped that must, on dark nights, be a serious drain on Haitian man power.

Smart life in Haiti – the dazzling white tropical suits, the dark heads and hands – resembles a photographic negative. Only white chauffeurs at the wheel of the grand limousines are absent to complete the illusion. *Cabane Choucoune*, the fashionable night club of Port-au-Prince, is perched on the mountain-side above the capital in the cool suburbs of Pétionville. It is a replica of an African kraal, a great cylinder of bamboo with a steep conical roof which simultaneously achieves, by a skilful twist of sophisti-cation, the amenities, the low lights and the luxury of an expensive night club with the atmosphere of the dwelling of an equatorial monarch.

But there was nothing remotely primitive about the Christmas Eve gathering. Men in beautifully made white suits and dinner jackets danced with women dressed in the height of fashion. They were superb, far the best-looking we had seen in any of the islands: tall, broad-shouldered, narrow-waisted and long-legged, with a fine carriage of the head and great elegance of movement and gesture. What a relief to see this colour and splendour and extravagance after the shapeless dresses of the colonies! Many of our neighbours were pale in complexion, but the majority were of an imposing ebony. A woman sitting at the next table was perhaps the most beautiful in a room full of sable Venuses. She had fine dark features of extraordinary delicacy and regularity, and sat with her elbows leaning on the table, clasping and unclasping her long ringed fingers as she talked, and each time she did so the heavy diamond bracelets on her forearm flashed. Enormous pearls glowed in the lobes of her ears, and her dress was made of stiff scarlet taffeta.

It was about an hour short of dawn before we got back to our hotel. When, at last, slightly dizzy, I went upstairs, I must have mistaken the door, for suddenly I found myself in a strange room. A small fire of logs and charcoal had been built on a sheet of tin in the centre of the floor, filling the upper half of the room with smoke. Round it squatted a peasant family, a man and three little girls of diminishing size, and an old woman who was cooking their breakfast. Their gourd-plates were being filled with ladlefuls of hot maize. Five startled black faces turned in my direction, their dark features and the whites of their eyes very distinct in the firelight. We might have been in the heart of the Congo.

Our second hotel, for the first proved too lugubrious to remain in for long, was cheap, and entirely frequented by Haitians. It was built above a *pâtisserie* and bar on the Champ de Mars. This leafy expanse is the Haitian equivalent, not of its Parisian namesake, but of the Place de la Concorde, and it is about as large. It is the real heart of Haitian civic and national life, a clearing covered by a network of paths, and adorned with statues and bandstands and trees. It was here, during the Revolution, that the patriot Sonthonax erected a guillotine. An immense crowd, according to Sir Spencer St John, assembled to witness the execution of a suspected royalist. 'But when they saw the bright blade descend and the head roll at their feet, they were horror-stricken and, rushing on the guillotine, tore it to pieces, and no other has ever been again erected in Haiti.'

I was woken every morning by a bugle just below my window, and standing on the balcony I watched an officer and a platoon of the Haitian guard breaking the colours from a mast among the trees. The brazen notes of the National Anthem rang through the air as the little packet of bunting jerked its way up the mast. The soldiers stood with presented arms, and the passers-by remained riveted to the ground. The flag fluttered open, the final notes died away, and the Haitians thawed into mobility again. The Haitian banner is the Revolutionary tricolor of France from which the offending white stripe has been torn: a red and blue bicolor. The centre is charged with a warlike panoply that symbolizes the Haitian War of Independence: a palmiste surmounted by the cap of liberty on a pike; a drum and cannon-balls at the foot of the tree, and cannon pointing their muzzles to dexter and sinister. Round the central palm half a dozen furled banners radiate in a vainglorious peacock's tail. The two-coloured flag and its martial insignia are virtually a heraldic expression of the cry of Boisrond-Tonnerre when he drew up the Haitian Act of Independence in 1804: 'What we need,' he affirmed, 'is the skin of a white man for parchment, his skull for a writing-desk, his blood for ink and a bayonet for a pen.'

The statues of the heroes of Haitian liberty form a scattered population in stone, and for many of the simpler Haitians they have almost the mystic attributes of totem-poles. The most representative of these is the effigy of Dessalines, the first emperor of Haiti, an imposing figure with strong Negro features, a braided military frock-coat, enormous epaulettes and a cocked hat, and a fiercely flourished sabre. On the many anniversaries of the Haitian calendar, these paladins are the objects of a public cult. Peering through my window over the tree-tops, I could observe the crowds assembling round the image of Dessalines, and the police persuading them back on to the pavements; and I would hurry downstairs and run across the grass to join them. A body of the Haitian Guard came swinging through the sunlight from the direction of the barracks, with pennants waving overhead, each platoon headed by an officer with a drawn sword. Wheeling into line with Potsdamlike precision, they formed a guard of honour. There we would wait, while a brass band discoursed military music to the morning air. Beyond the soldiers and the tree-tops and the stone sword-wielder appeared the steep Tyrolean-chalet roofs of the villas which surrounded the Champ de Mars, and beyond them the mountains were gracefully assembled. Their bare, clean lines, the shadows branching like leaf-veins in their ravines and the crystalline purity of the sky recalled the mountain satellites of Athens. My gaze would sink again to the ranks of Haitian soldiers. They wore their American uniforms with extraordinary dash. With my mind still lingering on Athenian themes, and the flashing fustanellas of the Evzones at similar functions, I regretted that a crack regiment of the Haitian Guard was not also dressed in the ancestral war trappings of Africa. How splendid these black warriors would appear, naked to the waist, equipped with the head-dresses of ostrich feathers, and armed with the vast almond-shaped shields of antelope-hide, the heavy knobkerries, and the tall and glittering assegais ...! Such reveries were interrupted by a movement in the crowd: all heads were turning in one direction, as a procession of limousines came purring down upon us through the haze. Words of command rang out, and fanfares sounded as the vehicles glided up to the foot of the statue and discharged their loads of officials in uniform and evening clothes: the generals, the military household, the cabinet and, at last, the President himself. M. Estimé had reached presidential office a year before as a result of Haiti's one bloodless revolution. (The Mulatto government of M. Lescot had been criticized for its increasingly fascist tendencies, and had been turned out in favour of an all-Black régime.) The President, a figure of great dignity, descended from his motor, and, making his way through the galaxy of notables, placed an enormous wreath before the statue. Bayonets flashed in salute, the band played the National Anthem, the air trembled with the boom of saluting ordnance. A sizzle and hiss was followed by a loud swish as the first of many rockets sailed upwards and popped in the limpid air. The cars filled up again and purred away, and an open limousine, escorted by a moving crackle of applause, carried the President slowly down the avenue. The sun gleamed in the spectacles and the ebony contours of the President's face, and added lustre, against the black serge and the starch, to the ribbons and orders. It flashed resplendently from the top hat that was raised in a motionless attitude of acknowledgement. Then the crowd broke over the scorched grass and we would follow the fleet of cars at a trot in the direction of the statue of Toussaint L'Ouverture ...

Along one side of this expanse of sward lies the presidential palace, an immense rectangle pierced by a multiplicity of windows and crowned by a groined dome which is flanked by two attendant cupolas; and all of a white so uncompromising and refractory to the sun that it appears, in that setting of parched earth and superabundant green, to be an edifice of snow magically transported from the polar wastes. At periods of national solemnity, it is adorned at night by thousands of electric bulbs, so that, with its vast bulk immaterialized, it hangs in the night as insubstantially as a pier which has been illuminated for a regatta. On its highest dome the Haitian banner in neon-lighting flashes on and off every second as though it were flapping and beating in a non-existent wind. It is often the background for the trajectories and the expanding sheaves of fireworks. The Haitians gaze up through the leaves at this magic foliage, and a whiff of cordite and saltpetre floats to their nostrils on the warm air.

Late one afternoon during the three days of festivity that mark the anniversary of independence, I paused outside the railings of the President's palace. On the shady lawns inside, a great garden party was in progress. Innumerable groups conversed under the palm trees. There were many uniforms, and scattered fragments of black or violet signalled the participation of the clergy. The hats and dresses and parasols of the ladies had sought and achieved the exact equipoise between gala and formality. The occasional pallor of a European, as the member of a foreign mission sauntered in colloquy with some grave legislator of the Republic, looked almost ghost-like. Splendidly dressed footmen moved through the elongated shadows with silver trays of champagne, and from the orchestra under the mangoes came the notes of the *Invitation to the Waltz*. It was a scene of singular and authentically Firbankian charm.

The day after Christmas is celebrated in Pétionville by a succession of cockfights. I wonder if this, and the kindred ceremony of the Boxing

Day Meet in England, commemorate in some obscure and atavistic fashion the stoning of Saint Stephen? And the Easter Bull Fights in Spain? Do they combine with their Mithraistic traditions a memento of the Passion, the Via Dolorosa and Golgotha, with the Lamb symbolism expanded to a sacrifice of Mithras and the Spectators in the role of the Hierosolymite mob? The banderillas would commemorate the scourging, the crowning with thorns, the bulrush-sceptre. The incident of St Veronica is plainly referred to in the sporting jargon of the *afición* and the kill, the Moment of Truth, would equate to the Roman's ultimate and dissolving lance-thrust ... It is a problem that could be profitably debated by Wyndham Lewis and Hemingway and the College of Cardinals.

The cockpit in Pétionville is a rectangle of beaten earth enclosed by a barrier of plank and sheltered from the sun by a roof of matting. After the blinding glare, the interior seemed almost pitch dark. There were about two hundred Negroes and Mulattoes, most of them belonging to the working class, clustering in little groups round the feathered champions. Tipsters and bookies circulated everywhere, and pedlars selling Coca-Cola and beer and rum. Some of the bets placed looked enormous, and bulbous rolls of *gourde* and dollar notes appeared from the pockets of the humblest labourers. The *gourde* is equivalent to a fifth of the U.S. dollar, and is divided up into centimes and *cobs*; and as American currency also circulates as legal tender, it is a long time before you are fully abreast of the intricacies of *centimes or, centimes Haitiens, cobs*, U.S. dollars and *gourdes*. I heard two explanations for the curious name of the larger Haitian unit. One was that it derives from the old Spanish *peso gordo*; the other that Christophe commandeered all the actual gourds in the kingdom (those hollowed, pumpkin-like globes are almost the only domestic utensils in the country areas) and issued them again as currency. The vision of shopping with a hundred gourds, or banks whose vaults contained them by the million, is so bewildering that one is unwillingly driven back to the first explanation.

We sat on a bench surrounded by standing Haitians. Most of the feet at the end of the forest of legs were bare, and so calloused with walking that they were virtually equipped, like espadrilles, with soles of fibre or rope. Occasionally a pair of legs was enclosed in white linen and shod with bi-coloured shoes which wove their way like raffish pythons through the groves of darker extremities. These were usually owned by business men and fight-promoters smoking large cigars.

It was the Haitian equivalent of a Regency sporting occasion. Jet black Bang-Up Corinthians stood with arms akimbo, discussing form with the Hawbucks and the Gemmen of the Fancy. The game-cocks were passed from hand to hand, prodded and fumbled and appraised and held at arm's length for display, or placed on the ground and pressed up and down as though to test the resilience of their legs. There were, to judge by the conversation, three crack breeds: the Rajah, the Cuban and the Dominican from the neighbouring republic.

A red cock and a white were the first two antagonists: Rouge and L'Homme à Surprises. They were subjected to an intricate toilet by their seconds, who first dosed them with haemoglobin, and then, filling their own mouths with water, pressed the birds to their lips, sucking and soaking the feathers so that they should cling to the body and afford no hold for the enemy. For the same reason their lower neck-feathers had been plucked, and their combs cropped flush with their low brows. No steel spurs were used, but their natural spurs were sharpened to a last, perfect point with penknives, and the birds were placed beak to beak.

Till then they had been crowing and flapping their wings threateningly. But now, craning forward and moving their heads up and down, or gyrating them with their beaks still touching, they fell silent: streamlined instruments of destruction on stilts, glaring at each other through wary, bloodshot and ferocious eyes. Their remaining neck feathers stiffened into ruffs, and then, slowly turning inside out as their anger rose, surrounded the purposeful heads in bristling funnels of plumage. Their prolonged sparring evoked a chorus of encouragement and jeering. As if they felt that their valour was impugned, the birds closed with each other. Pecking and lunging, they sailed into the air with their claws palm to palm, and hung there, poised with beating wings for a few seconds like a pair of heraldic supporters. Turning over and over, they subsided in a turmoil of flying feathers, and resumed their tussle in the dust while a typhoon of noise swept through the crowd. The spectators leaned forward over the competitors in a close circle of heads, working their arms up and down as they screamed, in a strange, unconscious imitation of the contestants. Again the two cocks shot up into the air. Last minute bets were placed, and greasy bundles of *gourdes* sailed to and fro across the ring. Both were bleeding round the neck, and it was evident that Rouge was growing weaker. L'Homme à Surprises went for him again and again, making wicked staccato pecks at his throat. At last, with a deafening roar of applause and encouragement, they closed again, and, as the dust and feathers cleared, Rouge rolled over on his back with a deep wound at the junction of his breast and neck. His claws clenched and unclenched once or twice and then froze. The victor mounted the corpse and, spreading his wings, let out a long, triumphant crow. Jumping into the ring, his owner snatched him up and kissed him. Straw hats were flying in the air.

After a pause for drinks and the settling of accounts, two new cocks took the ring. It was plain from the start which was going to win. One of them repeatedly turned his back on the other, and attempted to escape, but he was forced by his partisans back into the range of his opponent's murderous and unerring attacks. Finally he seemed to abandon all ideas of flight or resistance and stood in a species of coma. His enemy strode round him, pecking terrible gashes in his neck, and then aimed at his eyes. His victim stood inert and helpless, his head stretched forward, gasping slowly, with the blood gradually filling his open beak and dripping on to the dust. A savage jerk of his tormentor's head sent a shower of blood splashing across the shirts and forearms of the spectators, and the noise, the scores of crowing cocks, the claustrophobic heat, the dust, the smell of sweat and the flying drops of blood combined to form an oppressive atmosphere of crime and collusion. The remaining eye grew glazed, and the loser fell on his side with one wing hanging open ... It was about then that we realized that we had bitten off more than we could chew and, extricating ourselves from the crowd, slunk into the open, three hang-dog sporting coves. A Negro ran after me and thrust a handful of guilty winnings into my hand, gave me a friendly pat on the shoulder, and ran back. We headed down the road into Pétionville, in search of stiff glasses of whisky and soda, discussing the scene we had just left and our debility in the presence of the robust amusements of our ancestors. The ringing of the bell and an outburst of shouting in the hut behind us marked the opening of another main, the third of about fifty billed for that morning.

The telephone wires running beside the road to the capital were bearded, every few inches, with the wispy little hanging nests of humming-birds.

Port-au-Prince is a sprawling, loose-knit town, and quarters and atmospheres juxtapose and overlap each other with surprising fortuitousness. Government buildings, smart villas and monuments change, with no perceptible click, into arcaded streets of shops, or regions of dock and timber yard, rusting small-gauge railway and patches of dead land and savannah. Minute clumps of forest, with grazing oxen and disintegrating shanties, appear, and then, with half a dozen steps, you are surprisingly back in the heart of the metropolis. Gazing at the site of a demolished building which used to be called Fort Caca, after the perishable materials from which it was built, I would become aware of a cohort of little boys taking up positions of attack, and at the first opening an onslaught of begging would begin. *'Blanc,'* they cried, *'blanc, ba'moin une gourde, blanc.'* Worse still, a small *élite*, steeped in the culture of the Occupation, would trot behind me repeating, 'Gimme ten cents, boss,' like an incantation. Haitians possess fewer inhibitions about mendicancy than any race in the world; even plump and well-dressed children, small shopkeepers and soldiers would momentarily, at the approach of a mug, adopt the profession. *'Hé,'* a shoemaker would shout across the road, rising from his last, *'Ba'moin une gourde.'* But the children were the worst; at the alert of sighted game they remained, whip in air, till their tops ran down and then came padding across the dust.

The Market is a great arched iron structure painted green and red, and its echoing vaults enclose a bawling, arguing and bargaining Timbuktoo. Powerful hags preside over pyramids of wares – shoes, sandals, bags, trays of trinkets hammered out of old coins, and wooden objects carved from mahogany and *lignum vitae*. New and old clothes hang on rails, and broad-brimmed straw hats lie in snowdrifts. Women insinuate their way through the stalls, carrying on their heads globular baskets of colossal size, some of them as much as six feet in diameter, and weighing as light as a feather. Piles of them vanish into the vaults like towers constructed of enormous bubbles. One old woman was nesting like a jackdaw in a bastion of plaster images, holy water stoups, medals, bunches of rosaries and painted candles of every length and girth. I noticed a number of unfamiliar utensils among all this – painted gourds, earthenware and china pots with lids, and sets of three con-joined wooden bowls carved out of the same log. I asked what they were for. The old woman laughed, and indicated that it was too difficult to explain. When, intrigued by her reticence, I pressed her, she gave a toothless cackle and said, *'C'est pour le Voudou.'* And so they were: vessels, as I was to learn later, for containing the souls of the initiates of the Haitian rites.

The Republic of Haiti occupies the westernmost third of the island of Hispaniola. Its history follows, for a while, a familiar pattern: the extinction of the Indians and the arrival of the first Negro slaves, and the relaxation of Spanish interest and control; the haphazard settling of French and English filibusters on her coasts, the use of her waters and hideouts by the buccaneers of both nations; the arrival of great captains and organizers like Levasseur, de Poincy, du Casse and D'Ogeron with Royal Commissions; the discomfiture and exit of the English filibusters; and the Treaty of Ryswick that granted the colony of Sainte

Domingue* – modern Haiti – to France. A series of grandees succeeded each other: de Gallifet, de Blénac, de Vaudreuil, d'Estaing, de Rohan, de Vallière, de la Luzerne and the remarkable Barbé de Marbois, as Royal Governors and Intendants, bringing in their wake an influx of French noblemen in search of colonial estates. During the eighteenth century, over a million slaves were imported from Africa. Estates prospered, towns and country houses sprang up, and *les Grands Seigneurs de Sainte Domingue*, at Versailles, outshone even the Martinicans in affluence and splendour. (At the beginning of this colonial period, Père Labat strides for a month or two through the dull territory of the chroniclers; captious, pragmatical, humorous and greedy; dining with the governor, commenting on crops and morals, noting down recipes for roasting *cochon marron*, and sailing away again to be captured by Spanish freebooters; soon, of course, to escape. But out of these pages, alas, for good.)

The outbreak of the French Revolution found Sainte Domingue in a condition of suppressed ferment. This was mainly due to the freedmen (of whom there were a large number, mostly Mulattoes) to whom the French refused the full recognition of their privileges. When the Revolution broke out, the Mulattoes pressed their claims, and friends in Paris began a serious agitation for the emancipation of the slaves. In 1791, the tension was suddenly broken by direct action. Boukman, a Jamaican Negro of colossal size and a Houngan of the Voodoo rites, assembled a large number of slaves in the forests, and, after the sacrifice of a pig and the sacramental drinking of its blood, launched a wholesale massacre of the whites. The movement spread to all the slaves of the north, and for eight days a merciless and wholesale slaughter continued. Extraordinary tortures, such as sawing the colonists in half, were practised, and the burning of houses and crops was on so large a scale that the British colonists in the far Bermudas were bewildered and alarmed by the red glow in the sky. The slaves carried their destruction from plantation to plantation, and contemporary documents recorded that bloodshed reached such a pitch that the revolted Negroes appeared to be wearing gloves and stockings of scarlet. Then for days and nights 'an oppressive silence hung over the north, broken only by the distant crackling of burning forests and the mournful winding of the conch-shells'. It has

---

*Haiti is the old Arawak name for the island. The Spaniards at first called it Hispaniola (or Little Spain) and the name is still valid for the whole of the island. It came to be called Santo Domingo, after the capital: a name that the French, when they settled in the West, gallicized into Sainte Domingue. To mark the break with the colonial past, the victors of the Independence War returned to the primitive Arawak name. The remainder is still called Santo Domingo or the Dominican Republic – not to be confused with the British island of Dominica.

also been set down that in many cases the slaves of humane masters, although wholehearted supporters of rebellion, rescued them from the indiscriminate fury of the mob, and guided them to places of safety until this first orgiastic violence should have consumed itself.

The commissions dispatched to the colony by the National Assembly all proved abortive, and the French of the island were compelled, in 1794, to decree the abolition of slavery. Spanish forces under Toussaint L'Ouverture were driving the French back in the north, and the English had landed in the south and west.

The Negroes, under brilliant leadership by generals of their own race, by skilful exploitation of the contentions of the European powers, and above all by prolonged and bitter fighting, succeeded in throwing off the yoke of the whites. The struggle was characterized by extraordinary bravery, by massacres and by minor civil wars between the Blacks and Mulattoes, and by acts of cruelty and treachery on both sides. From this long flux of events, several figures emerge, and of these the most notable by far is Toussaint L'Ouverture.

Toussaint was a pure Negro whose family had only been a generation in the colony. An old tradition in the island makes him the grandson of Gaou-Guinou, King of Allada (Rada or Arada) on the Guinea Coast. In the campaigns which followed the Boukman *putsch*, he quickly reached the summit of command. He compelled the French governor to leave the colony for France, defeated the refractory Mulattoes of the south, and made himself ruler of Sainte Domingue. He next invaded the neighbouring Spanish colony and carried through a swift and successful campaign that culminated in his reception at the gates of Santo Domingo by the Spanish governor, offering him the keys of the capital on a cushion. All the Negroes of Hispaniola, at that particular moment, were free.

His flair for administering the enormous regions that now lay in his power was astonishing. He made laws, appointed governors, organized the plantations, levied taxes, and implemented his edicts with a thoroughness and a vigilance that were almost uncanny. Sloth was punished with the rod, and disobedience or defection with the firing squad or the gallows. His rigours reached such a pitch that he was obsessed towards the end by the caution and loneliness of a despot.

The colony was still nominally a part of the French Republic. But fearing its secession, the First Consul dispatched a force of 25,000 men and 70 warships, commanded by his brother-in-law Leclerc, the husband of Pauline Bonaparte.

The French army, after a series of hard-fought actions, reduced the opposition of the Negroes to the level of guerrilla warfare and then to a precarious peace. To seal the restoration of goodwill, the French invited Toussaint to a ceremonial banquet in Cap Français (now Cap Haitien), and he was allowed to enter the town at the head of a battalion of his troops. A month later Leclerc, on secret orders from Napoleon issued before the opening of the campaign, engineered the treacherous abduction of Toussaint under the guise of a friendly meeting with one of his generals on board a French warship. Transported to France, he was imprisoned in a mountain fortress of the Jura. Locked in this glacial dungeon, he passed his time writing impassioned and bewildered letters to Napoleon. These documents in self-taught and misspelt French make pathetic and tragic reading; Napoleon, out of indifference or some curious twist of Corsican vindictiveness, remained silent. His jailor finally received orders to withdraw pen, ink and paper from his cell, where, a year after his abduction, on the morning of the seventeenth of Germinal, the year XI, Toussaint was discovered dead in a chair by the fire, with his head leaning against the chimney-piece.

In contemporary portraits the long, intelligent face of this strange black Spartacus is poised above gold lace and epaulettes on the pedestal of a frilled and starched cravat and shaded by a cocked hat with a plume of ostrich feathers. He remains the foremost of the Negro chain-breakers and the first modern hero and herald of slave-emancipation throughout the world. Wordsworth was among the many contemporary poets and writers to applaud his struggle and mourn his end. There is, indeed, more intrinsic tragedy about his captivity and his death than that of his former warder, a couple of decades later, in St Helena. It is interesting to observe the consistent ignobility of Napoleon's dealings with the Negroes.

When Napoleon reinstated slavery in the Lesser Antilles, the war blazed up again under the command of Toussaint's generals, Dessalines, Christophe, Clervaux, Pétion and Maurepas. Yellow fever, as much as death in battle, thinned the ranks of the French. They succumbed in swarms, including the general himself. Before he died, reduced to despair by the hopelessness of the situation, he instituted a reign of terror that was ably continued by his successor Rochambeau.

This is a curious figure. He was extremely handsome, with his powdered hair still tied in a queue, despite the change of fashion – brave, insolently proud, and obsessed by a pathological loathing of the Blacks. He inherited Leclerc's tactics of mass shootings and hangings, and the Jacobin custom of *noyades*. He revived the English and Spanish Maroon-catching habit of hunting the Negroes with bloodhounds, and asphyxiated his prisoners with sulphur in the holds of warships. He even occasionally achieved those dizzy heights of unutilitarian harm, of absolute and disinterested wickedness that historians of the Renaissance ascribe to figures like Sigismondo Malatesta, the tyrant of Rimini. One of these is worth recording. When he was commandant of Port-au-Prince, he gave a ball for the coloured women of the capital. It was an unexpected success, as the dancing was general and notable for its gaiety. But at midnight the guests were led into a large chamber next to the ballroom, full of people dressed as priests who were chanting the *Dies Irae* before a row of coffins covered by a black cloth. When the chant came to an end, Rochambeau frigidly informed his guests that he had invited them to his palace to celebrate the obsequies of their brothers and husbands. The removal of the cloth then proved the truth of his little speech, for each coffin contained the corpse of a relation of each of his guests. The same figure was notable in battle for his chivalry and courage, and for those large and noble military gestures that one associates with the French *Régence* and the Maréchal de Saxe.

The campaign was a contest that forced Rochambeau to his knees, and finally, after the battle of Vertières, to surrender. This disaster for the armies of the Consulate was abetted by the British, who, as the Napoleonic Wars were at their height in other theatres, blockaded the ports and traded arms to the rebels. Haitian independence was declared at Gonaïves on the 1st of January, 1804, and a rough-and-ready constitution proclaimed. It was an amazing, an almost unbelievable achievement. The fierce and heroic Dessalines was crowned sovereign of Haiti as the Emperor Jacques I, on the 6th October; five months later than Napoleon's May Day coronation as Emperor of the French. One of the notable early actions of the new state was an important participation with Simon Bolivar in the struggles for freedom of the Spanish colonies of South America.

The history of Haiti since then is scattered by a startling catalogue of ephemeral empires and kingdoms, *coups d'état*, civil wars, conspiracies, Caco insurrections, outbursts of anarchy, murders and revolutions; it is characterized also by remarkable and steady progress in building up the machinery of a state, and in literature and science and the arts. The most recent event of lasting importance, before the fall of the Lescot government three years ago, was the occupation of the Republic, after the murder of President Sam in 1915, by U.S. Marines. This period of Haitian history achieved a number of material advances in the direction of road building, finance, sanitation, military matters and the formation of a rural gendarmerie. Socially, as I have said before, it has left little mark, except, superficially, the common heirloom of all occupations: a rise in prices and a cheapening of moral values.

When the French were expelled a century and a half ago, the Haitians really had to begin all over again (in the post-Montesquieu cliché of the day), as Lycurgus did at Sparta. The phrase can never have been more aptly applied.

It has been necessary to touch, in this summary fashion, on the history of Haiti because of its total divergence from the rather stereotyped background of the other Antilles, and because the memory of the War of Independence, and its results, pervade and stress the whole of Haitian life.

All these events have complicated the social affairs of the Republic. The situation of the Mulattoes, for instance, is anomalous and involved. The presence of the contending strains of black and white in the same organism may, under certain circumstances, be an excellent thing. But an adverse ideological climate turns the two elements into a ferocious antagonism, a life-long Zoroastrian duel in which Ormuzd and Ahriman drive each other from the battlefield of the brain to that of the subconscious and back again for ever.

The large number – in Haiti perhaps larger than the other Antilles – of Mulattoes affranchised before the Revolution, and the infinite social gradations that existed in the strange limbo between the African and French worlds, made the question of more or less white blood one of great importance. Moreau de St Méry, the French eighteenth-century writer of Ste Domingue, draws out elaborate tables of descent of the varying degrees of mixed blood ranging between the two unadulterated extremes, and each degree had its own name. Advancing, for the sake of simplicity, from black to white, first comes the *Sacatra*, seven-eighths African; then the *Griffe* and *Griffonne*, thirteen-sixteenths; the *Marabout*, five-eighths; and half-way up the scale, the Mulatto in its precise and original sense (which has since been extended), exactly half and half; then the Quadroon, one-quarter; the Métis, or Octaroon (in French *Quarteronné*), and sometimes the *Sangmêlé*, one-eighth; and, finally, some varieties of *Sangmêlés* and the *Mamélouc*, one-sixteenth. It will be seen by this system, which is far more complicated than the sixteen quarterings of *Hoffähigkeit* in former European courts, that *Maméloucs* and some varieties of *Sangmêlés* had only one Negro great-great-grandparent, and fifteen who were pure white. Should two of them marry, the remote Negro ancestors of their children and grandchildren became a smaller and smaller minority among a growing army of white ones. And this, indeed, has been the tendency, with the result that a small quantity of Haitians are no darker than Italians. They are inclined to form a slightly alien clique in the Haitian world, and as in pre-Revolutionary times many of them were not only free and able to read and write, but comparatively well off, they had a long start of their fellow-countrymen. Paris was often more a home for them than Haiti, and, in a world that is so fiercely organized against the black race, it is hard to blame those that tried to banish from their minds all memory of their African past. It is an attitude neither guilty nor laudable: merely extremely human. For many of these, the inevitable home-coming, the confrontation with the truth that had been locked away in the backs of their minds, was a painful event. Among many Mulattoes and Negroes who have adopted exclusively European values, anything that reminds them of Africa, like, for instance, the mention of Voodoo, causes extreme discomfort.

This attitude is in exact opposition to another section of the intelligentsia that derives all its pride and inspiration from the idea of the African past, from the fact that they are the descendants of the warriors of the forests of Guinea and of the revolted slaves that defeated the imperial armies of Europe. It often leads to a form of intellectual isolationism, a most human distrust and repudiation of the values of the white world by which they and their fellow-countrymen have been penalized for centuries; and this, in some cases, develops, out of over-compensation, into an aggressive Negro Chauvinism; again, an understandable mental attitude, but no more agreeable in practice than other nationalisms. Many of the Mulatto intelligentsia belong themselves to this group and join in the derision and distrust of the half-sarcastically termed Mulatto aristocracy of Pétionville. For the Mulattoes in Haitian history, in spite of great leaders like Pétion, and any number of her rulers and legislators and intellectuals, have always had a bad press and a reputation for instability and for a lack of concord with the ambitions and ideals of the Negro majority. In the early days of Haitian history this tension led several times to civil war. I suspect that, the rest of the world being as it is, pale-skinned Haitians are secretly pleased at their pallor, whatever their public statements may be. The great number of hairdressers that advertise *repassage des cheveux* – a system for ironing the hair out flat – is significant. And, of course, lightness of skin is an advantage outside Haiti. The result of all this is that being a Mulatto is personally a source of secret self-congratulation; and socially or nationally, often a target for abuse, with a nuance in the abuse of something hybrid and unpatriotic.

This internal contradiction, added to the already existing Mulatto dualism, is a hallucinating thought. If the conflict is further embroiled by a spiritual tug-of-war between Catholicism and – through atavism, or, with certain of the intelligentsia, through a conscious espousal on historical or nationalist-aesthetic grounds – Voodoo, and if this is sub-divided again into the ambivalence which is implicit in the Voodoo psychosis, the mind begins to reel at the proliferation of mental complexities. This huge gamut of emotions at war often seriously hinders normal contact between blacks and whites, in spite of the friendliest intentions on both sides.

The theatre was full when we found our places. At first glance, it appeared that the audience apart from ourselves was exclusively Haitian, but we were able later to pick out four American friends and acquaintances among the rest: De Witt Peters, of the *Centre d'Art*, Selden Rodman the poet, John Godwin, dressed in a blue sailor's jersey, with a thin gold ring in the lobe of one ear, and a tall young man who had come to Haiti for the sympathetic purpose of studying drums.

There was a warm ovation as the curtain went up, for the play was concerned with one of the first gestures of insurrection in pre-Revolutionary Sainte Domingue. Mackandal, after whom the play is named, was a runaway slave – a Maroon – from the Sudan, who may or may not have been a Moslem, though he is known to have spoken Arabic. He was reputed, in spite of having only one arm, to possess almost superhuman strength. He was almost certainly a Voodoo initiate, probably a priest. From his hiding-place in the *mornes*, he incited the slaves on the neighbouring estates to rebellion of a peculiarly subtle and terrifying kind: a widespread campaign of poisoning which took heavy toll of the colonists, and terrorized the whole white population. He was captured finally at a country dance and condemned to be burnt. He contrived to break the chains that secured him to the stake, but was overpowered and forced back into the flames, where he perished. (It is recorded that, for some time after Mackandal's death, five or six slaves were burnt monthly, in order to stamp out the secret network he had organized. The figures are known by the record of the 600 *livres* indemnity paid by the King of France to the owners for each executed slave.)

The play seemed at first a lively affair, and the early speeches evoked a great deal of patriotic applause. But it soon became clear that the amateur company on the stage had not a glimmering of how to act. Most of the dialogue was inaudible, all the gestures were wooden. No effort had been made to reproduce the clothes of the period; in fact, the eighteenth-century French villains of the play were dressed in modern cowboy hats and armed with toy revolvers. It was thoroughly, embarrassingly bad. But most grotesque and mysterious of all was the device of make-up by which the performers contrived (or rather, for a long time, failed to contrive) to indicate which of the cast were playing the rôles of white people and which of Negroes. The colonists, instead of applying white grease-paint, had remained as they were, while Mackandal and the slaves had smeared their faces, it appeared, with soot, lending a musical comedy appearance to the actors, without in any way modifying their complexion. I am still bewildered by the mental processes that prompted this odd convention.

Part of the audience began to show signs of protest at the poverty of the acting: a reaction with which at first I heartily agreed. The shuffling of feet became an organized stamping, and, by the end of the first act, shouts of derision were more and more frequent. When the second act started, the heckling had swelled to a steady and organized roar, of which the tone was so menacing and savage that our sympathies veered back again to the dismal figures on the stage. This body of noise soon called an opposition into being in the front rows of the stalls, whose occupants began to rise to their feet and hurl back insults at the hecklers. It was impossible to distinguish what the first party were shouting, but the shouts of their opponents in the front row were very plain. '*Mulâtres!*' they shouted. '*Sales mulâtres! Bâtards!*' The noise became a deafening shindy, and things were beginning to look ugly. Our neighbours thought some sort of riot was about to break out and slipped away. The actors were still moving clumsily about the stage in a pathetic attempt to make the show go on, like figures in a really bad silent film. The lights were switched on and the manager walked to the footlights with suppliant and ineffectual gestures for a hearing. The lights revealed that the original hecklers were mainly working-class toughs, and all of them Negroes, while the group in the front row, who were accusing the first interrupters of bastardy and Mulattohood, were well-dressed members of the *bourgeoisie*; and (until one worked it out this appeared inexplicable) Mulattoes almost to a man. It was, at that particular moment, mental, not physical, pigmentation that mattered.

We were herded from the theatre in a shouting mob. As the audience seethed into the starlit Champ de Mars, the gang of interrupting Negroes broke into a run across the grass, pursued by shouts of '*Lâches! Sales mulâtres!*' and vanished. They escaped just in time to evade a large-scale fight.

A few minutes later, in a café next to the theatre, under a sign which said, '*Demandez un Hot-Dog*', we were discussing all these events. We gradually became aware that someone was standing near by and watching us. It was a peculiarly striking figure, a very pale Haitian – or was he

Spanish or Italian? – of a haggard, tormented type of distinction, dressed in sandals and a shabby shirt and trousers. He was standing with his hands in his pockets, contemplating us with great ravaged eyes, and his face wore an expression that was half amused and half sardonic. His gift for relaxed immobility was admirable. Seeing that we had fallen silent, he said very distinctly, 'Eh alors?' and slouched off into the Champ de Mars. There was something so arresting, and at the same time almost sinister, about this apparition that we forgot to continue our conversation, and speculated instead on the nationality and identity of the stranger.

The presbytery was whitewashed and impersonal, and as dim, after the sunlight, as an underwater cavern. The pale, cleanshaven face of Father Cosme, on the other side of the table, was extremely remote from the Haitian scene. He came from Artois, near the border of Flanders, but had spent twenty years in the Republic as member of a mission of which one of the main duties was to wean the Haitians in the country districts from the elements of African religion that still survived. It sounded, as he talked, a difficult charter.

The hard part of it was that the Haitians were all, officially, Catholics already, and, in the country districts, nothing could make them understand why Christianity and Voodoo should not be practised side by side. In fact, Father Cosme had often heard country people ingenuously maintaining that Christianity was an essential part of Voodoo. It was a hopeless task. Many of the saints of the Christian Church, he explained, were confused in their minds with the gods of Africa. 'Take Erzulie, for instance.'

'Erzulie?'

'Yes, Erzulie Fréda Dahomin. This creature is the Dahomeyan Aphrodite, the goddess of love. She is supposed, in the superstitions of the natives, to be the wife of several of the greater African deities, and also unites herself in mystic marriages to mortals. *Elle est, en somme, une fameuse trainée.*' The priest's face was lit for a moment by a sparkle of frosty levity, which immediately disappeared. 'Well, that is the Haitian tradition. But,' he continued gravely, 'who do you think this wretch is identified with in the minds of the adepts of Voodoo? With the Blessèd Virgin herself. One shudders to think of it. The emblem of Erzulie – for all these gods, alas have their distinguishing signs, which is the root of a lot of the trouble – is a heart; and so, in the cult, their hateful goddess is held to be the same as Our Lady of the Seven Sorrows. Here is a print which we removed from a Voodoo temple.' He opened a drawer, and took out a lamentable oleograph of the Blessèd Virgin, from a painting in the style of Sassoferrato. The head of the Blessèd Virgin leant to one side, and her eyes were turned upwards in ecstasy or pain, while a waxen forefinger pointed to her scarlet heart, which was transfixed by seven rapiers. 'There are thousands like this in use. Worst of all, those Negroes who are the secret husbands of Erzulie dedicate every Tuesday and Thursday to the goddess. If they are married, their wives are driven from the house on those two days, for Erzulie is famous for her jealousy. Then,' his voice sank, 'quite alone, and with the auxiliary of certain herbs, they somehow contrive to pass the night in a state of orgy, into the details of which I will not enter.' He paused a moment; I did not dare to ask for further elucidation. 'And all this goes on under pictures like *this*.' He placed a finger on the edge of the oleograph. 'It is impossible to make them understand the abomination of such practices. Owing to the same confusion of emblems, sacrilegious use is made of a great number of images of the saints. Portions of the liturgy are incorporated into their savage ceremonies, and many is the time, when I have gone into the church to say Mass in the morning, that the congregation has consisted entirely of *voudouisants*, who have just left their temples, after spending the whole night dancing to tom-toms and worshipping the gods of Africa. But there they are, streaming with sweat, and one or two of them in an almost trance-like state, kneeling in the church with the utmost piety. What is one to do? We have to work with the material we have, however unrewarding. If the adepts of Voodoo were all, *ipso facto*, to be ex-communicated, we would remain with only a handful of true Christians in Haiti.

'Of course, the country people are not to blame, and there is no intention of sin. The guilty ones are the Voodoo priests, the N'gans or Houngans, as they are called, who exploit the credulity and superstition of the peasants for purposes of gain and power; though most of them are of ordinary country stock themselves and probably believe all this *fatras*, as well. They are the Church's most bitter enemies.

'Some years ago we were making a certain headway. A great deal of ground was cleared by systematic anti-superstition campaigns.'

'How did you set about them?'

Father Cosme's eyes kindled a moment. 'There was only one way: to pluck up our courage, and strike at the root! We began by cutting down trees which were said to be inhabited by their gods. At first we had to tackle them with an axe by ourselves, as the villagers ran away in terror and watched us from a distance. But after a while, when they saw that nothing happened to us, a few of them would help us in our work. We demolished any number of trees and caves and "sacred" rocks, and even cut down the centre poles of Voodoo temples, and made bonfires of the drums and instruments of the cult.' He showed us photographs of these curious conflagrations, of the enormous tom-toms and gourds and feathered emblems blazing away under the gaze of a crowd of Negroes, with a priest or two standing in the centre. Several were pictures of himself, or one of his party, with an axe raised, about to deliver the first blow to an inhabited tree. Joan asked him if there were ever any countermeasures. Father Cosme nodded.

'These creatures used to come with their followers and beat drums and blow horns outside the churches and drown the priest's voice with howling and shouting during the celebration of Mass. Once or twice priests have died mysteriously, and one can only assume that they were poisoned. Placing the juice of a certain leaf on the rim of a drinking vessel is a favourite method. The Houngans often combine Voodoo with the practice of Wanga.'

'Wanga?'

'Black-magic. All the apologists of Voodoo maintain that the two things are distinct. The practitioners of Wanga are called Bocors. But the Houngan and the Bocor are often united in the same person, so their separation is relative.'

Father Cosme spoke of Wanga at great length. In its simplest form it is little more than bush-medicine, the use of certain leaves for medical purposes. The next step is the invocation of evil denizens of the Voodoo pantheon – such as Don Pedro, Kitta, Mondongue, Bakalou and Zandor – for harmful purposes, for the reputed practice (which is of Congolese origin) of turning people into zombies in order to use them as slaves, the casting of maleficent spells, and the destruction of enemies. The effects of the spell, of which the outward form may be an image of the intended victim, a miniature coffin or a toad, are frequently stiffened by the separate use of poison. Father Cosme enlarged on the superstitions that maintain that men with certain powers change themselves into snakes; on the *Loups-Garous* that fly at night in the form of vampire bats and suck the blood of children; on men who reduce themselves to infinitesimal size and roll about the countryside in calabashes. What sounded far more sinister were a number of mystico-criminal secret societies of wizards, with nightmarish titles – *les Mackanda*, named after the poison campaign of the Haitian hero; *les Zobop*, who were also robbers; the *Mazanxa*, the *Caporelata* and the *Vlinbindingue*. These, he said, were the mysterious groups whose gods demand – instead of a cock, a pigeon, a goat, a dog or a pig, as in the normal rites of Voodoo – the sacrifice of a *cabrit sans cornes*. This hornless goat, of course, means a human being. Father Cosme, during his ministry in the remoter *mornes*, stated that he had encountered two or three well-substantiated cases of the disappearance of children for these purposes. One secret society had, for obscure reasons, compelled a woman to kill and eat her small infant, and a man was at that moment, he continued, serving a sentence for ritual murder.*

'Please understand,' he said, raising a hand, 'that I do not mean that such things are common; or that they have any but the remotest link with the normal practices of Voodoo; for they are extremely rare. But they occur.

'Things have taken a turn for the worse recently, in the new government's decision to allow the free practice of Voodoo. It is gaining ground and prestige daily. One wonders, sometimes, what good we are doing here, and whether,' he said, with a sorry smile, 'Voodoo might eventually develop into a sort of state religion. It is being given every possible encouragement. By some, because they really believe in it; by others, who are atheists, anyway, out of Chauvinism, because it represents the national idea. Worst of all, the practice of Voodoo is becoming rationalized, codified almost, by a certain school of writers.' He referred to Mars, Herskovitz and Dorsainvil as if they were virtually the Seraphic Doctors of Voodooism. 'It is similar to a small movement which hopes to replace French, as the official language of the country, by a phonetic Créole. They detest the whites and anything to do with us. *La situation est odieuse . . .'*

It was night when we said good-bye, and the air was beginning to throb with the sound of drums from several different parts of the town, rising and falling and then ceasing altogether, and, after a few moments, beginning again: a peculiar and disturbing sound. Father Cosme pointed to the direction from which it came and, with his frosty smile, raised his shoulders in a faint gesture of resignation.

I would like to say at once that there are several points, as will appear in the following pages, in which I am not in agreement with Father Cosme. But I have put down as much as I can remember of his conversation in order to have the point of view of a priest *vis-à-vis* the extraordinary phenomenon of Voodoo.

He left the Republic soon after, and is now in charge of a large parish in the west of Senegal.

---

*I will say more of this subject in the next chapter.

CHAPTER 11

Haiti Continued

It was hard to remember that these alley-ways were scarcely ten minutes' walk from the Champ de Mars. The women leaning and squatting in the lighted doorways and the glimpses of brass bedsteads and rocking-chairs grew more scarce, and the shanties that bordered these lanes looked, in the light of the setting moon, blank and extinguished; jet black on one side of the road, on the other, pale as asbestos. Only an occasional thread of light showed that there was any life bolted in there behind the planks for the night. The pulse of the drums grew stronger until, at a turn in the flank of a little cliff, it became all at once very loud, and augmented now by a steady metallic clangour and the sound of singing. Rodolfe led the way along a path between broken fences and waited for us outside the entrance to the *tonnelle*. The noise, the throng of Haitians, the scene that was taking place, and, above all, the idea of intruding three pale faces into a gathering so exclusively Negro, made us pause.

Slowly, out of the turmoil and the smoke and the shattering noise of the drums, which, for a time, drove everything except their impact from the mind, the details began to detach themselves.

The *tonnelle* was a roof of woven palm-trash, supported in the middle by a wooden pillar painted in spirals of blue and red. The trees and bushes, and the Haitians gathered round the edges, blocked out the moon, and the only light radiated over the beaten mud floor from an oil-lamp that hung from a nail on the pillar. At one end stood the Houmfor, the small white temple, and the three Rada drummers sat at the other, gripping their long wooden tom-toms between their knees.

These instruments are the dwelling-places of gods of whom the drummers are the especial ministers, and each of the brightly painted sections of tree-trunk is of a different size and key. They taper in both directions from the broadest point just below the top, and rawhide is stretched across the upper end and lashed to massive pegs. The fourth instrument is the Hogan, a hollow iron vessel with a handle on which an iron rod beats with continuous clangour. The rhythm of the last two is unchanging and the second sometimes alters, but the first drum, which dominates everything, is subjected to countless changes of rhythm and mood and pitch.

The floor was covered with dancers, but at their centre about twenty women danced round the main pillar in a more formal fashion. They wore identical white dresses, and white kerchiefs were tied round their heads. One of them, a middle-aged virago of enormous bulk, was plainly some kind of a leader. They were the hounci-bossales and hounci-canzos, Voodoo adepts of the first and second stages of initiation, who form the staff of the *tonnelle*, and act as acolytes and chorus to all the ceremonies under the direction of the woman of more commanding aspect who was the mambo, or high priestess.

Backwards and forwards, very slowly, the dancers shuffled, and at each step their chins shot out and their buttocks jerked upwards, while their shoulders shook in double time. Their eyes were half closed and from their mouths came again and again the same incomprehensible words, the same short line of chanted song, repeated after each iteration, half an octave lower. At a change in the beat of the drums, they straightened their bodies, and, flinging their arms in the air while their eyes rolled upwards, spun round and round.

A thin clanging, caused by the shaking of the *açon* and the ringing of a little bell in the priest's left hand, cut across the sound of the four musicians. The *açon*, symbol of the priestly office, is a long-necked gourd enclosed in a loose cage of snakes' vertebrae and coloured beads. When the chanting subsided, the Houngan would intone a new couplet. He was seconded in everything by the Houngenikon, whose name means a candidate for the Voodoo priesthood, for the rank of Houngan.

So crammed were the three square yards of the houmfor with the stage properties of the cult, that it took some moments to become aware that these manifold appliances were arranged with the utmost care.

On the massive white cubic altar stood a heavy wooden acute angle, an A without a cross-bar, about a yard high, festooned with coloured necklaces. A recess filled with water lay to one side of the altar, and above it leant the twisting iron serpent of Damballah. Serpents were also frescoed round an old lithograph of St Patrick trampling the snake of Ireland. Next to this a schooner was painted, the emblem of Ogoun Agoué, the God of the Sea. Calabashes adorned with beads and red rags stood in rows, interspersed with wooden bowls and china pots. These are the containers, at different junctures of their progress, of human souls. A cross and an image of the Blessèd Virgin were almost hidden among bottles full of ambiguous liquids, with dried flowers in their necks. In the ground had been struck an old-fashioned cavalry sabre, the emblem of Ogoun Ferraille, the war god. Two sequin-embroidered flags were crossed above the altar, each displaying a bird with its wings outstretched, and the remaining wall space was covered with pictures of Christian saints who have also attained high rank in the Voodoo pantheon. At the striking of a match, pictures of Our Lady of the Seven Sorrows, St Anthony, St Nicholas, St Charles Borromspeo, St James the Major, St Rose of Lima and the Archangel Michael appeared out of the shadows.

At the edge of the crowd we came upon a little hut, scarcely larger than a dog kennel: *Le caye Zombi*. The beam of a torch revealed a black cross inside and some rags and chains and shackles and whips: adjuncts used at the Ghédé ceremonies, which Haitian ethnologists connect with the rejuvenation rites of Osiris recorded in the Book of the Dead. A fire was burning, in which two sabres and a large pair of pincers were standing, their lower parts red with the heat: *le Feu Marinette*, dedicated to a goddess who is the evil obverse of the bland and amorous Maitresse Erzulie Fréda Dahomin, the Goddess of Love.

Beyond, with its base held fast in a socket of stone, stood a large black wooden cross. A white death's head was painted near the base, and over the crossbar were pulled the sleeves of a very old morning coat. Here also rested the brim of a battered bowler hat, through the torn crown of which the top of the cross projected. This totem, with which every peristyle must be equipped, is not a lampoon of the central event of the Christian faith, but represents the God of the Cemeteries and the Chief of the Legion of the Dead, Baron Samedi. The Baron is paramount in all matters immediately beyond the tomb. He is Cerberus and Charon as well as Aeacus, Rhadamanthus and Pluto.

Men were now scattered among the ranks of the female houncis, and the dance had grown more violent. The dancers, simultaneously with the advance and recoil of buttocks, shoulders and chin, shook their frames from side to side in quadruple time so that their bodies were trembling and jerking in every possible direction. The mambo moved across the *tonnelle* with her shoulder-blades shaking in a palsy while her great hind-quarters, slowly evolving, rolled up her spine and flowed forward and sank again with the motion of a surfacing and plunging whale.

In slow response to these cumulative hours of incantation, the gods were stirring in their distant home in Africa. Each couplet and each step of the *yanvalloux* brought them closer, and the night above the heads of the dancers was becoming populated with the denizens of that remote Valhalla: Legba, Loko, Damballah Wédo, Zaka, Agoué Arroyo, Erzulie, Bossou Comblamin, Ogoun Ferraille, Ogoun Badagris and the whole company of the Lwas, the divine spirits of the tribes of Guinea and Dahomey and the Congo, who can only be summoned by drums and dances and sacrifices. They lurk in the air above the palm roofs and peer down at the dancers in search of devotees in whom to incarnate themselves. The atmosphere of the *tonnelle* was heavy with their impending presence.

There was a sudden flurried movement, and the ranks broke. In the space which was suddenly cleared, a young man staggered, catching at the forearm of one of the houncis to prevent himself from falling. The others ran to his help. He remained stiff and inert in their arms, with his mouth wide open and his eyes revulsed, and one shoulder-blade gyrating at great speed, the shining black mesh of his shoulder muscles shuddering with the lift of the bone. Two of the girls bent down and rolled up his trousers. Then, breaking from his supporters, he began a staggering, unconscious dance in the middle of the *tonnelle*. The tempo of the drumming changed to an ominous roll, and the Houngan followed his erratic progress, dipping his *açon* into a can of water and sprinkling the dancer in the manner of a priest with a hyssop-twig. The young man snatched the can from him and spilt three pools round the pillar and then one in front of each of the drums, and, falling on his face, licked up the mud. The Houngenikon and the mambo took him in turn by both hands, and pumped them up and down with the motion of Oranges and Lemons. He made a few more steps and then, falling against the pillar, with his chest heaving as though it would break through his ribs, he collapsed into the arms of the dancers. The houncis gently wiped his face with a red cloth and his eyelids slowly fell, and his head sank to his breast. Covering his face with the cloth, they carried him, with his feet dragging behind him, from the floor.

Just before his collapse, a universal cry had broken out, and the beat of the drums had again changed. It was the beginning of an incarnation, and, by some mannerism in the dancing limbs of his human habitation, the descended Lwa had been recognized. It was Ogoun Ferraille. The anthem of the War God burst from every throat, and the dancers, crouching in a frog-like position with their knees almost touching the floor, once more filled the *tonnelle*. They advanced once more, working their way slowly round each other back to back, and then retreated quaking and stamping to their own sides. The Houngan, meanwhile, stooping before the pillar, was drawing in white maize-flour the *vévér*, or heraldic emblem of the god. Filling his right hand, he turned the circle formed by closing his thumb and forefinger into a spout, through which the white powder was poured. Then, with the speed and precision of a pastry cook with an icing-funnel, he limned on the beaten dust the intricate white curves and triangles and loops and stars. The invocation that accompanies this office makes curious reading: *Par pouvoir St Jacques Majeur, Ogoun Badagris, nègre Baguido Bago, Ogoun Ferraille, nègre fer, nègre ferraille, nègre tagnifer nago, Ogoun Batala, nègre, nègre batiocoue nago, Ogoun Achade Bokor, nègre gouegui malor, nègre Ossangne malor, Ossangne Aquiquan, Ossangne Agouelingui, Jupiter tonnerre, nègre blabla, nègre oloncoun, nègre vanté'm pasfiém. Aocher nago, Aocher nago, Aocher nago.* Straightening up and blowing into the hollow of his hand, he sent a white cloud of flour into the air.

The drums had changed and the Houngenikon came dancing on to the floor, holding a vessel filled with some burning liquid from which sprang blue and yellow flames. As he circled the pillar and spilt three flaming libations, his steps began to falter. Then, lurching backwards with the same symptoms of delirium that had manifested themselves in his forerunner, he flung down the whole blazing mass. The houncis caught him as he reeled, and removed his sandals and rolled his trousers up, while the kerchief fell from his head and laid bare his young woolly skull. The other houncis knelt to put their hands in the flaming mud, and rub it over their hands and elbows and faces. The Houngan's bell and *açon* rattled officiously and the young priest was left by himself, reeling and colliding against the pillar, helplessly catapulting across the floor, and falling among the drums. His eyes were shut, his forehead screwed up and his chin hung loose. Then, as though an invisible fist had dealt him a heavy blow, he fell to the ground and lay there, with his head stretching backwards in a rictus of anguish until the tendons of his neck and shoulders projected like roots. One hand clutched at the other elbow behind his hollowed back as though he were striving to break his own arm, and his whole body, from which the sweat was streaming, trembled and shuddered like a dog in a dream. Only the whites of his eyes were visible as, although his eye-sockets were now wide open, the pupils had vanished under the lids. Foam collected on his lips. The priest stooped over him with his rattling implements, and after a few minutes the young man rose to one knee and, like a sleepwalker, regained his feet; and at last, with the same painful expression, as though his whole body were on fire, danced a few disjointed steps. The howling anthem and the drums burst upon him. Slowly, slowly, though his face lost nothing of the blank agony of its abstraction, his limbs regained their co-ordination. 'He's mounted by the Lwa,' the whisper ran, as the possessed figure began to evolve. *'Li gain Loa!'* It was the beginning of a long, unconscious ballet.

Now the Houngan, dancing a slow step and brandishing a cutlass, advanced from the fireside, flinging the weapon again and again into the air, and catching it by the hilt. In a few minutes he was holding it by the blunted end of the blade. Dancing slowly towards him, the Houngenikon reached out and grasped the hilt. The priest retired, and the young man, twirling and leaping, spun from side to side of the *tonnelle*. The ring of spectators rocked backwards as he bore down upon them whirling the blade over his head, with the gaps in his bared teeth lending to his mandril face a still more feral aspect. The *tonnelle* was filled for a few seconds with genuine and unmitigated terror. The singing had turned to a universal howl and the drummers, rolling and lolling with the furious and invisible motion of their hands, were lost in a transport of noise.

Flinging back his head, the novice drove the blunt end of the cutlass into his stomach. His knees sagged, and his head fell forward as he sank in a mock death. In the instant that he seemed about to crumple up, a dancer rushed from the ring of spectators and bound a scarlet cloth round his middle. A dance of death-agony followed. The Houngenikon gyrated and sank and recovered, the muscles of his arm taut with the effort to thrust the sword home. Shuffling and singing, the dancers crept back on to the floor, closing round the throes of the young priest, who, lurching round and round across the floor, disappeared into the houmfor as the wave seemed about to submerge him. The monotony of flux and reflux began again.

But not for many minutes. The door of the houmfor swung open, and the drums beat a retreat. The young priest burst into the emptied peristyle, and danced violently to the middle. His back was hollowed, his shoulders squared and his head carried arrogantly erect. It was a complete metamorphosis. In every line in his body and every step and movement, death and dissolution had been replaced by pride and triumph and life. The cutlass was still held to his middle and the cloth still made its scarlet smear. But in his left hand he held a bottle of rum, and in the corner of his mouth a long cigar was stuck, leaving in the air, as he twirled and sprang, spirals and arabesques of smoke. Leaping backwards on his heels in a flaunting hornpipe, he took the cigar from his mouth, bent his head back and swallowed a long draught from the bottle. Then, leaping across the *tonnelle* with his legs bent at right angles, he began to revolve on one heel with the other leg, raised high in the air, swept him round on this pivot with a scythe-like revolution. As he appeared about to lose his balance, he changed legs with a stamp, looping and coiling in this manner round the amphitheatre in a series of arcs which dwindled in radius until they brought him to the middle for the triple libations to the pillar, and then to the drums. Halting here, he stuck the neck of the bottle between the teeth of each of the drummers in turn.

The dancers had fallen to their knees in a ring. The Houngenikon wove his way towards a young hounci, and, striking her on the arm with the flat of his cutlass, danced round the circle and back to her once more, and forced the bottle-neck into her mouth. Then, remaining in one place, but marking time with a complicated step, he held out his arm. The hounci rose, and, resting her hand on his crooked fingers, pirouetted in a complete circle, then back, and then round once more, and retreated shuffling and shaking in the steps of the *mahi* dance. Moving to the next kneeling figure, he repeated the same gestures, and the girl made the same stately revolutions, motions as grave as the pirouette in a seventeenth-century *pavane*, and danced away. The delicate urbanity of this evolution struck a surprising note among the prolonged barbarian spasms of the dance. Could it have slipped into the ritual in the time of Louis XV? At the same period, perhaps, that St Claire and St Rose of Lima unwillingly gate-crashed the Olympus of Dahomey? When the cycle of salutes had finished, all were dancing again, many of them with an almost stationary, burglarious prowl, or in couples which stalked round and round each other, or leaped up and down in solitary accesses of elation. The floor could hold no more. In the centre, dominating everything from the plinth of the pillar, stood the Houngenikon with his head and torso reared backwards and his legs planted wide. His right arm was still downstretched with the thrust of the cutlass, and his left hand, grasping the nearly empty bottle, rested on his hip. He was bathed in sweat and quivering slightly all over. The bared teeth and the whites of his eyes shone like the apertures of a dark mask lying on the snow, while the combustion of his cigar and the long dragon-like prongs of smoke that he fired down his nostrils turned his head into a steaming black thurible. Although the pupils were slowly reappearing, his eyes retained a look of the remotest abstraction.

Motions of disorder erupted at short intervals as the Lwas effected their entrance into one or other of the dancers. They writhed and staggered and fell and lay twitching and gasping, and slowly rose again transformed, and evolving with the impotence of somnambulists under the control of their immanent deities. The road from Olympus had been thrown open.

Less ceremony attended these later avatars. Each time the drummers battered out a pattern of deafening impacts, their slapping and rod-wielding hands rising high over their heads, while their heckling snarls stressed the fury of the music. The Lwas were falling out of the sky as thick as leaves, and by the time, hours later, that we extricated ourselves to go, the *tonnelle* had become a running, stamping, howling, gasping and shrieking theodrome.

Climbing through the squatting figures into the outer darkness, I caught a sudden glimpse of the gypsy figure that had struck me so forcibly, on the night of the Mackandal play, leaning relaxed and aloof against one of the supporting posts. He was gazing sardonically into the lighted circle with a cigarette in the corner of his mouth. Half a dozen Negroes stood up and he was blotted out.

The moon had set half a dozen hours ago, and the rattle of the drums faded as we followed the beam of Rodolfe's torch. Faded, but as they died, others sounded and, as we advanced, grew louder. Going home was unthinkable. Plainly the only thing to do was to continue till we fell asleep, or till everything had come to an end.

The following hours were spent in two different *tonnelles* – theatres, like the first, of multiple incarnation.

The drums all fell silent at last. On our way home we passed our original temple. The fire of Marinette was smouldering to extinction. An odd sandal and a number of empty bottles had been tidied into a corner, and two of the drums leant against the step of the pillar. The other had rolled a couple of yards away near the door, and two or three of the dancers were sleeping on mats. The Houngenikon lay quite straight on his back outside the houmfor, sound asleep. The Lwas had abandoned the husks which had been their temporary dwelling, and were already half-way across the Atlantic on their homing flight to the Guinea forests. Dust hung in the air, and the tarry smell of sweat betrayed that the *tonnelle* had only been empty a little time. The tired Houngan was smoking a last cigarette. He appeared pleased to see us and, sitting half asleep on the bench, we had a last gulp of rum with him over the ashes of the fire. The phantasms of the night were fast vanishing.

Colour crept back into the mango trees and palms as we walked home along the lanes. Dawn was breaking with its startling tropical swiftness. Just before we reached the Champ de Mars, across which a platoon of soldiers was already marching briskly to break the Colours, we overtook a troop of Negroes. We recognized them as our companions from the first *tonnelle*, and exchanged *bonjours*.

'Where are they going to, Rodolfe?'

He looked slightly surprised at the question.

'*Où? Mais à la messe.*'

Indeed, the bells of the neo-Gothic cathedral were clanking for early Mass, and every instant the sunlight filled the sky with a brighter radiance.

> Ecce jam noctis tenuatur aura,
> Lux et aurorae rutilans coruscat,
> Supplices rerum Dominum canora
>   voce precemur.

This is all very well. But what would St Gregory have thought of the little procession of the faithful which was at that moment trailing across the areopagus? As the cathedral swallowed them up, one, at least, of the houncis was still half-dancing and half-walking in a diminishing spasmodic aftermath of possession by Erzulie.

A young peasant in an immense wicker hat trotted past on horseback, the unshod hooves clicking in the dust. A bugle sounded from the midst of the soldiers at the foot of the flagpole, the Haitian bicolor broke loose and fluttered in the morning air. A new day had officially begun.

When we awoke next afternoon, the sequence of the night's events seemed remoter than a dream. The most interesting thing, apart from the general mystery of Voodoo and the astonishing virtuosity and, sometimes, beauty of the dances, remained without question, the phenomenon of possession.

There is nothing singular about the first part of the crisis, the falling flat on the ground in a movement of violent religious emotion. Such events were common in the Dionysiac mysteries, and they were caused by the same factors: the semi-hysterical state coupled with the knowledge of divine presence which accumulates through many hours of gregarious dancing. The rum-drinking is not as important as it might be supposed, for, medically speaking, few of the subjects are drunk when the phenomenon presents itself. Similar cases, without any of these adjuncts except the feeling of the divine presence, are recorded again and again in the history of Christian mysticism, and are especially remarkable, for instance, in the writings of St Angela of Foligno, or the fascinating records left by Marie de l'Incarnation, the Ursuline nun; and when the wind of inspiration was blowing through him, Schiller fell flat upon his face.

The schizophrenic phase which follows this temporary extinction of the ego, the domination of mind, will and body by an intruding spirit, is much harder to explain. Dr Price Mars, who, with Drs Dorsainvil and Herskovitz, is the greatest of the writers on the Haitian popular religion – almost, according to Father Cosme, the Aquinas of Voodoo – describes it as 'a mystic state characterized by a delirium of theomanic possession and splitting of the personality'. Dorsainvil is more prolix: 'It is a religious and racial psycho-neurosis characterized by a splitting of the ego with functional alterations of sensibility and mobility, a predominance of pythiatic symptoms.' Dr Louis Mars succinctly refers to it as Emotivo-Kinetic Mysticism. But these formulae, invented especially to apply to this isolated phenomenon, define obscurity with obscurity. Dr Louis Mars, who has written an excellent clinical report on his observations of the crisis of possession, is the most helpful writer on this particular problem. It is a phenomenon in which Haitian scientists and ethnologists are passionately interested and the brief attempt at explanation which follows is based on his essay, on the opinions of the other writers who have come to roughly the same conclusions, on conversations with various Haitians, and on limited personal observation. I think their conclusions are right, inasmuch as a foreigner who has witnessed this difficult phenomenon no more than a couple of dozen times can be allowed an opinion.

Rhythm and the dance are probably the single most pressing need in the organism of the Negro in his primitive state. They are an outlet without which his very life seems threatened. For thousands of years his whole being has been conditioned by the beat of the drum, and experience has taught the drummers, in a way that has become an instinctive tradition, which beat, speed, pitch and volume of the drums control the motor and the sensitive centres in the dancer. African mysticism, as opposed to the Yoga of the Orient, the *peyotl* drug of the Mexican Indians and the solitary *askesis* of Europe and the Levant, is always gregarious, always promoted and fostered by the closeness of co-religionaries undergoing the same experience; and always, as Dr Mars would say, kinetic.* Every Haitian, through atavism, religious training and ambience from his earliest childhood, is spiritually geared for the event of incarnation; and he knows that the moment of miracle occurs in the dark *tonnelle*, where the air is afloat with mysteries, and where the drums are already violently reacting on his nerves and brain. He knows, too, that he is a vessel that the Lwas

---

* In point of fact, Emotivo-Kinetic Mysticism has, apart from Negro sects like the Holy Rollers, occasionally appeared in the Christian world. The rage for producing religious ecstasy by dancing which was launched by Montanus, Priscilla and Maximilla in Phrygia in the second century, held sway in many eastern and north African bishoprics. Tertullian himself became a modified Montanist. The other instance – *Les Convulsionnaires*, whose antics represent the death-throes of Jansenism in eighteenth-century France – is more remarkable.

may at any moment inhabit. And so, when he has been brought by the drums, the dance and the divine presence to a state of hysteria and physical collapse, a dormant self-hypnosis, finding no opposition, leaps to the surface of his brain, and takes control.

To understand this self-hypnosis, it must be remembered that the Lwas have undergone none of the abstraction and sublimation that is the lot of most divinities. Haitians from childhood know the Lwas as well as their own fathers or mothers, and they believe in them in a far more real, literal and immediate way than is conceivable to all western believers except the most accomplished mystics. The Lwas are coarse, vital, almost human figures of his own race; they eat, drink, dance, sleep and make love, and every Haitian knows their habits, their clothes, their appearance and their tastes. He longs to be possessed by them, and in the critical second when artificially created outside events and suggestion, auto-suggestion and hypnotism – the hypnotism, of course, being the sum of his mental processes since childhood, and his heredity – when all this has reduced him to a state of hysteria, his dream comes true. Under the spell of this hypnosis, the immanent Lwa becomes the truth. All else vanishes, and the impotent host of the Lwa knows what to do in the same way that the truth emerges unconsciously through drunkenness, or on the tongue of a sleeping man, or as sleep-walkers unerringly guide themselves to the scene of some hidden obsession of their waking hours, or as ghosts are said to haunt the scenes of their great joys or sorrows. We shape our gods as we wish them to be, and if we think about them enough, they break and enter.

Violent physiological symptoms precede these metamorphoses. The first warning of possession is a feeling of vertigo, a sensation of being thrust over forwards. The subject attempts to regain his balance by leaning back on one heel, and throwing out the other leg; and falls, losing consciousness completely for a moment. As he recovers, this is succeeded by the feeling of an intolerable clamping weight at the nape of his neck which slides down the spine and spreads along the arms and legs. He feels as though he were in a strait-jacket and, shaking his limbs with violence, struggles to free himself. The possessed is observed, at this point, to make attempts to tear or wipe away, or to unwrap something which clings to his hands. Next he feels that he is straightening up, that his eyes are brilliant and his gestures ample and free. All this meanwhile, is quite unconnected with his actual gestures, which are becoming the first steps of the signature dance of his temporary inhabitant. It is the moment when the Houngan, the drums and the other dancers recognize and salute the god.

A Voodooist possessed by Papa Legba, the most ancient of the Lwas, becomes old and lame, and the dancers, recognizing at once who is in their midst, run to supply him with a walking-stick and a crutch. Ogoun Agoué Arroyo, the god of the sea, rows indefatigably with invisible oars. Agaou climbs the central column or swings from the branches of trees to approach the thunder clouds that are his kingdom; Maîtresse Erzulie, even when she is perversely lodged in the body of a man, is flaunting, mincing and vain. Ogoun Ferraille fights desperate and bloody battles. The Petro Lwas, the evil gods of force and bloodshed and disaster, twist their incarnate servants into terrible convulsions and their faces become masks of cynicism and wickedness. The Ghédés, half myrmidons of the underworld and half Eumenides, become insanely agitated, ribald and ghoulishly erotic. Zaka, the telluric deity of the woods and the fields, at once declares himself by his peasant oafishness, his rustic gait, and a facial expression that is a caricature of bucolic ruse.

The possessed retains a dual awareness of himself and of the Lwa. He knows, though his awareness of himself and of his surroundings is dim and reduced, that he is both. His limbs react automatically to the changing behests of the drums, and the bell and *açon* of the Houngan can also control and direct him. The Houngan has the power (I imagine it is one of the secrets of his particular degree of initiation) of halting possession. In many sessions after our first contact with Voodoo I saw this happen, presumably because an untimely incarnation might interrupt the progress of the ritual. The only observable gesture was the prolonged Oranges-and-Lemons shaking of the hands, and the use of the *açon* and the bell. Sometimes the person on the brink of possession withdrew and fell asleep, or sat down in a coma that took about an hour to dissipate itself.

The crisis usually lasts between two and three hours. The feeling of immanence dies down, the drums salute the departing Lwa, and his deserted human palace either returns to normal or sinks into a deep sleep.

Possession often entails deep disturbances in the sensibility. Adepts have been observed to hold their hands in boiling water, or to allow molten lead to be dropped on to their naked flesh, without reacting in any way. (Melancholic Negroes in Africa are able to cut off their own fingers without turning a hair.) A Haitian doctor records the case of a man on whom a testicular operation was being performed with an insufficient anaesthetic. The patient suffered atrocious pain until, breaking into a Voodoo incantation, the pain subsided, and the agonized grimaces on his face grew calm. He had entered a state of possession, and the operation followed its course in complete serenity. Some adepts have been known to live in a state of complete possession for days, automatically fulfilling all their ordinary duties but remembering nothing, or almost nothing, when they emerge.

Strange sounds may accompany the phenomenon, sounds which, when observers have stooped to record them, approximate to the syllables *rounyou! rounyou! rounyou!* repeated interminably, and frequently punctuated by hiccoughs, grunts and sobs. Sometimes words find utterance in disconnected sequences which demonstrate, in the elegant terms of one expert, the complete emancipation of the tongue from the brain. The symptoms of Voodoo possession are akin to those that ancient chronicles ascribe to people possessed by the Devil, a state which was no doubt attained by the same processes of hysteria and self-hypnosis, and by the same conviction of the presence of a supernatural being; in this case, of the Evil One. For, like Hell as opposed to Heaven, the Devil has always been distinguished by a more intense aura of immediacy, and by characteristics more understandable to many laymen than those of the God of Light. A witches' coven must have had much in common with a Haitian religious ceremony.

The majority of Haitians are thus in a permanent state of divine gestation. Every Haitian devotee is a Dr Jekyll whose personality is split up into an enormous and invisible phalanx of Mr Hydes. I wondered, at first, if this strange religious delirium could in any way be compared to the ecstasy of the Unitive period in Christian mysticism. Could these African paroxysms be a short cut to the feelings which inspired, after such devious and terrible journeys, St Theresa on reaching the innermost dwelling, or St Juan on the summit of Carmel? I learnt with relief that the adepts, on emerging from possession, feel little beyond a sensation of the great honour that the Lwa has paid them, and a feeling of lassitude. 'Otherwise, nothing in particular ...'

The slaves of Sainte Domingue were drawn from four main areas of western Africa. The smallest number, about ten per cent of the whole, came from the confines of the Sudan: Senegalese, Wollofs, Peuhls, Bambaras, Quimbaras, Soussous, Mandingos, Haussas and Malinkis. Next in numbers, about twenty per cent, were the Negroes of Dahomey: the Alladas, Fongs, Mahis and Mines. These tribes, before leaving Africa, had overlapped and interacted culturally with the inhabitants of Guinea proper, notably with the Nago, Ibo and Kaplaou which contributed about twenty per cent of the new Transatlantic population. The largest single group came from the basin of the Congo – the Fangs, the Mayombés, the Monsombés, the Bafiotes and the Mondongos, who formed the remaining percentage of the whole slave race. Each kingdom and tribe brought to Hispaniola its own language and religion, and, just as their languages fused and solidified into the universal Créole, bit by bit, the innumerable beliefs coalesced into a single whole in the dark secrecy of the barracoons. Each tribe was represented by a number of Lwas who possessed the religious and physical characteristics of the race that had created them. The new religion had two main branches which were eventually believed and practised by all: the Congo Rite, originating among the slaves of Congolese origin, and the Rada Rite, named after the town of Allada, which, along with the territory of the Mahi and Nagos tribes, was conquered by the warlike Fongs of Dahomey early in the eighteenth century. So, before their enslavement and embarkation for the islands, much of the Dahomey-Guinea* group of tribes – the Alladas, the Fongs, the Mahis, the Mines, the Nagos and the Ibos – were under the influence of the religion of Dahomey; and it was the religion, the legends and customs of the Dahomeyans which, through their greater strength of character, or a higher culture or religious dynamism than all the others, dominated the new hybrid Negro race which was growing up. The Congo Rite fell into a secondary place, and Rada remained supreme.

Many of these religions had become inextricably tangled by foreign influences long before they were thrown into the same alembic and melted into one religion by the fire of a common evil. Faint rings of sound from Luxor and Athens and Bethlehem and Mecca had crossed the empty wildernesses, and their remote messages had become garbled and woven into the animism of the forests. Neighbouring tribes left inevitable deposits of belief and practice, and it was already an amalgam of complexities that, as they united and merged into a single faith, was exposed to its last great influence, the factor that was to provide its final and definitive twist: the teaching of Christianity.

It was with reluctance that Louis XIII granted to the first colonists the right to make use of slave labour. He did so, rather naïvely, because it was urged that slavery was the infallible and only means of converting the Africans to the Christian faith. The colonists were able to satisfy their consciences with the thought that the Hell in this world which was the corollary among their slaves of their own mounting revenues was an apprenticeship for the Negroes' eternal felicity in the world to come. The work of conversion would begin soon after the Negroes had landed from the slavers and the exciting new stories were eagerly listened to, and gratefully incorporated into the fabric of the other new belief which was being so rapidly built up out of more familiar material. Christianity

* Centred upon the seaboard and hinterland of the Grain Coast and the Ivory Coast.

won a special and privileged position, and the observances of the Church became the overt and public side of the occult rites which they performed in private. Missionaries had early misgivings about the profundity of their new conversions. Father Labat shakes his head over the task of the missionaries to Angola and the Congo. 'These Negroes,' he sighs, 'have no scruple in imitating the Philistines. They couple the Ark of the Covenant with Dagon, and secretly preserve all the superstitions of their ancient idolatrous cults with the ceremonies of the Christian religion. One can judge what sort of Christianity is the result ...' It was exactly the case of Haiti.

New religions pass through a bower-bird period when elements from any neighbouring faith are joyfully woven into the half-built nest. When the structure is complete, dogma and canon harden into orthodoxy. After this theological closing time, anyone welcoming late-comers or questioning the credentials of earlier arrivals becomes guilty of schism or heresy. This hour with Voodoo (as the new religion, after the Dahomeyan word *Vodun*, meaning 'spirits', soon came to be called), has not yet struck. Possessing no dogma at all, Voodoo is wonderfully elastic. It has a vast mythology, and a ritual which custom has formalized, but as primitive Negro spiritual demands are uniquely magical and talismanic there was nothing heterodox in the incorporation of vast lumps of Christian practice. Any saints who caught their fancy were enlisted on sight, on the strength of the similarity of their external attributes with those of the great Lwas. Only one of them seems to have attained the status of a Lwa on an equal footing with his African colleagues: St James the Major, who is, however, nearly always invoked in the company of the Ogoun group of Lwas. I have been unable to discover why St James occupies this exceptional position, unless the military ring of his title rendered him especially welcome to the Lwas' warlike Valhalla. His *vévér*, his coat of arms in maize-flour, is a sword flanked by two banners, and *Santiago!* of course, was the battle-cry of the Spanish conquistadors.*

With the principal actors of the Christian religion and an irregular battalion of the saints, many of the prayers of the Church, and a few fragments of the liturgy have found their way into the Voodoo rites. There the Christian contribution ends. But there were other elements in the new world suitable for incorporation. When the first Africans arrived, the Indian natives of Hispaniola, whose thinning ranks they had been brought to supplement and finally to replace, were not yet extinct, and

---

*This raises the suspicion that Jackaminory, whose brief life story is such a disappointment in the nursery, is none other than St James the Minor, *St Jaques Mineur*, and that he owes his position in nursery lore to a similar fortuitous cause.

Dr Louis Maximilian maintains that the snake cult attached to the name of the Lwa Damballah may – though other authorities trace it to the serpent-worship which throve in the Dahomeyan town of Wydah – owe something to a Carib or an Arawak cult of the feathered serpent similar to the Aztec worship of Quetzalcoatl or to the Kukulkan of the Maya. Bits of European magic, of the Kabbalah, the books of Hermes Trismegistus, the Rosy Cross and Mesmerism, and all the French eighteenth-century fads, slipped into Voodoo. Pentacles appeared among the *vévérs*, and the word *Adonai* occurs frequently in the language of the cult. Freemasonry has left its traces, and in Guadeloupe the secret African rites and those of the Grand Orient are practised side by side.

Some of the Lwas (like Baron Samedi and his consort Maman Brigide) actually originated in Haiti. The most important of these is Petro. Don Pedro is a fierce and shadowy figure, a Negro from the Spanish part of the island who played a part in the Independence War. Some, alternatively, maintain that he was an African god, the spirit of a great king, worshipped first in Surinam in Dutch Guiana. Whatever his origin, he introduced new dances and ceremonies into Voodoo and then vanished, leaving his sinister observances behind him, so that Voodoo now has three rites (each of which is subdivided into a number of ceremonies): Rada, Congo and Petro.

Four and a half centuries have passed since the Spaniards, in the time of the Emperor Charles V, imported the first slaves from Africa; so it is to that date – 1503 – that the first bubbles of religious fusion must be ascribed. But the chemico-religious process achieved its most intense activity under the French, when the shipping of slaves from the whole West Coast of Africa took place on a much larger scale. By the middle of the eighteenth century, Negroes were arriving at the rate of 30,000 a year. The period immediately before the War of Independence brought the mixture to the point of boiling and overflow, and all through the nineteenth century, when Voodoo, though officially forbidden, was in practice connived at, the crucible simmered, steadily furnishing new accretions to the vast mass of the religion which had already become solid.

So voluminous and complex is the ritual of Voodoo, so numerous its traditions and its obligations, that it is hard to discover what skeleton of theory underlies the unwieldy body of actual practice. The most fervent Voodooist would be nonplussed if he were suddenly asked to formulate a simple *credo* of his religion, and the learned Haitian writers are all at variance about its more abstract side. There are many opinions, for instance, about the identity of the chief of the heavenly hierarchy. And the fact that this diversity of opinions should be a matter of little concern is a proof of the purely instinctive nature of the cult.

Some maintain that the all-powerful demiurge is a nebulous figure called *le Grand Maître*, successor of a divinity called Mawu* in the religion of Dahomey. But if this Great Master is the main God, he is a personality of great remoteness, and certainly not a paternal god or a god of Providence. Even the sex of this Being is not certain, for he is sometimes appealed to as *Bon Dieu maman moin*. But the usual term for him is *Bon-Dieu-Bon*. Other authorities maintain that Schango – who is, alternatively, merely one of the prominent Lwas of the Ogoun group (he has given his name to cults equivalent to Voodoo in the other islands) – is the Omnipotent One and the Demiurge; and that Schango has gracefully stepped aside to cede his high place to the Word, the Creative Spirit of the Christian faith; indeed, Christ himself, and so, according to Christian logic, God. But the nature, name or sex of this Divinity arouse neither interest nor deep controversy. He is too lofty and dim for any practical purposes. His (or Her) immediate subordinates are so powerful, so well known and so real that Voodoo is virtually a polytheism. Prayers are addressed to them, not for intercession or advocacy with a higher power, but for direct action on their own account. It is hard to say whether they are more exactly gods or saints.

The Lwas have many different definitions. The word in Créole is usually written *Loa*, but they are also called *voudous*, *z'éspwits*, *mystères*, *z'invisibles*, *z'anges* and *lessaints*; gods, angels, saints, daemons, numina and genii all contribute something to their complex nature. They are guides, counsellors, judges, punishers, consolers and advocates who give divine sanction to human frailties and aspirations, and daily prove their love for their devotees by the miracle of incarnation. I have been able to count over seventy, and there are many more of them, possibly a hundred and fifty or two hundred. They seem to be subjected to the loosest sort of hierarchy. Papa Legba is always first to be invoked, as he is the protector of cross-roads, journeys and beginnings, but the great Damballah has a position not far removed from that of Zeus. Erzulie Fréda Dahomin is the third who appears with most frequency, and Ogoun Ferraille and his warlike fellow Ogouns have a special prominence. The air is governed by Brisé, the wind by Aida Ouèdo, the rainbow by Damballah la Flambeau and Agaou-Tonnerre; fire by Marinette-Bois-Chèche, Lemba Zaou, Zaou-Pimba, Ogoun-z'yeux-Rouges and a number of

---

* Or Amo Ama, Nabulaku or Anyambé.

Congolese immortals. The water falls under the dominion of Agoué-Arroyo and his queen, Chorché, and his brothers. The earth is controlled by a problematical Sainte Terre, Grand-Bois and Zaka. Guédé Nibou is the protector of flocks, Loko Atissou of the hearth, and Lisa, with her obverse of Saint Clara, rules the moon. The sun is sometimes represented by St Nicholas, and Azès is the patron of blacksmiths; and so on. The proliferation of the Lwas is like those Byzantine frescoes of the company of saints where haloes overlap in receding vistas like the scales of a fish.

The Lwas invoked in the Petro rite are a gang of maleficent wretches whose worship consists of propitiation or of the supplication of their help for evil purposes. Petro is thus a first step to the practice of Wanga or Black Magic. Many of these Petro gods are the cruel and ruthless obverses of the magnanimous Lwas of the Rada and Congo rites. One of the most notable is Erzulie z'yeux Rouges or Marinette, whose attributes lie half-way between those of Medusa and of a celestial executioner. The Mondongo Lwas also form part of the Petro rite. They are the representatives of the Congolese race of the Mondongos, who were notorious in colonial times for cannibalism. The official sacrifice of these Lwas has now been reduced to the tamer fare of striped dogs, but they still have the reputation of being harsh and gloomy brutes. Other Petro Lwas – Bakalou, Kitta, Zandor, etc. – also have a hateful renown.

There is no doubt that human sacrifice has, in the past, played a certain minor *rôle* in the rites of the Petro Lwas. But, as Dr Dorsainvil suggests, these ritual murders were the equivalent of Agamemnon's sacrifice of Iphigenia to enlist the favour of the gods, or of Abraham's abortive immolation of Isaac to appease Jehovah. It is the expression of a psychological state fairly general in primitive humanity. And it is, above all, a characteristic of primitive religions in which the gods may be unkind, harmful and wayward powers which can only be appeased with human blood. So, though the offering may, in point of fact, be eaten, such sacrifices must be absolved of the vulgarity of ordinary cannibalism.

This is a delicate theme. Ever since, in 1864, eight people were publicly executed for sacrificing and eating a small girl called Claircine, the youthful Republic has had a bad time from foreign writers. This reached such a pitch in the last century that Froude, disembarking for an hour or two in the Haitian port of Jacmel, records, with an insincere coyness surprising in such a writer, that he hardly dared to glance at the butchers' booths in the market for fear of the disquieting wares that might have been exposed for sale. To me, ritual murder seems more remarkable by its scarcity than by its actual occurrences. A very large number of the slaves originated in the Congo, and of these, many were drawn from the populous Mondongo tribes. After the War of Independence, when repugnance to the defeated western ideas slowly subsided, internal upsets of the state prolonged the illiteracy of the rural masses, and the peasant approach to the teachings of the Church was a purely negative one. There was nothing to veto the prolongation of the customs to which, in the happy freedom of Africa, they, or their fathers and grandfathers, had been accustomed. Whether Mondongo anthropophagy was religious or merely gastronomic – Moreau de Saint Méry hints that it was the latter – atavistic beliefs certainly spiritualized and elevated it. Instances, with the infiltration of western prejudices, became steadily rarer, and authorities are today agreed that human sacrifice, in Voodoo, does not exist.

Whether ritual murder exists outside Voodoo is another matter. Many Haitians affirm that it is still practised, extremely rarely, in remoter districts, by the nightmarish secret societies of wizards and necromancers of which Father Cosme had spoken – the Vlinbnidingues, the Zobops, the Mazanxas and the rest – in which the Wangaters, the Mauvais Mounes and the Werewolves invoke the Petro gods, who still secretly demand, and here receive, their ancient offering of a hornless goat.

It is maintained that Black Magic, or Wanga, stands in the same relationship to Voodoo as the Black Arts to medieval Christianity. In practice the chasm is bridged by the fact that there is no prejudice against 'working with both hands': combining the duties of a Houngan of the rites of Voodoo with the less reputable office of a Bokor, or practitioner of Wanga. Many clients of the Bokors are members of higher social strata than the run of Voodoo adepts, usually women in search of charms or love potions or revenge, who would no sooner resort to a *tonnelle* than many European consultants of fortune-tellers or mediums would dream of going to church.

African animism subsists in the attribution of souls and divine powers to inanimate objects, to plants, stones, rocks, trees, caves or drums, which are known as the Resting-Places, the *reposoirs*, of the Lwas.

It was the unifying force of Voodoo, far more than the advent of New Ideas from Europe, that impelled the slaves at the time of the French Revolution to revolt. The new ideas merely provided the opportunity and implanted in their opponents the mood of doubt. The first chain-breakers – Mackandal the poisoner and Boukman, whose terrible *jacquerie* struck the first overt blow – were both Voodoo initiates, and the Haitians were carried to victory by the inspiration of their equatorial numina, for, like Castor and Pollux at Lake Regillus, the Lwas appeared on the battlefield and participated in the rout of the whites. Now the heroes of the war are themselves triumphant denizens of the Voodoo pantheon, worshipped in the Petro rites with fanfares and drums and with the explosion of gunpowder and the clashing of sabres. Mackandal and Boukman, and the cocked-hatted colossi of Toussaint l'Ouverture, Pétion, Rigaud and, above all the Emperor Dessalines, have undergone canonization or apotheosis. This, for Haitians, is the sovereign importance of Voodoo: the memory and the worship of their great ancestors and heroes and a melancholy and triumphant nostalgia for their lost home in the forests of Africa – the remote and legendary green kingdoms of *Nan Guinan*.

The organism of a Voodoo adept is divided into three parts: the body; the *p'tit bon ange*, or tutelary spirit; and the *gwos bon ange*, or soul. When the body sleeps, the *gwos bon ange* roams the ether, dances with gods and devils, and visits the ghosts of his ancestors and only returns to his tabernacle at the moment of waking. The strange dreams that it brings back form, in the brain of its owner, a life that has as much importance and reality as that of the hours of waking. The adventures of the soul, should its owner pass through the preliminary stages of initiation, are very complex. At one arcanum, at the moment of becoming a hounci-canzo, it is confined by proxy in an earthenware *pot de tête*, and kept in the houmfor. This captivity or dedication is symbolized by placing in the head-pot tufts of hair from the scalp, armpits and pubic region of the candidate, alongside his nail parings, and the beak, blood and fluff of the bird which was sacrificed to mark the occasion. The soul is equipped with a personal Lwa, which has to be replaced by a similar ceremony after death. This is performed by the Houngan sitting astride the corpse under a sheet, or – though it was long forbidden by the police – astride his grave after dark. After this rite, which is called Dessounin, the *animula vagula blandula* is released from its prison of china. It then takes refuge in the element of water. A year after death, a service called Withdrawal from the Water takes place, when the Houngan, surrounded by sheeted houncis, obtains permission from the Baron for the release of the soul. Then, raised to a status not unlike that of a minor Lwa, it flies away to join the shadowy throng of his ancestors. Unwithdrawn spirits are dangerous, and spend their time circling the air and wreaking damage.

The early years of life are considered to be adequately equipped by the ceremonies of the Church, though Christening is sometimes supplemented by a secret baptism of fire to solicit the favour of the Lwas and the *manes*. The child is thrown through flames crackling with salt and gunpowder and in certain regions, fortified against danger from *loups-garous* by a bath of ox's bile, tortoises' blood, magic leaves and faecal matter. The first serious stage of initiation takes place, some time in the 'teens, at the ceremony of *Haussement*. The catechumen, dressed in first Communion clothes, performs his (or her) first libations and swears to respect the Voodoo hierarchy and the mysteries of Guinea. He is hoisted aloft in an armchair, to a chorus of 'Ah! Bobo!'; emerging afterwards as a Hounci-Bossale. The next step is from Hounci-Bossale to Hounci-Canzo, a long and arduous process which culminates, after six days of preparation, in the solemn rites and sacrifices of *Brûler Zin*. The later rungs of initiation, which are reserved for very few, are the secret gnosis of the priesthood, which carries the candidate by slow degrees through the ranks of Hougenikon, Houngan and Mambo or Papalwa and Mamalwa. There is no higher central authority or synod which pronounces on liturgical or doctrinal or disciplinary matters.

It is hard to say exactly what this final priestly matriculation entails. Knowledge of the function and choreography of the dances, the many rhythms of the drums, the conduct of the ceremonies, the invocations and the duties of the houmfor; *'langage'* (a kind of inspired and meaningless articulation) and the abracadabresque jargon of the liturgy, which is a mixture of African, Créole, French and Latin; the ability, aided by the use of the bell and the *açon*, which are the pontificalia of his office, to control, assist or suppress possession; the practice of white magic for curative purposes; a knowledge of the meaning of dreams; the ability to 'call the god on a Govi' – to prophesy, that is, and make oracular pronouncements over a draped pitcher containing a god (long dialogues take place behind a curtain, and the god announces his presence in a cavernous voice, with the words: *'Messieurs et dames la Société, bonjour!'* Delphic pronouncements follow, and the Houngan or Mambo emerges, as from a trance, exhausted and with bloodshot eyes); the handling of the souls in their various phases; a knowledge of the complex hagiography of the Lwas, their habits, their many names, attributes, sacrifices, colours and armorial bearings, and the knack of marshalling their escutcheons in maize-flour; and the use of the bizarre and dust-covered stage properties of the cult: the pots, pans, basins, calabashes, gourds, crosses, images, rosaries, oleographs, drums, horns, conches, leaves, herbs, blood, bile, offal, salt, gunpowder, sheets, ribbons, feathers, lingams, skulls, cross-bones, chains, whips, pincers, cutlasses, sabres, goggles, frock-coats, top-hats and bowlers that make the inside of the houmfor such a bewildering sight.

What is the final goal of this ladder of initiation? Mawu? Schango? Jesus? I do not think anybody knows. Again, as with the Lwas, the religion loses itself in a jungle of detail, and (I think) goes no farther. One writer says that Voodoo, like all ancient religions, is impatient of explanation.

It was developed instinctively to lead the slaves to a private liberty that the state of things in their world forbade. The open air and the sunlight meant the cane-fields, the sweat, the chains, the whip, the endless toil and misery of a slave's existence. So, like children who build up a dark and secret world of freedom and womb-like intimacy out of chairs and carpets, and sit there in felicity for hours, the slaves went warrening back into the darkness, farther and farther away from the heartless glare. There they crouched in the warm secrecy of their own sounds and spirits and joys and terrors, and, above all, with memories of Africa which grew, with every passing generation, dimmer and more wonderful. It was the *chère petite grotte*, the *grand-fonds de Malampia* of Melanie Bastian, Gide's sequestered girl of Poitiers, who, withdrawn from the darkness and squalor of her prison to the blinding asepsis of a hospital ward, languished for a day or two of homesickness for her grotto, and expired. They were not heading *for* but *away* from something, and that is why I think Haitian writers are wrong to look any farther than the Lwas. It is also why theories are so vague and conflicting about a higher celestial hierarchy, why Mawu or Schango or *le Grand Maître* or *Bon-Dieu-Bon*, or any of their African alternatives, are so unreal, and Christ such a misfit. It may also be the reason why so few of the Lwas have the actual names of African gods, and so many of them the names of regions and rivers and towns, which slowly turned into gods as the nostalgic generations succeeded each other. And so, as the child in his dark lair surrounds himself with corroborative detail to make his myth more real, the adjuncts and the gear accumulated. Initiation can only lead deeper into the dark burrow, into the secret. The burrow led nowhere. It was being there that mattered.

So the point of Voodoo, and the whole of the religion, is its practice. If the drums and the dances and the *tonnelle* were to cease, the whole vast structure would collapse into a débris of superstition, and of vague memories that would soon vanish as they have vanished in America. It exists for itself. The ideas that it represents – the memory of Africa; unity against a cruel and hostile world; survival; the enthralling miracle of possession, the mystery, the warmth, the drums and the dances – are all part of the religion's actual performance. No theory, not a written line, embraces them. I was at first mystified by its lack of rules, of a code of ethics, of a logical hierarchy. It was as if, in the study of Christianity, the next step, after the genealogy of Christ, were the function of a bishop's mitre. For in Voodoo there is nothing in between. How could there be? But, to the masses in Haiti, it is far more than a philosophy, a dogmatical or metaphysical system or a code of ethics. It is the past, the present and the future, the air they breathe, the entire universe.

The weeks that followed were obsessed by Voodoo. It seemed impossible to talk or think or read about anything else, and, as night fell, we would listen for the first faint roll of drums with the anxiety of dipsomaniacs waiting for opening time.

Rodolfe accompanied us to our first few Voodoo sessions, but after a while we ventured out on our own, visiting, sometimes, several in the same night. The poor quarter of Morne Marinette in the hilly northern fringe of Port-au-Prince proved the most profitable region for our purposes, as the peristyles here are as numerous as chapels in a mining town. Sliding quietly into the back row, we would sit in the darkness for unnumbered hours, watching the development of the ritual, the evolutions of the dancers, and the never-failing phenomenon of possession. The terrors of mendicancy that reigned in the street suddenly ceased inside these precincts. No kind of financial levy was laid on us in the way of a collection, but after a while we learned to take half a bottle of rum to contribute to the common supply. In the excitement of the events taking place, the presence of whites seemed to pass unnoticed and we were treated with indifference or with shy hospitality. At some *tonnelles* the ceremonies continue for five or six nights on end, the intervening days passing in a trance of sleep which is cast off at nightfall with the first reverberations of the tom-toms.

The adepts, all of whom belong to the poorer working classes, pass an attractively idle and bohemian life. Army officers, and members of the *bourgeoisie* in collars and ties, would occasionally appear among the ragged Negroes, but on catching sight of us would melt away again into the darkness, as though disturbed at the prospect of our meeting in more formal circumstances. (We soon noticed that the mention of Voodoo, in the higher levels of Haitian life, caused distress. It was almost a *gaffe*. There is a tacit ban on the subject, a negation, though the air may be throbbing with remote percussion, of its existence.)

The Houngans, as the controllers of the spiritual life of Haiti, were specially interesting figures. Some of them appeared little different from the rest of the community. Others looked sinister scoundrels, or humorous, verbose cards. One or two were imposing, powerfully built men. But all of them had an aura of portentousness and command. Their positions as priests and, frequently, wizards at the same time, put them in a position of enormous authority, and many of them wield unchallenged political as well as spiritual sway. This makes their goodwill an important factor in Haitian political life. There is much talk in the capital of their influence in politics, and of the lengths to which politicians will go to conciliate them and obtain the suffrage of their flock. *'On dit que le vieux,'* an opponent of the present régime said, referring to a prominent figure in the government, *'a sacrifié un boeuf avant d'être élu . . .'*

A *Brûler Zin*, the most important ceremony in Voodoo, was being solemnized to celebrate the initiation as hounci-canzos of two neophytes from Curaçao. In order to attend the rite, they had crossed the Caribbean Sea in one of the schooners plying between the Greater Antilles and the Spanish Main: a journey which suggests that there is more connection between the secret Negro sects in the islands than is generally supposed.

The *tonnelle* lay behind a large breadfruit tree in the heart of a populous quarter near the tramlines and rum-shops. The drummers were plainly virtuosi, and the twenty white-clad houncis danced with the cohesion of a *corps de ballet*. Everything was disciplined and organized to the smallest detail. The ceremony had been going some time when we arrived, but, though there were about a hundred people in the *tonnelle*, the mud floor was only occupied by the Houngan, the mambo, the houncis and the various postulants and acolytes of the peristyle.

The candidates, meanwhile, for whom the impending *Brûler Zin* was the last act of initiation, were invisible inside the Rada houmfor. Their six rigorous days of preparation were nearly ended. The first step of this preparation is confession and absolution in a church, followed by a second plenary confession to the Houngan, who repeats it aloud to his personal Lwa. Two days are then spent in rest and meditation and certain specific ablutions, and then there is another compulsory period in church. Next, as all this week is aimed at making the candidate a fitting vessel for the visitation of the Lwas, the Houngan and the mambo conduct a ceremony in honour of Aizan-Véléquété, the Lwa of purification and exorcism. After further ritual lustrations, the candidates are enveloped in sheets so that only their faces are exposed, and then stretched out on mats in the houmfor with their heads resting on pillows of stone. Here, living on a liquid mixture of maize and mushrooms and herbs, they remain in the darkness for four days of silence and prayer. Sacrifices and unctions and a kind of baptism punctuate this symbolic death, and the Houngan removes their souls and places them in a head-pot. The vigil was about to finish.

The swordsman and his two standard-bearers were engaged in a prolonged dance of salutation. The swordsman, the *Laplace*, wove a path among the houncis, leaping and turning, and twisting a cutlass in the air, while two girls, slowly waving their red and blue silk banners on which eagles were embroidered in sequins, danced on his left and right. They remained together throughout the evening, moving and turning perfectly in line, rhythmically prostrating themselves and recovering in unison, and making the elegant pirouette-salute to all the staff and to the congregation.

At one moment the houncis were dancing in two lines, at another round the pillar, falling rhythmically to the ground in a circle and kissing the ground, so that the radiation of their white figures formed a white corolla; rising again with the dust grey on their lips and foreheads, chanting, all the time, to the clatter of the drums. The mambo appeared laden with their long necklaces of coloured beads, which they knelt in turn to receive. She arranged them so that they crossed in saltire on their breasts and backs. Libations were spilt, and a magic ring of white maize-flour drawn round the pillar, encompassed, in a circle about a yard in diameter, by the white cognizances of each great Lwa. The drums fell silent, and the initiates sank to their knees in a compact group and bowed their heads. In the universal hush the Houngan softly intoned a long series of prayers in French. The first (as copied by Dr Maximilian from the notebook of a Houngan) is: *'Venez mon Dieu, venez, venez mon doux Sauveur, venez régner en moi au centre de mon coeur, venez mon Dieu, venez ...'* This is succeeded by prayers to St Gabriel, St Philomena, the Blessèd Virgin, St Mary Magdalen (*'Hélas, Hélas, Hélas, la Madeleine mérite le pardon ...'*) and to Our Lord, followed by a litany to St Antony of Padua, St Nicholas, St Joseph, St Andrew, St Moses, St Augustin, St Gérard, St Ulrich, St Patrick, SS Cosmo and Damian, the Twelve Apostles, St Charles Borromspeo ... *'Vierge Altagrace, vierge Caridad, vierge des Mont Carmel, St Claire, tout les Saints et Saintes qui sont dans le ciel'*; then it slowly slides into the queer sacerdotal language, *'tout rondi-oroum dans le ciel. Zo lissandole zo, zo lissabagui zo, lissabagui wangan ciqué lissandole zo.'* Next, beginning with Legba, comes the invocation of the Lwas, a prolonged rubaiyat that grows more cabalistic in suggestion, until the names of the Lwas cease, to be replaced by a monody of pure sound from which all apparent significance has been purged: *'Lade immennou daguinin soilade aguignaminsou ... Oh! Oh! Oh! ... Pingolo Pingolo roi montré nous la prié qui minnin africain ... Wanguinan Wannimé ... En hen mandioment en hen ...'* And so on for six pages. It seems that only a minimum of these words are of African origin, and their meaning is totally obscure. Nobody knows where or how they originated; whether they evolved in Haiti, or whether they are a memory of some hermetic language of the priests in Africa. Softly towards the end of these orisons the drums began to throb, first a tentative tap, then another, then half a dozen, until, after a pause, all the voices and drums had struck up again louder than ever, and the houncis were shuffling and revolving their way through a *yanvalloux*. They danced slowly into the temple and the doors were closed. The peristyle was bare for a while of all but the drummers.

After half an hour of this emptiness, the door was thrown open and the swordsman and standard-bearers, waving their emblems, sprang down the steps in a single flying arc. The others streamed after them, howling, rather than singing, at the top of their voices. The procession, ceremoniously carrying little cauldrons, bottles, iron pegs, bundles of firewood and sheaves of green branches, began to revolve round the pillar at breakneck speed. The mambo danced at the rear of the saraband, waving flurried trusses of live white chickens above her head. Some of the dancers continued their round, while the others drove sets of iron pegs into the ground, sloping inwards to form primitive tripods, at three points round the pillar. Fires were kindled and flames were soon leaping up. The green branches were spread out all round them in a rustic carpet. Pouring liquids into the flames, the mambo flourished the clucking fowls along the proffered limbs of the houncis, and ceremoniously waved them to the four cardinal points: '*A table*', '*Dabord*', '*Olandé*', and '*Adonai*'.* When the birds had pecked at the scattered maize in token of their willingness to be offered up – an omen which was greeted by jubilant shouts of 'Ah! Bobo! Ah! Bobo!' – they were consigned to the various officers of the *tonnelle*, who crouched with them beside the fires, over which the earthenware cauldrons – the *zins* – had now been placed on the tripods.

The method of sacrifice is swift and inhumane. Simultaneously all the chickens' tongues were torn out, and their legs and their wings were broken; then, with a dexterous and violent movement, their heads were wrenched off. The sacrificers were soon up to their elbows in blood as the chickens, with savage expertness, were pulled to pieces. Blood was poured into the cauldrons. Tufts of the neck feathers and the gutted and dismembered carcases soon followed them. The battery of tom-toms continued without a break, the drummers leaning forward at each roll with their long heckling snarl. The cauldrons and the flames, the flying feathers, the blood, the ring of serious black faces in the firelight above the carpet of green leaves, were a wild and disquieting sight. If a goat, a dog or a bull is to be sacrificed, scent is first poured all over the victim, and it is dressed in ritual trappings. It is suspended in the air by its four outstretched legs; the priest castrates it and severs its windpipe with two

*E, W, N, and S.

deft cutlass-blows. It was impossible not to wonder what the sacrificial technique had been in the obsolete Mondongo offerings. The modern observances of the Zobops and the Vlinbindingues were an even more irresistible theme for conjecture.

The door of the temple had again opened, and the gyrating swords and flags were leading into the open a procession which advanced with unnatural slowness. Surrounded by an escort of houncis, an object like an enormous white slug with an immense hump was crawling out of the shadows of the houmfor. As it worked its way towards us, guided by the houncis, it still remained problematical. It was, one finally realized, a white cloth with a man inside it. But how could he be twisted into that extraordinary shape? The houncis, crawling along beside it on all fours, were holding the edge of the sheet to the ground, so that not an inch of the person inside it could be seen. It drew level with the fires and stopped. The mambo fumbled with one corner of the cloth, the edge was slipped up a couple of inches, and two clasped hands were revealed, one black, the other dark brown, and both, I noticed, left hands. One man must have been crawling on his hands and knees, while a second, kneeling behind him with his body hunched over his arched back, stretched down across his shoulders to clasp the hands of his mount for support. The mambo pushed the black hand back under the cloth and rubbed the pink palm of the other with oil. She reached into a cauldron and scooped out a handful of hot maize-flour, and, working it with grimaces of pain into a paste, she moulded it to a cylinder and pressed it into the pink palm, forcibly closing the fingers over it and thrusting it back under the sheet. The boiling maize on the oil must have been almost unendurable. A tremor, accompanied by a long gasp, ran along the white shape, which slowly resumed its circuit. When it came round again, the other hand was subjected to the same ordeal. On the next two journeys, feet were in turn extricated and held for a moment in the flames. The white mass slithered, like some legless mammal, unwieldily up the steps and vanished inside the houmfor. The second candidate appeared and the operation was repeated. When he was in the temple and lying once more on the floor beside the other candidate, the dancing and the invocations began again. The huddling mambo emptied flasks of oil into the *zins*, and scattered a pool of rum all round the fires which at once burst into a blaze. The houncis, falling to their knees, plunged their hands into the flames. The cauldrons cracked and disintegrated with the heat, the boiling oil was mingled with the rum and a great flame leapt into the air. The remains of the sacrifice were ceremoniously buried and a rhythmic stamping dance took place over the grave.

Soon afterwards the first crisis of possession occurred. Shaking off the usual initial paroxysm, a bulky hounci-canzo rose from the ground in a metamorphosis whose symptoms resembled an amorous delirium. Gabbling and leering, she careered unsteadily round the *tonnelle*, rubbing her loins against every person and object that she encountered, in an erotic simulacrum.* Her fellow houncis seized her and began to force her arms into the sleeves of an old morning coat several sizes too small for her. For a Ghédé had been recognized, and these myrmidons of Death all wear the Baron's livery. A hounci-bossale swiftly appeared with a collection of headgear, and, in spite of the Ghédé's shouts and her jerks to free herself, they contrived to hold her while a broken bowler hat was crammed over her ears. A battered trilby was thrust on top of it, and on the very summit of this pagoda, an ancient top-hat. A great pair of black glasses was hastily straddled across her nose, and the moment she was released the Ghédé flew galloping round the *tonnelle* once more, screeching and laughing and firing a child's cap-pistol into the air. The drums thundered, and the drummers roared and snarled over their cylinders like three jaguars. As she cavorted past us, we could see that her eyes were turned back in the revulsion that had become so familiar. Soon another Lwa descended, and by the first light at least half a dozen dancers had fallen and died and risen again, each of them possessed and transformed into members of this ghoulish horde – Baron Cimetière, Général Criminel, Capitaine Zombi and the rest, whose rites are celebrated with cracking whips and gunpowder and the wielding of colossal bamboo phalli – until the peristyle seemed to be filled with the top-hats, coat-tails and goggles, the shrieks and the cantrips of a troop of demented and nymphomaniac scarecrows.

I spent the next afternoon, as usual, in the library of the Institut de Saint Louis de Gonzague. It is a miraculously cool and neutral refuge from the incandescent streets. Recognizing me with a smile, Brother Yves, the little Breton librarian, would climb up the ladder and descend with his arms full of vellum-bound memoirs of the colony of Sainte Domingue, and all the nineteenth-century works about the War of Independence and the ephemeral reigns of King Henri Christophe and the Emperor Faustin Soulouque. Occasionally another cassocked figure, a fellow-countryman from Morbihan, would come rustling in from the cloisters, and I could hear their quiet conversations in Breton as I turned the pages. I asked

---

* These ceremonies never end, as might be supposed, in an orgy. The Ghédés leave them within a couple of hours, and their abandoned lodgings are far more prone, as the community breaks up, to think of the Church than the alcove.

Brother Yves what he thought of people who practised Voodoo. He looked at me with tolerant amusement, and said: '*Mais ils sont tout à fait coucou.*'

Cuckoo. It was a new ecclesiastical standpoint, and a more reasonable one, I thought, than that of poor Father Cosme. There had been something really tragic about those photographs of the abandoned anti-superstition campaigns, the felled Resting-Places, the holocausts of idolatrous gear. Yet what should be the attitude of the Church in these extraordinary circumstances? A pretty strong anti-clerical bias exists in many of the Latin-American republics, a delayed-action Voltairianism which aims at the influence of the Church the conventional accusations of obscurantism and reaction. But the defective religious practice of the Haitians springs from exactly the opposite reasons. For if the Church is reactionary, it reacts to a different and an alien past, and the only drawback of its obscurantism and its magic is that they are not, compared with the intoxication of Voodoo, obscure or magical enough. A religion thrives on proscription, but, failing through competition on grounds such as these, it can only repine. It is an undeserved reverse, for the Catholic Church has done more than any other form of Christianity to mitigate the essentially unpromising circumstances of the West Indies.

We went back to the *tonnelle* after dinner to see the new initiates emerge from the houmfor. The hounci-canzos of either sex were dressed in their best Sunday dresses or in neat blue suits. Several girls wore high-heeled shoes made out of celluloid, so that the feet inside looked as though they were in aspic. Coloured sweets and glasses of liquor were being offered on trays, and only the softly beating drums, the fire of Marinette, and the dismal cross of Baron Samedi reminded us that we were in the precincts of a *tonnelle*.

The two new hounci-canzos were sitting side by side near the drums. I had imagined, for some reason, that they were men, and was astonished when they both turned out to be women. One was a young girl with round and bewildered eyes, the other middle-aged: plump, homely figures, looking, among the strong-featured and flamboyant Haitians, phenomenally domesticated and Dutch. The elder was dressed in a severe, rather governessy dress of pale lilac, the other in green with a lace collar, and both of them wore their new hounci-canzo necklaces crossed over the breast. The Haitian houncis were at pains to make them feel at home. But, as their new fellow-initiates could speak neither French nor Créole, it was heavy going, an intercourse of smiles and rolled eyes and friendly gestures. The two initiates would exchange a few words between themselves in Papiamento from time to time. It was as though two rather timid visitors from a Dutch provincial town had arrived in Paris with letters of introduction and had first encountered their new hosts in the middle of a bohemian party where nobody spoke a word of Dutch.

CHAPTER 12

Haiti Continued

How does an artistic renaissance begin? The great Italian movement of
the fifteenth century needed the destruction of an empire and the sack
of the imperial city to set it in motion; an event scarcely less momentous
in history than the fall of Troy. The minor but undeniably valid
renaissance in the painting of Haiti came into being through no more
startling an event than the arrival, during the war, of an American painter
in Port-au-Prince to teach English at the Lycée Pétion.

As, a few years ago, sociologists were agreed that all traces of Haitian
art were dead, there is something akin to the miracle of Lazarus in the
resurrection that has taken place. Mr De Witt Peters received his first
hint of the existence of primitive painting in the Republic from the frescoes
of brightly coloured birds and fruit and flowers on the doors of a bar
beside a country road. The quest for the disinterment of Haitian primitive
painting from this initial clue – a painted mug here, decorative designs
on wood or cardboard there, or a sudden efflorescence of colour on whitewashed walls in the remotest *mornes* – until the opening of the *Centre
d'Art* and the sudden constellation of painters and sculptors that have
been summoned out of oblivion or brought into being under its auspices,
is an exciting story.*

For Haitian art, the authentic vernacular painting of the race, lulled

---

*It has been admirably told by Selden Rodman in his book *Renaissance in Haiti* (Pellegrini
& Cudahy, New York), a long and thoughtful essay which traces, with the help of numerous
plates in colour and monochrome, the sources of the phenomena and examines in detail the
work of the individual painters. It is one of the most lucid and readable books on an artistic
movement that have appeared for a long time and one which, in its explanation of the tie-up
between primitive painting and the history and social and political trends of Haiti, furnishes
invaluable sidelights on the whole Republic.

by official ignorance of its existence and the indifference of the *élite*, was not dead, but sleeping. The *élite*, faithfully reflecting in this their equivalent in the French provinces whose appreciative scope stops dead at Ingres or David, are chary of acknowledging anything in art that differs from the academical standards of a provincial *bourgeoisie*. The aversion of the Mulatto aristocracy is increased by the obvious affinities of these paintings with the forbidden, the would-be-forgotten theme of Africa. For atavistic survivals of the plastic formulae of Dahomey are clearly detectable, and much of the wood carving displays uncomfortable reminders of Ashanti. The policy of the present government, in line with its general tolerant attitude to Afro-Haitian tendencies, has bestowed its support on the move-ment. But the wealthy men of Pétionville reserve their approval, and (which is more to the point) their money, for paintings that resemble more nearly the standards of the Paris *Salon* in their student days fifty years ago. Haitian primitive art thrives almost entirely on the encourage-ment and the purchases of foreigners, and of a handful of Haitian intellectuals.

Fortunately, the artists belong, by the very nature of their work, to the humbler strata of Haitian life – cobblers, bakers, tailors, part-time Houngans, and so on – and their modest financial demands are amply satisfied from this source. The great success of their work at the Unesco exhibition in 1947 and of those paintings which have been shown in New York, and the astonishment of travellers in Haiti have assured them the respite from financial worry that creative work demands. The *Centre d'Art* is a permanent exhibition of their works and, if they choose, a studio for them to work in. It is also a meeting-place from which they can draw encouragement and, on occasions, advice. Under the wise direction of De Witt Peters it has become not only an institution that enables these artists to live and work, but the impulse that has unleashed the entire Haitian artistic revival. Its opening was, for the Republic, a miniature Fall of Byzantium. Rodman records the reaction of André Breton when, on a visit to the island with Wilfredo Lam a year after its inauguration, he bought a number of Hyppolite's paintings. 'This should revolutionize French painting,' he is reported to have said; 'it needs a revolution.'

They are astonishing pictures. The influences that lie behind them are manifold and diverse. The dwindling hangover of African traditions, the painted drums and banners of Voodoo, the obsessive, *kris*-like writhings of the serpent of Damballah, the multi-coloured plumage of the globe-shaped Congo charms, the heraldic and geometrical precision of the maize-flour *vévérs*, and the horned head-dresses, the bats' wings and the great animal masks of carnival are some of the most apparent. To these must be added the sleek formalism of religious oleographs from Europe and Latin America, cinema posters, the covers of dime-magazines, and the omnipresent portraits of the Haitian heroes. These things are all registered and remembered in brains that abound already with the miracles of Voodoo and Wanga and Christianity and the deeds of the great Lwas, the *loups-garous*, Haitian battles, zombies and African fairy-tales, while all round them, as a permanent and unconscious background, lie the mountains, the forests, the intricate forms of the leaves, the sea and the luminous thin atmosphere of Haiti.

The pictures that emerge from this maelstrom of currents prove once more the overwhelming primacy in the Haitian mind of the imaginary world over the real. Less than a quarter of them are recordings or trans-positions of what lies before the painter's eye, and portraits are scarcely attempted. There is a profound unconscious wisdom in this choice of themes, a true feeling for the limitations of their scope, and a reluctance to force it beyond itself into alien channels. One has the feeling, too, that many of the landscapes – the cross-roads or crowded markets or those wooded mountain-sides with their dazzling angular scaffolding of roads – are inventions or memories. The others are all, as it were, literary: the recording of a great event in Haitian history, as in the case of Philomée Obin – a procession of heroic rebels, the funeral of a patriot, an historic incarceration, a ball – or an imaginary scene drawn from religion, mythology, folklore or magic. Once the subject is chosen, nothing – absolutely nothing – daunts these artists, and the paint is applied with the strength, conscientiousness and diligence of a grown man, and all the intrepidity of a child; and, with regard to any academic rule of thumb, with a flair for the combination of colours and a pristine and almost miraculous heterodoxy that make the observer gasp.

What is it in these primitives, apart from the bewildering fearlessness in the application and the juxtaposition of colours, that gives one such pleasure? Much of it comes from delight in the fact that the painter has not been compelled with gritted teeth to break the shackles of proportion and linear perspective. It comes from his very unawareness of these bonds, from the fact that he is unfettered, free, has never worn chains and does not know that they exist.

These painters reflect the brilliant colours of their habitat, and their pictures are filled with an aura that appertains to the worlds of dream and nightmare; even if it is only a picture of a plate of tropical fruit by Cédor, or a fish stretched on a dish of sliced vegetables by Bazile, or a barnyard scene by Auguste where the animals cluster like prehistoric cave figures. Many of the group pictures – market-places, wakes, Voodoo ceremonies, *bamboches*, the pursuit of runaway slaves – are packed with tiny figures placed among hills and trees and stilted palm roofs, as though they had been cut out and glued on, so immobile are they; or so agitated that each animal and manikin is whirling, leaping or gesticulating in an epileptic and independent access of activity which has suddenly been frozen into silence and immobility by the baleful stare of Medusa. Such are the pictures of Rigaud Benoit, André Bouchard and Wilson Bigaud. Very often the themes are religious, legendary or hermetic or drawn from the *mythos* of Black Magic. The bodies of angels project through coal-holes in the clouds, archangels fly by on magic carpets, the Blessèd Virgin appears transfigured in the sky; serpents writhe; a mermaid-tailed minotaur, by Gourgue, coiled among the ironmongery of Voodoo on a grey table in a green claustrophobic chamber, fires white cataracts of light from its eye-sockets; a wizard or a Houngan, ensconced among his triangles and magic circles, conjures, with an exòrcising pass of his conductor's baton, horned and bat-winged demons from the surrounding cactus forest.

Scenes of violence, as one might expect, are frequent. Horses stamp, javelins fly, blood flows and zombies with their hands bound behind them are driven through the tombs with whips. But the vague dream atmosphere that weighs upon these pictures, and the Gorgon-struck stillness, place their impact several removes from that of mere horror.

The painter Louverture Poisson has unearthed a curious Baudelairian vein of *romantisme du bordel*. A naked Negress combs her hair in front of a looking-glass. A murdered girl, equally naked, sprawls to the floor from her cocoon of tumbled sheets in a room that is littered with an enamel basin, a man's hat, some dirty towels and the tell-tale and blood-stained cutlass. The artist has discovered the technique of unloosing his pictures into movement, and the mood of these pictures is both frightening and tragic. A third picture, a shadowy and aqueous corridor receding in a tunnel of diminishing doors all swinging ajar to a distant and inaccessible garden, is hallucinating in its obscure erotic implications and its suggestions of anguish and disaster.

But the most remarkable of these painters is, without doubt, Hector Hyppolite. His were the frescoes of fruit and birds on the tavern door that first intimated to De Witt Peters the possibilities of Haitian art. Coming from a family of Houngans, and, until the time of his death a few months ago, a desultory Houngan himself, he had been steeped in Voodoo all his life, and he had, to the total neglect of his apprenticed trade of cobbler, always painted. He wandered away to Cuba and New York and, perhaps (for his accounts were always rather vague) to Dahomey and Abyssinia.

His life was one of paint, travel, poverty, love affairs and religion. His house, at the time that we made friends with him, was a trash-roofed shanty by the sea in one of the poorest quarters of the town, half *tonnelle*, half studio, with his easel in the middle of the peristyle. The floor was crowded with canvases, paint pots, drums and Voodoo gear and streamers, tinsel crowns, stars and witch-balls hung from the rafters. The black cross of Baron Samedi stood in one corner, duly bowler-hatted, and with a bucket and a bottle hanging from either arm. Along the crossbar were painted the words *Ecce agnus Dei Dieu Qifer Imedevi*. A tablet nailed farther down bore the words 'St Georges. *Hodie!*' and at the very bottom, among a pile of cannon-balls, another, between a skull and crossbones and the trellised heart of Erzulie, was inscribed with his own initials: H.H. The whole place was penetrated with air and light, and the earthen floor was striped like a tiger's back with the shafts of sunlight that slanted through the bamboo walls. A little *sobagui* behind a partition contained a painting of his crowned and fish-tailed patroness and *lar familiaris*, Maîtresse la Sirène, who, with St John the Baptist, was his guiding numen. A model sailing ship, dedicated to Ogoun Agoué, projected from the wall, and outside, on the narrow stretch of sand by the lagoon's edge, stood the skeleton timbers of a full-sized sloop half-way through building. He explained that when it was completed he intended to travel about in the realms of his divine spouse, the water-goddess. In speaking of these matters the expression of his distinguished features abandoned their cast of diffident and scholarly abstraction and the eyes behind the gold-rimmed glasses kindled for a moment into enthusiasm. His face can best be described by saying that it looked as though it belonged to a member of the Huxley family mysteriously transformed into the blackness of coal. Like coal, it offered to the light a series of smooth and glittering facets.

We determined, at the risk of skipping a few meals at the end of our journey (when financial shock-tactics, anyway, would have to be employed to rectify our dwindling supply), to buy one or two Haitian primitives. For a very few dollars, I became the owner of a beautiful Wilson Bigaud, the *Mango Thieves*, and Costa bought three very fine Hyppolites.

Hyppolite is the only one of these painters who does not pursue the realism which is the goal of his colleagues. His paintings are impressionistic and full of movement and, alongside the massive solidity of his central figures, of a fluid and sinuous quality that the others lack. And they are, without for a moment crossing the primitive borderline into sophistication, much more subtle in colour and treatment. Some of them are pure decoration and design – rich proliferations of leaves and hibiscus and convolvulus, for instance, twining round birds' nests that are arbitrarily tilted to display the little family of birds inside, or the three white eggs, while colibris hover in the threshold of the pistilled trumpets. The ease and the balance of these sheaves and swags and panoplies of vegetation (painted in Nile green, perhaps, and russet, maroon and slate grey) must surely derive from the Houngan's expertness in marshalling the complicated and beautiful maize-flour emblems of the Lwas. A poetical discipline – the poetry of the idyll, the epic or the *Dies Irae* – focuses the mood of dream or nightmare into visions of celestial and Hadean significance. The decorative jungle withdraws to the edge of the picture to reveal the grave and monolithic gods in conclave, their almond eyes gazing from the sable arcs of their eyebrows with the black intensity of Byzantium and Ethiopia. A black lover stoops beneath a chevron of giant hibiscus towards a reclining Shulamite; a lonely beauty, dusky and Gauguin-limbed, meditates under a pavilion of blossom. Leaf-winged and tusked, the genii and the cacodaemons carry the implements of magic through the nocturnal sky; a paladin in a bicorne shoulders his epauletted torso through a loophole of flowers and banners. Cocked-hatted, too, and lance-bearing, Ogoun and Zaka gallop towards us into battle like the Gemini; and outside his hut a Negro gesticulates, while from the twirling palm trees overhead, a great green coconut falls and hangs embedded for a moment in the mysterious air.

As his paintings were inspired and their execution guided by the Lwas, Hyppolite's conviction of his genius was free of the taint of ordinary vanity. Picture after picture by these Haitian artists was placed before us in the *Centre d'Art*, and his soft voice from behind would aid our deliberations in tones of detachment. Each time that one of his own pictures appeared, a thoughtful murmur would escape him, *'Ça, c'est bon; c'est twès bon,'* or *'Achetez plutôt ça, c'est un Hyppolite ...'* Turning round, we would encounter the features of Theodore Gumbril. The very faint smile hovering round the lips and behind the gold-rimmed spectacles was only just detectable.

The art form of primitive painters is directly comparable to the genius for description and story-telling that thrives among the illiterate peasants of Spain and Italy and Greece; a brilliance inherited from innumerable generations which dissipates itself at once when they learn to read and write. The virtue vanishes, and their conversation declines into chatter, or a tissue of clichés, or awkward silence. What, then, is the future of the younger of these primitive painters? Adaptability is a dominant characteristic of the Negro race, and the comparative prosperity secured for them by the recognition of their work brings them into contact with more sophisticated trends. There must be some danger of their experimenting with the *pompier* art forms that receive the approbation of the Haitian *élite*, and of being strangled into inertia or tenth-rate painting by the pot-hooks and hangers, the copperplate and the copy-book maxims of academic painting. But a much greater peril, because it is so much more akin to their own plastic feeling, lies in the work of the great modern painters of Europe. What is to prevent them from imitating, say, Matisse, or straggling into the rearguard of the vast armies spellbound in mimicry of the different periods of Picasso?

How can the fatal apple of knowledge be withheld? If their experimental curiosity or their mimetism impel them to new departures, it would plainly be impossible and wrong to expect them to pass the rest of their painting careers as stuffed *naifs*. Yet what should their future developments be? In their present formula (which, within its limitations, is one of the most exciting discoveries of the century) they are supreme. In any other they are almost inevitably condemned to mediocrity or worse. The predicament is full of unknown hazards. The Haitian Renaissance is only seven years old, and only the coming decades can answer these questions.

You may say that Hyppolite, by dying, has discovered the only safe issue. But he had, by delving deeper and deeper into the territory he had already marked out for himself, found it long before. Urbanism and success only drove him to mine for his buried heirloom of atavistic wealth with more vigour and singleness of purpose. And this, of course, is the right solution to the problem.

Mystical preoccupations even affect the names of the buses. They stood in a row down one side of a square near the market, antique conveyances with wooden superstructures painted all over with green and orange and scarlet. Their names were picked out in large characters: Ste Therese, St Charles Borromée, les Trois Josefs, St Jacques Majeur, Notre Dame de Perpetuel Secours, and, lastly, our own, Ste Rose de Lima (*La Bolide en Action, Toujours en Eveil*).

The road carried us out of the capital, through the concourse of horses and mules and into the country, and ran northwards then as straight as a rifle bullet. The rough surface shook the vehicle so mercilessly that every pothole threatened to break it to bits. Breakdowns and halts for rum-drinking were mercifully frequent, and long after we had stopped, an empty cylinder of fine white dust lingered for miles above the road as though the whole army of Sennacherib were on the march. My two neighbours in the back carried game-cocks on their knees, and, under the temporary roof of interlocking hat-brims, dodging the random savagery of their beaks and the criss-crossing trajectories of spit was an added hazard to the journey. Our presence appeared to be a welcome change and a source of chaff and entertainment. Our fellow-passengers, all of them peasants from Gonaïves or the North, would point us out to their acquaintances as we rattled through the villages. 'Z' *avons twois blancs-là,*' they would shout, indicating three figures that must have seemed as strange in such surroundings as three Negroes would have appeared in the Outer Hebrides. Now and then they interrupted their endless conversation in Créole to turn to one of us and ask, '*Ça va, blanc?*' The blazing sun had soon reduced us all to liquefaction, and the dust that settled in our mouths and throats and all over our bodies had reduced everybody, *blancs* and *noirs* alike, to a spectral uniformity.

For hours on end there was no change in the scenery. The straight vista of road vanished ahead, and the flat sheet of dust stretched away towards mountains as dry and wrinkled as the hide of an elephant. In the neighbourhood of the straggling villages, dusty cane-fields appeared, a field or two of Indian corn and a few plantations of yam and cassava. Then a derelict assembly of huts would fly past, where the old pipe-smoking crones in their scarlet kerchiefs thumped away with their great wooden pestles and mortars, surrounded by a swarm of naked children who waved deliriously as we passed. Lean pigs, their necks bound in pillories of sticks to keep them from breaking through the fences, dispersed squealing at our approach, and moth-eaten donkeys reared up at their tethers with a deafening bray. For some reason their ears had been cut off, a mutilation which lent them the bald, unfurnished appearance of sea-horses. The villages vanished, and the monotonous plain returned. Only cactus throve there, candelabra-cactus growing singly, or assembling into clumps and spinneys of barrenness, or the larger organ-cactus which springs from the plain in great gatherings of pipes. Desiccated weed flourished sparsely among them, and thorn bushes whose roots had withered away. The lightest breath of wind would detach and send them spinning aimlessly along the plain like overgrown globes of thistledown. The landscape was disturbing in its sterility. Only less disturbing than the parched hamlets that rose a few feet above its dusty surface.

In the late afternoon the blank limestone mountains came rolling towards us. Their foothills were clothed with serried lines of maguey or sisal, from which fibre for rope-making is extracted, and whose roots, pulped and fermented, supply the Mexican Indians with their fiery liquor, tequila. The plant springs from the ground like a pineapple, and from its summit radiates a panoply of stiff blue-green spikes. Sheaves of bayonets, they resembled, or wickedly destructive obstacles against cavalry. A small-gauge railway curled in to join us on the other side, and, a little later, the sea, and as we entered the even dustier wilderness of the Artibonite, my neighbour, who had buttoned his fighting-cock into the bosom of his shirt so that only its hateful little cropped head appeared, began to discourse of religion. He had repudiated Voodoo, he said, and along with it (as though it was a subdivision of Voodoo), Catholicism. All that idolatry! The Lwas, the saints, the Virgin Mary, Jesus Christ, he'd finished with all that. 'I only believe in the Old Testament,' he surprisingly went on; all the rest was rubbish. He was, he maintained, a convert to Wesleyan Methodism. 'No more idols!' he said, and fell asleep. An empty rum bottle fell from his lap and rolled about the floor. The head of the cock, oscillating with the jolts of the bus, fixed me with a severe and bloodshot eye, which plainly stated that the same sentiments went for him too. The sun set, and a mood of depression, closely resembling despair, overcame me.

This cheerless region of the Artibonite saw much of the fighting in the Caco Revolt in 1918, when, armed with obsolete weapons, a force of Haitian guerrillas engaged the invading American marines. It was a savage campaign of which the most memorable event was the betrayal to the enemy, at Petite Rivière de l'Artibonite, of the guerrilla leader Charlemagne Péralte. He was stripped naked, and then, as a warning to others, crucified to the door of the American headquarters. The funeral of Péralte in Cap Haitien is one of the best and most celebrated pictures of Philomée Obin.

The headlights, plunging ahead into the night and illuminating the stunted acacia trees at the side of the road, invested our itinerary with the appearance of an interminable journey up the drive of a country house. Between sleeping and waking, we pretended that the welcoming light of a château would soon appear, with the doors flung open to reveal a glowing interior richly equipped with food and drink and the Pickwickian silhouette of our host with arms outstretched: the Comte de Limonade ... But the road went on and on. Every bone seemed to be navigating loose in our dust-caked frames, and all that our sore eyes encountered was an occasional village where not a light glimmered, and the sudden flash of a pair of dog's eyes in the road was the only evidence of life.

We woke up at last in the moonlit town of Gonaïves. It appeared wonderfully empty and noble. Not a figure moved under the high silver tiers of colonnades and the deep velvet of architectural shadows. We walked through the warm dust like somnambulists, dazedly registering the moonlight along the boles of the palm trees, and a painted statue of St George spearing a newt-like dragon in the coping of a wall. We seemed to be the sole inhabitants of a deserted and planetary city.

A Negress unbolted the door of the hotel, and, scarcely less solicitous than the imaginary count, cooked us a meal of Wiener Schnitzel and black beans and rice, and miraculously produced a bottle of Chianti. Black beans and rice are a Haitian staple. Haitian food, if one escapes the peasant horror of salt fish, is not at all bad. We remembered as, in a trance, we dined, the delicious conch, *lambi flambé au rhum*, and the *biscuits de manioc*, the brittle discs of cassava, which we had eaten at the Rodmans' the night before. Drugged with sleep and wine, we were led upstairs by our kindly guardian, who tucked the mosquito nets round us in our little wooden partitions, turned down the wicks of the lamps and opened the shutters to let in the moonlight.

A young Haitian of extraordinary beauty was standing at the bottom of my bed when I awoke. His shoulders and arms were draped with snake skins. Observing without a word that my eyes had opened, he spread all these treasures across the bedclothes and placed a little stuffed alligator on my breast. Many of the skins had beautiful markings, and one, which, judging by its breadth, must have sheathed an enormous brute, was over seven feet long. But our finances were in such a bad state that I had to refuse them. In slow Créole sentences that I could just grasp, he explained that he spent all his time in the woods hunting snakes, and, hearing that some whites had come to Gonaïves, he had walked in to offer them for sale. What about school? He said there were no schools within miles of his village, and nobody there could read or write. (About ninety per cent of the peasants are illiterate, and schools are, indeed, very scarce. Until recently the Catholic Church, by building schools and instructing the peasants, was the only authority that did anything to modify this high level of illiteracy.)

He made himself our guide through Gonaïves. Robbed of the moonlight, it appeared much smaller and less imposing than it had seemed last night. The streets petered out in coral rocks by the sea, and a limestone bluff loomed over it inland. The market was the same African turmoil as in Port-au-Prince: the pitiful mounds of wares, trussed chickens, tethered animals, and market women, crouching in the sun, clad in coarse dresses made out of grain sacks cut up and stitched so that the great stencilled lettering and trade-marks formed symmetrical designs. He showed us the place where Haitian independence had been declared by Jean Jacques Dessalines in 1804.

The Saint Rose of Lima had mysteriously left without us, and we had to wait in the road in the hopes of getting a lift for Cap Haitien. But no car of any description came, and it began to look as though we would have to spend another night in Gonaïves. We sat on, with sinking hearts, on stools under an acacia tree.

The sun had cleared the streets. For three hours the only passer-by was a young girl who shuffled along with a tin of Vim balanced on her head, and her hands hanging idle. Every hour a corporal came out of the barracks of the Haitian Guard opposite, blew a fanfare on his bugle, and withdrew. Somebody had dropped a bull's-eye in the dust in front of my chair, which was the centre of a whirl of activity, the only one in the town, among the ants and flies. We felt, as the time dragged past, that the sun was treading the life out of our souls. What business had we got to be here, anyway? In Gonaïves, lost in the interior of Haiti in midwinter?

At last a car appeared, the *Camion poste*, and, thank heavens, bound for *le Cap*. The driver, a tall, active man armed with a vast pistol slung in a bandolier, threw our luggage in the back with the mail-bags, made room for us beside him on the broad front seat, and away we went.

We drove on through the Artibonite: a landscape of angry desolation. The derelict villages huddled in hollows. Occasionally we overtook a young man riding along on a mule saddled with sackcloth, and women poured water on the green leaves of tiny vegetable gardens that were strangely planted on racks a few feet above the ground. *Pepinières*, explained the driver, for young vegetables which are planted on these raised beds in soil that is specially imported from more fertile regions. The soil of the Artibonite is too salty and poor and rainless for anything to prosper. Flocks of sheep grazed on the weeds among the clumps of organ-cactus. We scarcely saw a church all day, but all the villages were equipped with a *tonnelle* and a dusty cemetery in which the Baron's cross was prominent.

These country regions and the *mornes* of the southern peninsula are the places where Voodoo (and the superstitions of which Father Cosme had spoken) prosper unconditionally. I wondered sleepily whether one of them which I had discovered in the pages of Moreau de St Méry was still in force: the transformation of all who were guilty of sexual intercourse in Holy Week into frogs. Sir Algernon Aspinall, who had been such a helpful authority in all the preceding islands, is disappointing on Haiti. 'The late Sir Henry Johnston,' he says, 'declared that the black points of Haiti had been exaggerated ... The Haitians were certainly in love with military pomp and display, but too much had been made of their revolutions ... He characterized the stories connected with Voodoo worship as "exaggerated nonsense", and ridiculed the "bosh" talked about cannibalism ...' Well, I suppose Sir Henry was attempting to neutralize the harm done by a third English knight in the Republic, Sir Spencer St John. His book, based on the famous *affaire Bizoton* of which

I spoke in the last chapter, consists entirely of lurid accounts of cannibalistic rites. Poor Haiti! It seems to be condemned for foreigners to the two extremes of denigration and whitewash. Like all other countries in the predicament of swift evolution, it deserves *ni cet excès d'honneur, ni cette indignité*. One must thank one's stars for Herskovitz and Leyburn and, now, Rodman. The only danger, a natural and rather noble one which springs from disgust at misrepresentation in the past, is to bowdlerize Haiti, and turn it in print into a sort of black Switzerland or Holland. It is something much more vital and interesting than either. If (as I think they do) obsolescent, superstitious excesses still occur once in a blue moon, there is as little purpose in pretending they do not as in denying the various atrocities that occasionally impair the civilizations of France, America or Great Britain.

I woke up in a completely different world. The road, climbing higher at each twist, was flung like a tangle of white tape over beautiful rolling hills as rounded and smooth as the parts of an anatomy: shoulders, flanks, breasts and thighs. Forests and woods appeared in the valleys like curling green moss in the hollows of a human body. A distant pool was eyelashed with slender trees, and all was soft, gracious and feminine, as though the *Camion poste*, reduced to the size of a ladybird, was scaling the contours of a lovely recumbent giantess. *J'eusse aimé vivre auprès d'une jeune géante* ... The landscape supplied a long-felt want.

Streamside villages of conical huts, *à l'ombre de ses seins comme un hameau paisible*, gathered under the mangoes and the breadfruits in the mild Arcadian ravines. Hibiscus and the pale bells of datura brushed the side of the truck, and the air was loaded with the scent of sweet-smelling trees. Then the road sailed up again on to the clear and delectable highlands of the next mountain ledge. Clematis and morning glory, the scarlet dogs'-tongues of poinsettia, wild maguey and aloes grew at the side of the track. Stalks fifteen feet high issued from the heart of their savage blades to hold aloft great round yellow flowers like miniature suns. Solitary cabins, shaded by a mango or a ceiba tree, appeared on the slopes below us, and little circular granaries of cane and thatch were perched in the air on flimsy-looking stilts which swelled, just below the granary floor, to peculiar globes. They were hard lumps of clay plastered there by the peasants to foil the inroads of rats on the garnered maize-cobs.

The ascending curves raised us high into the clear mountain air, until, from the pass of a lofty water-shed, we looked down into the north of Haiti, and up and away to the mountain ranges that lay all round us in an amphitheatre of massifs. Feathered with woods and darkened in the hollows by the shades of evening, the road sank through succeeding ranges of hills. As we drove on, the driver, deceived by our talking French though we were ignorant of Haitian Créole, asked us if we were from Canada or from Louisiana. We explained ourselves. French people come so little to Haiti, he said, and the Americans seldom speak French. English people and, above all, Greeks, are even rarer birds. He had travelled to the United States and spent some time wandering about in Louisiana. Speaking of the Mississippi and the Negroes living in the swamps, he described the old French houses – *'comme,'* he said with a wave, *'il y avait ici dans le temps'* – the creeks and the *bayous* mantled in weeds and lilies and the trees draped in the grey tatters of Spanish moss; *la barbe espagnole,* as it is called in Haiti. The Negroes, he said, spoke a French patois called Gombo, which he was just able to understand.

He was an extremely intelligent man, and seemed touched and diverted by our preoccupation with Voodoo. He had been a hounci-bossale in his youth, he said, and he regaled us, driving at a hair-raising pace, with an invocation to Damballah. This was followed by a charming song called *Erzulie, né né oh!* and a stirring call to Papa Inglessou.

> *Lo m'songe z'enfants m', m'coeur, m'fait moin mal*
> *Bam couteau!*
> *Bam poignard!*
> *M'pwal' piqué Ibo!*

He was still intoning when, half an hour after nightfall, we rattled into the narrow streets of Cap Haitien.

Our awakening was as grey and depressing as a midwinter morning in Huddersfield. The sky was overcast, and Cap Haitien was lost in a damp sea-mist. From the windows of the old-fashioned hotel where we had found lodging, the great dome of the cathedral and its cluster of attendant cupolas were just distinguishable. How strange and unsuitable is such Nordic weather in the tropics! A gust of wind from time to time blew a hole in the swirling grey film, and a couple of palm trees would appear, or a barefooted Negress balancing a trayful of pineapples on her head. Then the wind dropped, and all was Huddersfield again. We had a queer apocalyptic vision of the interior, visible through the open windows, of a Wesleyan Methodist chapel: whitewashed walls, the Tables of the Law, a grandfather clock, a wheezy harmonium and two dozen Haitians droning away at the tune of *Ein Fester Burg ist unser Gott.* In their midst I distinguished my cock-fighting neighbour from the St Rose of Lima.

The Cathedral was a rather fine lofty Louis XV building of pilasters and semi-circular arches and marble slabs under the misty concavity of the domes. We examined the usual ferocious statue of Dessalines in the centre of the untidy square. Next to it lay a memorial of tremendous national import. *'Honneur et gloire,'* ran the inscription, *'aux martyrs, Mackandal, Lacombe, Ogé, Chavannes qui furent éxecutés sur cette Place d'Armes; à Boukman dont la tête y fut exposée et aux milliers d'Esclaves revoltés qui furent pendus. A ces héros de la Liberté, Reconnaissance.'* For this, in French colonial times, was the emplacement of the gibbet, the wheel and the block, and all the country surrounding *le Cap* speaks of the terrible and heroic events that led to the Independence of Haiti.

The earlier place-names and events, though important in themselves – the reef at Petit Anse where Columbus's flagship, the *Santa Maria*, went aground and sank; the site of the fort built from its timbers, which was the first Spanish building in the New World; the scene of his meeting with Guacanagaric, the cacique of the Arawaks of northern Haiti; the later battles of the buccaneers – all these fade into insignificance before the stupendous doings at the beginning of the last century. The north has monopolized most of the great happenings of Haitian history, and *Le Nord* is always mentioned in a different tone of voice to the west and south. Port-au-Prince was the headquarters of the more tractable Mulattoes, and Cap Haitien is considered to be blacker, more authentically African, Haitian and revolutionary. The mist had cleared, and our driver of the day before, who proved remarkably learned in Haitian history, pointed across the bay in the direction of the Bois Caiman, where the sacrifice of the pig and the oath of the Maroon Negroes unloosed the first massacre of the whites and the firing of the plantations. Below the mountains stretched the Plaine du Nord and the malarial coast where Napoleon's armies had melted away. *Le Cap* itself, at the approach of the French fleet, had been set in flames by the grim and determined Christophe, so that when General Leclerc and Pauline Bonaparte landed, the town was a smouldering ruin. The port was the scene of Rochambeau's atrocities, and the same mountains had echoed to the howling of the bloodhounds with which he hunted the straggling guerrillas.*

* I came across a faint but interesting survival of this business of hunting runaway slaves with specially-trained dogs – a practice that occurs with surprising frequency in the history of the Antilles – in one of the Windward Islands. 'Fido's such a clever dog,' our hostess observed after dinner, 'he can always tell when a black man's hanging about, even in the dark; he just goes on barking until they leave.' Roused by the sound of its name, an appalling brute materialized at her elbow, and lowered a heavy Bismarck-like head into his mistress's mauve lamé lap. My sympathies immediately went out to his nocturnal quarry. 'But,' she went on, 'he never makes a sound if a white person comes up the drive. Not a sound. Does 'oo then, clever boysie-woysie?'

Somewhere in the same region lay the house where Pauline had lived during the campaign. She conducted herself, it is said, with a frivolity which incurred, on her return to Paris after Leclerc's death with General Humbert as her lover, the sharp censure of Napoleon. Following the direction of the driver's forefinger, we were just able to make out the steep outline, perched on a peak in the distant sunlight, of Henri Christophe's citadel.

We called at the *Centre d'Art* of Cap Haitien and spent a pleasant hour with the grave and charming Philomée Obin and the group of younger painters there. Much of their work, like the punctilious and beautiful primitives of Obin himself, we had seen in Port-au-Prince. Then, making my way to the outskirts of the town, I visited an elderly *savant* who is entirely immersed in the archives of Haitian history, M. Villardouin Lecomte. Books and papers were littered on every table. Seeing that I was interested in the same things as himself, he allowed me to return in the afternoon and browse among them at leisure. He sat under a fine portrait of President Boyer with his single gold ear-ring, and explained each new document as it appeared – the letters of Leclerc or Christophe, ancient gazettes and decrees and a quantity of old coins and maps and almanacs. One of these marked the estates of the pre-revolutionary land-owners of the district. Many of their names had associations quite un-connected with Haiti – d'Estaing, Gallifet, Fouché, Montauban, le Vicomte de Choiseul, and, most evocative of all, Villiers de l'Isle Adam. Could this vanished sugar-planter have had any connection with the kings of Cyprus or with the author of Axel? Or, were that possible, both? My host shrugged his shoulders. They were all killed, he said, wiped out in the great August massacre of 1791. It was hard to tell whether pride as a Haitian or regret as an antiquarian and a student of history were dominant in his voice.

He gave me, as I left, a piece of random information that filled me with perhaps exaggerated pleasure. We were talking of the Créole patois. The Haitian word for hibiscus is *choublac*, and I asked him how it came to have such an odd name. His eyebrows went up. Didn't I know? It was the word the old English buccaneers had used, because they were accustomed to blacking their shoes with hibiscus. Picking a blossom from the wall of the courtyard, he gave it to me. I rubbed the beautiful flower sacrilegiously on to my shoes, and, sure enough, a purplish juice ran out of the crushed petals and dried on the leather in a shiny black varnish.

At Joan's instigation, we wandered, towards the evening, through the narrow streets of projecting beams and upper storeys to the cemetery. The usual emblems of the Baron and of Maman Brigitte, smeared with the smoke of offerings, stood in the centre of a forest of ornate tombstones.

A little six-line poem marked the resting-place of the hero of the Caco rebellion. It ended –

> *Face à l'Américain, lui seul a crié halte;*
> *Découvrez-vous devant Charlemagne Péralte!*

The mountains rushed steeply up into the forest behind the cemetery, and under the trees an assortment of headstones, crosses and coffins were enclosed in the fence of a humble undertaker's establishment. A signboard advertised the identity of the owner. At the top was painted a little white tortoise, and at the bottom a death's head. Between them were the words *Enterrements. E. La Tortue*, and then, in larger letters, *L'ami des morts*.

After a steep ride through the sodden woods, we emerged into blinding sunlight and the Citadel appeared before us above the treetops.

I was prepared for something remarkable, but not quite for this formidable Bastille. The forest wavered some distance up the peak of the Bonnet d'Evêque, and then ceased. The rock continued the line of ascent until the main bastion sailed up into the air, aiming at the only approach a sharp angle like the bows of a great stone ship. It soared into the sky to a very great height; to such a height indeed that gazing up at the battlements momentarily filled us with vertigo. It is difficult to believe that anything so essentially a part of the Dark Ages could have been built during the last century, for no castle on the Rhine or the Danube or Calabrian fortress of the Hohenstaufen is so uncompromisingly feudal, stern or precipitous. The weathered rock of the blank walls and the colossal perpendicular bastions look as though they had stood there for a millennium. The vast size of the thing, its brooding impregnability and its atmosphere of inviolable strength quite literally, and for some time, rob the beholder of speech.

After the sunlight, the inside of the fortress, isolated by walls ten feet thick and a hundred feet high, was piercingly cold and dank, and, until the eyes became used to the shadows, almost totally dark. Our footsteps raised echoes along the gloom of the cellars and the dungeons. Looking down into cylindrical cavities, we could see thousands of cannon-balls faintly glowing like kegs full of caviar. Dungeon followed dungeon, and the tiers of galleries, thirty feet wide and a hundred and fifty in length, commanded through their embrasures a landscape that grew smaller in detail and more distant with every mounting step. Broad flights of stone ascended from tier to tier until we came out on to a roof that seemed to be hoisted into the heart of the wind and the flying clouds. We were on the edge of a large aerial parade ground which, considering its lack of any surrounding wall, must have been a frightening place for military exercises. A Haitian student sitting on a cannon told us that it was Christophe's custom to drill platoons of his troops here. To test their discipline, he marched them now and then clean over the edge. I have found no written verification of this extraordinary tale, but, apocryphal or not, it is an illustration of the type of myth that surrounds this figure. Over they went, the student said, and a twirl of his forefinger illustrated the descending arc of the uniformed insects as they spun down into the gulf.

But Henri Christophe needs no rhetorical gift to supplement his biography. Everything he did was on the same exaggerated and titanic scale. A giant himself and possessed of enormous physical strength, he proved a very capable and quite fearless general throughout the War of Independence. The destruction of Cap Haitien (where, as a young slave, he had been a waiter in an hotel) gives an idea of the lines on which his mind worked. He sprinkled his kingdom with palaces, many of which, including the palace with three hundred and sixty-five doors, were never completed. During the building of the citadel, the people of the north were, temporarily, virtually re-enslaved, and it is a popular saying in the island that each of the great blocks which they hauled across the mountains was paid for by a human life. It was built 2,500 feet above the sea, as a stronghold against the return of the Napoleonic armies, and the castle was capable of garrisoning ten thousand troops. Hundreds of cannon were mounted. Storerooms for food and cisterns for drinking water and magazines of powder and shot were built to withstand a siege of several years.

When one reads of Christophe, of his executions, his tyranny and his palaces, the creation of his Haitian nobility and the erection of a presidency into a monarchial institution, one is prone to get the man out of focus. He was much more than a despot or a megalomaniac, and his measures were destined for his personal aggrandizement, certainly, but also to wipe from the mind of his subjects the memory of slavery, and to establish the dignity of the Negro race in their own eyes and those of the world. He was a tireless worker and possessed an excellent brain. The Constitution and the mass of Royal edicts which were issued when he had himself declared King Henri I of Haiti in 1811 prove that every detail of the organization of his realm had been minutely prepared in advance. The monarchy was pronounced hereditary, an aristocracy was established, and a heralds' college to matriculate their arms. Ministries were set up, the administration of Justice was co-ordinated in the Code Henry, with a sovereign court and a system of regional seneschalsies. A navy was built and manned, the army and finance were successfully reorganized, hospitals were founded, and agriculture was fostered. He hated Voodoo, as a survival from the time of slavery. Marriage was enforced and Catholicism was established as the State religion. Priests bearing the viaticum to a death-bed were supplied with a guard of honour, and the whole army turned out to escort the monstrance at the feast of Corpus Christi. He set up a State printing press, built schools in the provinces, and summoned a staff of foreign professors to his new Academy in Cap Haitien. Christophe had a passion for education, and his letters prove that he himself had learnt to read and write very adequate French. A governess was brought from Philadelphia for the Royal princesses, and they had drawing lessons from the English painter Evans, who had been an assistant of Sir Thomas Lawrence in London, and now directed the Royal Academy of Art* which Christophe installed in his palace of Sans Souci. He was, until the movement and the widespread interest generated by the *Centre d'Art*, the only patron of the arts in Haiti.

But although the kingdom prospered under his rule, his despotism, and the curtailment of liberty that was the corollary of his attempt to turn Haiti, overnight, into a world power on the European scale, brought about his downfall. Repeated insurrections broke out, and, as a Negro and king, he was the natural enemy of Pétion, the civilized Mulatto republican (and friend and ally of Simon Bolivar in his fight for the freedom of the South American states), and of his successor Boyer, who in turn ruled the other half of Haiti from Port-au-Prince. After a nine years' reign, this combination of internal and external forces finally disintegrated his kingdom and caused his death. In the inner courtyard, a small white tomb and a pile of whitewashed cannon-balls mark the place where his body, carried here from Sans Souci, lies buried. A bronze plaque bears his device: *Je renais de mes cendres*.

The roof of the citadel extends for acres round this central well, and here and there the caretaker has cultivated vegetable gardens among the battlements. Seeds, blown by the wind, have found lodging in the cracks of the stones, and produced a small wilderness of weeds and flowers. Everywhere, among the thistles and dandelions and pimpernel, old bronze cannon lie prone. Only a few bear the crowned H of Christophe. The others must all have been captured at some period from the various European powers in the Caribbean. Lion-mouthed and dolphin-swivelled, they are embossed with the arms of Aragon, Castile, Navarre and Leon

---

* A number of extremely interesting portraits of contemporary Haitian notables by this school – so dirty, alas, that some of them are hard to make out – hang in the National Museum and the Chamber of Deputies in Port-au-Prince.

surrounded by the chain of the Golden Fleece, or with the lilies of France, and with gorgons and radiating suns. A British gun, dated 1742, is adorned by the Royal Arms with the Hanoverian inescutcheon, and farther along the barrel, by another coat under a ducal coronet: three lozenges within a bordure quartering an eagle with wings displayed, with the motto *Spectemur agendo*. Searching, months later, for the identity of these arms, I discovered that they could only have belonged to the Duke of Montagu, to whom, in 1722, George I had made a grant of the Windward Islands. Four years before, the King of France had made a similar grant to the Marshal d'Estrées. Both of them sent out expeditions to colonize their estates, and the two parties came to blows in St Lucia and St Vincent. The Duke's gun must have been captured in some skirmish by the Marshal's men before the islands became neutral at the Treaty of Aix-la-Chapelle, six years after the gun was cast in London. It would then have been brought to Sainte Domingue by the French Fleet, and here, during the revolution, have fallen into the hands of the revolted slaves of the north to be finally dragged up to the Citadel by the myrmidons of Christophe.

Lying on my stomach, I gazed down the expanse of wall to the point where it joined the rock in a green constellation of banana trees. The Bonnet d'Evêque is the highest peak in this particular range, and the forested mountains, seen from above, rolled away like a relief map. Here and there the shadow of a cloud, twisted out of shape by ravines, floated across the upheaval. Disturbed by my presence, a kestrel peered up from his hole in the wall, and then plunged down like a plummet towards the treetops. The air trembled in the heat, and to the north the distant line of sea could only be distinguished from the sky by the dim outline of the island of Tortuga, the most notorious haunt of the old buccaneers and filibusters in the whole of the Caribbean. The kestrel returned and flew past the keep with its flagpole and the languid Haitian flag, and dropped down the other side. I got up and joined Joan and Costa in one of the gun galleries, and descended through the chill depths of the Citadel towards our wilting horses. *Si monumentum quaeris* ... I wonder which is the more apt memorial to the genius of Henry Christophe – this great martial acropolis, or the ruined palace, miles below, of Sans Souci?

The tropics are merciless to ruins. So savage is the onslaught of the rain, the creepers, the insects and decay, that dwellings which are abandoned for a single year have the appearance of centuries of dereliction. But something uncompromisingly stubborn in the fabric of Sans Souci has redeemed it from this dateless anonymity. From a distance, the great staircases, converging like a truncated pyramid, lend it the appearance of an Aztec or a Maya ruin, but with every advancing step through the wooded valley, the columns and arches and balustrades become clearer and assign it more unmistakably to the heroic era of its construction.

The drive leads through great gateways of clustering pillars and sentry boxes past the white Palladian rotunda of the chapel with its pillared portico surprisingly crowned with a dome that is almost Moorish. And then it leads onwards, in a royal sweep, to the foot of the grand staircase: a portentous colonnaded zigzag that branches at a platform with a romantic rockery, and joins and then branches again in beautiful shallow flights in the fashion of the grand staircase of Saint Cloud. It was this palace, indeed, that King Henry, as he leant over the designer's shoulder, had in mind: a staircase that would outsweep its French equivalent, and a palace that could compare in splendour with that of any monarch in Europe. And he got it. Yellow plaster now peels from the massive ribs of brick and stone, and brambles smother the recumbent pillars. But the main skeleton still stands, and it is easy, in the mind's eye, to reassemble this venerable wreckage into the splendid building that it must once have been, that old prints and paintings prove that it was.

Brother Yves, in the library of Saint Louis de Gonzague, showed me a picture of Sans Souci painted, it is supposed, by one of the royal pages.* The palace, flying with arbitrary perspective above the dome of the chapel, stands among brilliant palm trees and mangoes: an opulent, golden, graceful building surrounded by lawns and pleasances and embowered in trees. In the centre of the façade, pillars support a pediment and a cube of masonry roofed with rose-coloured tiles that rise above the main economy of the palace. Corresponding towers are lifted at either end, and between them, rows of windows look down on a noble promenade which seems to be held aloft by the spreading tributaries of the staircase.

Here, on state occasions and birthdays, the king would receive his nobles and his officers of state. Unlike the pictures of the other Haitian heroes, he is not always smothered in gold braid and feathers. Sometimes he wore a blue cutaway coat, a high white stock, breeches, and buckled pumps: a tall, handsome-looking man, with a complexion of the darkest ebony, of immensely powerful, bland Olympian aspect. The queen would stand at his side with the princes and princesses of the blood. Behind them, anomalous figures among the Negro grandees, Dr Stewart, his Scottish physician, and the Philadelphian governess, could be singled out;

* I searched in an old Royal Almanach for the name of this page. It was Numa Desroches. Could this be the name of the earliest of all Haitian primitive painters? The picture is unsigned.

Evans the painter, perhaps, and sometimes a visiting British admiral, for Christophe's hatred of Napoleon had strongly tinctured his politics with Anglophilia.

A fanfare of heralds' trumpets scattered the birds from the trees. Stepping from gilt and emblazoned coaches, their Serene Highnesses the Princes of Gonaïves and Limbé, carefully gathering their long black and golden embroidered cloaks, proceeded slowly up the staircase. Their tunics were of white satin, their knee-breeches of scarlet silk, and their white silk stockings ended in red-heeled shoes with gold buckles. One hand rested on a gold hilted sword, and the other, ready for the deep obeisance stipulated in the court protocol, held a black hat laced with gold, the brim of which was fastened back with a gold clasp from which sprang five ostrich plumes of red and black. After them came the seven dukes and their duchesses, led by the Ducs de l'Artibonite and Toussaint Brave de la Grande Rivière, and the fifteen counts and countesses, notable among whom were the Counts of Marmalade, Laxavon, Limonade, Mirebelais, Leogâne, Ouananinthe and Yacinthe du Borgne. A host of barons followed, each rank of the nobility in gala robes carefully adjusted to their station; and finally the knights of the Order of St Henry in blue coats, red taffeta vests and breeches, white stockings, green maroquin shoes with square gold buckles, swords slung on green baldricks and hats with a panache of two flowing green feathers. Like Napoleon, Christophe had omitted the rank of marquis from his nobility, as it savoured too strongly of the *ancien régime*; except in the case of the Marquis d'Avelasse, who was, however, also Duc de la Grande Rivière. The Royal princes were *Altesses Royales*, the princesses, *Madame Première* and all the *Mesdames*. As the assembly moved across the grass, the conversation crackled with honorific forms of address: *'Majesté'*, *'Monsieur le comte'*, *'votre grâce'*, *'Monseigneur'*, *'Ah, chevalier!'* ...*

Christophe loved these occasions. Never, indeed, in the melancholy procession from Timbuktu to Harlem can the Negro flair for colour and clothes and pageantry have been crowned with a more splendid or more authentic fulfilment. All the misery of the past generations seemed effaced among the titles and the trumpets and the sound of saluting cannon; a noise which now subsided as the court musicians, seated under the trees, tuned their violins and their 'cellos ...

The end of this colossus was as tragic, in its way, as that of Toussaint L'Ouverture in his dungeon among the snows of the Jura. His subjects

---

* At the dissolution of Christophe's kingdom, this tropical Almanach de Gotha seems to have vanished completely. Robbed of his determination and his iron will, none of these ephemeral honours remained. Today there is not a trace of them.

were in rebellion and his enemies were threatening the kingdom when he was suddenly struck down by paralysis. As he lay in canopied immobility at Sans Souci, the news spread through the kingdom that he was actually dead. His European doctor could not help him, so an African Houngan was called, who massaged him for many hours with a mixture of rum and red pepper. Putting on his regalia of white and gold and blue, he contrived to walk to the front of his palace. His troops were assembled for review, and a large concourse of the people, summoned to see that the king was still alive, waited in silence. He made a few steps towards his charger, intending to mount it and receive the salute of the troops and populace. But, still a yard or two away, he suddenly crumpled up and rolled between his horse's feet. It was the end. He was helped back into the palace, where, deafened by the noise outside the windows, he took a pistol that was ready loaded for such a contingency, it is said, with a silver bullet, and fired it through his heart.

The kingdom collapsed. The enemy was triumphant everywhere, and in a few days the streets of Cap Haitien were resounding with cheers for Boyer, the Mulatto president. Some faithful servants carried the king's body up the mountain-side and buried it in the Citadel in secret. The crown prince was assassinated, and the queen and the princesses, fleeing the country under the protection of the British admiral, Popham, found refuge in London and finally, after a long, impoverished hejira, in Pisa. Prince Ferdinand, the last of the dynasty, later expired in Paris in the utmost misery.

Little now remains of the mosaic floors, and the panelling of precious Haitian woods has been torn from the walls where the tapestries and portraits and the great French looking-glasses used to hang. We followed a little Negro, his bare feet pattering over the flagstones, through derelict saloons and halls and libraries where the evening shadows were assembling. The palace is open on all sides to the weather, and anybody can wander through thresholds from which the doors have vanished. Grass flourished everywhere, and a sound of birds was audible in the rafters overhead. Behind the royal stables, a stream fell in little cascades under the archways of the breadfruit and paw-paw trees, and in the centre of a lawn the branches of a great star-apple tree, under which the king used to hold council and deliver justice, opened its great umbrella. A pedestal supporting the white marble bust of a woman who might be a heroine of Chateaubriand now moulders there romantically under the leaves. A long colonnade on the garden-side of the palace runs along a terrace. The lawns descend in unkempt stages to the gloom of a valley where everything, in this last moment of daylight, glowed with colours that dwindled as we watched them, and died. Large white moths flew past, and the last shoals of crimson faded from the mackerel sky. The fireflies kindled erratically against the dark foliage of the mountain-side, and the song of the crickets and the frogs grew louder, while the broken arches around us signalled through the dusk more legibly than any of the sonnets of Du Bellay or the engravings of Piranesi, their obsolete messages of grandeur and decay.

The lives of these great Negroes of Haiti (and, above all, their deaths), the ferocity of their battles, the pinnacles of power that they achieved and their ineluctable disasters unroll with the tragic inevitability of the Atridae; and the atmosphere through which these trajectories soar from slavery to the throne thickens as the curves ascend into a mould from which there is no escape: the despotic solitude, the overclouding of their lustre in the fumes of conspiracy, the last blinding flash of the tyrant's fall and the final dark whirlpool of bloodshed. It is the unbreathably heroic and doomed air, heavy with magnificence and horror and the grotesque, that weighs on the pages of the *Duchess of Malfi* and *Tamerlane*. It is scarcely astonishing, one reflects, that these tremendous figures who lived and acted little more than a century ago, still obsess the imagination of the whole of Haiti; especially when it is remembered that the last outcome of all their gestures was not the destruction of states and empires, but the final victory over slavery and the birth of a free republic.

Listen to Dr Dorsainvil's account of the death of the Emperor James I of Haiti, Jean Jacques Dessalines; an event which was to prove a model for the end of several subsequent rulers –

Surrounded by a feeble escort and revolving in his mind projects of vengeance, the Emperor arrived. Suddenly a voice cried, 'Halt! Surround him!' and soldiers rose from the bushes and made a ring round Dessalines. But respect and fear prevailed, and nobody obeyed the officers' order to fire. 'I am betrayed!' the Emperor said. He struck at those round him with his cane, shot a soldier dead with his pistol, and attempted to withdraw on his tracks. Then Garat fired a tremulous shot that only struck the Emperor's horse, and Dessalines and his mount rolled together on the ground. The Emperor struggled to free himself, crying, 'Come to my help, Charlotin!' Charlotin, leaping from his horse, had seized Dessalines round the body when a hail of bullets mowed them both down.

A terrible scene ensued. The Emperor was stripped of his clothes and his arms, his pistol and his sabre were stolen. The fingers were hacked from his hands in order that the rings might be more easily removed, and Yayou had him laid out on a stretcher of rifles. 'Who would think,' he sneered, 'that only a quarter of an hour ago this miserable little wretch made the whole of Haiti tremble!'

While they made their way, drunk with joy, to Port-au-Prince, the body of the

Emperor was allowed again and again to fall, and the crowd hurled themselves on it and stoned it and slashed it to bits with their sabres. When, half an hour later, they threw it into the middle of the Place du Gouvernement, the Emperor was no longer recognizable. The skull had been beaten in, the hands and the feet cut off. For hours he was left there, frequently stoned by children who were encouraged in their violence by their seniors.

When evening fell, an old mad woman called Desirée put the bleeding remains of the Emperor in a bag, and carried them off to the Inner Cemetery....

The idea of a monarchy cropped up again in the middle of the century, when an illiterate and not very intelligent Haitian called Soulouque made himself Emperor Faustin I in 1849. The fact that this strange event took place so soon after Louis Philippe had been driven from his throne, when crowns were still shaking on most of the royal heads of Europe, is another illustration of the entirely individual trend of Haitian politics. But, except for his tyranny and his executions and the vast nobility that he created – four princes, fifty-nine dukes, ninety-nine counts, two hundred and fifteen barons and three hundred and forty-six knights, to be exact – the fantastic splendour of his coronation and the showers of medals, crosses, ribbons and stars that he scattered among his subjects, he was a feeble version of Dessalines and Christophe. He ruined the economy of his Empire and finally lost the support of the whole country. The usual conspiracies began, and he only avoided the inevitable murder by escape. Trollope, on his West Indian travels, encountered him in Jamaica on his way to obscurity and death in exile.

A last, faint and rather comic echo of these emperors and kings occurred in the 'twenties of this century. A rather simple-minded N.C.O. in the U.S. Marines, called Faustin Wirkus – a man of Polish origin – was stationed, as commander, on the small Haitian island of Gonave. On the strength of the similarity of his Christian name with that of the Emperor Soulouque, the islanders, at the instigation of a very intelligent Mambo, persuaded him that they proposed to regard him as their king. I think he was actually crowned. Gratified by the deference, real or simulated, by which he was surrounded, his rule was very much milder than the normal rigour of an occupation, and everybody was happy. The white king of Gonave died some years ago, and his daughter is now married to the painter Louverture Poisson.

Compared to our other island sojourns, we had stayed so long in Haiti that our departure was almost a deracination. Acquaintanceships had begun tentatively to take root, and the mood of departure hung heavily upon us.

We had spent the morning in Morne Marinette, talking, in her *tonnelle*, to Madame Luc la Forêt, a beautiful priestess of Erzulie. It was a very different place from most of the Voodoo temples we had seen. It was whitewashed, spotlessly clean, and, in the sober light of mid-morning, free of the sinister, brooding atmosphere that pervades them at night. The great painted drums were neatly piled and sunlight poured on to the smooth earthen floor of the peristyle. The pillar in the centre was painted in brilliant spirals of blue and white. The houmfor was surprisingly unencumbered with implements – a few frescoed serpents and a painting of St James the Major in polychrome on the blank wall, the silver comb, hair brush and looking-glass of the goddess, the usual crossed flags, little else. Like the peristyle, it was empty and clean. The fastidious and house-wifely scrupulousness in the temple, it appears, is a characteristic of the votaries of Erzulie. In answer to our requests, the Mambo took a plateful of cornmeal, and covered the beaten floor round the pillar with *vévérs*. It was delightful to watch the deft sweep of her hands, and the speed and precision with which the emblems grew – the criss-crossed heart, the swords and flags and sailing ships, the skulls, the serpents and the sickles. She straightened again, patting the white powder from her hands, and a few errant specks that had settled on her flowered dressing-gown and silk turban, and smiled. Her movements possessed a grace and dignity and simplicity of which only certain Negresses seem to own the secret.

The afternoon had lapsed in packing, and the evening in farewells. After dinner we had sat for an hour or two round one of the little metal tables of the *pâtisserie* under our hotel, drinking coffee and hopefully listening; but no far-off beat of drums came to our ears. It was, from a Voodoo point of view, a dead season.

I stayed on alone to write my notes, and, having brought them up-to-date, sat smoking in one of those infrequent moods when one feels entirely quiet and at peace with everyone. Lamps among trees! How beautiful and mysterious they always are, and how beautiful were these, stretching away across the Champ de Mars, along the diminishing pathways with which that expanse of trodden grass is traversed. A national holiday was in progress, and the president's palace at the other side had assumed its festive garlands of lamps. Haitian couples were strolling idly under the lamplit leaves, and the ring of their laughter, every now and then, came floating through the tree-trunks and the statues. A radiogram across the road in the Café Kalmar played *Choucoune* – a lulling and charming sound – again and again.

The reader may remember a couple of oblique and mysterious

references, in the last chapters, to the stranger that had so impressed us, on the night of the play, by his air of deep-eyed and spectral aloofness, his pallor, his fragility and the gypsy-like neglect of his appearance. Turning my eyes, now, from the Champ de Mars, I saw him leaning against one of the pillars of the *pâtisserie*. I must have been in a frame of mind when human contacts occur with ease, for our eyes met, and we exchanged a friendly smile. It was not difficult to introduce ourselves – 'Fermor': 'Clément Magloire-Saint-Aude' – and to sit down again at the same table. Before many minutes had passed, we were embarked on a fascinating and close-knit conversation about French literature of the most diverse kind: Villon, Baudelaire, Verlaine, Heredia, Gide, Dali and Breton, of which my new friend discoursed with a ruminative and mature familiarity. It was difficult after some time to believe that the lights before our table were those of Port-au-Prince, and not those of the left bank of the Seine; still more difficult to believe that he had never left Haiti. And English literature? Yes, he loved it, although, he protested, he did not know it very well. Which of our writers, I asked him, did he prefer? There was no hesitation in his answer:

'Sir Walter Scott.'

And which of his books in particular? He was equally decided: *'Ivan-o-é'*; and for a minute or two the talk revolved round Robin Hood and Sir Brian de Bois-Guilbert. His discourse ranged with an ever-increasing charm and unexpectedness, and after an hour he asked me what my profession was. With a truthfulness that was only anticipatory, I told him, a writer. On what? Well, I said, on the Caribbean islands, among other things. On Haiti? Well, yes. A friendly and commiserating smile spread across his face, and his hand, for a moment, rested on my shoulder. *'Vous allez écrire des bêtises, mon pauvre ami.'* We both laughed, knowing that it was bound to be true. I asked him, in return, what way of life he had chosen. He blew a long thread of smoke into the air, and answered, with a lapidary decisiveness that was becoming familiar:

'Je suis poète.'

Lyric? Epic? Romantic? Symbolist? He shook his head with a slow and negative motion. No, none of those. He was a surrealist. At my entreaty, he recited two of his poems which I found so remarkable and so good that I copied them down next day from his two books* in the public library. Here are fragments of them.

---

* *Tabou* and *Dialogues de mes Lampes.*

Sept fois mon col,

he began

Dix sept fois mon collier.

His eye catching mine, we both laughed again.

Informe, froid
Les yeux sans eau comme la fatalité

And then, in a deep, slow voice –

A l'horizon des fièvres
Pour la voix au bal du Poète
Le poète chant lugubre, au rire de chat,

Le coeur, léché, fêté par les veilles
Dites aux litanies délacées Edith
Le lieu, le buste, au gré de mon reflet

Cloué, incomplet, aux éventails
Dans ma douceur morne.

Torpeur dans mon sang déganté sans amour
Après-midis dénués a tire d'ailes

ending in still deeper tones –

Je descends, indécis, sans indices
Feutré, ouaté, loué au ras des poles.

We sat there talking into the small hours. Next morning, in the aeroplane, I met a dapper little Mulatto acquaintance, to whom I mentioned the poet's name. He smiled tolerantly: '*Magloire-Saint-Aude? Un garçon d'excellente famille.* But he does nothing, nothing at all, and he's always abominably dressed. Nothing, that is,' he continued as his shoulders and eyebrows lifted in a shrug, 'except write those poems of his. *Et il est noctambule dans l'âme.*'

CHAPTER 13

Jamaica

A stupendous and echoing dome of metal swallowed us up, and the roar of aeroplanes landing and taking off was replaced by a babel of English, American, Spanish, Portuguese, French and Dutch as the swarm of travellers from Europe and North and South America and from every point in the Caribbean Sea were slowly churned through the formalities of departure and arrival. Jamaica is in the very heart of the Central American waters, and every air line seems to cross there.

As we penetrated this great enclosure a black nurse plunged, with intimidating briskness, a thermometer into every mouth. As soon as this was removed, a smiling emissary of the Sugar Manufacturers' Association placed in each of our hands a large glass of rum punch, and, as soon as it was empty, another, equally delicious and even stiffer, as though a normal temperature had proved our fitness for the rigours and delights of Jamaican life. Rubber stamps thundered down on to the pages of passports, and customs officers inquired if there was anything to declare – not only the usual things, but stranger commodities. Birds? Insects? Earth? 'Are you quite sure,' they asked, 'there's no earth in the baggage? No?' Reassured, they marked each sordid bundle with a chalk hieroglyph, and we moved along into the orbit of a waiting reporter from the *Daily Gleaner*, who subjected each newcomer to a deft and high-powered inquisition. Light-headed with vertigo and rum, we were driven off down the slender peninsula, and then westward along the shore of the mainland in the direction of Kingston; wondering if the pace of all Jamaican life would be as rapid as this.

It would be idle to pretend that Kingston is an attractive city. It is bigger and uglier than any other town in the British West Indies. The centre resembles the nastiest of London outskirts, and the outskirts are equal to the most dreary of West Indian slums. It was a relief to discover, after a few days, that it is quite unrepresentative of the rest of this beautiful island. The evil streets, the red brick Victorian Gothic, the Chinese general stores, the goitrous and stunted statues, the rusty field guns and howitzers of the First World War placed as memorials in meanly conceived squares, the profusion of chapels dedicated to depressing sects – all these dismal adjuncts told us nothing of the country that we were to encounter outside its walls. But even Kingston had its compensations.

One of these was the obsolete splendour of breakfast, a sparkling still-life that could only have fallen from the volutes of a tropical cornucopia: paw-paw, sour-sop, mango, pineapple, and ice-cold mandarines peeled and impaled on forks were the merest forerunners of a multiplicity of eggs, kedgeree, sausages, bacon, fried banana, a cold wing of fowl, hot rolls, a week's butter ration, and marmalade. It was a breakfast fit for a tropical potentate or a Regency prize-fighter. Thus fortified, I left the pleasant coolness of the South Camp Road Hotel and wandered into the blinding town. The heat soon turned the smart white suit (with which, after humiliating sartorial reverses in Puerto Rico, I had prudently equipped myself) into a sopping envelope of rags.

The strains of a brass band came panting through the air from the garden of the Myrtle Bank Hotel, and I hastened my steps towards that great centre of Kingston social life. The khaki drill of army officers' uniforms, the first, apart from the occasional police, that I had seen in the West Indies, interspersed the white-duck elegance of the swarms of English winter-visitors. Caps with the two sphinx-badges of the Gloucestershire Regiment lay about on tables. The Sam Brownes and shorts and swagger-canes and the rumour of forgotten military terminology lent to this hotel a savour of Shepherd's, the Cecil or the King David. But strangest of all were the musicians. For, against a background of palm trees, deck-chairs, lawns and the noisy transports of a swimming pool – Egyptian scenery, in fact, that is all too familiar – appeared a group of Negroes attired as Janissaries and Bashi Bazouks and Grand Eunuchs. Their plum-coloured tarbooshes were bound, turban-wise, with thick cords of yellow and white. Waistcoats and Moroccan boleros of brilliant canary and scarlet were frogged and braided in elaborate Eastern designs, and, below striped sashes, blue trousers piped with yellow spread their oriental volume, while the calves of their legs and their ankles were covered with dazzling white pipe-clayed spats. Some of them – the 'cello, the violins, the clarinet, oboe, fife, bassoon, and trombone – were seated. The big drum and the double bass players attacked their enormous instruments standing up. Here and there a pair of spectacles reflected the Sunday morning sunlight. It was the most surprising vision, and one that I contemplated with absolute mystification until a knowledgeable acquaintance explained it. The musicians, I learnt, were the band of the Royal West Indian Regiment. Queen Victoria, in the middle of the last century, was consulted about a suitable uniform for this distant corps. She had just returned from a state visit to Paris, and, after a few moments thought, she said: 'You know, like those French ones with red hats and baggy trousers.'

'Zouaves, ma'am?'

'Yes, yes, that's it.' And Zouaves they have remained ever since, puffing away very adequately, in this particular moment, at *Orpheus in the Underworld.*

Kingston is not altogether to blame for its unpleasant appearance. It was intended to be neither the principal port nor the capital of the island. History, the exigencies of trade and the violence of nature have turned it into both.

The original capital which the English inherited from Spain when the island was captured by Penn and Venables during the Commonwealth, was Spanish Town, thirteen miles inland and westwards from Kingston. And the port of the island lay at the tip of the Palisadoes, the slender filament of land down which we had driven from the aerodrome; a barrier which almost separates the harbour and the Bay of Kingston from the Caribbean.

Port Royal, of which only a few buildings subsist, must have been an extraordinarily wicked and absorbing town in the last half of the seventeenth century. 'Babylon of the West' is the epithet of one writer, and 'A gilded Hades where Mammon held sway' another. Its central position between the Caribbean and the Gulf of Mexico turned it into the market and warehouse of the New World and a species of fair in constant session. Merchandise was landed here and bartered to all the races of the Caribbean for 'bars and cakes of gold', a contemporary records, 'wedges and pigs of silver, Pistoles, Pieces of Eight, and several other Coyns of both Mettles; with store of wrought plate Jewels, rich Pearl Necklaces, and of Pearl unsorted and undrilled several Bushels ... beside which ... the purest and most fine sorts of Dust Gold from Guiney, brought by the Negro ships who first come to Jamaica to deliver their Blacks'. Goldsmiths turned these precious raw materials into plate, and sold them to the burghers, all of whom, it appears, were accustomed to eat off nothing but gold and silver. Cups of silver and gold were the ordinary ware of the drinking shops where seamen and buccaneers 'gambled with heavy gold coins whose value no one cared to estimate'. The cups were embellished with 'gems torn from half a hundred cathedrals'. Ordinary 'bearded seamen', the same writer declares, were dressed in the finest silks and loaded with jewellery, and their ears were adorned with heavy gold rings studded with gems. Dagger thrusts were so common that if a man were stabbed, his body would remain on the floor until the dancing was finished. Pirates were hanged on a promontory near by, now overgrown with mangroves. As many as two dozen were sometimes strung up at the same time, and left there as a warning.

A retribution worthy of Babylon was in store for the town, for on the 7th of June, 1692, three earthquake shocks, breaking under Port Royal with a noise like thunder, shook down, sank and overwhelmed almost the whole town. Wharves, warehouses, the sumptuous residences of the planters and traders, the taverns and the stews disappeared in the space of a few seconds. Of the houses and churches, 'the spires only of the latter,' writes Dallas, 'were visible, intermingled with the masts of the ships ...' A frigate, hove down to careen, was righted in a moment by the sudden rush of water and driven over the tops of the drowned houses. The rector* describes 'whole streets being swallowed up by the opening of the earth, which, when they shut upon them, squeezed the people to death'. A number were left with their whole bodies enclosed in this sudden matrix and only their heads projecting above the ground. The scene closely resembles the frescoes of Luca Signorelli at Orvieto. The harbour was afloat with the bodies of people 'of all conditions', rubbing shoulders with the corpses of English and Spanish burghers long dead, who, as though summoned from their shattered graves by the Trump of Doom, had sailed buoyantly to the surface ... *Quantus tremor est futurus!* The descriptions of this, more than those of any other disaster, sound like a hideous rehearsal for the Resurrection. Oddly enough, exactly the reverse occurred in another part of the island where an upheaval of the earth in a few minutes drained the River Cobre of its waters and left vast quantities of the fish to flail their lives out on the slimy soil.

As though this sharp admonition had not been enough, the partly reconstructed town was burnt to the ground a few years later, every single house. A hurricane demolished it again in 1722, and another fire in 1816.

---

* In case a pious student of such disasters should read celestial partiality into his exemption, it must be remembered that a condemned murderer was the only survivor of the eruption of the Montagne Pélée in Martinique.

Another notable survivor of the Jamaican tragedy was a French Huguenot called Galdy, who was swallowed up by the earth and then thrown forth again into the whirlpool.

But the inhabitants had at last abandoned it for Kingston, and the ruins only survived as a base for the Navy. Long before, Admiral Benbow, after his fight with Du Casse on the Spanish Main, had sailed back here to die of his wounds. The town was a haunt of Sir Henry Morgan, and it was to Port Royal that the triumphant fleet of Rodney repaired, escorting their prizes and the captive de Grasse after the Battle of the Saints. The arms of Nelson surmount one of the doorways of Fort Charles, and a nearby inscription enjoins the traveller that should tread in his footsteps here to remember his glory.

To Kingston, then, flowed all the trade of the old port, and the town grew at such speed in prosperity, size and importance, that, during the nineteenth century, the seat of government was shifted here from Spanish Town, and Kingston became and has remained the political as well as the maritime and commercial capital of the island. The benighted planters who ruled the country were too breathless keeping pace with their growing fortunes to bother about anything so unprofitable as decent public architecture. Some of them, no doubt, were people of discrimination and taste; but the others, perhaps the bulk of them, sound pretty terrible. Lady Nugent, the Governor's wife in the first decade of the last century, talks of them slightingly. Halting at the inn half-way between Kingston and Spanish Town, she observed 'a host of gentlemen who were taking their *sangaree* in the Piazza; and their vulgar buckism amused me very much. Some of them got half tipsy, and then began petitioning me for my interest with *his Honour* – to redress the grievance of one, to give a place to another, and so on. In short it was a picture of Hogarth.' Too supercilious and metropolitan, perhaps, but from this and other sources one gathers that quick returns through slave labour, followed by a splash in London, a multiplicity of coaches, and a smart marriage for their daughters were, at this period, nearer their hearts than cultivating the humanities in Jamaica. Only the Nabobs could compete with them in riches. It was to one of these immensely wealthy West Indian heiresses, a Miss Phipps, that Charles Fox, ruined by racing and gambling debts, was packed off by his friends to pay his court; but only as a practical joke, for they assured him that the lady, coming from the West Indies, had a horror of all but the fairest complexions. Poor Fox, cursing his matted black eyebrows, swarthy Stuart complexion and permanently blue chin, arrived in her presence under stifling layers of rice-powder ... The marriage did not take place.

I found it hard to stay away from the Institute of Jamaica. It possesses the best library in the West Indies, far better, even, than that of the priests of St Louis de Gonzaque in Haiti; nearly thirty thousand volumes, all of them beautifully kept, and also, it appeared, every existing work concerning the Caribbean – a far larger and more imposing array than one might think. Stuffed animals and birds and cases of botanical and geological specimens fill another part of the building, and the walls of the basement are covered with portraits of island dignitaries. The old maces of the island's Chamber and the bell of the drowned church of Port Royal are preserved here, and a fine exhibition of old prints of the island. Best of all, I thought, was a series of coloured engravings of the late eighteenth or early nineteenth century, depicting, in the manner of Rowlandson or Gilray, the perils and pleasures that beset a subaltern stationed in Jamaica: the routs, the rum, the yellow-fever and the unsuitable sentimental imbroglios.

I could return to the bosky shelter of the South Camp Road by a roundabout route past the Good Tidings Chapel, the Synagogue, the Chinese Club and the Catholic Cathedral, which is a reinforced-concrete version of St Sophia. The Synagogue, though nothing much to look at, is alone of its species in the whole world, for the fire of 1882 destroyed both the Sephardic Synagogue of the Spaniards and Portuguese – who, impelled by the Inquisition, arrived here in the same fashion as in the other Caribees – and the English-German Synagogue of the Ashkenazim. The two communities, driven together by adversity, pooled their funds and built a synagogue in which they now both worship. So these two branches of Jewry which separated so many centuries ago in the Levant – the Ashkenazim travelling northwards through Russia, and westwards through Poland and Germany to England, and from England here, and the Sephardim migrating westwards with the Moors into Spain, and then, driven forth by Ferdinand and Isabella to Amsterdam, eastwards to the Ottoman Empire or across the Atlantic to Brazil, and then north to the Antilles – have at last met and amalgamated in this West Indian island. Only here, among the coconut palms and the mangoes, does a Henriquez or a de Cordova bow down in worship beside an Eisenstein or a Weintraub. Rothschild and Sidonia unite.

But the shorter way back led through Hanover Street, down the smouldering length of which a dejected and unconvincing brothel-quarter damply blossoms. Here, on the balconies of bars and ramshackle hotels with jaunty names, strapping West Indian girls diffidently conjure the passers-by with their artless blandishments: a dumb crambo of soft whistles and inexpert winks. Some were veterans, others were bluff viragoes, and yet others quite young, but nearly all, for an island with such a high standard of good looks, surprisingly plain. Under the trees that line this milder Babylon of the West a straggling population of sailors or dock workers indecisively moons. The filibusters of Port Royal would not have tolerated anything so dismal as this. Not architecture only, but everything, even these humble delights, has gone downhill.

A number of rum-shops do busy trade round this quarter. In one of them, of which the customers were mostly middle-aged black sailors, I made a habit of halting on my homeward walks. I discovered that it is wiser to choose one place and to stick to it, so that the initial distrust of an alien complexion might with familiarity be gradually relaxed. Though, indeed, colour difficulties were far less inhibiting in Jamaica than in many other islands. I remarked on this to an old sloop-captain who had travelled widely in Central American waters, and now plied between Jamaica and the southern U.S. ports of the Mexican Gulf. I asked him how Jamaica compared with the States. After a pause he said, 'It's much better in the States – plenty better. They've got discrimination there, they've got the Jim Crow laws, they call you a nigger and they call you a jig, but the black folk know where they are, and among black folk life's pretty good. But here,' he waved his arm round the room, 'they tell you we're all brothers, all the same and equal. They put their arm round you and call you a brother, and when you're a child it's all fine. But time goes on, boss, and the buckra, he's way, way ahead, you don't see him no more. But the black man, he stays right where he is. Right here.' He lit his pipe. 'We're always going somewhere. But we never get there.' There was a sound of assent from the others at the table. 'That's right, boss. We're all equal but we ain't *equal*.' I was surprised by this general agreement, though it confirmed feelings that had first occurred to me in Barbados: that our middle course between the French and American extremes – that is, a colour bar that is non-existent in law but in social practice violently alive – leaves the coloured race stranded in a limbo of uncertainty whose invisible frontiers materialize when touched, and only then, into walls of adamant. Being invisible, it is often impossible, without collision, to gauge their distance. The fingers may feel the cool surface of this mysterious masonry within arm's length; or it may seem to recede step by step until, gaining confidence, the adventurous explorer may quicken his pace through the psychological Tom Tiddler's ground, only, in the end, to collide with greater force and retreat with more lasting bruises.

But the fact that, in the West Indies, all the whites live in a privileged fashion, that most of them own motor-cars and pleasant houses, converts the whole white race into an Equestrian Order. Their distinctions and discriminations among themselves are too far from the humbler West Indian to be discernible. Ignorant of the slums and poverty that exist in Europe, they are prone to think that the Negro race has a monopoly of the world's social injustice. Black means poor and White, rich. How can they know that a system operates in Europe which relegates white humanity to the equivalent status of Negro, Mulatto and buckra, as savagely and inevitably as any colour feeling in the West? Unaware of all this, they conclude that they are the only victims of a universal conspiracy. Propaganda has taught the poorer classes in the West Indies to attribute all their disadvantages not to a world-wide evil, from which all races suffer, but to the specific handicap of their colour. The class war becomes a colour war and the propaganda-line is painfully easy.

Places of worship abound. The Church of England, the Catholics and the Jews represent the main religious currents, but a hundred protestant sects flourish in the back streets of the capital, developing, from orthodox Anglicanism, through the Methodist Connection, the Quakers, the Seventh Day Adventists, the Good Tidings and the Salvation Army into the odder revivalist cults of the Shakers and the Holy Rollers and the queer excesses of the Pocomaniacs.

Religious instruction among the slaves of the Church of England planters was, as we have seen, purposely neglected until the beginning of the nineteenth century. When the work of conversion began, some Christian elements were eagerly grafted, as in Haiti, on to the surviving remnants of the religions of Africa. But the African survival was less robust than in Haiti, and Pocomania, in spite of its curious practices, is naively considered by its adepts to be merely another protestant sect. The Trinity, the Angelic host and the company of Saints have won the contest against any straggling deities from the African pantheon. Not one of them remains.

Indeed, in the first barn-like fane that we visited, much of the service resembled an ordinary nonconformist assembly. Hymns were sung by the congregation on the benches and the preacher, sitting on a rostrum, delivered a little homily. 'De Lawd,' he cried, 'is on the telephone. His number is Heaven One. When in trouble, brothers, and sisters, we must dial the Lawd.' He went through the motions of doing so. 'Hello? Hello? Is dat de Lawd? Is de Lawd there? Hello? Hello?' He rattled an invisible hook, and at last, sadly replaced the imaginary receiver. 'There's no reply. And for why, brothers and sisters? For why? *Because I am a sinner and the wires have been cut.*' Repentance, the electrician, had to be called in, but even then the line was unobtainable until Faith, the switchboard operator, had come to the rescue, and at last put him through ... Another hymn was sung, and the first symptoms of oddity appeared when a woman with a white and gold flag danced slowly to and fro before the rostrum, while another near the door rattled a peculiar implement like a thyrsus or a caduceus of plaited cane, from the terminal loop of which hung two rings of wicker. An old woman on the front bench began softly moaning, and then, rising to her feet, rocked slowly about the barn in a mild, rather drunken-seeming trance. An hour passed, and there was little change. But during a moment of silence, our expert ears pricked to the sound of a distant drum. We slipped out into the moonlight.

Trench Town is a labyrinth of slender alley-ways. Warm and sinuous troughs of dust uncoil between tall hedges of candelabra cactus. In the blaze of the moonshine it looks secret and mysterious and astonishingly beautiful. Gaps in these bristling palisades revealed huts of timber and palm-leaf and dusty courtyards: cool and silvery expanses with here and there a donkey or a couple of goats – portentous figures in that brilliant light – munching above the dark pools of their own shadows. The little torch-lit temple that we discovered at last at the end of an arcade of branches was, virtually, a Haitian *tonnelle*.

The single drummer was invisible among the adepts. These, like the *yanvalloux*-dancers of Port-au-Prince, shuffled in solitary evolutions round a table loaded with calabashes and flowers and feathers. The priest, standing beside his altar, gyrated in dervish-like circles, goading the dancers on, and ringing, from time to time, a large bell. He was arrayed in a mauve silk dressing-gown and a coronet of gilded cardboard, and a sparse curling beard framed the lower part of his face. The troop of girls that formed the core of the dancing were all, like houncis, dressed in white, with white Indian-looking turbans. It was plain that the dance would continue interminably, and I was able to inspect at my leisure the equipment of the shrine at the far end of the hut.

Behind an altar adorned with a cross lay a round cement pool like the *bassin* in a houmfor for Damballah Wedo or Ogoun Agoué Arroyo. Suspended above the cross was a board covered with cabalistic inscriptions. An enormous A, inscribed at its summit with a pentacle, bore, upon the two converging bars, the words: 'By Moses and Jehovah Jah Bear reb Aaron', and underneath, in uncouth capitals: 'Peter James John walk with me Daniel Reynolds, set me free.' Upon the crossbar, among a profusion of symbols, and signs of the Zodiac, was written: 'Holy Michael Holy Adonay Archangels and Spirits deliver me.' Another board carried the words: 'Aijel Agoni, Eliaou joena ebreel Eloijela. Mephiniaj Phaon, God of Gods plea for me.' A circle was filled with a number of letters which at a first glance appeared to be Glagolitic or Etruscan, thus:

I gazed in mystification at this assembly of letters, and (to anticipate a few hours) came back next day to ask Daniel Reynolds, the Shepherd (as a Pocomaniac priest is called), what language it was. He told me that it was a runic alphabet that he had invented himself. He wrote it out for me. The inscription transliterated from the disc, reads AQA MY GOD STAND BY MY [*sic*] DANIEL REYNOLDS; the right-angled boomerang in the second line seems to have slipped in by mistake. No more than that, a primitive and purely personal *eon* of gnosis; fascinating, nevertheless, as a symptom of the need for mystification. The pool served for the curative lustrations of Balmism, a form of African bush-medicine based on a knowledge of the properties of plants and leaves. When I asked him if he had any acquaintance with Obeah – black magic or sorcery – he flung his head back with the scandalized vehemence of a Haitian Houngan against whom an imputation of Wanga is levelled. And the Hebrew-looking words – what did they mean? Just words, he said, magical, white magical, words that he had learnt when he became a Shepherd. He did not know what they meant. He made an impression of complete candour, to which his willingness to part with the key to the alphabet lent verisimilitude. So, if this were true, we were back once more in the child's secret palace with its arsenal of corroborative impedimenta – deep, deep down once more in the darkness of Malampia, the *chère petite grotte* of Melanie Bastian, surrounded, in the reeking darkness, by the matted hair, the chicken bones and the mountains of oyster shells ... We must return to the previous night.

Turning from the scrutiny of this peculiar iconostasis, I saw that the ceremony had altered. The gold crown of the Shepherd had been replaced by a lofty turban of white linen like the headgear of a Wallachian hospodar, and a swarm of white-robed devotees were assembled round the central table. All were stationary. The Shepherd intoned a number of prayers from which the Blessèd Virgin and the Catholic Saints were notably absent. Their place was taken by the Trinity, the Apostles, the prophets of the Old Testament, and by Archangels, Cherubim, Seraphim, Dominions and Thrones. Among the other prayers, we were moved to hear the Celestial Host implored to keep kindly watch over the white sister and two white brothers in their midst. As the last Amen died away, the whole congregation leant forward and made a long guttural grunt – an alarmingly animal sound. Recovering with a jerk, the same motion and noise were repeated, and then again and again, until it developed into a violent syncopated roar. With each cry, the devotees jerked forward from the waist, hunching their shoulders back and craning their jaws as each lion-like cry – half-way between a snarl and a howl – rose from their windpipes. For half an hour this savage sound continued, slowly gaining in speed and volume as the minutes passed. Eyes were closing, and it was plain that the trance-like state that ushers in possession was slowly approaching. Every few seconds the Shepherd leapt, with astounding agility, about a yard into the air with a cry that sounded like 'Bo-bo-bo-bo-bo-bo!', a sound made by filling his cheeks with air and expelling it through his thick and flexible lips. A peal on the bell followed each of these leaps, and as the collective numinosity increased, he raised his hands and his face towards the roof and invoked the assembling spirits. 'What are you waiting for, Jesus? Come down, Gabriel; come down, Michael and Moses and Abraham. We're all here, we're ready, what are you waiting for?' The roaring had waxed into an agonized fortissimo; and soon, sure enough, down the celestial beings came.

The speed and the violence with which the crises of possession occurred was as strange as anything we had witnessed in the practice of Voodoo. One after the other of the adepts fell to the ground as though they had been mown down by rifle fire and lay there kicking and writhing and shuddering in desperate pangs. I counted thirty-four at one moment, all prostrate. Their flailing feet raised a cloud of dust. The barking and howling had sunk to a chorus of moans and gasps and sobs as the vessels of possession squirmed and writhed, or, with arms outstretched, rolled over and over. The throes of incarnation were reminiscent of a net-load of fish which has just been hauled out of the water and emptied on the sea-shore. The Shepherd remained upright in this squirming tangle of humanity, leaping and whirling and clanging his bell and summoning, in stentorian apostrophe, the last of the lingering celestial beings from the clouds.

Nearly an hour passed before the congregation were all on their feet again. As we left, they were drawn up in a ragged file before the Shepherd, their white uniforms dirty and crumpled and torn, their turbans awry or lost, the foam drying on their lips. Their eyes were still revulsed in the retreating aftermath of immanence. The Shepherd, as each of his flock approached, rubbed her all over with his hands in a sort of vigorous massage that covered the skull, neck, breast, back, arms, waist and thighs. While this was taking place, the subjects stood docile and patient, shivering slightly now and then. When it was over, they lurched, one by one, wearily out into the lanes. It was about four o'clock in the morning.

Riots, often begun by entirely different parties and sometimes for the most trivial reasons, are fairly frequent events in the streets of Kingston. The town, while we were there, was still in convalescence from a recent outbreak. Frequent glimpses of Mr Bustamante and Mr Manley, the first cousins and bitter political enemies whose factions are as firmly embattled against each other as those of the Capulets and the Montagues in Verona, are constant reminders of this split. What seems very surprising is that Mr Bustamante, the pistol-packing, hard-living and humorous ex-rabble-raising demagogue, whose every word and gesture have an engaging histrionic phoneyness, should be the leader of the more moderate party; while Mr Manley – darker, equally aristocratic in appearance, but whose reserve and poise and purity of speech remind one constantly that he is a Rhodes scholar and a K.C. – should be the leader of the extreme left P.N.P.; as far left, he told us, as it is possible to be, short of revolution and public violence; but (he dropped his low voice still lower to lend emphasis to what he was about to say) entirely unconnected with the Communist Party. He had failed to win a seat in the House of Representatives in the last elections, so had no official platform for his views. I only had one opportunity, and for a very short time, of conversing with this very impressive-looking man, and of appraising his rather diffident and academical distinction. Mrs Manley is English. It is rumoured in Kingston that, as a gesture of protest against colour-prejudice, she would prefer (though there is no actual foundation for it in fact) to be thought of partly African descent. She is a fine sculptress in wood and eagerly encourages the beginnings of a Jamaican artistic renaissance which, although it is a long way behind the Haitian phenomenon, is beginning to produce interesting work.

Mr Bustamante, then, the former riot leader and *enfant terrible* of the island, is forced, by the politics of his cousin, to divert his overwhelming energies from their former turbulent channels into the sluices of Empire and of partisanship of law and order. He champions the cause of moderation and the middle course with a positively incendiary violence. Thanks to the kindness of Miss Esther Chapman,* we spent several hours, on two occasions, with this most disarming of egocentrics. It was a delight to see the sense of drama, that antique faculty so pitifully lacking in the dramatic events of our century, surviving so robustly here. For in Mr Bustamante's unstaunchable flow of bravura, humour, invective and peroration, men and events grouped and regrouped themselves about his own protagonistic centre in an endless sequence of astonishing subsidiary combinations. A splendid *dramatis personae* of Spanish generals, Cuban ministers, Arab leaders, British governors, lords, Secretaries of State, menacing opponents, howling mobs and shy beauties walked on and off the fluctuating scene, a stage which he alone never abandoned, and which extended from the camp of the Spaniards opposing Abd-el-Krim in the Riff wars, embracing police headquarters and street fights in Cuba, New York skyscrapers, and Kingston thoroughfares tumultuous with rioters, to the very curtains of the alcove. I listened in fascination to that slow nasal delivery in the Irish-Welsh intonations of Jamaica from the other side of the whisky glasses. The expressions of those long aristocratic features underlined each change of scene and mood. His face has the form and colouring of an Iroquois chief, and, in repose, the same expression of supercilious aloofness, anomalously backed by a Liszt-like shock of white hair; anomalously poised, too, on a high white collar and white butterfly bow. Leaning forward to repeat exactly what he said to the Secretary of State, he would thrust his cuffs slowly back from sinewy forearms, and his long hands would perform gradual motions of strangulation. In the House of Representatives it was a stirring sight to see this tall and magnificent histrion lope to his place and settle there, searching the roof with his wild eyes as he allowed his torso to fall back in his seat of office with the languor of a tired statesman or of a theatrical knight. Nobody who has seen such a performance can complain that the sense of gesture has entirely drained away from the parliamentary life of the Empire.

Jamaica is bewilderingly prolific in unusual groups of human beings. Amalgamated Jews, Pocomania, Garveyism, the extinct Bedwinites,

* Now Mrs Hepher.

Balmists, Obeahmen, the Maroons, the Rastafari – the list could be still further extended. Some of them, to be sure, possess exact equivalents elsewhere, but nowhere do they exist in such profusion.

None of them is more peculiar than Rastafarism (or the Rastafari), a thoroughly eccentric movement named after the Emperor of Abyssinia. The word is pronounced, by its adepts, Răstăfări, the final *i* sound being long, as in the first person singular and the stress falling on the second syllable.

The Rastafari live in a patch of waste land by the railway in the western slums of Kingston known as the Dunghill – pronounced Dungle, to rhyme with jungle – a collection of huts built of the same flimsy materials as the hovels of San Juan de Puerto Rico. Some of the slightly more luxurious dwellings are composed of the rusting bodies of old motor-cars from which the wheels have been removed. The whole is embedded two feet deep in the ground. The glassless window space is filled in with paper; holes cut in the hood do service as chimneys. The other houses are constructed throughout of cardboard and paper. From flagpoles above these hovels flutter the red, yellow and green tricolour flags of Abyssinia; and noticeboards bear messages in clumsily-formed letters, which say 'Long live Abyssinia' or 'We are Ethiopians.'

Among their other characteristics, the inhabitants of the Dungle are passionately anti-white, and I had been warned by coloured Jamaican friends that it was insane even for coloured people who were not initiates to set foot inside it. It was the refuge of all the robbers and footpads and murderers of Jamaica, and policemen, they said, could only venture there in twos and threes; a real Alsatia. Curiosity, however, triumphed over caution, and I made an intrepid descent.

It was plain to see that the Negroes lounging among the trees and huts regarded this white intrusion with extreme dislike. They looked a terrible lot of people with expressions of really frightening depravity. All were dressed in the most sordid rags, and all equipped with curling black beards. Three boys of about eighteen, of slightly less forbidding appearance, were throwing dice on a biscuit-tin. I asked them for a light and after a pause, to avoid the appearance of haste, offered cigarettes; which, after a pause, were accepted.

'What are you looking for here?' one of them asked. I had thought out my line rather carefully, and answered with what I hoped was a nonchalant unconcern.

'Nothing, thank you. I was just going for a walk.'

'The white folk don't come to the Dungle.'

'Where's the Dungle?'

'This is the Dungle. This is where the Rastafari live. Don't you see the beards?'

'I'm sorry. I've just got off the boat from England, and don't know Kingston at all. What are the Rastafari, and what about the beards?'

Their hostility seemed to waver a little.

'Come inside,' one of them said, getting up. 'I'll tell you.'

The hut was about two yards square and constructed entirely of copies of the *Daily Gleaner* glued together. Three of us sat on the plank bed that filled half the cabin. The owner settled down on the biscuit-tin that he had brought with him. A photograph of the Negus, nursing a bat-eared lap-dog with enormous eyes, was stuck to the paper wall. Underneath it was written in charcoal, 'My one hope. Signed Paul Fernandez'.

The Rastafari, he explained, were Ethiopians, and they had all come to live in the Dungle before going back to Africa and their King – but not, he said, before they had conquered the West and driven away the white men. But, I said, none of the slaves that came to the West Indies were from Ethiopia, which was inhabited by a different, a Semitic race. He waved this aside. 'That's all lies,' he answered, 'that's what the history books say, but the history books are all written by white folks to make a fool of the black men. We're from Abyssinia. We got wise men, and they tell us the truth.' There was no more to be said about that.

There were, he continued, only a few hundred Rastafari in Jamaica – but there were millions in America and millions and millions in Abyssinia, all ready to conquer the white race and make Haile Selassie king of the world. 'Do you stand up when they play "God Save the King"? Well, I don't, no *sir*. I sit down and drive the legs of the chair into the ground.' He made the gesture of doing this with his biscuit-tin. The others grunted their agreement. 'That's right, Haile Selassie is the only king. Long live the red, yellow and green!'

'We don't want no English king, no president of the United States, no bishop, no pope, no police, no white men. You know what we call England? We call it Sodom, the place of the wicked. We want the Negus, Ras Tafari, the Emperor Haile Selassie, the King of Kings and the Lion of Judah, the Elect of God. We want King Alpha and Queen Omega!'

'Who are they?'

'They are the same thing.' I began to understand that Rastafari, like all primitive religions, as Dr Maximilian remarks of Voodoo, is impatient of explanation. I said that they ought to have a soft spot for the English, as we had driven the Italians out of their country and helped the Negus back to his throne. Paul was ready for that too. 'That's another lie the white folks say, to win us over.' But they were not to be fooled. They were going to make war on the whole white race.

'Not the Russians, Paul,' one of the others said.

'That right. Not the Russians. They're good folk and they love Haile Selassie. But on all the rest.' They were all members of the P.N.P., he said: 'All for Manley and Communism.'

'But,' I remonstrated, 'it's not the same thing at all.'

'It's the same. Manley loves the Russians. And he loves Haile Selassie.'

Thereupon they sang, to the tune of a hymn, a political song beginning 'Jamaicans, Jamaicans, one and all, Listen to the clarion call ...' which ended with a chorus: 'It's the remedy for all the ills we see, So rally to the P.N.P.!'

I wondered how pleased Mr Manley would be.

The air in the hut was beginning to smell very strange – a sweetish, vegetable reek that awoke memories of Piraeus and Beirut. I noticed that the boy on the end of the bed was smoking a home-made cigarette as blunt and as unwieldy as an ice-cream cone. He smiled as my eyes fell on it, and waved it in the air. 'It's the wisdom weed, boss,' he said. 'This is what makes us see everything so clear ...' He hospitably rolled me one, and handed it down the bed. I asked him how he got the stuff – didn't the police put a stop to it? They all laughed and pointed to a clump of weeds outside the door that turned out to be, on closer inspection, hemp. 'They can't take that away from us,' Paul said. 'The police don't come here. We smoke it all day.' The Dungle, apparently, is a fanatics' lair, like the refuge of the Old Man of the Mountains and his Hashasheens, in more senses than one.

They had a Dungle King – a sort of stand-in for the Negus – in the past, they said, but he had been hanged for murder some years ago, since when the office had remained dormant. The hill, too, from which the Dungle had taken its name, had been levelled when the railroad was laid – 'The whites pull down the old Dungle,' the smoker tearfully observed, 'so now we got no view of the sea ...'

There was something pitiful about my hosts. They had all three been in jail – two for theft and the third for using a razor in a fight. None of them had known homes since they were ten years old, and not one of them could read or write. The only controlling influence they had ever encountered were the wise men they kept referring to. They pointed one out as we crossed the waste land towards the railway – a shrewd middle-aged man in spectacles, reading the evening paper in one of the half-buried motor-cars. His eyes followed me out of sight with a look of detestation. It occurred to me that his presence there was for quite different

purposes than for the organization of a return to Ethiopia. There is a
strong streak of madness in the Dungle, induced, perhaps, by continual
marijuana-smoking and propaganda as well as by the aid of crime and
disaffection; and the rallying-call of an organization for a return to the
Abyssinian Canaan is as good a means of keeping those poor wretches
together as another. Not one Rastafari, since the birth of the cult twenty-
odd years ago, has ever undertaken the journey to Addis Ababa. I could
not help speculating what the reactions in Ethiopia would be if all the
denizens of the Dungle suddenly appeared there, and whether the Negus
had ever heard of his distant worshippers. Nothing else – except Communism and the P.N.P. – is talked about all day. What a curious, dreamy
and lotus-eating life they lead! Their existence consists exclusively of
dodging the police, singing songs in praise of a monarch who knows
nothing about them, planning the downfall of the white world, drinking
rum, throwing dice and smoking reefers.

I must have been there several hours. The street lamps were growing
brighter as the dusk fell round this pseudo-Ethiopian wilderness. Candles
appeared in the flimsy little huts, making them appear more than ever
like card-houses that a breath of wind could demolish. The outlandish
banners fluttered in the evening breeze.

A group of bearded Dungle-men, a really abominable-looking gang,
were heading for the town on some dubious errand. Their passing
reminded me to ask Fernandez about the beards.

'We grow the beard,' he said, 'to look like our Emperor.'

'But why haven't you got a beard?'

I wished I had not said it, as he was all at once utterly downcast.
He caught hold of my hand and ran it across his smooth cheek.

'I can't grow no beard,' he said sadly. 'But, boy! I'm beard-minded.'

The road climbed higher and higher round the flank of Mount Diabolo
through the Blue Mountains into a world of cool and gentle valleys, which,
by a recurring miracle which is not infrequent in the tropics, but which
is nevertheless always a surprise, resemble the most lyrical English
countryside. It is a region of ghostly English pasture harnessed by a
network of lanes and as velvety and green as any in Devonshire or
Somerset. Trees grow in the meadows as spaciously and as aloofly as
English oaks, and cast their shadows over hollows where the sleek
northern cattle slowly graze from shade to shade.

Ancient writers assess the numbers of Arawaks that inhabited the four
Greater Antilles at two million, and it is agreeable to think of the gentle
and tractable creatures inhabiting these regions. Their life was one of

blessed indolence. Dancing and singing, to the accompaniment of a drum and a small timbrel, and a game called *bato*, played with an elastic ball, were their passions. One can easily picture them lying in hammocks strung between these shady trees, talking to their tame parrots and smoking through branching calumets, or wandering into the woods with their bows and arrows, their *alco* at their heels: 'that little mute dog,' writes John Cutting, the friend of Dallas, 'caressing and sequacious, which, once loved and cherished by its poor Indian masters, is now like them, exterminated'. Their dwellings were beehives of timber and wild cane clustering among the trees. The floor was strewn with palm leaves. Sometimes the houses were surrounded by a little garden, and the hut of the cacique would slightly overtop those of his neighbours. They never quarrelled among themselves, and the Spaniards, when they arrived, found them pathetically docile. Their life in these dreamy hills and savannahs must have been akin to that of our first ancestors in the Garden of Eden, a prelapsarian existence evolving without land-mark or history until the steel-clad Christians, with their armoured horses and fire-breathing culverins, strong in the authority of Pope Alexander VI Borgia, suddenly irrupted into this private paradise. For this part of Jamaica, Saint Ann's Parish, is precisely where the Spaniards first landed: the first messengers (for there were no poisonous serpents in the island) of the Fall.

Here, then, the Arawaks throve among the woods of ceiba, lignum vitae, silk-cotton and pimento. The forests were shared by monkeys, parrots, macaws, humming birds – 'hovering atoms of emerald, and amethyst and ruby' – parakeets and mocking birds. The trees rang with the cooing of doves and ringtailed pigeons, and in October myriads of ortolans flew southwards from the Carolinas. An abundance of wild fowl challenged their skill as archers, and the fens of Westmoreland were scarlet with the plumage of flamingoes – elegant and princely birds, now also extinct, like the *alcos* and the Arawaks themselves. The island teemed with agoutis, peccaries, opossums, racoons, alligators, iguanas and armadilloes. Plentiful fresh-water fish swam in the mountain streams and the landcrabs whose habits Father Du Tertre so minutely observed were a food that never failed them. In April and May they leave their clefts and hollow tree stumps in the highlands and set off, several million strong, on a pilgrimage to the coast. So direct is their course that if they encounter a house they attempt to scale it. At the approach of danger, their claws are raised in the air like the swords of a mighty army. Lying up during the sunny spells and marching only in the rain or the dark, their journey may take them two or three months. Safely arrived in the shallow water, they scatter their spawn; then, reinforced by several more tiny millions, the long anabasis back to the mountain begins. Once in their fastnesses, each crustacean immures itself in the darkness to change its shell. The seams of the carapace unlock, the plates are shed, the soft carcase hardens and at last the crab emerges again in full armour. This is the period when they are best to eat.

The hunting technique of the Arawaks was as ingenious as that of the Caribs and even more peculiar. For salt-water fishing they trained the murderous remora, or sucking-fish, as falconers train their hawks. Putting to sea in dug-out canoes, they launched these finny hunters on the end of a long line, and, paddling swiftly after them, retrieved their prey, catching turtles, on some occasions, that were too heavy for a single man to carry. Their method of hunting wild fowl was also engagingly simple. Lurking near the ponds and the meres where the waterbirds congregated, they scattered calabashes on the water and waited until the birds became accustomed to the floating globes. Then, sawing one of them in half and drilling two holes for their eyes, they crammed them over their heads, and waded into the deep water until only their innocent-looking helmets were visible among the other calabashes. Working their way into the crowded waterfowl, they seized them one by one by the legs and, jerking them deftly under water, tied them to their girdles 'and so, without creating the least alarm among the remainder of the flock, they loaded themselves with as many as they could carry away'.

Hardly a trace remains of these gentle savages. Nothing but half a dozen clumsy rock carvings, a few utensils, a kitchen midden or two, and a random heirloom of flattened skulls.

The stigmata of elderly *villeggiatura* are detectable at many points of the northern shore of Jamaica. And no wonder. Long stretches of the coast-road are only divided by a balustrade and a few rocks from the sea, and the country that lies along it is all that a stranger, bred on tropical visions and adventure stories in sterner climates, could hope for. Here, at last, are the creeks plumed with palm trees, the sleeping islands lying a furlong out to sea, the extravagant profusion of tropical vegetation, the beautiful rivers pursuing a wild course through crags and forests. Collecting in pools beneath a penumbra of leaves they spill in white and foaming waterfalls down rocky staircases to the sea. The hotels and the rest houses, built among trees on the edge of the water, only very slightly dispel this authentically romantic atmosphere. At Ocho Rios, east of Oracabessa, the bather swims under water through a complex submarine wood of coral where the great blue fish and the vast shoals of small fry striped like convicts or wasps are only just learning to swim away at the sight of black and yellow goggles and a harpoon gun.

Here, on a headland, Commander Ian Fleming has built a house called Goldeneye that might serve as a model for new houses in the tropics. Trees surround it on all sides except that of the sea which it almost over-hangs. Great windows capture every breeze, to cool, even on the hottest day, the large white rooms. The windows that look towards the sea are glassless, but equipped with outside shutters against the rain: enormous quadrilaterals surrounded by dark wooden frames which enclose a prospect of sea and cloud and sky, and tame the elements, as it were, into an ever-changing fresco of which one can never tire.

East of here, our road lay through country that a recent hurricane had strewn with the broken trunks of palm trees. Only the gigantic silk-cotton trees – whose trunks when excavated sometimes furnished the Arawaks with a boat capable of holding a hundred mariners – had resisted its violence. Their vast and whirling branches, all spiked with parasites and roped with wild vine, gesticulated indestructibly above the wreckage of their frailer neighbours.

Half an hour's drive away from our new headquarters at Port Antonio ('The most exquisite port on earth', writes Ella Wheeler Wilcox with excusable over-statement), the Rio Grande unwinds through the hills. This river offered us one of the most delightful experiences in the West Indies. At a little riverine port, a silent Negro embarked us on a long, Japanese-looking raft of bamboo-poles which slowly carried us down-stream through a willow-pattern landscape. We slid overboard and drifted with the current under the branches and the lianas and climbed on board again to bump innocuously over the miniature rapids; to dive, half an hour later, into deep and shadowy pools. Then we clung once more to the raft as it ferried us through whispering vistas of wild cane. Herons perched ibis-like on the shore or circled languidly overhead until the craft reached the bridge and the flat country that ended this watery adventure.

Scattered along this northern coast lie some of the most important places in Jamaican history: Dry Harbour, where Columbus landed in 1494, and the point where Penn and Venables invaded the island in 1655, and Runaway Bay, whence the defeated Spaniards escaped to Cuba. The whole coast-line is fretted with the secluded creeks which were the refuges of the pirates who tormented the Spanish towns of the isthmus and the Main and lay in wait for the returning Plate Fleet.

In the centre of this region lies the beautiful little town of Falmouth – a town that forces one straightway to retract any hasty strictures on the former planters of Jamaica that the hideousness of Kingston may have prompted. The early nineteenth-century law courts – allowing for the usual time-hiatus of the Antilles – are fine examples of English provincial architecture at the period when solidity and elegance united with their greatest success. From this magnificent stone building, with its branching staircases and its pediment resting on a row of Doric columns, the streets radiate seawards, full of old wooden, or stone and wooden houses that also pursue, as far as the medium allows, a classical mode of columns and pilasters and wrought-iron balconies, many of them of great delicacy.

In a Falmouth shop called Antonio, the shelves are filled with the most brilliant and uninhibited shirts in the world; shirts of which even the Saga boys of Trinidad cannot have dreamt. Flaming colours are printed on light summer materials in patterns of leaves, drums, African dancers, sunsets, castles on fire, sunflowers and marching grenadiers. These amazing garments make Montego Bay an exhilarating sight.

This Jamaican pleasure-resort, lying some miles farther west than Falmouth, is dominated by several luxurious hotels and built over golden beaches and an incredibly blue sea. It succeeds in capturing much of the atmosphere of ease and gaiety for which the French Riviera is so highly prized. It is the world of barracuda- and bonito-fishing, sunburn lotion, striped umbrellas, expensive motor-cars and yachts, and it draws to itself a steady airborne stream of holidaymakers from America, Canada and England, from European capitals even, and from palaces in Europe that have been emptied by unrest and revolution. The atmosphere is a compound of Wall Street, the *Tatler*, *Vogue*, *Tout Paris* and the *Wiener Salonblatt* anomalously transplanted in a background of palm trees and blazing sunlight. The *Daily Gleaner* capably fills the function of all these publications, and, in winter, the pages are full of social news and the photographs of fashionable visitors. Ice clatters in shakers and poker dice are thrown unceasingly on the bars of this Jamaican Nineveh, and, for the uninitiated visitor, the chasms of tedium yawn deeper every second.

Inland, among the hills and the coconuts and the immeasurable cane-fields are scattered a number of old houses which are closely connected with English and Colonial social history. Some of these – notably Cardiff Hall, an ancient hurricane-house which still possesses its old dungeons – have been in the possession of the same families for many generations. This house, until almost yesterday, was still in the possession of the Blagroves, descendants of one of the parliamentarian regicides who, after having appended his signature to King Charles's death warrant, found sanctuary in the remote island which the Commonwealth had so recently acquired. Not far away, Fonthill, which is named after the English architectural phenomenon, is the home of a branch of the Beckford family, collateral kinsmen of the author of *Vathek*. The architectural, bibliophile and antiquarian adventures of William Beckford were paid for out of the revenues of his vast Jamaican estates, and it was the same source that enabled his uncle Peter, the author of *Thoughts upon Hare and Foxhunting* to devote his life so elegantly to scholarship, gastronomy, travel and the chase. His work was Jorrocks's bedside book. 'He would bag a fox in Greek,' a contemporary writes, 'find a hare in Latin, inspect his kennels in Italian and direct the economy of his stables in exquisite French.' His companions on the continent were Voltaire and Rousseau and Sterne; a second-rate life, perhaps, by absolute standards, but a stinging rebuke nevertheless to the present irreconcilable antagonism that severs the active from the intellectual way of life.

One of the most remarkable of these houses is the ruin of Rose Hall, a ruin that heavy outlay might still breathe back to life. It was built in 1780, and its remains show that it must have been a magnificent building. It stands dramatically on the summit of a hill, and from the edge of its abandoned garden the sugar-cane surges down to the sea. Scars on the wall show where the staircase has been ripped away. The floors and ceilings have disappeared, and the sun streams through the rafters. Strange and rather disquieting sounds come from the cellar, caused, it soon appears, by a donkey which has strayed from the fields and wandered down the steps, miserably tearing now at the thistles that abound there. Rose Hall is celebrated in the annals of Jamaica as the house of a terrible Mrs Palmer. She has proved a theme for novelists and her complex love-life and her brutality to her slaves are still proverbial.

The epitaph of a lady a couple of miles away tells a very different story. She died at the age of twenty-seven – 'beloved and bewailed not by her immediate friends only, but by all her Negroes, for whom she laboured both by precept and example to make known the true God and eternal life'. It is the tomb of Mary Clementina Barret, lying not far from the earliest of her dynasty, 'Eduardo Barret', who died on the 'kalends of December MDCCXCVIII'. The little overgrown cemetery was filled with Barret tombs, derelict stones with the writing half-effaced, and half-buried in the long grass. One of these slabs – broken clean in half, with a green lizard poised in frozen alertness above the lettering – commemorated the death in London, in 1857, of Edward Barret Moulton-Barrett, father of Elizabeth Browning. It was difficult to connect the uncompromising Caribbean glare with the stuffy sitting-room in Wimpole Street, with the Halls of the Ca'Rezzonico, murmurous with the muted rumours of the

Grand Canal; or with the cool rooms of the Brownings' house in Florence, where, still unreconciled to her father, the poetess was established at the time of his death. Her father had added a second and final Barret to his surname when, as a young man, he inherited from his aunt, together with a substantial fortune, the surrounding cane-fields. It is interesting that the prosperity of Elizabeth Browning's family and that of Gladstone should have owed so much to slave-labour. Both of them, prompted no doubt by a feeling of remorse about the guilty origins of their affluence, were violently opposed to slavery. Two Barret manor-houses, Barret Hall and Cinnamon Hill, lie close by: white, solid country seats pleasantly shaded by spreading trees in valleys that wind downhill to the seashore.

The island has many connections with literature. Lady Holland, the formidable friend of Sheridan and Byron and Macaulay, who for so many years made Holland House the most exciting place in England, belonged to a plantation-owning family of Jamaica; and when she inherited her father's estates, both she and Lord Holland prefixed her maiden name of Vassall to that of Fox. Dallas, the friend and cousin by marriage of Byron, was likewise a Jamaican squire. He has claims on the traveller's attention, as we shall see later, which are quite unconnected with the poet. It is an odd coincidence that Byron should also have been the friend of a third remarkable Jamaican figure of that period. It is as though his restless spirit spread tentacles all over the world. This third Jamaican is none other than Matthew Gregory Lewis.

One imagines 'Monk' Lewis far more readily in a European setting – devouring the novels of Mrs Radcliffe, and, under the influences of *The Mysteries of Udolfo* and Horace Walpole, scribbling *The Monk* and its melodramatic successors in a fever of romantic medievalism; calling on Goethe at Weimar and arguing with Madame de Staël; simultaneously boring and charming Byron in London and Geneva and Venice – boring him by his earnestness and his prolixity, and charming him by his engaging ingenuousness and his kind heart. But 'a jewel of a man', Byron admitted him to be.

But in his Jamaican diaries,* he is neither tedious nor prolix, and the account of his two short visits to his newly-inherited estates, which he undertook with the sole purpose of inquiring into the conditions of his slaves, give us a vivid picture of life in the island during the interregnum between the abolition of the Slave Trade and the Emancipation Act. True, there are occasional traces of silliness, and, from time to time, he plunges into almost unreadable verse. The hawks that swoop so unnaturally from

---

* *Journal of a West Indian Proprietor.*

the sky to inflict rape on the turkey-hens of his backyard become, in his prose, feathered Tarquins and their victims are hapless Lucretias. His outdoor privy, whose walls are so transparent the passing slaves tactlessly raise their hats in homage when he is inside, becomes a 'Temple of Cloacina ...' One sees what Byron was getting at. But his high spirits, his sense of fun and his kindness are never obscure for long beneath the buckram and the horsehair.

Many of the regular planters in his pages are hard and illiberal men, and nearly all the overseers and bookkeepers are perfidious and cruel. But a large number of them emerge from 'Monk' Lewis's pages as humane masters who did their best to mitigate the horrors of slavery. His cabin companion was, like Lewis himself, one of the new and advanced school of planters. 'Hedicating the Negroes,' he kept repeating, 'is the honly way to make them appy; indeed his umble hopinion, hedication is hall in hall ...' Although the slave-owners' power of life and death, the use of chains and the fiendish flogging of the last century had been abolished or curtailed by law, brutalities still occurred. But by the time he visited the island in 1815 and 1817, a change was well on the way. The slaves were being converted to Christianity, and were slowly assuming the status in their masters' eyes, of human beings. Sunday had at last been allotted to them as a day of rest, and, on Lewis's plantation at any rate, Saturday was kept free for the cultivation of the slaves' own garden produce. Each family had its own cottage. Their wooden houses were equipped – it sounds almost incredible – with four-poster beds, and plentifully stocked with food and wine and porter. They grew their own vegetables, and reared their own livestock, and appear to have been allowed considerable freedom of movement from place to place. Baskets of vegetables were carried to market in Savannah-la-Mar or Montego Bay – the 'Bay' and the 'Bay Girls' were a great attraction for the more adventurous and unruly – and the life, compared to the bad old times, seems almost normal. Lewis's first reform was to abolish the use of the terrible cattle-whip. The threat of selling delinquent slaves to a less benevolent master was, he records, the worst punishment he needed to inflict. He drew up a mild code of laws for the management of his estate. He affirms that it functioned perfectly. Hospitals were built, doctors and midwives employed. His presents of meat, salt-fish, calico and clothing seem to have been almost daily events, and the parties of country-dances with free food and rum, when his slaves danced the jam-jam and the kitty-katty all night to the sound of the 'banja and the gumbo drum', were scarcely less frequent. The practice of Obeah, the casting of spells, the use of malign herbs, poisoning with corrosive sublimate, petty larceny, unreliable bookkeepers, a runaway or two and a number of lovers' quarrels, seem to have been the only things that marred this earthly paradise. 'If only his friend Wilberforce could have seen!' Poor Lewis was only six months altogether on his Jamaican estates ...

He gives an account of the Myal dance practised by Obeahmen in their secret gatherings – a dance which sounds very close to Voodoo and Pocomania – and records the terror of duppies, or ghosts, by which all his slaves were obsessed. 'Nancy-tales', charming folk-stories of the Negroes, and the legends of the elderly Ibo slaves were carefully recorded, and the fancy dresses and the contests of the 'Reds' and the 'Blues' – Britannia, Nelson, Wellington, Royal Princes, Jesters, and Duchesses – at the New Year Carnival, are extensively described. The names of the slaves themselves are interesting: Neptune, Catalina, Oscar, Epsom, Sully, Marlborough, Hazard, Nato, Hercules, Toby, Pickle, Plato, Strap, Damon and Priam were the names of the men. The girls were called Psyche, Polly, Phillipa, Jug-Betty, Delia, Moll, Venus, Martia, Big Joan, Juliet, Minetta, Phyllis, Pam and Sappho. 'What other Negroes may be,' he wrote as he prepared to sail, 'I will not pretend to guess; but I am certain that there cannot be more tractable or well-disposed persons (take them for all in all) than my Negroes of Cornwall. I only wish that in my future dealings with white persons I could but meet with half so much gratitude, affection and goodwill.'

He died at sea a few days later of yellow-fever. Byron was genuinely moved. He wrote in a letter to John Murray, as soon as he learnt the sad news:

> I would give many a sugar cane
> Nat Lewis were alive again.

Months earlier, I had begun to be fascinated by the idea of the Maroons, those Negroes that ran away from their owners and lived as outlaws in the mountains and forests. Their name probably derives from the Spanish word *Cimarrones* or Peak-dwellers. Sometimes they joined themselves together in armed bands. They were hunted without mercy and subjected, if they were caught, to the direst penalties. But if they happened to have run away from Spanish plantations, they often secretly leagued with the English, and, when the English made piratical descents on the Spanish towns of the islands or the Main, the Maroons would descend like a fifth column from the interior, and simultaneously attack the Spaniards in the rear.

But in Jamaica the usual process was exactly reversed. For, when the

Spaniards were driven from the island, they armed their slaves and set them free, and the presence of these formidable enemies in the interior, determined at all costs to retain their freedom, was a constant trouble for the new arrivals. After eighty-three years of liberty, during which time their numbers were steadily augmented by the arrival of runaways, they were becoming such a menace to the peace of the island – roving the mountains on marauding parties, plundering, burning estates, and murdering whites – that in 1734 the government built barracks and forts on the edges of their territory and organized a military expedition against them with the purpose of wiping them out for good. Such was the skill of the Maroons, however, in guerrilla warfare and in exploiting their knowledge of the Maroon mountains, that the government forces, in spite of the employment of Blackshot troops and of two hundred Mosquito Indians specially brought to the island by sloop from the coasts of Nicaragua, met with reverse after reverse. They narrowly escaped annihilation, and in the end were forced to withdraw with heavy losses. There was nothing for it but to come to terms with them. Dallas describes in detail how the enemies met. The Redcoats halted at the foot of the Maroon mountains, and a Doctor Russel was sent forward to parley. He shouted an offer of peace towards the wooded slopes, knowing that hundreds of invisible Maroons were hiding, with their muskets cocked, under the leaves of the overhanging ledges. Two wary Negroes emerged, and when they were sure of the peaceful intentions of the enemy, called back to their leader in the Koromantee tongue. The undergrowth became alive with black warriors, and the doctor and old Cudjoe, the Maroon chief, advanced towards each other. Dr Russel held out his hand in friendship, and Old Cudjoe seized it and kissed it. As a further sign of concord, they exchanged hats. A faded etching on the frontispiece of Dallas's book commemorates the incident: under an indeterminate tropical tree, Old Cudjoe, a short, stout Negro with a wild aspect and a hump, dressed in campaigning rags and armed with a musket, a powder horn, a pouch of slugs and a cutlass, has already put on the Doctor's cocked hat with its enormous cockade. The Doctor, in a modish full-tailed coat, white breeches, stockings, and buckled pumps, a rapier at his side and the curls of his wig impeccably powdered, is reaching forward for the hat in Cudjoe's hand, which looks like a battered pudding-basin ... Cudjoe called up his chief followers, the Captains Accompong, Johnny, Cuffee and Quacko. Colonel Guthrie approached with his staff, and a general embracing and exchange of hats took place between the Maroon and the British officers. A treaty was signed under a cotton tree in Trelawny Town: 'Whereas peace and friendship among mankind, and the preventing the effusion of blood,' it ran, 'is agreeable to God, consonant to reason, and desired by every good man, and whereas His Majesty George the Second, King of Great Britain, France and Ireland and of Jamaica, Lord, Defender of the Faith, etc., has by his letters patent ... granted full power and authority to John Guthrie and Francis Sadler, esquires, to negotiate and finally conclude a treaty of peace and friendship with the aforesaid Captain Cudjoe and the rest of his captains, adherents and others of his men, we ...' The terms were that all hostilities should cease for ever. The Maroons were granted their freedom and the fifteen hundred acres* lying between Trelawny Town and the Cockpit Country were ceded to them and their posterity in perpetuity. All runaways must be sent back, and the Maroons swore to be allies of the King in the case of internal rebellion or invasion from without. The succession to the chieftainship was laid down. The administration of justice, except for cases involving the death penalty, was left in the hands of the Maroon leader, and a white representative or adviser – a sort of ambassador – was to reside permanently in the Maroon capitals of Trelawny (or Maroon Town, of which several are dotted about the island) and Accompong. Harmony was general. The whole affair was a great triumph for the Maroons. It was virtually the creation of a vassal, almost a sovereign state, within the colony.

All went well for nearly seventy years, and the contract was punctiliously held on both sides. But in 1795 the Trelawny Maroons worked themselves into a state of faction over two issues: the replacement of their resident white representative (who had become a great favourite of the Maroons; a cheerful, hard-drinking swash-buckling fellow called James) by a sober-minded and unsympathetic successor; and the public flogging of two delinquent Maroons in Montego Bay at the hand of a slave of the Magistracy. All attempts at conciliation failed, a deputation of Maroon leaders were arbitrarily arrested and imprisoned in Spanish Town, and the Maroons broke loose on the surrounding plantations in a sudden wave of arson and slaughter. A formidable expedition was launched against them, and for a year the Second Maroon War followed the same distressing course as the first. The Redcoat columns were ambushed everywhere. They would advance into the woody defiles of the Cockpit Country, and the Maroons, warned by their scouts and disguised in leaves from head to foot, would stealthily surround them. When the troops were deeply engaged in these natural labyrinths, they were suddenly attacked from all sides by staggering volleys. And, again

---

* The *Jamaica Handbook* states that 2,500 acres were granted.

and again, the troops were forced to retreat with appalling losses. The Negroes were such skilful marksmen that, while the soldiers blazed away recklessly and ineffectively into the forest, scarcely one of the Maroon shots went wide. Again, their knowledge of every inch of the mountains put them at an advantage, and their system of scouts and inter-communication was faultless. They were able to signal long and compli-cated messages to each other by blowing the horns or conch-shells that all of them carried and for which they had evolved a primitive but most efficient morse code. Months dragged by and, at each new attempt to subdue them, the troops were driven back in disorder. Losses were heavy, and several of the best officers were killed, while scarcely a Maroon had even been sighted. A general gloom settled over the colony.

The war was finally brought to an end by the importation from Cuba of two dozen Spanish chasseurs and sixty couples of Maroon-hounds: huge mastiffs specially trained for man-hunting, of an aspect so terrifying that when they were led ashore, snarling and baying though securely muzzled, the streets of Montego Bay were empty in a second. These brutes were not actually used in a single instance, but their moral effect among the Maroons was devastating. The Negroes had been victorious so far, but they were exhausted by the war, and, when General Walpole made an honourable peace offer, they began to surrender and throw down their arms. The leaders, fearing some trick, failed to give themselves up till a few days after the expiry of the stipulated time, and this delay gave the government the pretext to revoke their promise that the Maroons should not only be pardoned, but permitted to remain on their land as before. Lord Balcarres, the Governor, and the Assembly decided that the rebel Maroons, though still in possession of their freedom from slavery, should be deported from the island.

But General Walpole, the commander of the British troops all through the campaign, had acquired a strong liking and respect for them, and when he learnt that the government proposed, on a legal quibble, to go back on their promise, he refused the sword of honour that was offered him by the Assembly, angrily declaring that the Maroons had relied on his word of honour that they would be fairly treated (without which they would still be armed and at war), and that he had been forced into the position of 'a deceiver or a catspaw'. He resigned his commission in the Army on the spot and left Jamaica in disgust.

Five hundred of the Trelawny Maroons were shipped to Nova Scotia. A blaze of glory, rather than any disgrace, surrounded their departure. The authorities were feeling rather unboastful about the hounds from Cuba, the Spanish chasseurs, the questionable justice of their final decision and General Walpole's resignation. The behaviour of the Maroons in Nova Scotia was on the whole exemplary. When they arrived, the Governor, Prince Edward, George III's younger son, inspected them and voted them a fine body of men and a plucky lot. They only remained in that unsuitable climate a season or two – that winter the colony had the heaviest fall of snow for many years – and they were finally embarked for Sierra Leone; back to the continent from which, a dozen generations earlier, their ancestors had all originally come. Here, when Dallas, in 1803, finished his account of their adventures, they were settled on the land and doing well. They sank back into the life of Africa, and history makes no further mention of them.

The other Maroons of Accompong, however, in the south of the Cockpit Country, had taken no part in the revolt and were still, I learnt with astonishment, living in their free mountain kingdom, under the dispensation laid down in the 1738 treaty between Old Cudjoe and George II. Realizing the implications of this, we began packing almost immediately.

These days among the Maroons were one of the pleasantest of our sojourns in the Caribbean. What a singular community they are! The constitution of the mountain hegemony has scarcely changed since Old Cudjoe's day. He was succeeded as the treaty laid down, by the eldest of his surviving captains and then by a long sequence of elected rulers until the present day.

The chieftainship had now devolved upon Colonel Rowe, a dignified and charming old man of eighty-three, with the appearance, strength and alertness of a very much younger man. Indeed, only his grizzled hair gives any hint of his age. There is no hint of it in his dark and energetic features.

'What's your job?' the Colonel asked me out of the blue. It was so sudden that I had to think hard before answering, 'I'm a writer.'

'Shorthand?'

'No, longhand, unfortunately.'

'Ah. That's hard work.'

Although, compared to the peaks of the Blue Mountains, Accompong lies at no very great height, I had the feeling that the Maroons lived on a raft sailing high above the dark river-bed of Jamaican life. And looking out of the window of the shanty in the early morning at the descending layers of mist that were entangled in the millions of leaves, a whole world seemed to separate us from the plains. Maroon life unfolds in an airy floating world of its own that has no particular link with any definite place or century.

Old men of amazing age and robustness sat in their doorways and shouted a greeting as we passed, and the Colonel and the school-master took us on a sort of state visit to the little school. The pupils jumped to their feet as we came in, and subsided again at a wave from the Colonel, who questioned them about their lessons with a stern benignity. We sat down for a while and listened to the children reading aloud from their history books: 'Ethelred the Unready,' a small girl read, 'was a weak king. He attempted to keep the Danes out of his kingdom, not by going to war with them, but by giving them money. This was known as the Danegeld ...' The children were intelligent and prompt, and, perhaps because of the Colonel's presence, magically well-behaved. When the bell rang for the end of the class, they pelted out in the sunlight and began wrestling and chasing each other over the grass, climbing into the branches of a ceiba tree, or swinging through the air on the ropes of a primitive merry-go-round. They were, like nearly all Negro children, engagingly active and lithe and extremely pretty. It was pleasant to learn that the Maroon population is slightly on the increase.

Leaving the Colonel to his official duties, we set off for the Cockpit Country with his brother, Emmanuel Rowe.

A ravine swallowed us up. After a mile or two it grew narrower and then so dense with vegetation that it seemed to close entirely. It was only by scaling the tree-covered rocks through a spider's web of liana and convolvulus that we could go any farther. Dripping with sweat, we emerged at last into a glade at the bottom of a circle of precipices. Escarpments of limestone jutted through the trees, which throve on every roothold. A beautiful place, but ghostly and forbidding in its windless hush. Not a leaf moved. Emmanuel shouted and his voice came echoing back from the wall of rock at the other end, and then the silence settled again.

'A cockpit,' Emmanuel said.

He led us across the silent place to a cleft in the rock wall. Scrambling with hands and feet up a ladder of limestone boulders and then twisting through the tree trunks and the creepers, we climbed into a second abysmal corridor which brought us, after a heart-breaking scramble, into another cockpit slightly larger than the first and equally sinister and silent. And so the country continues for many miles, proliferating in all ways: an endless maze of gullies and hollows running through a chaos of limestone and forest. A stranger can wander for days through this without finding the way out. We began to understand the misgivings that must have oppressed the files of Redcoats as they advanced through these

337

endless convolutions of rock. The noonday sun falls into them perpendicularly and heats the stagnant air to stifling point. The motionless vegetation begins to vacillate before the retina. All is hostile and withdrawn, and the meridian demon that is the genius of the place binds the air and the rocks and the forest in a conspiracy to send the intruder to Coventry. And how much more frightening, when, from the still girdle of the woods, might blow at any second a tempest of Maroon bullets, while the gunfire and the wailing horns shattered this spellbound vacuum with a sudden pandemonium of echoes ...

As though reading our thoughts and feeling that it was indelicate to keep us longer in such surroundings, Emmanuel conducted us through a hidden corridor into a peaceful valley at the bottom of which a stream ran merrily under the pimento trees. We watched his tall figure running and leaping barefoot downhill, negotiating the rocks with an agility that left us plodding far behind. One hand grasped an antiquated fowling-piece with a long barrel, and each leap made his cutlass slap against his thigh. He was a few years younger than Colonel Rowe, he was not quite sure how many. He must, he thought, be somewhere in his late seventies. Lean, erect, athletic and indefatigable, an expression of friendliness and alacrity radiated from his bright eyes and informed his impulsive and eager way of talking.

By the time we caught up with him he had cut and spread some leaves under a tree and filled a calabash with water. He carefully halved four avocadoes with his cutlass. Afterwards, puffing at his little home-made pipe, he discoursed of old hunts after the wild boars that live in the forests. He told us of the guile and savagery of the beasts and the special bullets needed for penetrating their hide. The pursuit of one particular enemy had lasted for days. When, quite alone and miles from any habitation, he had laid it low at last, the beast proved too heavy to carry. He had cut it up and hidden it, and carried some of the carcase back to the village, sending his friends to recover the remainder. It was the biggest wild hog (we learnt later in the village) that had been shot for over a hundred years. I cannot remember when Emmanuel said that the beast was killed – I think when he was a very young man; in the late 1880s or the early 90s perhaps ... To celebrate the event there was a great banquet of rum and jerked hog; pork, that is, sliced and smoked over a slow fire. When Joan asked him what it had tasted like, he joined his hands in prayer, and turned his eyes to heaven.

We felt weary after our trek through the Cockpit Country, and Emmanuel's quiet voice and the cooing of the ring-tailed pigeons slowly lulled us to sleep. When we awoke, evening was coming on. Emmanuel led us home through a region of calm savannah with long evening shadows streaming down the slopes. He interrupted his recollections now and then to tell us the names of the fields and valleys through which we were passing: Good Hope, Hill Middle, Saucy Train Cross-roads, New Lumber Road, the Old Mill. We strolled down the valley leading to Accompong, past scattered huts and gardens where the ginger was laid out to dry in armies of tiny gesticulating manikins. The forest ruffled in the breeze, and the silhouette of Accompong rose on its cone like a Biblical city. It was a dark shape against the wastes of turquoise where the sunset was shaking loose great stooks and sheaves of crimson cloud.

On our last night, the Colonel, at our request, donned his uniform as Colonel of the Maroons. It was a splendid affair, thought out, I imagine, by himself: a grey military jacket stiff with black braid, a Sam Browne belt, grey pantaloons with black stripes down the seams, and a helmet the same shape as those worn by colonial governors. He wore it with a nice combination of solemnity and dash. After a dinner of eggs, cassava, and yam – the best yam I have tasted – and a pineapple which still trailed its long green plumes, we sat on over our rum and sweet pimento-wine: Emmanuel, the Colonel, their pretty, intelligent niece, and a few neighbours; going through old Maroon documents of the Colonel's and listening to his comments. Later we began to sing, and Emmanuel, in a high and lively voice, sang a song with a sprightly air like an Irish jig –

> Cheer up, young ladies, and don't be afraid,
> Cheer up, my lady, and don't be ashamed.
> We have the clarinet and the French horn and the bugle that blow.
> On the first day of Christmas, young girl win the race.

and another, rather sentimental, Tom Moore-ish one, that began

> The rain is gathering over the hill, it's time for us to go ...

and,

> When you want to get money to send to the war
> They gather up thousands of pound.
> The Obeahman visit the parishes then
>   And drives in a buggy-go-round.

Prompted, I suppose by the mention of Obeah, we asked him if he knew any African songs. They all laughed, and said 'Only one, and only Emmanuel can remember it.' It ran as follows:

Ho minni wey – oh
Ho minni wey – oh
Ya seki a-brahé
Yekko, tekko
Yekko tekko
Yum, tum sayé,
Aya! Aya-yé!
Aya! Aya-yé!
O – se – oh,
Yekko Tekko,
Apasha – yé!

What did the words mean? Nobody knew. The sense had been lost. But it was in the Koromantee language, they said, the language that the old people, that their grandfathers and grandmothers, used to speak. It was a song that old Maroons sang while they were digging graves for their dead. The air is so authentically African, and so sad, that I will write down the music in case anybody with a knowledge of West African races and tribes can trace its origin –

Of another song, equally African sounding, he could only remember one couplet –

which he sang several times over, as though, like many of the Voodoo incantations, the two lines were sufficient in themselves.

I feel a slight pride in saving these two fragments of music and libretto from oblivion, for I think Emmanuel Rowe is the last of the Maroons to remember it. When he dies (which may God defer for many years) this last remaining link with Africa will be broken. Unless the tunes were brought here in a slave-running ship, the latest possible date of their arrival in Jamaica is 1807, when the Slave Trade was abolished. But they may have been in the island ever since the Spaniards brought the first shiploads of Negroes here four and a half centuries ago. The sad part of it is that neither of the songs is really in Koromantee, unless the words have been garbled by time out of all recognition. I asked Emmanuel if he knew any other Koromantee words, and he produced the following: *Yang kung kung?* How do you do? *O Sef-Sef*, quite well; *Ajuma*, a Negro; *wembo*, a gun; *afenna*, a knife; *opami*, come to visit me; *Abrowno*, a white man; and *Nyankopong ossassé*, God on top of the Earth.

Now Koromantee is a small town, almost a village, on the seaboard of the Gold Coast; so small that it is marked on very few maps. I think that the term 'Koromantee Negro', which occurs in all the memoirs, embraced all the Fanti Negroes in whose territory Koromantee lies, probably all the Ashanti, and indeed all the Africans belonging to the Twi and Akan group of languages of the Gold Coast, as all the dialects are similar. Knowledge of one of them gives an understanding of all the rest. I repeated Emmanuel's phrases later on to a Twi-speaking Negro lawyer from Accra, the capital of the Gold Coast. Some he did not understand – they are probably corrupted, or acquired from the language of other tribes that they encountered in the West Indies – but *afenna* is the Akan word for knife all right, *Obroni* is a white man, and *Nyankopong* (Accompong) *ossassé* means the God of the Earth. The songs were quite incomprehensible to him. My lawyer friend thought they might belong to the Ewe group of languages, which is spoken in the neighbouring Togoland and Dahomey.

All the old books on Jamaica, notably those of Dallas and Brian Edwards, and the Maroons themselves, are unanimous in saying that the Maroons are of Koromantee descent, drawn together in the mountains by their community of language and tribal tradition. There were accretions from other sources; namely the Kencuffee Negroes who, judging by their name, were also of Akan-speaking origin; and a small number of the problematical 'Madagascars', whose origin is a riddle, as no slaves were drawn from the island of Madagascar. Dallas describes these mystery-men as smaller than the Koromantees and very dark, with delicate features and soft loose hair. Koromantee, anyway, was the common Maroon language during both the Maroon wars. The names of the early Maroon leaders – Cudjoe, Quacko and Cuffee – are the Ashanti words for Monday, Wednesday and Friday, and today, still, the days of the week are widely used as names in the Gold Coast. Accompong, as we have seen, is the Akan word for the Supreme God, the single shadowy Being that lies beyond the polytheism of fetish-worship. If the word Koromantee covers all the Akan-Twi-speaking Negroes, the Maroons must be the only pure, or, at least, the purest, racial group of African origin in the West Indies. Everywhere else the many tribes became, almost at once, inextricably mingled. As we were finishing the bottle, the Colonel declared that the Maroons were largely of Arawak descent but there are no indications of this in the old chronicles, and the poor Indians were well on their way to extinction by the time the first Africans arrived.

The main races of slaves in Jamaica at the end of the eighteenth century, according to Brian Edwards, were the Fuli, the Negroes of Wydah on the coast of Dahomey, who practised circumcision, the cannibalistic Iboes from the land beyond the Bight of Benin, and small numbers of Mandingoes. He owned two Mandingo slaves himself, both of them gentle and civilized creatures, able to write beautifully in Arabic, and accustomed to bow down in prayer at sunrise and sunset. One of them, he writes, would repeat the words 'La illah La illah' at these moments of worship. The price of a full-grown Negro at that period was £40 or £50 in the slave market at Montego Bay. A baby went for under £5. Large numbers of newly arrived slaves admitted that they had been born into slavery in Africa and captured by hostile tribes, or sold as children by their rulers to other Negroes in discharge of debts, and enormous numbers were kidnapped or captured in the forests by Africans with the express purpose of selling them to the West Indian slave-merchants.

Edwards and Dallas give much the same account of the Koromantees. They were remarkable for their extraordinary strength and symmetry, their distinguished appearance and proud bearing. They were blacker and taller and handsomer than their fellow-slaves; vigorous, muscular and agile, intelligent, fierce, ruthless in war, fanatically attached to the idea of liberty, and strangers to fear. Large numbers of them, apart from the Maroons, were scattered about the colony. They were excellent workers in the cane-fields, but prone to revolt. An uprising of Koromantee slaves occurred on one of the Beckford estates in 1760, led by a slave called Tacky, who, it was rumoured, had been a chief in Guinea. (His claim was almost certainly well-founded. The name Tackie is used right down to the present day by the king or chief of Accra.) There was much bloodshed and arson and the hills resounded with the terrible 'Koromantee war-yell'. When the revolt was suppressed, the ringleader was burnt alive. Two of them were hung to perish in irons, another was condemned to have his legs slowly burnt off. All endured their fate with stoicism. The two that were starved to death in chains, Dallas writes, talked and laughed with their fellow-tribesmen almost until the moment of death, and the one that was sentenced to suffer the leg punishment succeeded, when his legs were half burnt away, in releasing one arm from his bonds and flinging a burning brand in the face of his executioner.

In the library of the Jamaica Institute in Kingston I found and copied, from some old book whose name I have unfortunately lost, the following note on Nanny, the wife of Old Cudjoe:

The notorious Nanny ... was ten times more ferocious and bloodthirsty than any man among the Maroons. She was possessed of supernatural powers, and spirited away the best and finest of the slaves from the outlying estates. She never went into battle armed like the rest, but received the bullets of the enemy that were aimed at her and returned them with fatal effect in a manner of which decency forbids a nearer description.

This is the only recorded instance of a Maroon turning his back on the foe.

The hospitable Colonel seemed as sad as we were at our departure. Why didn't we stay a couple of weeks or a month? Why not indeed? Alas, we had to return to Kingston to see if our telegrams to Havana had at last resulted in the granting of our Cuban visas. Three Maroons aged fourteen or fifteen were detailed to carry our luggage to the railway station five miles away. They hoisted our bags on to their heads, and trotted off down the hill as though it were a pleasure-outing rather than an intolerable grind. We followed them down the steep path. It was 6 a.m., and a slight shower had washed the woods to a clear and brilliant green. Their voices, singing, 'Give me back me shilling with de Lion upon it' and then 'Linstead Market', sailed up the pathway.

Looking back, we saw a tall figure leaping down the slope, gun in hand and cutlass flying. It was Emmanuel. We waited for him to catch us up. He put something into Joan's hand that looked like a great log of wood. 'There,' he said, 'she said she liked the Maroon yam. Here is a piece from my garden to eat in London ...' He waved his gun in the direction of the city as though it lay the other side of the forest: the vague metropolis of which he had spoken in the Maroon mountains with such wonder; palaces and fluttering banners and spires and the King and Queen driving diamond-crowned over airy bridges in coaches of solid gold. He halted half-way up the slope. 'From my garden,' he shouted down to us, 'the finest yam in Jamaica.'

The train from Montego Bay and Ipswich steamed into the station. What pleasure to be in a train again! to pull the armchair round to the window – for the seating in the Jamaica Government Railway is sybaritically arranged – light a cigar, and glance at the news of the island in the *Daily Gleaner*. The news of the rest of the world seemed too remote and irrelevant to bother about. But the attractions even of this splendid newspaper failed to hold out for long against the quiet and sylvan landscape that streamed past the windows, the darkly-timbered uplands and sloping fields, and the weeping trees heavy with white flowers that dropped so lyrically over the alligator-haunted meanderings of the Black River. Silk-cotton trees, sleeved and bearded with beautiful parasites, sailed past the windows and, beyond their branches, the pale-green mountains uncurled. Prospects of parkland and glade and the deep clearings of the forest unfolded like great flowers drawing the path of the eye deep into regions of almost dream-like beauty. It is not surprising that 'Monk' Lewis, riding at the head of a cavalcade laden with hats and handkerchiefs and knives and lengths of Oznaburgh cloth as gifts for the slaves on his eastern estates, drew rein under the trees here. He paused and gazed across the celestial valleys of the May-day Mountains, and then marshalled his Byronic musings into the pronouncement that this must be the most beautiful landscape on earth. The journey became a second Childe Harold's pilgrimage. He forded rivers in spate, laboured through precarious passes in the mountains, rode in the dark through gloomy forests while forked lightning sundered the heavens. In one of the inns where he slept the night his heart beat faster at the sight of a beautiful coloured girl from Cuba, 'quite brown', he quoted from the dramatist Colman, 'but extremely genteel, like a Wedgwood teapot'.

At Appleton a posse of boys climbed in with baskets of oranges, sour-sops and avocadoes for sale, and the train steamed on into the Parish of Manchester – called, like so many of the places in the island, after one of Jamaica's numerous ducal governors. We stopped again at the little towns of Balaclava and Green Vale, and at Kendal climbed out to catch the bus to Mandeville, which also perpetuates the Montagu name. Here we stayed in a 'guest house' kept by an English lady. We stepped from the glare of midday into shuttered chambers looming with mahogany furniture and bead curtains and revolving bookcases packed with the English classics and best-sellers of many decades ago.

After a quiet afternoon with *Countess Kate and the Stokesby Secret*, by Charlotte M. Yonge I was woken by Costa and Joan. We strolled past the parish church and across the ultra-English square to the Manchester Club.

The members on the verandah were all English, but most of them, it appeared from the conversation, had alighted in this little backwater after half a lifetime in India. Elderly ex-soldiers and civil servants meditatively contemplated the golf-links over their whiskies and sodas, exchanging stories of Rawalpindi, Simla and Darjeeling and half a dozen outposts of empire that had cruelly pre-deceased them. They were joined in their reminiscences of khitmagars and khansamahs and the Saturday Club by an elderly memsahib, sadly dethroned and transplanted.

> ... Prim and trim as a tongo-pony
> her tortured curls are planted like a lawn
> and fenced across her forehead with a ribbon ...
> Where is an indication of her date?
> Only the whiskered regimental groups,
> cantonment champions
> framed and frozen, stamp her dynasty.*

The verandah was heavy with nostalgia. It was all rather moving and sad.

The hills, next day, gradually subsided as the train carried us eastwards. The sugar-cane rose in a flood, and the Blue Mountains reappeared, heaving into the sky a winding chain of spikes. Hidden among these peaks lie dark ravines which hang there in the alien gothic shade of pine trees. But seen from the south, nothing in their steep and wrinkled contours suggested those chill interior regions. We could just descry the ledge of mountain where Bellevue (which was, without any question, the most beautiful of the old Jamaican houses that we had seen) lies

---

* Xan Fielding, *Six Poems*, Cyprus, 1946.

poised; built above a steep cataract of coffee-wood and forest, and over-shadowed by giant trees in the topmost branches of which the Night-Blowing Cereus, one of the loveliest and most mysterious of tropical epiphytes, opens its nocturnal corolla of petals. Cool and finely pro-portioned eighteenth-century rooms open one from another in a vista which leads through the central window of a long library into the sky. From here or from the lawn below one can gaze down at a relief map of the southern Jamaica coast and an astonishing expanse of the Caribbean. During his sojourns at Bellevue Nelson must also have gazed at that gulf of water. It was from Jamaica that he mounted the Rio San Juan and raided the Spanish forts of the Nicaraguan interior: an expedition the hazards of which I was able to appreciate months later when we sailed down the same peculiar river.

The Caribbean sea between the shores of Jamaica and the Venezuelan coast is almost empty of islands. Thirty-odd miles south-east, however, and forty-odd miles south of the colony, lie the Morant and the Pedro Cays. The former are three small islets, valuable only for the guano that accumulates there, and for the vast concourses of birds which assemble in spring and litter the island with their eggs. They are carefully gathered and dispatched to Jamaica by the schooner load.

A hundred and seventy-eight miles north-west of Jamaica floats another minute trinity of islands, the Caymans. For a long time they were the haunt of the Corsairs and of every kind of picaroon vessel: outlaw craft which shifted their headquarters northwards to the banks of the Mississippi when the archipelago became a place of call for warships. Their cannon still remain embedded in the sand. The inhabitants, who are either pure white or pale Mulatto, are nearly all Baptists. They ship turtles and coco-nuts to Jamaica and plant sugar and raise cattle, and, as late as the 'eighties, there was scarcely any money in circulation, nor any need of it. Coral reefs encompass these lonely places, and the sands are en-cumbered with the skeletons of sloops and schooners, for the Cayman Islanders are skilful ship-builders. This calling, according to a Kingston sailor, is charitably fostered by nature, for the steady pressure of the Trade Winds camber the tree trunks into the exact curve that is needed for the timbers of the hulls.

Another little cluster of coral satellites, the Turks and the Caicos Islands, lie over four hundred miles to the north-east: outposts, geologically speak-ing, of the Bahamas, but administratively dependent on Jamaica. The populat amounts to over five thousand souls, Negroes for the most ith a strong Mulatto minority and a sprinkling of whites. slanders are descendants of the slaves of Loyalist landowners who took refuge here from Georgia after the American War of Independence. The whites soon evaporated, the Negroes sank into a state 'little short of savagery', and scrub was allowed to run wild over the plantations. The inhabitants are still reputed to be very much more backward than those of the mother colony. The Negroes of the Turks Islands, which are named after the scarlet fez-like blossom of the local cactus, subsist almost entirely on the sale of the salt which they gather from the numerous lagoons and salt-flats. Apart from a few brackish springs where the cattle are watered, there is no drinking-water but the rain which they husband in catchments. Poultry is scarce on these flat stretches of land and vegetables and fresh meat are even scarcer, so the hardy islanders live entirely on fish. Visiting ships are rare, and only the hurricanes, sweeping northwards on their way to Florida and Carolina, make an occasional change.

Sponge-diving into the rich underwater forests that surround the reefs is one of the chief sources of livelihood among the Caicos Islanders. The work is carried on under the instruction and example of the most expert of sponge divers, the Greeks from the small Dodecanesian island of Kalimnos, who for countless generations have made their living in the southern waters of the Libyan Sea. The Caiconians' other submarine quarry are the conch shells, in about one out of a thousand of which the valuable pink pearl forms. Prices are high, and one pearl suffices to buy the fishing-boat which is the final crown of every islander's ambition. The labour involved in the discovery of a single pearl is not wasted, points out a Jamaican writer in the 1890s, for the conch is a universal article of diet among them 'and when curried, it is not to be despised even by more educated palates'. Patronizing ass! Not to be despised indeed! *Lambi* is one of the most delicious things in the world.

The Venezuelan coast used to be the most profitable hunting-ground for pearls. In the early days of Santo Domingo, vast quantities were fished and they were unloaded in the sea-ports of Spain 'as though they were hay'. Hawkins lost four hundredweight of them at the battle of San Juan de Ulua. The islands are the rumoured hiding-place of immense quantities of treasure and elaborate expeditions have been mounted in the attempt to discover it; so far, fortunately, perhaps, for some adventurer of the future, in vain.

The train was bowling along through the flat cane-fields and every turn of the wheels bore us closer to the tramlines of Kingston. Our Jamaican journey was almost over.

But not quite. Before traversing by road the last thirteen miles to Kingston, via Bog Walk and then past a monumental and duppy-haunted ceiba tree, we got out at Spanish Town: Santiago de la Vega, the ancient capital of the Spaniards, and for two centuries the seat of the British government in Jamaica.

The streets were almost empty of citizens. But they were full of sunlight and heavy with that late-afternoon atmosphere which is peculiar to towns that have lost their importance. For Kingston, with its outlet to the sea, its docks and its trade, was too much for the old island capital. The languid mechanism of Spanish Town came to a halt and the government was reluctantly transferred to its urchin usurper.

A minute's walk from the central square stands the Cathedral of Saint Catharine. Although it is no bigger than an English parish church, it is the oldest in the British colonies, and every passing decade has contributed something to its architectural character. The recurrent earthquakes and even the restorations have failed to destroy its charm. Grandiloquent Georgian epitaphs to dead governors and administrators have thickly silted up the walls of the interior. Bulging and inadequately pinioned brats in marble pine over torches reversed, or shrouded urns, and pale sibylline figures mourn in attitudes of pensive melancholy beside the stately eighteenth-century obituaries. The floor of the nave is virtually paved with memorial slabs of black and white marble. The charges on the shields that nest there in a whirlwind of carved mantelling have been rubbed smooth by the tread of generations, and the seventeenth-century lettering of the brief biographies beneath them, telling the tales of early colonists from York or Somerset or Connaught, is all but indecipherable. Many of the tombs in the churchyard have been fissured or smashed by earthquakes and tossed into restless attitudes. They lie there under the branches like ships on a tempestuous ocean of grass.

There are few vestiges of the grandees that once ruled the island for Spain. Indeed, the brocade and the Velasquez-moustaches of those figures – Diego Colón, the son of the great admiral Columbus himself; Don Juan de Esquivel, de Ganay, and the last governor, Don Cristoforo Arnaldo – now seem as dim and far away as the plumed headdresses of the Arawaks. Why the Spaniards suddenly abandoned Sevilla Nueva, their first capital on the north coast, is as mysterious as the sudden departure of the Maya from their great cities in Central America. Even Sir Hans Sloane, gazing at all that remained of it in 1688, was unable to determine the cause. Various reasons have been advanced; the total annihilation of the inhabitants by an Arawak onslaught, which hardly sounds likely; a m͟a͟s͟ ͟i͟n͟s͟ion of ants, or of French filibusters, or merely because the ͟ ͟ ͟unhealthy. Nobody knows.

͟ ͟ ͟s House in Spanish Town, the Governor's residence, still stands. From here a succession of wigged and fastidious magnates administered Jamaica for the King of England – a sequence whose orthodoxy was only interrupted by the governorship of the pirate Morgan. Not far away, a tamarind tree marks the place where two Cromwellian colonels were shot for mutiny.

Three sides of the main square are formed by a school, the former court house and an old House of Assembly where the dust thickens over the Royal Arms and the spiders stretch their threads from window to ceiling. (The town, even in Lewis's day, though still the capital, was in a ruinous state.) The houses are built of stone and wood, in a classical, almost Palladian style. But the fourth side of the square is flanked by a really important achievement. Between the two finely proportioned eighteenth-century houses at either end, a stately Ionian colonnade sweeps in a shallow crescent. It is broken in the middle by a heptagonal rotunda of Corinthian pillars. This is balustraded round the cornice and enclosed with a groined cupola which in its turn is crowned by a small heptagonal lantern of the slenderest columns. The elegance of the building is slightly impaired by the lowness of the Roman arches which spring from the capitals of pilasters running half-way up the flank of the seven great pillars; the expanse of wall between the arches and the architrave of the rotunda is a shade heavy. It makes the upper part look a little too enclosed. Above the central semi-circle flaunt the arms of Lord Rodney: a coroneted shield, three eagles with wings displayed and reversed, and a scroll of stucco with a bellicose device, *Non generant aquilae columbas*.

Under this canopy stands a pedestal sculpted with the symbols of triumph in tropical waters. Britannia, drawn by a team of dolphins in a cockle-shell, travels victoriously through a bas-relief of destruction. Fleur-de-lys banners trail humbly in the water and brigantines and frigates and men-o'-war, the wreckage of the entire French fleet, litter the marble background; tritons emerge, and a fanfare of conches wafts her onward while sea-lions and porpoises and strange sea-monsters gambol beside the vainglorious car. The fishtails of marine unicorns uncoil through the breakers, and an alligator, anomalously basking here, reveals its teeth in subtle approbation. Olympian above his attributes stands Bacon's statue of Lord Rodney himself. There he postures, the intrepid admiral, brilliant sailor, confirmed gambler and philanderer; fantastically dandified, eaten up with vanity, racked by gravel and the gout and bowed down with premature old age; changed here, by apotheosis, into a Graeco-Roman hero in toga, chlamys and kilt, and a thorax embossed with the Medusa's head. He points with his baton in a superbly Augustan gesture towards the drooping palm trees of the square. Two captured cannon from the flag-ship of Count de Grasse, their barrels wreathed with the cipher of Louis Charles de Bourbon, Comte d'Eu, Duc d'Aumale, lie at his feet.

The Jamaicans erected this memorial as a sign of gratitude for the victory of the Saints, a naval triumph that is, I suppose, subordinate only to the destruction of the Armada and the Battle of Trafalgar. The sculptural balance between dignity and bombast is brilliantly maintained and the impression of these flaking yellow columns and the derelict and beautiful square in the evening light is reminiscent of the patina of an Oxford college.

The sunlight faded from the tops of the mountains. It had vanished long ago from the weary and desiccated palm trees of the square, and the kites huddling among the branches were almost invisible. Two Negroes, returning laden with baskets from the market in Kingston, crossed the road, their cigarettes glowing in the falling dusk. It was time to move on.

ENVOI

The night train from Camagüey to Havana was hurrying us towards the end of our Caribbean journey.

In the south-eastern corner of the island, far beyond the shimmering cordilleras through which we were travelling, lay the city of Santiago, the first capital of Cuba. What a wonderful town it sounds, with its High Renaissance churches in the Florentine style, its Tuscan altars and its castles, museums and palaces. It epitomizes for Spaniards who have not crossed the Atlantic all that is most exotic and beautiful in the islands of their lost empire, and it has proved the theme for a poem by Lorca that is almost a metrical litany of nostalgia. Nothing is omitted: the sound of the Trade Winds in the palm trees, the click of the wooden instruments, the rhythm of the dried seeds, the tobacco flower, the alligators:

> *Cuando llegue la luna llena iré a Santiago de Cuba*
> *Iré a Santiago*
> *En un coche de agua negra.*
> *Cantaran los techos de palmera*
> *Iré a Santiago . . .**

The moon that hung so low over the mountains was as full, as expanded as it is possible for the luminary to be; filled to the point of brimming over, as it were, with lunar substance, until only a circumference ten times her normal size could accommodate it; a lamp that drowned the lustre of every star and quickened the wild surrounding mountain ranges and every tree of the unflurried woods that throve in the valleys; and, with the same impartiality, struck everything dead. The branches hung with a metallic and thunderstruck rigidity, and only the sleek elongated reflections of the moon in the railway lines were subject to movement or change.

A strange landscape rose from the mists of the dawn. It was a vista of symmetrical and juxtaposed hemispheres of pale green, and each mound was placed in relationship to its neighbours with the precision

*When the moon is full, I will go to Santiago de Cuba
I will go to Santiago
In a coach of black water.
The roofs of the palm trees will sing
I will go to Santiago.

of a cell in a honeycomb. The white mist still lingered in the ravines, so that the country rolled away in an infinity of green discs floating on a pale and softly moving network. Across this vague landscape the Royal Palms wandered away in Indian file, each of them taller and more slender than any imaginable tree. This wonderful plant, the *Orodoxia Regia*, is indigenous to Cuba, and it has become the emblem of the Republic. It appears again and again in the embossed and gilded panoramas inside the lids of cigar-boxes; those landscapes that so faithfully capture, as truth is captured by a parable, the atmosphere of Cuba. The smooth trunk, grey-green and perfectly cylindrical, shoots into the air to a phenomenal height, and, on its journey, swells and diminishes with the most gentle curves like the pillar of an Egyptian temple with its girth melted to the exiguity of a pencil and its length drawn ever higher into the sky to explode there in a miraculous corolla of leaves. These dark masses of foliage hung like enormous birds flying parallel to the track of the train or migrated in long winding flights towards the prim-rose and scarlet daybreak. Isolated *haciendas* floated past with the columns of their verandahs lost in the mist, surrounded now and then by palm-thatched colonies of huts. The little stations were thronged with Negroes and Mulattoes waiting for a later train to Havana: white assemblies of sombreros that all slanted upwards and rotated together as the express rushed past and above them. Yards full of ox-carts appeared for a few seconds, and heavily-caparisoned horses up to their hocks in mist. Then the tobacco-fields or a sudden lake of sugar-cane swept them away, and the strange ballooning savannah returned once more. Grey cattle meditated on the convexities under the palms or moved along the misty labyrinth like ghosts of which only the great emerging horns were real.

The humble Perla de Cuba had infinitely more charm than the luxury palaces that abounded in the more fashionable quarters of Havana. My great wooden bed was more elaborate and unwieldy than a Spanish galleon, and there was something pleasingly austere and monkish about the bare white stone walls of the room and the high ceilings. A single metal spigot fed the washbasin with water. The basin itself was a shallow fluted scallop-shell of marble, destined, one would have said, more for some symbolic sacerdotal purpose than for any mundane ablutions. During the heat of the afternoons, this tall white cell was a priceless refuge. Safely immured here behind closed shutters from the glare and — would lie and read the history of the Spanish empire. A jug —beer stood within easy reach and only a muted suggestion — penetrated the cool and watery dimness. A ship's siren was audible now and then and every quarter of an hour the bells of Havana sounded. The sweetness of their tone, the Cubans say, is due to the quantities of silver and gold that their ancestors poured into the molten bronze when the bells were cast three centuries ago.

What an astonishing race of men these early Spaniards were! As I turned the pages of the chronicles and histories that record their gestures, the shadowy bearded figures assumed reality and life: the entire Columbus family, Diego Velasquez, Panfilo de Narvaez, Ponce de Leon of Puerto Rico and Florida, Hernandez de Cordoba and Juan de Grijalva who explored the islands of the Mexican Gulf and the coasts of Yucatan; Hernandez de Soto, the discoverer of the mouth of the Mississippi, Vasco Nuñez de Balboa who penetrated the swamps and forests of Darien and first contemplated the waters of the Pacific; the great Cortes* himself, who conquered the empire of the Aztecs with a handful of soldiers and wandered speechless through the saloons and aviaries of Montezuma; Olid and Sandoval, the knights who accompanied him, and Bernal Diaz, the soldier who recounts their adventures; the Montejos, who reduced the city-states of the Mayas, and Alvarado, the lieutenant of Cortes and the conqueror of Guatemala; Pizarro, who scaled the Andes and defeated the Incas of Peru. Volume after volume is filled with the expeditions through the jungles in full plate-armour, the battles with the Indian hosts, the victories and disasters, the sudden astounding visions of Popocatepetl and Chimborazo. The mind winged forward to these new realms, to the caciques and emperors in their palanquins of parrots' feathers, the warriors armed with weapons of chalcedony and obsidian, the cathedrals and the grandees' palaces which sprang up in the jungle. Their adventures made it hard to restrict one's thoughts to the confines of this island from which so many of them had set forth; from which, in a couple of days, we were to follow them.

The end of carnival coincided with our last night in Cuba. We forced a passage through the mob which thronged the sides of the Prado, the great boulevard that runs into the central square under the dome of the capitol, and sat on the kerb with a family of Cubans. Decorated grandstands receded behind us in tiers, and the small boy beside me pointed out the President and other prominent figures. Posses of police roared up and down the empty street on motor-cycles. It all seemed too organized and civic for a carnival. The first beauty-queens, floating at a snail's pace on edifices like huge wedding-cakes of tinsel through

---

* Who never, except by poetic right, sat upon a peak in Darien.

dutiful outbursts of clapping, augured badly. It looked as if the whole thing might turn out to be a bore. Hold-ups of three-quarters of an hour turned the effulgence of their smiles to cardboard, and the bare arms that waved in acknowledgement of the languishing plaudits lent to the triumphal cars the purposeless, fluttering motion of sea anemones. They shrank, as the clapping subsided, into immobility, to unfurl and wave again only when the cortège moved on.

At last the final chariotload of Venuses sailed by, and a fanfare of trumpets heralded the arrival of a far stranger procession organized by the Chinese community of Havana. Little men in the costumes of Buddhist priests swelled their cheeks over the mouthpieces of long wind instruments resting on the shoulders of the boys in front of them. A cohort of pikemen followed. They were dressed from head to foot in Chinese armour and they grasped in their hands long halberds with fantastically shaped blades. After them came standard-bearers with silk banners which were embroidered and tasselled and fringed and charged with gleaming stars and with dragons. Others bore aloft on poles enormous three-dimensional dragons made of paper, lit from inside and spiked along their backs, with beams of light blazing from their eye-sockets; resplendent pterodactyls whose tails uncoiled for many yards overhead.

Other light-bearers accompanied them, supporting, in the slots of their baldricks, poles ten or fifteen yards high that poised on their summits many-coloured parchment globes. Some of them were several yards in circumference, the upper parts tapering into the air like pagodas. The curling gables of the superstructure were strung with coloured lights and tassels and bells and Chinese ideograms were painted on their illuminated parchment panels. As they moved along, the light-bearers twirled the staves in their sockets, and the airy palaces and temples, glowing with a soft lustre against the stars, swung and gyrated high over our heads to the sound of bells and trumpets and far-oriental music.

There was something unspeakably charming and almost magical about this flimsy flying architecture. Chinese girls in gold litters came after them, and then, trotting among pikemen, little piebald horses splendidly caparisoned, and miraculously emerging, one would say, from the T'ang dynasty. They bore upon their backs fairy-tale Manchu princesses whose heavy silk and gold-embroidered robes, sweeping to the ground with the stiffness of metal, entirely enveloped them. Under winged and pinnacled head-dresses, ivory Chinese faces of extreme beauty gazed into the night, as motionless and grave under their gleaming accoutrements as those saints on ikons of the Eastern Church whose faces and hands alone the silverwork reveals.

Like a length of Chinese embroidery the procession coiled away. The sound of the bugles and bells grew fainter, and the shining edifices receded; a diminishing Chinese Venice floating into the distance on a lagoon of stars.

An African sound now struck our ears: the clatter and boom of tom-toms, the sneezing jerk of the shack-shack and the scraping of plectrums over slotted gourds; and, again in the wake of a forest of lights and escorted by the flames of torches, an interminable but orderly horde of Negroes came dancing down the street. They heaved backwards and forwards with the advance and the recoil of the authentic Negro dance of Cuba: the *Conga*. On they came in hundreds, each dancer evolving alone; surging three paces to the left, stopping with a sort of abrupt choreographic hiccup on a half beat, then three paces to the right (crash!), and then to the left again as all the barbaric instruments underlined the beat. As the impact of the music grew, the approaching dancers themselves increased every second in size, until they were dancing past like an invasion of giants.

They were tall, jet black Negroes and handsome Negro women in the slave costume of the plantations. The latter were dressed in white blouses and red billowing skirts with three rows of frills. Red scarves were tied round their heads and tartan shawls about their shoulders. The men were barefoot and sashed with scarlet. Their trousers ended in a fringe half-way down their calves, and a length of tartan stuff was bound about their loins. At their waists hung a tin cup and a plate and red handkerchiefs were tied round their foreheads under broad-rimmed wicker hats of which the front of the brim was fastened back with a large black scorpion. Enormous scorpions were also painted on the drums and banners, and below them were hung scarecrow figures of eighteenth-century plantation owners in powdered wigs. Each of the dancers held in one hand a length of green sugar-cane and in the other a cutlass which he flourished in rhythm with his steps. They were singing a deep repetitive African chant that rose and fell and abruptly ceased and then began all over again in the mode of a Voodoo incantation or one of the Koromantee songs of the Maroons.

In the middle of the throng danced the drummers, some with toms-toms slung from their shoulders and others moving along locust-fashion with their instruments between their bent knees. Troops of Negroes carried drums on their shoulders that were seven yards long; cylinders, like the Assotor drums of the Haitian forests, hollowed from the boles of large trees. Held high above the heads of the dancers, the drummers crouched forward astride these great instruments like demoniac jockeys, the palms

355

of their hands beating the drumheads of membrane with a frenzy that sent each blow booming down the cavern of the drum and out into the air like a shot from a cannon. In this stupendous *Conga*, there was nothing frivolous or carnivalesque. The combination of dance and symbol and song was in the nature of a summing-up of the history and the revolts of the Negroes and of the lament for Africa. It was an apocalyptic intimation, too, of Voodoo, Obeah, Cambois, Schango, Ñañigo, Los Santos, Batonga-Naroca, Candomble, Caboclo, Ubanda, Macumba, and Wanga and all the secret Negro cults of the Americas, and the admiration evoked by the precision and the abandon of the dancing and the magnificent volume of the singing and of the music of the drums was closely allied to awe.

Gradually the Scorpion dancers moved on. They were succeeded, as the hours passed, by armies, each of them over a hundred strong, of Negroes and Mulattoes. First came a party of mock Spaniards in Andalusian dress. Then a Harlem group. The men sported top-hats and tail-coats and gold-knobbed canes and danced gravely along with cigars between the white gloved fingers of their right hands. On the sleeve of their gallantly crooked left elbows rested the gloved arms of their partners: tubes of silver or scarlet or lilac attached to sinuous figures in superbly exaggerated evening dresses that might have been designed by Balenciaga. From the naked shoulder to the knee, they clung as tightly as snakeskin and then flared out behind the stilt-heeled golden shoes in peacock's tails of coloured feathers and sequins. Panaches of ostrich-plumes rose from hip and shoulder and the towering Carmen Miranda head-dresses, ascending from their sleek coiffures and climbing and branching and expanding in the air like multi-coloured pineapple foliage, tossed and coruscated with each advancing step.

Then came the Dark Town Strutters; the blazered and straw-hatted, banjo-strumming minstrels; *Charros* and *Vaqueros* with big spurs and sombreros; conquistadores in full armour, musketeers, courtiers in silk and brocade, animals, tumbling dwarfs, and a hunchback with his head flung back who, for mile after mile, balanced a glass of water on his forehead. As the last troop passed the Capitol, the spectators surged round and among them, and the procession simultaneously fanned out and disintegrated among the crowd in many brilliant islets of colour; all, dancers and crowd alike, swelling and seething and shuffling in a dazzling confusion, until the town became a universal *Conga* under a heaving roof of lanterns and streamers and confetti, and stars.

Holding hands lest the human currents should carry us off into different maelstroms, we headed back to the *Perla de Cuba* to collect our luggage.

Breaking free from the main tide of dancers, we raced along the back streets, for our plane was leaving in half an hour. The rum-shops in the colonnaded lanes were packed to capacity with disguised Negroes. A party of Scorpions, with their cutlasses scattered about the tables, were drinking straight out of the bottle. One of their number still hammered away at a drum while a Minotaur span round and round, slowly clapping his hands. Confetti was scattered everywhere and tangled balls of streamers had collected in the gutters. Under a street lamp at the corner six amazing figures stood in colloquy. They were horses' heads ten feet high, like gigantic chessmen with bared teeth and staring eyes, their lower lips, articulated to mimic the action of speech, hanging inanely loose. Little portholes in their breasts revealed the faces of six Negroes smoking cigars. Intrigued by our three running figures, the great heads swung ponderously round and followed us out of sight with their great fatuous eyes.

The lights of Havana grew smaller and finally merged into a luminous smear. The only distinguishable object was the revolving beam of the lighthouse on the Morro, and in a little while we were flying over a bare tract of the Caribbean. The aeroplane was almost empty. Joan and Costa, exhausted like me by the doings of the last few hours, had turned off the lights over their seats and settled down to sleep. I felt I should soon do the same. The water was scarcely visible by the light of the stars, but in a little while the remains of a moon began to appear and a faint radiance was spread over the eastern rim of the sea.

Well, I thought, as I gazed out of the throbbing cocoon at the emptiness, that was the last of the Antilles. The Negroes had come to an end, and, except for the narrow red quadrilateral of British Honduras towards which we were flying – which is little more, really, than a landing-stage on the shores of Latin America – so had the colonial world of the British, the French, the Americans and the Dutch. All that lay ahead was Spanish, of which I knew very little, and Indian of which I knew nothing at all; a region of great rivers and swamps and steaming forests inhabited by baboons and jaguars and the quetzal, the semi-divine bird with the two long green tail feathers; waterless sierras and the pyramids and the ruined cities of the Mayas, baroque cathedrals and ruined cities of the Spaniards. The tapering sequence of the central American Republics, through which our travels for the next few months were about to begin, waited the other side of the night; dwindling southwards from the bulk of the Mexican mountains to the narrow filament of Darien in a long-drawn-out plague of volcanoes whose smouldering cones stood like a barrier between us and the Pacific Ocean. These tenebrous regions approached through the darkness while the curving line of our past itinerary streamed away behind us into memory. There lay the islands in the night, suspended between the stars and the sea's bottom with the abstraction of thoughts: the stages of a thesis that was still to be unravelled. Guadeloupe was the exordium. The Lesser and then the Greater Antilles and Haiti swelled into a ponderous exegesis waiting to be clinched and driven home at last with the triumphant peroration of Cuba. And what was the conclusion to be?

The day that was about to begin happened, by a coincidence that is no literary device, to be my birthday. Rilke mentions an old superstition, in one of his letters, that a microscopic chink exists between the ending of one year of a lifetime and the beginning of the next. For a split second, he says, one can peer through this fissure in the joinery of time and behold the Truth. This moment was now approaching, and no place surely could be more propitious for taking full advantage of it than this undetermined point two or three thousand feet above an empty sheet of water. Making my mind a blank, I watched the minute hand of my wrist-watch move forward.

But the moment of revelation failed to occur. Nothing happened. Nothing, that is, except a smell of garlic that ensnared me like a noose and the sound of a voice asking me the time. I opened my eyes again and saw that the fourth passenger, who had appeared till then to be asleep, was leaning across the alleyway. It was an ugly, cheerful, intelligent, and rather charming face made raffish by several days' growth of beard. He seemed inclined for conversation, and questioned me about my provenance and my destination. When he was duly informed, I asked him the same questions; where was he from – Cuba, Guatemala, Mexico? No, no, he said, he was a Greek from Sparta returning from a family visit in the Peloponnese to his grocery business in Nicaragua. Things were pretty bad in Greece, he continued. Prices were rising, the cost of olive oil was enormous, the drachma was falling every day; there were scarcely any caiques sailing between Crete and the Aegean islands – all sunk in the war; the civil war was wrecking the country's economy, and there were bandits even in the mountains of the Morea. No stability anywhere. 'But still,' he concluded, 'the wine is cheap and the people don't change.' His gold teeth appeared for a moment in a rather melancholy smile. 'It was bad to leave just as spring was coming on.' We talked of such matters for an hour or two, and then fell asleep.

INDEX

READ MORE IN PENGUIN

In every corner of the world, on every subject under the sun, Penguin represents quality and variety – the very best in publishing today.

For complete information about books available from Penguin – including Puffins, Penguin Classics and Arkana – and how to order them, write to us at the appropriate address below. Please note that for copyright reasons the selection of books varies from country to country.

In the United Kingdom: Please write to *Dept. JC, Penguin Books Ltd, FREEPOST, West Drayton, Middlesex UB7 OBR*

If you have any difficulty in obtaining a title, please send your order with the correct money, plus ten per cent for postage and packaging, to *PO Box No. 11, West Drayton, Middlesex UB7 OBR*

In the United States: Please write to *Penguin USA Inc., 375 Hudson Street, New York, NY 10014*

In Canada: Please write to *Penguin Books Canada Ltd, 10 Alcorn Avenue, Suite 300, Toronto, Ontario M4V 3B2*

In Australia: Please write to *Penguin Books Australia Ltd, 487 Maroondah Highway, Ringwood, Victoria 3134*

In New Zealand: Please write to *Penguin Books (NZ) Ltd,182–190 Wairau Road, Private Bag, Takapuna, Auckland 9*

In India: Please write to *Penguin Books India Pvt Ltd, 706 Eros Apartments, 56 Nehru Place, New Delhi 110 019*

In the Netherlands: Please write to *Penguin Books Netherlands B.V., Keizersgracht 231 NL–1016 DV Amsterdam*

In Germany: Please write to *Penguin Books Deutschland GmbH, Friedrichstrasse 10–12, W–6000 Frankfurt/Main 1*

In Spain: Please write to *Penguin Books S. A., C. San Bernardo 117–6° E–28015 Madrid*

In Italy: Please write to *Penguin Italia s.r.l., Via Felice Casati 20, I–20124 Milano*

In France: Please write to *Penguin France S. A., 17 rue Lejeune, F–31000 Toulouse*

In Japan: Please write to *Penguin Books Japan, Ishikiribashi Building, 2–5–4, Suido, Tokyo 112*

In Greece: Please write to *Penguin Hellas Ltd, Dimocritou 3, GR–106 71 Athens*

In South Africa: Please write to *Longman Penguin Southern Africa (Pty) Ltd, Private Bag X08, Bertsham 2013*

BY THE SAME AUTHOR

A Time of Gifts

'More than just a Super-travel book ... it is a reminder that the English language is still a superb instrument in the hands of a writer who has a virtuoso skill with words' – Philip Toynbee in the *Observer*

The story of Patrick Leigh Fermor's walk to Hungary at the age of eighteen, *A Time of Gifts* won the 1978 W. H. Smith Literary Award.

Between the Woods and the Water

Here Patrick Leigh Fermor resumes the account of his journey to Constantinople, beginning where *A Time of Gifts* ended, taking him from Hungary to his destination.

'Indescribably rich and beautiful ... a masterpiece' – *Guardian*

'Absolutely marvellous ... Buy it at once ... this book belongs in the highest travelling-company ... it is irresistible and I think will remain so long after our time' – Robin Lane Fox

Between the Woods and the Water was the winner of the 1987 Silver Pen Award and the Thomas Cook Travel Book Award.

Roumeli

Travels in Northern Greece

'Roumeli is the man himself. He lives in Greece, speaks Greek, knows the Greeks themselves as well as any man can, and loves what he knows. And so the focal point of the work is a masterpiece of intellectualism softened by warm, human understanding' – *Sunday Telegraph*